SCHOOLS FOR SCANDAL

SCHOOLS FOR SCANDAL

THE DYSFUNCTIONAL MARRIAGE OF DIVISION I SPORTS AND HIGHER EDUCATION

SHELDON ANDERSON

UNIVERSITY OF MISSOURI PRESS
COLUMBIA

Copyright © 2024 by
The Curators of the University of Missouri
University of Missouri Press, Columbia, Missouri 65211
Printed and bound in the United States of America
All rights reserved. First printing, 2024.

Library of Congress Cataloging-in-Publication Data to come

ISBN 978-0-8262-2308-1 (hardcover : alk. paper)

∞™ This paper meets the requirements of the
American National Standard for Permanence of Paper
for Printed Library Materials, Z39.48, 1984.

Typeface: Minion Pro

Sports and American Culture
Adam Criblez, Series Editor

This series explores the cultural dynamic between competitive athletics and society, the many ways in which sports shape the lives of Americans, in the United States and Latin America, from a historical and contemporary perspective. While international in scope, the series includes titles of regional interest to Missouri and the Midwest. Topics in the series range from studies of a single game, event, or season to histories of teams and programs, as well as biographical narratives of athletes, coaches, owners, journalists, and broadcasters.

For all the college athletes who really are dedicated students or want to be.

CONTENTS

Acknowledgments	xi
List of Abbreviations	xiii
INTRODUCTION	3

CHAPTER ONE
    The "Accidental Industry":
    The NCAA and the Myth of the Amateur Athlete   11

CHAPTER TWO
    The Big Gamble:
    Peddling College on the Front Porch of D-I Sports   33

CHAPTER THREE
    You Play, We Profit: The Exploitation of College Athletes   67

CHAPTER FOUR
    The D-I Rap Sheet:
    Point Shavers, Sexual Predators, Escorts, and Cheats   91

CHAPTER FIVE
    Take the Money and Run:
    Carpetbagger Coaches and Recruiting Ruses   117

CHAPTER SIX
    Good Ol' Boys' Club:
    The NCAA's Fight Against Minorities and Women   139

CHAPTER SEVEN
    No Contest: Sports Rout Academics   167

Contents

CHAPTER EIGHT
 Cheating to Make the Grade:
 Keeping Athletes Eligible 197

CHAPTER NINE
 Exercises in Futility:
 Reforming the Unreformable NCAA 211

CHAPTER TEN
 On Defense:
 Pom-Pom Presidents, Booster Boards,
 NCAA Bureaucrats, and the Status Quo 237

CHAPTER ELEVEN
 A New Game Plan:
 Free Market Campus Sports, the American Way 249

CHAPTER TWELVE
 Student-Athletes for Sale:
 Making Millions on NIL Deals 275

Afterword 279

References 283

Index 289

ACKNOWLEDGMENTS

Two scholars contributed mightily to this book. David C. Smith provided numerous references to relevant newspaper articles, especially from the early era of intercollegiate athletics. Chris Elzey did a careful proofread of the manuscript and made many important suggestions and corrections. I am indebted to them both. Delaney Ross-Shannon deserves special mention for her valuable contributions to the early drafts of the book. I would also like to thank my editor at the University of Missouri Press, Andrew Davidson, and series editor Adam Criblez, who guided the manuscript to publication. I also owe a big debt of gratitude to expert copy editor Lindsay Oliver, who polished up the final version. She deserves a raise.

ABBREVIATIONS

AAU	Amateur Athletic Association
AAUP	American Association of University Professors
ACE	American Council of Education
AGB	Association of Governing Boards of Universities and Colleges
AIAW	Association of Intercollegiate Athletics for Women
BSC	Bowl Championship Series
D-I	NCAA Division I
CFA	College Football Association
FBS	Football Bowl Subdivision
FERPA	Family Educational Rights and Privacy Act
HBCU	Historically Black Colleges and Universities
IAA	Intercollegiate Athletic Association
IOC	International Olympic Committee
MLB	Major League Baseball
MLS	Major League Soccer
NAIA	National Association of Intercollegiate Athletics
NBA	National Basketball Association
NCAA	National Collegiate Athletic Association
NFL	National Football League
NHL	National Hockey League
NIL	Name, Image and Likeness
NIT	National Invitational Tournament
WNBA	Women's National Basketball Association

SCHOOLS FOR SCANDAL

INTRODUCTION

> "When will we admit that some college sports are professional in structure and in practice?"
>
> —Late historian Pellom McDaniels III, who played football at Oregon State and with the Kansas City Chiefs, 2013[1]

Is yet another book on the incongruous, anachronistic, and corrupt system of big-time intercollegiate sports necessary? Sports journalists and historians, among others who pay attention to the issue, might have the cynical reaction, "Tell me something I don't know." There have been repeated exposés of the shady business of Division-I (D-I) football and men's basketball. However, when I discuss the subject with non-academics—many of them avid sports fans—I am surprised by this common response: "Really? I didn't know that." Many people just like watching college games, and they are happy to believe in the pure amateur ideal—the student-athlete whose first priority is the classroom and who competes for the love of the game, free of the evils of greed and profit-making. The average fan either willfully ignores the contradictions and inequities of D-I sports or believes in the myths that the National Collegiate Athletic Association (NCAA) and athletic departments have so successfully marketed.[2]

This book has three main purposes. First, it provides an overview of the long history of corruption in college sports. If this has you wondering whether *corruption* might be too strong a word to describe the system of big-money D-I athletics, ponder how Merriam-Webster defines the word: 1) "dishonest or illegal behavior especially by powerful people" (check); 2) "inducement to wrong by improper or unlawful means (such as bribery)" (check); and 3) "a departure from the original or from what is pure or correct" (again, check).

Introduction

The numerous scandals plaguing D-I sports are—as broadcasters term the incessant replays on the field these days—"under review" here. For well more than a century, big-time college sports has been a business enterprise that has consistently undermined the mission of higher education. The treatise here serves as a legal brief calling for the stakeholders—college administrators, boards of trustees, athletic departments, the courts, and politicians—to do the right thing: end the sham of the "student-athlete" and the myth of amateurism.

Although similar issues exist at the D-II and D-III levels,[3] the focus of this study is on D-I football and men's basketball, programs that have the potential to rake in millions of dollars for a university, even though most such programs do not do so. Even those teams that are vastly profitable do not cover the costs of all other sports programs offered by their respective universities.

The very old problem of college athletic scandals seemingly will never desist. More than one hundred D-I schools have had major rule violations in the last half century, from academic cheating, point-shaving, illegal perks, and blatant cash payments to players, to running "escorts" for athletes and recruits. And those are only the infractions that have come to light.

Second, this book seeks to correct the many commonly held misconceptions about D-I sports, including the following:

1. *The corruption of the mission of higher education by D-I intercollegiate athletics is a relatively new phenomenon.* At the turn of the twenty-first century, former University of Michigan president James J. Duderstadt wrote, "In a very real sense, the problems in college sports that are of so much concern today are not significantly different from those a century ago."[4] Duderstadt was right: The history of rampant rules-breaking in intercollegiate sports started in the late nineteenth century, exposing the endemic dysfunction in the marriage between universities and athletics, with one seeking to educate and other needing to win at all costs.

2. *College sports is a shining example of a pure amateur system—a pursuit of athletic excellence without the corrupting influence of money, as in the early period of modern team games and the Olympics.* College athletics is the last vestige of a nineteenth-century amateur ideal that all other major sports in the world discarded long ago. Sports historian Ronald A. Smith, author of several books on intercollegiate sports, dispels the myth of the amateur college athlete: "There was never a shining

period, a golden era, of college sport when amateurism was upheld, and when professionalism and commercialism were not in existence."[5] *Wall Street Journal* columnist Jason Gay, among many other pundits, concurs: "We are long past the point of purist outrage in big-time college sports. Flimsy notions of amateurism and loyalty evaporated from the landscape generations ago."[6]

3. *Division I athletic departments make money.* Fact: Only about twenty D-I and a handful of D-II athletic departments in the country make money on sports. The vast majority of D-I athletic programs are millions of dollars in the red, subsidized by mandatory student fees and university budgets. Most regular students have no idea that they help fund athletic scholarships and the exorbitant salaries of coaches through their student fees. College administrators and the NCAA have tried to mask the inequities of the system, but repeated scandals have uncovered the corruption behind the façade and the (mostly) men propping it up.

4. *College sports teach integrity and good moral character.* This is a presumption about sportsmanship that is impossible to prove or disprove, but at the highest levels of college sports, recruits and players are pampered, winning is a must, and financial incentives are paramount. Playing fair is optional at best.

5. *The NCAA has been in the vanguard of promoting athletic opportunities for minorities and women.* Sadly, college sports has not traditionally been a pioneer in promoting civil rights. Discrimination against Black people on the playing field has mirrored societal racism, and even lagged behind other institutions in breaking the color line. The NCAA turned a blind eye to Southern schools discriminating against Black athletes long after the ruling in *Brown v. Board of Education* in 1954 and the civil rights legislation enacted in the mid-1960s. Furthermore, White males dominate athletic departments and coaching positions. Likewise, it took federal Title IX legislation in 1972 to mandate that colleges give women equal opportunities to play sports. The NCAA and athletic departments fought hard against that legislation, and, after it went into effect, tried to undermine it. In some cases, athletic departments still underprivilege women's sports programs and treat women athletes as second-class citizens.

6. *College players are students first, athletes second.* This is perhaps the biggest fiction in big-time college sports. The "student-athlete" is *la grande illusion* invented by the NCAA in the 1950s to make sense of

the peculiar link between higher education and intercollegiate sports and to absolve schools of having to classify players as employees who would have to be paid workman's compensation for serious injuries. Most coaches are unconcerned with their players' courses of study, caring only whether they stay eligible. There is no other major part of a university more disconnected from its educational mission than a D-I athletic department. The imperative to win works in contravention to every school's mission statement, none of which mention fielding a winning sports team.

7. *The expenditures on intercollegiate athletics have no impact on academic budgets.* The money spent on sports reduces outlays for academics, including academic scholarships for serious, qualified students. At the same time that athletic budgets are steadily increasing, better-paid tenure-track professors are becoming an endangered species, replaced by poorly compensated short-term contracts, adjuncts, and visiting professors.

8. *The best way to promote a university is to field winning men's basketball and football teams.* Many university administrators pitch their product to prospective students on the basis of their football and basketball teams, rather than on the excellence of their academic programs. The millions of dollars saved by eliminating elite sports programs could cover generous advertising campaigns to promote the school as a top educational institution. Furthermore, most athletic boosters do not give to their school for academics.

9. *Reform of the current system is possible.* The tip of the iceberg of corruption in the NCAA is already melting, and the bigger underwater chunk is surfacing. It has been more than a century since college presidents and faculty first recognized that intercollegiate athletic contests were undermining the mission of higher education as well as siphoning money away from academics. Reform efforts have repeatedly failed; the money in college sports has grown exponentially in tandem with more and more incidents of rules breaking. None of the stakeholders who profit so handsomely from big-time college sports have any incentive to change the system. To put it simply, reforming the current NCAA system is impossible.

Third, and perhaps most importantly, this book addresses the salient question: What is to be done? There is a way forward. The book offers bold, realistic recommendations to end the current system of big-time college sports to allow it to function as an unfettered entertainment business—one in which the players would be paid their fair share. After all, free economic choice is an integral part of the American way.

My Perspective
My contribution to the substantive literature on the topic (see Afterword) is a synthesis of the many studies illustrative of the long and tortured history of the NCAA's attempt to maintain the myth of amateurism and the student-athlete, along with the attendant fiction that players' academic achievement is the top priority of D-I athletic programs.

I also bring a unique perspective to the debate, having played on basketball teams in high school, college (D-III), West Germany, and communist Poland.[7] I have first-hand knowledge of the differences between the school-based American system of "amateur" sports and the European club system in which a basketball junkie like me could still play in an organized league (I am in my seventies as I write this). For the vast majority of college athletes, their serious sporting careers end at the age of twenty-two.

For over thirty years, I was a professor in the History Department of Miami University, a mid-major D-I school whose athletic department lost $17 million in 2019. Three years after I was hired to teach history, I applied for the head basketball coaching job at Miami, hoping that the search committee would at least consider prioritizing academics by considering a well-qualified faculty member. Having played basketball at all levels under some great coaches and having had success in the classroom teaching history to undergrads, my application was no joke. After all, all good coaches are good teachers. The search committee did not even bother to send me a rejection letter.

In the last three decades, I witnessed the increasing isolation of Miami University athletes from the rest of the student body. Eventual pros like cager Wally Szczerbiak and quarterback Ben Roethlisberger used to show up at the Miami rec center in the off-season. I played with the likes of them, but no more. Varsity athletes now have their own workout centers, training tables and dorms, year-round workouts with coaches, and fine-tuned, easy courses of study guided by personal academic tutors.

Unfortunately, male football and basketball players rarely enrolled in my sports history course, in which evaluation was based on writing essays rather than on true-false or multiple-choice tests. I also didn't see many athletes in my history courses that fulfill university requirements.

Introduction

Full disclosure: I love watching D-I college sports. While I don't go to many games these days, I am indirectly complicit because I watch them on TV, from which much of the NCAA's profit derives. What is more fun than watching March Madness?

It is a tale of two cities—Division 1 schools everywhere are living the best of times and the worst of times. Team sports is a beautiful thing; players subordinate their individual goals for the good of the whole community. Sports *can* teach the value of hard work, teamwork, and friendship. Whether in a military, business, educational, or athletic setting, there is nothing like the feeling of accomplishing a shared goal that transcends personal gain. I have experienced that.

The tale of the other, darker city is one of corruption, immorality, greed, and exploitation under the pretense of giving young football and basketball players a meaningful college education. If I walked the walk, I would turn off televised college games. Perhaps that is one of my motivations for writing this book, which I see as a call to revolutionize the system, so I can enjoy football on Saturdays just as other people do on Sundays—guilt free.

The following is a compilation of evidence that implicates the NCAA cartel in running an anti-democratic, anti-capitalist system full of unjust rules of play. I bring to the witness stand university presidents, athletic directors, professors, journalists, and politicians who have had the courage to point out the inequities of the current system. Mine is not just one voice in the wilderness but one in a chorus that has long been singing for reform in college sports.

I do, however, have one caveat to this indictment: athletic directors and college coaches do not belong in the front row of the dock. Many of them are well-meaning and sincerely concerned with their athletes' intellectual well-being. Those employed in D-I sports operate under a system not of their creation, and they will lose their jobs if they do not put winning teams on the field. Who can blame a coach for recruiting athletes first, students second, and keeping players eligible at any cost? What coach manages to keep his or her job for having a 90 percent graduation rate along with a 10 percent winning record? Cheating reaps its own rewards, and offending coaches—as long as they post a winning record—can always find another coaching job.

I invite the stakeholders in the system to engage in an honest and forthright debate over the corruption in and the future of big-money college sports. I implore them to stop handing us the myths, the

Introduction

prevarications, the obfuscations, and the hypocrisies. Let's just call D-I sports a huge entertainment *business*. That's fine. Remove it from universities, where the main mission, I thought, was to provide students with the best education possible. Maybe the sheer weight of all these critiques of the NCAA system will cause educators to listen to their conscience and move big-time college sports off its pedestal. This is my unvarnished polemic, and hopefully a contribution to a movement to end D-I college sports as we know it, for the moral, educational, and financial good of anyone associated with higher education.

There are many people working in big-money college sports who will be outraged after reading this book. Their very raison d'être is under fire. Welcome, then, to the debate.

A final note: The title of the book is borrowed from a comedic drama, and some of the chapter-opening quotes provide levity in an otherwise depressing story. Although I view the future of higher education with all seriousness, the problems of sport here are not existential, such as the proliferation of nuclear weapons or global warming, about which I would not joke.

Notes

1. Pellom McDaniels III, review of *Pay for Play*, by Ronald A. Smith, *Journal of Sport History* 39, no. 3 (Fall 2012): 567.

2. Joe Nocera, "The Difference Between Unpaid and Paid Student-Athletes? Not Much, It Turns Out," *New York Times*, October 25, 2021, B8.

3. See Alan Draper, "Innocence Lost: Division III Sports Programs," *Change* 28, no. 6 (1996): 46-49.

4. James J. Duderstadt, *Intercollegiate Athletics and the American University: A University President's Perspective* (Ann Arbor: University of Michigan Press, 2000), 187.

5. Sally Jenkins, "The Athletes Are the Only Thing Saving College Sports from the NCAA," *Washington Post*, April 6, 2021, accessed September 8, 2021, https://www.washingtonpost.com/sports/2021/04/06/ncaa-sports-cheat-college-athletes/.

6. Jason Gay, "How to Quit a College Football Job," *Wall Street Journal*, December 1, 2021, A14.

7. See Sheldon Anderson, *Jump Shooting to a Higher Degree: My Basketball Odyssey* (Lincoln, NE: University of Nebraska Press, 2021).

CHAPTER ONE

The "Accidental Industry"
The NCAA and the Myth of the Amateur Athlete

> "[Red Grange] will no more graduate from Illinois than will the Kaiser return to power in Germany."
>
> —University of Illinois at Urbana–Champaign head football coach Bob Zuppke after the Galloping Ghost left college for the pros in 1925[1]

The NCAA is the last adherent to the myth of amateurism in the sports entertainment business. Nowhere else in the world do big-time sports have a close connection to institutions of higher learning in which athletes are required to pose as college students. Every other major professional sport that began with amateur players has succumbed to economic realities. The NCAA is still defending this anachronistic, faux-amateur structure, denying players their fair share of the profits.

What is remarkable about the 150 years of intercollegiate sports is how little has changed; the corruption of the amateur ideal began at its inception and continues to this day. Intercollegiate athletics has never been purely amateur.

How did nineteenth-century rowing regattas and football games between American colleges on the East Coast become the huge money-making entertainment industry it is today? After all, more than a century ago, no one would have predicted that college men's basketball and football would draw millions of fans and take in billions of dollars every year.

Intercollegiate sports had inauspicious beginnings. Yale and Harvard rowed against each other in 1852. The first college football game was played at Rutgers University in the fall of 1869. The home team trounced New Jersey, later known as Princeton, six games to four (every score was considered one "game"). The teams had twenty-five players a side, and to the 100-odd spectators, the contest looked more like rugby, but who's quibbling? Undoubtedly, there were friendly wagers made among the fans, but the game itself made no money. Although the NCAA does not like to talk about it openly, gambling on college games is a time-honored practice and adds to their popularity today. At least $8.5 billion was wagered on the 2021 NCAA basketball tournament—and that was just the legal betting.[2]

Princeton and Rutgers were to play three contests that fall, but the third was canceled because the faculties on both sides thought that the series was taking the players away from their studies.[3] What a fantastic notion it is today that faculties should have any say in how Division I athletic departments are run.

That insignificant football contest between two neighboring colleges has evolved into what economists Allen Sanderson and John Siegfried have called the "accidental industry"—the NCAA's multi-billion-dollar business of intercollegiate college sports.[4] In 2018–19, a century and a half after that first Rutgers game, the top six bowl games and the national football championship made a nifty $549 million for the teams and their conferences. Players in those games got none of that pot of cash.[5]

Division I men's basketball is the other big NCAA moneymaker that grew out of an obscure contest—this one in 1895 at Hamline University in St. Paul, Minnesota. Hamline athletic director Raymond Kaighn had played in James Naismith's first basketball games in Springfield, Massachusetts, so he organized a game with the Minnesota State School of Agriculture. Each team had nine players on the court, and dribbling was prohibited. Minnesota won the high scoring shootout, 9-3.[6] This was an amateur affair, but almost 125 years later, NCAA revenue from the 2019 March Madness basketball tournament reached nearly $1 billion.[7]

The Myth of Amateurism

Since its formation more than a century ago, the NCAA has propped up an edifice that rests on flimsy theoretical foundations. There has never been, as historians Matthew P. Llewellyn and John Gleaves argue, "a clear-cut and homogeneous definition or universal comprehension of an amateur; it meant different things to different people in various local, regional, national, and international contexts."[8] In 1908, London's *Sporting Life* noted, "There are almost as many definitions of an amateur extant nowadays as games themselves."[9] Winning—and the money it takes to do that—made a mockery of the idea that players should just play for fun.

The upper crust in Britain, who created many of the modern games, could afford amateurism. The well-to-do had the leisure time and space to play games without the need to pay players. Their "lawn games" of tennis, golf, croquet, and cricket were genteel contests played on manicured greens in exclusive clubs, without the taunts and catcalls of the riffraff.[10] Amateurism was a way to make it difficult for wage earners and manual laborers to play these games and maintain upper class social status.[11] The 1879 Henley Regatta restricted participation from the lower classes, as did England's Amateur Athletic Club.

It was harder for the political and economic elites to keep money out of the rough and tumble games for the masses. Amateurism could not survive in urban, working-class, industrial Britain. Soccer and rugby were easier games to organize and play, and unlike in the golf and cricket clubs, the upper classes could not restrict participation. However, the laborers who fielded soccer and rugby teams could not afford to take off time from work with no pay, so in the late nineteenth century, soccer and rugby club owners in the North of England began to compensate their players. Using subsidized players, the Blackburn Olympics beat the Old Etonians in the 1883 Football Association final, entrenching professionals in English soccer. Rugby's "Great Schism" came in in 1895 when Rugby Union teams, mostly from the South, pledged not to pay players, even though the Rugby League already allowed it.[12]

Cricket, England's most class-conscious game, clung to this outmoded notion of amateurism. In the mid-nineteenth century, England's most famous cricket player, W. G. Grace, was one of the first to expose the "shamateurism" of the game because players were paid under the table. The sticky amateur wicket finally came down in 1963, when English cricket ended the distinction between professionals and amateurs—"players" and "gentlemen."[13]

For nearly a century, the International Olympic Committee (IOC) tried to adhere to the idealized amateur athlete, who competed for the love of sport rather than financial gain. Frenchman Pierre de Coubertin revived the idea of resurrecting the Olympic Games; he was determined that only amateur men would compete. Coubertin was, however, fully aware of the difficulty in keeping money out of the Games: "[Amateur] rules, which seem simple enough, are more complicated in their practical application by the fact that definitions of what constitutes an

Chapter One

amateur differ from one country to another, sometimes even from one club to another."[14]

The IOC fought a losing battle against paying Olympic athletes, banning allegedly professional athletes such as American Jim Thorpe and Finnish running great Paavo Nurmi. Thorpe, a Native American and gold medal winner in the pentathlon and decathlon at the 1912 Stockholm Olympics, had played some summer baseball for small cash payments, as had many college athletes in the early twentieth century, thereby also compromising the NCAA's attempt to keep its game amateur; major and minor league baseball clubs were professional from the start. After World War II, Brooklyn Dodgers general manager Branch Rickey called out the NCAA for criticizing major league baseball for signing young players. Rickey pointed out that universities—through scholarships, phony jobs, and illegal cash payments—were recruiting and paying impressionable young kids, too, but keeping them classified as amateurs.[15]

The NCAA declared that as long as a college athlete did not earn money for *anything related to sports*, he was eligible to compete. The Amateur Athletic Union (AAU)—the US organization that determined eligibility for athletes to compete in the Olympic Games—was even quick to disqualify anyone who had played an amateur game on the same card on which pro teams appeared. During the Cold War, the IOC turned a blind eye to both the blatant professionalization of Soviet bloc athletes and the scholarships and training facilities provided to American college athletes. As the money in its "amateur games" grew, and because fans wanted to see the best in the world compete, the IOC finally bowed to reality in 1988 and allowed professionals into the Games.

This left the NCAA as the last big-money sports organization still clinging to the myth of the amateur athlete. Profits in soccer, rugby, cricket, tennis, the Olympics, and other sports became too big to prohibit players from getting a bigger piece of the pie. Nevertheless, the money makers in D-I sports today want to hold onto their healthy slice. The NCAA still prohibits universities from paying their "amateurs" and limits compensation to a scholarship voucher to attend classes (in 2023 proposals were made to pay players a modest salary, but few schools can afford that).

Money corrupted intercollegiate athletics from the start; college administrators were having none of that stuffy British upper-class idea of playing sport just for the jolly good fun of it. Winning on the playing

The "Accidental Industry"

field reflected the fiercely independent, entrepreneurial American spirit. The demand for winning inevitably meant paying college players on the sly, whether they were serious students or not. It was a ruthless business. "The spirit of the American youth," wrote a *Nation* journalist in 1890, "as of the American man, is to win, to 'get there,' by fair means or foul, and the lack of moral scruple which pervades the struggles of the business world meets with temptations equally irresistible in the miniature contests of the football field."[16] Educators preached that games taught sound morals, but sportsmanship on the football field was optional, and if one had to injure the opponent, so be it.[17]

In the 1890s, Yale coach Walter Camp forged college football's best team, helped by $100,000 of dark money to hire bogus students to play football. Camp was instrumental in changing college sports from student-run clubs to teams managed by paid coaches. On the gridiron, Harvard challenged Camp with the infamous "flying wedge," which was supposedly based on "Napoleon's surprise concentrations of military force." Injuries abounded, and doctors often had to be called out on the field. Harvard faculty were appalled and called for banning the sport.[18]

For universities across the Northeast and eventually the nation, football became an irresistible moneymaker and publicity boon. In 1894, the *New York Times* reported that the Yale–Harvard football game had netted $119,000—more than three million in today's dollars.[19]

The competition to lure coaches via salaries bigger than those paid to most professors on campus began in the late nineteenth century when University of Chicago president William Rainey Harper hired Amos Alonzo Stagg, who was a star end for Camp at Yale. Harper charged Stagg to "develop teams we can send around the country and knock out all the colleges."[20] Chicago fudged the academic performance of football players, who took most of their courses in the Physical Education Department. To this day, finding soft courses and easy majors for athletes remains a tried-and-true strategy for D-I athletic departments to keep players eligible.

As intercollegiate sports became more popular in the late nineteenth century, universities also began to use "ringers" to win games.[21] It was common practice to enroll college baseball players who had played in professional summer leagues, sometimes under aliases.[22] The screenwriters of the Marx Brothers comedy *Horse Feathers* (1932) obviously knew that phony students were infiltrating college football. In the film, Professor Wagstaff (Groucho) wanted to enlist professional football

Chapter One

players to help Huxley College beat archrival Darwin. Wagstaff mistakenly hires a couple of bootleggers instead, and the usual mayhem ensues.

One of the most famous of the so-called "tramp athletes" was Fielding Yost, who played football for West Virginia before transferring to Lafayette College, right before Lafayette's key game with Penn. After helping Lafayette beat Penn, Yost, who would later become a great coach at Michigan, went back to West Virginia to finish a law degree.[23] In 1905, Alexander Meiklejohn, the dean at Brown University, called out colleges for hiring football players: "Thousands of dollars are expended annually in the work of securing for the teams men who have no right to play on them whatever."[24]

Players in the wild and wooly days of tramp athletes sold their talents to the highest bidder. In one game between two central Illinois towns, eight ringers from Notre Dame were paid to play for Carlinville. The gamblers betting on Carlinville were foiled when Taylorville out-ringered them by hiring nine University of Illinois players.[25]

At Chicago, Stagg was suspected of using professional players, but the administration of the university ignored it. Stagg is often credited (or blamed) for putting football on a more organized, business-like footing. In the Gilded Age, the generous payment of management (coaches) and the meager wages for workers (players) in college sports mirrored the private sector. More than a century ago, sociologist Albion Small made an observation that could be said of D-I players today: "The student-player lost control of his surpassingly enjoyable pastime—the adults snatched the joy from him, and his campus enjoyment became his campus employment."[26]

By 1905, Harvard was fed up with losing to Yale in football year after year, so the school hired coach Bill Reid for $7,000, about twice the average faculty salary, setting the precedent that sports were more important to a university than academics and faculty.[27]

The huge new venues that were built for the lucrative college football franchises also contradicted the mythical amateur system. In 1914, Yale finished its 70,000-seat stadium, the first of the big stadiums on college campuses. The Los Angeles Coliseum was built in 1923, where the nearby University of South California (USC) played football. In 1926, the American Association of University Professors (AAUP) decried the detrimental impact of college sports: "The distortion of values lasts throughout the college course [the students' years in college], if not through life." The huge spending on stadiums, the organization charged, "dwarfs the significance of the library, laboratory, and lecture hall."[28]

At least schools such as Minnesota and Illinois built "memorial" stadiums in honor of the 100,000 Americans who died in World War I. Dedicating stadiums to the fallen soldier is a tradition that is long gone in college athletics (there are few "memorials" left), having given way to the naming of sports venues after high-paying corporate advertisers. Today, there are eight college football stadiums with seating capacities of more than 100,000 (the NFL has none). Division I college football is a colossal spectacle—a secular religion with rabid, devoted disciples who worship at the weekly gridiron services. The temple's tables are flush with money.

The Intercollegiate Athletic Association (IAA) was formed in 1905 to end the mayhem in college football and bring an end to the corrupting influence of money in the game. The IAA was renamed the NCAA in 1910, but the organization could not put the greenback genie back in the bottle. Universities ignored the NCAA and its rules. Historian Kurt E. Kemper writes:

> With the home rule principle enshrined in NCAA bylaws and the growing necessity of public cover, big-time schools slowly joined the organization. The significance of home rule was that the NCAA maintained no regulatory power to govern college athletics for nearly a half a century. Nonetheless, many schools that belonged to the NCAA took advantage of the organization's annual meeting to espouse the principles of amateurism, faculty control, and athletics beholden to the mission of higher education.[29]

In 1916, the NCAA defined an amateur athlete as "one who participates in competitive physical sports only for pleasure, and the physical, mental, moral, and social benefits directly derived therefrom."[30] The reality suggested otherwise. In a Carnegie Foundation report of 1929, Carnegie head and former MIT president Henry Pritchett condemned college football for its hypocrisy:

> Athletics, in large measure professional in its methods and organization, fills a larger place in the eyes of students and even of the public than any other one interest. The paid coach, the professional organization of the college athletics, the demoralization of

students by participation in the use of extravagant sums of money, constitute a reproach of American colleges and to those who govern them.

The Carnegie report charged that "the paid coach is at the bottom of all difficulties in American college athletics."[31] A foundation survey of 112 colleges and universities revealed that only twenty-eight of them were running "ethical" sports programs. Even then, winning and making a profit trumped the teaching of fair play, honesty, and academic achievement.[32] Dr. Karl F. Wettstone, the president of the University of Dubuque (Iowa), witnessed the way sports was eroding the academic mission of his school and courageously eliminated the athletic department. "In view of the fact that college athletics have become so commercialized that coaches and athletic directors are paid three or four times the salary of the heads of other departments," Wettstone said, "I have come to the conclusion as the head of the University of Dubuque that I must step out of intercollegiate competition, or I must sacrifice my moral principles." Wettstone also criticized the recruitment of high school players, who he said were more interested in how much the school would pay them to play than in the school's educational standing.[33]

Paying "Amateur" Players

The popularity of college football boomed after World War I, rivaling baseball, boxing, and horse racing as America's favorite sport. Some previously parochial schools, such as Notre Dame and Southern Methodist, became nationally known through newspaper, magazine, and radio coverage of their teams. In 1926, Harvard created a "director of athletics" who would be "on the same footing in faculty deliberations as the professors in the university, and with the same authority as the deans."[34]

The big business of college sports was burgeoning. Shortly after the Carnegie Foundation issued its report, the athletic director at the University of Illinois, George Huff, said, "The problem of every university in the country should be to prove that the widespread criticism of modern athletics does not apply to them."[35] Creighton president Father Patrick J. Mahan agreed with Carnegie's conclusions: "I am convinced, and reasonably so, that no regular player is on a 'big team' without being paid. He does not, out of his own pocket, pay for his tuition fees, board, and lodgings. Yet authorities of universities decry the subsidizing of athletics." Mahan charged that some presidents were willfully ignorant of these illegal practices.[36] L. C. Boles, the athletic director and football coach at Wooster College (Ohio), implored "influential alumni, trustees, and curb-stone coaches" to exert pressure to reform the college game. Speaking to a gathering of physical education departments, Boles said that a sportswriter had it exactly right that college football was "one of the last strongholds of old-fashioned American hypocrisy." He added that "true educators" could not back college athletic departments "if we are sheltering hypocrisy, pseudo-amateurism or any shady practices."[37]

College football had already become too big to pay attention to the Carnegie Foundation or these few critics. For some schools, football subsidized all other athletic programs. In 1931, Big Ten football teams made $100,000 per school on average.[38] "The elements of 'professionalism' denounced by the Carnegie report eventually became standard practices," concludes sports historian Michael Oriard, "but not before three more decades of wrangling over the ethics of college football, with the economics trumping ethics at each step along the way."[39]

The imperative to win still describes the state of D-I intercollegiate athletics today. A school's academic reputation seldom plays a significant role in a top football or basketball recruit's choice of school. And with the hundreds of D-I players entering the so-called "transfer portal" to come out the other side playing for this or that team, it is obvious that they are not searching for a more suitable course of study but for a spot in the starting lineup or a better endorsement deal.

For more than a century, the NCAA has maintained the illusion that college athletes do not receive cash payments. Critics of college football in the interwar period called on school authorities to acknowledge that the sport had become "a stern and relentless business," as one journalist put it. It was obvious that players were being paid. In the early 1930s, Pitt football players were pocketing up to $650 a year.[40] Popular reporter Westbrook Pegler wrote that the practice should be brought out into the open. "[The problem was] the pretense and concealment, couched in resolutions and agreements of the most elaborate amateur piety."[41] The AAUP called the illegal payments to players "the crudest form of dishonesty."[42] Three years after the Carnegie report, former Columbia University student Reed Harris published *King Football: The Vulgarization of the American College* (1932), in which he wrote, "Watching college football from inside and out has convinced me that

Chapter One

the 'grand old game' has become a Frankenstein, threatening to throttle what is left of American higher education."[43]

In addition to illegal payments, college players found other ways to cash in on their talents. In the mid-1920s, the great University of Illinois halfback Red Grange ran roughshod over Big Ten defenses, but amateur purists were furious when "The Galloping Ghost" left school after his senior football season but before graduating to play for the Chicago Bears. Like cash-strapped college players today, Grange was supposed to eschew the opportunity to parlay his elusiveness on the gridiron into a needed payday. The NCAA still tries to restrict football and basketball players from going pro, relying on the NBA and the NFL not to sign younger players (the NHL and MLB, which do not rely on D-I teams as their minor leagues, have an age limit of eighteen).

As radio increased the popularity of college football in the 1930s and 1940s, more boosters showed up on college campuses to lure recruits, pay players, and hire ringers. Along with Oklahoma State's Hank Iba and Kentucky's Adolph Rupp, Phog Allen of Kansas is considered one of the greatest basketball coaches of the mid-twentieth century. He compiled a .729 winning percentage at Kansas, with whom he won the NCAA championship in 1952. Allen was an outspoken critic of college football, calling for it to "die of its own rottenness." He also decried the "rising professional tendency in college basketball" and castigated college presidents for allowing the recruitment of students for sports only: "Why should we sugar-coat and lie to high school athletes, when in the long run supplying them with an education is the basic purpose of college?" Allen denied any wrongdoing in his program, however, claiming that he had never promised "unsuspecting young rabbits [high school recruits] into the fold with glowing promises of board, room, laundry, and other chattels . . . it has always been by policy to rank schoolwork ahead of basketball. My present policy of not playing the boys who have lower than a 'C' average backs up this statement."[44] Sugar-coating its system of professional sports as an academic enterprise is an NCAA specialty.

Forest Evashevski, Iowa's football coach in the 1950s, confessed that winning was his only objective: "At most colleges, the pressure is on the coach from the president on down. The coach enters into a tacit understanding with the president that he will recruit good ball players by any means short of larceny. And if the coach doesn't come through with good recruiting, out he goes."[45]

The "Accidental Industry"

After World War II, the NCAA waived transfer rules for returning players, and the GI Bill gave veterans the chance to go to college. The black market for college football players ballooned. There were rumors that players were paid $100,000 or more, and that about half of college football players were veterans. The highly successful University of Kentucky basketball program was built on GI Bill players. "The mistake the NCAA made after the war," one coach said, "was to let boys go anywhere to college on the GI Bill, rather than back to where they'd [played before the war]. The rich got richer and the poor got poorer."[46] The same can be said for the liberalization of the so-called "transfer portal" today, which has created a free-for-all in recruiting players from other college teams, without any penalty for poaching.

Paying players for doing fake jobs was another way to circumvent NCAA rules. Illegal payments became so widespread that the NCAA passed the so-called "Sanity Code" in 1948 to "prohibit all concealed and indirect benefits for college athletes," save scholarships. Paying players, the organization said, was insane.[47]

The Sanity Code was a deadletter before the ink was dry. The Pacific Coast Conference folded in 1959 as the result of repeated illegal booster club payments to football teams, some of them with euphemistic names like USC's Southern California Educational Foundation, and UCLA's Young Men's Club of Westwood. The code might as well have been called the "Sanity Clause" from the famous "Party of the First Part" contract skit in the Marx Brothers' movie *Night at the Opera* (1935). Fiorello (Chico) objects at one point to a paragraph in the contract: "You can't fool me. There ain't no Sanity Clause." The same could be said about "amateur" D-I players.[48]

The Television Bonanza

Much of the money D-I college sports rakes in today comes from television contracts. Media money in college sports began modestly. In the 1920s, the advent of radio broadcasts helped to popularize college football. In 1931, the University of Minnesota signed an exclusive deal with Minneapolis-based WCCO radio to broadcast its games for $500 a year.[49] After World War II, television revenues served as the springboard to the NCAA's high-powered moneymaking machine. Penn was the first to televise its home games in the early 1940s, and by 1950, the school made $150,000 on its broadcasts.[50] At first, officials at the NCAA fretted that television might hurt live attendance numbers and tried to stop the practice. When Penn and other schools balked, the NCAA made its own deal for a weekly TV game, a twelve-game slate on which no team would appear more than once.

In 1950, 9 percent of Americans had a TV. By 1960, 90 percent of households had a set, and the NCAA procured a football television package for more than $3 million a year, to be shared with the nearly 1,000 members.[51] In the early 1960s, the NCAA was making more money on its television contract than the NFL.[52] The so called "Game of the Century" in 1966 between Notre Dame and Michigan State, the two top-ranked teams in the country, catapulted D-I college football as a competitor to the NFL and MLB for the biggest television sports draw (the game ended in a disappointing 10–10 tie).

In 1979, Michigan State was also involved in men's college basketball's leap into American living rooms when the Magic Johnson-led Spartans took on undefeated Larry Bird-led Indiana State in the NCAA championship, bringing the "madness" to the annual March tournament. According to the *New York Times*, "In the Big East Conference's first year of operation in 1979, it earned $305,000 for the right to broadcast all of its games; three decades later, ESPN would offer more than $100 million for those rights."[53]

The NCAA mistakenly thought that its TV money would be a bargaining chip to coerce schools to adhere to its picayune amateur rules. The NCAA had always been ruled by consent, like the British Empire, where most modern sports originated. The grand viziers (the NCAA) get relatively few satraps (athletic departments) to do their dirty work, keeping the profits of the enterprise from the exploited masses (the players). Like the empire, however, the members began to demand independence from the oppressive center.

The lucrative TV contracts inevitably led to squabbles between schools over revenue sharing. The big NCAA schools already resented the small fry for trying to save money by limiting the number of scholarships and coaches. The NCAA banned free substitution of players in 1953, but football costs ballooned when it allowed the two-platoon system again in 1965. Now, instead of eleven players playing both ways, players became offensive or defensive specialists, and rosters and coaching staffs expanded. Walter Byers, the NCAA executive director at the time, recalled, "The two-platoon system overtook college football with a vengeance. It was corporate and bureaucratic America at work; a head coach, offensive and defensive coordinators, position coaches, special team coaches, and plenty of recruiting coaches."⁵⁴ Byers said that for most of his tenure he fought a losing battle against athletic directors and coaches:

> When they sought more grants-in-aid [euphemism for an athletic scholarship], I campaigned for fewer. As they steamrolled their way to platoon football, I battled for limited substitution. When they wanted extra basketball games, I asked for a shorter season.... When I backed stronger enforcement, prominent coaches ridiculed the rules and damned the NCAA police force.⁵⁵

The price of fielding a football team continued to rise. In the 1970s, schools like California State University Long Beach were hemorrhaging cash on their highly unprofitable gridiron program. For its part, the school seldom, if ever, appeared on TV. In 1974, Long Beach president Stephen Horn sent a circular to other NCAA schools suggesting cutting D-I football scholarships by half, and that the NCAA share television revenues. "As far as I am concerned," he said, "Notre Dame and Ohio State can be on [TV] every weekend. If that were so, I think we [the NCAA] might get a $30 million contract for the season and it would help everybody." The big schools, however, were not in a generous mood, and the plan was never seriously considered. Michigan athletic director Don Canham fumed, "Hell, that's socialism, and we're not in a socialist state. Why should Michigan play for $40,000 rather than $450,000?"⁵⁶ "I don't want Hofstra telling Texas how to play football," grumbled Longhorns' coach Darrell Royal. Among those agreeing with Canham and Royal were football coaches Bear Bryant of Alabama, Oklahoma's Barry Switzer, and Indiana basketball coach Bobby Knight.⁵⁷

In 1981, the NCAA entered negotiations with ABC and CBS regarding televising college football games. Each of those companies had the rights to air fourteen live games per season as well as to negotiate individually with the competing schools, and they were required to pay a "minimum aggregate compensation" to the participating schools. The goal of the plan was to televise games in such a way as not to drastically decrease live attendance. The NCAA did not permit any of the schools to negotiate outside of this plan.⁵⁸

In the early 1980s, the big sports programs sought their own television packages. The launch of ESPN in 1979 had given D-I schools another programming option. The football powers decided to create the

College Football Association (CFA), taking the negotiation of television rights away from the NCAA. The CFA landed a separate contract with NBC for more games and money. In response, the NCAA announced that it would take disciplinary action against any school that complied with the CFA plan. The University of Oklahoma, supported by other members of the CFA, took the case to the Western District Court of Oklahoma, which found that the NCAA contract violated the Sherman Antitrust Act. When the NCAA appealed the decision, the Court of Appeals for Oklahoma affirmed the judgment of the lower court. Still unconvinced, the NCAA fought the ruling to the highest court in the land. In a 7–2 decision in 1984, the United States Supreme Court ruled that the NCAA's television plan imposed a restraint on the free market and thus violated Sherman. One University of Texas administrator crowed about the verdict, "We eat what we kill." Byers wrote in his 1995 memoir that this unbridled quest for revenue was "gnawing at the innards of college athletics."[59]

In the early 2010s, the CFA negotiated a contract with ESPN for $5.64 billion to televise the Bowl Championship Series (BCS) and six other bowl games from 2014 to 2025. The NCAA then turned to basketball for revenue, buying the National Invitational Tournament (NIT) in 1995. In 2010, the NCAA made a deal with CBS and Turner Broadcasting for March Madness: $10.8 billion for fourteen years. Today, basketball TV contracts comprise 95 percent of all NCAA revenues.[60] The NCAA made $1.06 billion on the tournament in fiscal year 2017, with $105 million in profit. Recently, the "non-profit" NCAA signed a new $8.8 billion TV deal for the amateur extravaganza through 2032.[61]

It is no wonder that former Duke coach Mike Krzyzewski lobbied for a basketball counterpart to the CFA—an association of the Power Five basketball conferences to control its own TV contracts. In 2021, West Virginia coach Bob Huggins also proposed that the big conferences hold their own basketball tournament, taking that revenue source away from the NCAA and excluding the little schools. "Those Cinderella schools are putting 200 people, at best, in their gym," he said. "We're putting 14,000."[62]

Teams and conferences have already created their own networks to bring more money directly back to their athletic departments. In 2011, Texas linked up with ESPN to form the Longhorn TV Network. When the Big Ten Conference launched the Big Ten Network (BTN) in the early 2010s, Conference Commissioner Jim Delaney defended the move

The "Accidental Industry"

as somehow connected to the work of a public broadcasting company: "When President Obama comes to the University of Michigan, we can televise it.... When there are flood-relief efforts in Iowa, we can be part of that."[63] It is difficult to decipher what Delaney was talking about. Don't look for news on BTN, which is solely dedicated to sports.

The competition for TV money from college sports continues apace. In 2006, the Big Ten landed a deal with ESPN for $1 billion over ten years to televise its football games. Two years later, the Southeast Conference (SEC) football teams picked up a tidy $3 billion, 15-year contract with ESPN and CBS. Minnesota's athletic budget was $130 million in 2018–2019, bolstered by $43.7 million paid to them by the BTN and other media contracts.[64] ESPN and ABC have a virtual lock on important college football games, including broadcasting forty of the forty-four 2021–22 bowl games. With the addition of Texas and Oklahoma to the SEC in 2025, the conference will distribute some $60 million to member schools annually.[65] In 1995, Byers pinpointed the dangers of the exploding profits from college sports: "As the rewards for winning multiplied, so did breaking the rules and cheating."[66]

With so much potential TV money, the CFA will undoubtedly expand the number of teams in the football playoffs as the NCAA did with the basketball tournament. Perhaps soon, a Fall Frenzy will tide us over until March Madness. Playing an extra two or three games on top of the twelve or thirteen D-I football teams already regularly schedule will negatively impact players' studies and final fall semester exams, but that is unlikely to be of primary concern to athletic departments.

The Student-Athlete Ruse

To keep the big television profits for themselves, athletic departments, coaches, and the NCAA doggedly clung to the legal definition of the athlete as a student and not an employee. In 1947, Congress ruled that the money that a pasta manufacturer had given to NYU law school could be taxed. According to the *New York Times*, "Sensing the threat, the NCAA pressed lawmakers to make sure that the new tax would not apply to money from sports programs. Accordingly, congressional committee reports declared that 'athletic activities of schools are substantially related to their educational function,' even citing the supposed educational benefits of football and basketball."[67]

In 1955, Ray H. Dennison died after sustaining a head blow while playing football for Fort Lewis A&M, a small school in Colorado. His widow sued the NCAA for workers' compensation, but the Colorado Supreme Court ruled that the college was "not in the football business."[68] The case went to the United States Supreme Court, where the NCAA won on the basis that Dennison was not playing for pay. Five years later, Cal State Poly player Edward Gary van Horn was killed in a crash of a university plane. Cal Poly refused to pay any compensation to his wife, arguing that his scholarship was a gift, not an employee's wages.[69]

In 1974, TCU running back Kent Waldrep was paralyzed from the neck down in a game against Alabama. Nearly two decades later, the Texas Workers' Compensation Commission ruled that Waldrep was an employee of the university, and he was awarded compensation of $70 a week for life. The university's insurance company appealed, arguing that a scholarship player was not a university employee. After a quarter-century of litigation, an appeals court handed down the final verdict in 2000: "[Waldrep] was not an employee because he had not paid taxes on financial aid that he could have kept even if he quit football." School officials told Waldrep that "they recruited [him] as a student, not an athlete." Waldrep called that "absurd." Waldrep's weekly seventy bucks were taken away. Waldrep died in 2022, having spent two-thirds of his life in a wheelchair.[70]

The free market imperatives of the business world, where the bottom line often trumps ethical behavior and fair treatment of workers, permeate the NCAA system. In effect, TCU told Waldrep to fend for himself. "So we occupy a world of hypocritical half-measures," observed journalist Steve Rushin. "We still end up in front of the TV, watching some sanctioned act of violence that wouldn't be countenanced if there were a People for the Ethical Treatment of People."[71]

The rulings confirmed the wisdom of Walter Byers, who led the NCAA from 1951 to 1987. Byers guided the organization and its members to unprecedented financial success, and his clever creation of the term "student-athlete" protected universities from workers' compensation claims and from paying state and federal taxes. Byers said that "[the term] was embedded in all NCAA rules and interpretations." Noted author Taylor Branch has criticized the NCAA's definition as self-serving and hypocritical:

> The term student-athlete was deliberately ambiguous. College players were not students at play (which might understate their

The "Accidental Industry"

athletic obligations), nor were they just athletes in college (which might imply that they were professionals). That they were high-performance athletes meant they could be forgiven for not meeting the academic standards of their peers; that they were students meant they did not have to be compensated, ever, for anything more than the cost of their studies. Student-athlete became the NCAA's signature term, repeated constantly in and out of courtrooms.[72]

After retiring as executive director in 1987, Byers' conscience spoke. Like Dr. Frankenstein and his monster, Byers came to rue his creation, which was tearing asunder the academic mission of higher education. "The colleges have expanded their control of athletes in the name of amateurism," he wrote, "a modern-day misnomer for economic tyranny." The NCAA claims to "promote the opportunity for institutions and eligible student athletes to engage in fair competition," but its rules are inherently antithetical to American dedication to the free-market system. The black market always plays the role of corrective to government restrictions on the free exchange of goods and services. Byers estimated that almost a third of D-I schools were breaking the rules and that illegal payments to athletes were commonplace.[73]

Under the heading "The Commitment to Amateurism," the NCAA Rules Book today hangs onto this nineteenth-century amateur ideal, even as the organization runs a multibillion-dollar sports industry:

> Member institutions shall conduct their athletics programs for students who choose to participate in intercollegiate athletics as a part of their educational experience and in accordance with NCAA bylaws, thus maintaining a line of demarcation between student-athletes who participate in the Collegiate Model and athletes competing in the professional model.

The Rules Book, which now runs well more than 400 pages in an endeavor to keep that sacred "line of demarcation," says nothing about the multimillion-dollar salaries paid to NCAA administrators, athletic directors, and coaches. Amateurism, such as it is and never was, is for athletes only. "I think in this day and age, as opposed to yesterday," NBA Hall of Famer Oscar Robertson concluded, "the concept of what they consider amateur basketball is gone forever."[74]

Chapter One

Notes

1. John Sayle Watterson, *College Football: History, Spectacle, Controversy* (Baltimore: Johns Hopkins Press, 2000), 154.

2. Will Yakowicz, "March Madness Gamblers Expected to Break $8.5 Billion Record Thanks to Mobile Sports Betting," *Forbes*, March 17, 2021, https://www.forbes.com/sites/willyakowicz/2021/03/17/march-madness-gamblers-expected-to-break-85-billion-record-thanks-to-mobile-sports-betting-draftkings-westgate/?sh=6e061e18776d, accessed May 5, 2021.

3. "The First Game: Nov. 6, 1869," Rutgers University, accessed January 15, 2021 https://scarletknights.com/sports/2017/6/11/sports-m-footbl-archive-first-game-html.aspx.

4. Allen Sanderson and John Siegfried, "Why American Universities Sponsor Commercial Sports," *Milken Institute Review*, July 31, 2018, accessed September 21, 2019, http://www.milkenreview.org/articles/why-american-universities-sponsor-commerical-sports?IssueID=29.

5. "College Football Business is Booming at Halfway Point, but Expansion Looms," *USA Today*, January 9, 2020, accessed November 2, 2020 https://www.usatoday.com/story/sports/ncaaf/2020/01/09/college-football-playoff-financial-success-expansion-future/2838495001/.

6. Sports books have a college basketball bet on the first team to get to fifteen points. Here the total for both teams for the whole game didn't add up to fifteen. In 1896, the University of Iowa played the University of Chicago in the first five–on–five game.

7. Unattributed, *Star Tribune*, February 3, 2022, C5.

8. Matthew P. Llewellyn and John Gleaves, "A Universal Dilemma: The British *Sporting Life* and Complex, Contested, and Contradictory State of Amateurism," *Journal of Sport History* 41, no. 1 (2014), 96.

9. Llewellyn and Gleaves, "A Universal Dilemma," 96.

10. See Ronald A. Smith, *The Myth of the Amateur: A History of College Athletic Scholarships* (Austin, TX: University of Texas Press, 2021), 11ff.

11. The so-called "mechanics clause" excluded workingmen from playing.

12. See James W. Martens, "'To Throttle the Hydra': The Middle Class and Rugby's Great Schism," *Canadian Journal of the History of Sport* 16, no. 1 (May 1991): 52–76.

13. Christopher Ford, "Cricket Ends Distinction Between Gents and Players," *The Guardian*, November 27, 1962, accessed September 8, 2021, https://www.theguardian.com/theguardian/2012/nov/27/cricket-gentleman-players-amateurs-1962.

14. Llewellyn and Gleaves, "A Universal Dilemma," 97.

15. Ronald A. Smith, *Pay for Play: A History of Big-Time College Athletic Reform* (Urbana: University of Illinois Press, 2011), 97.

16. Benjamin G. Rader, *American Sports: From the Age of Folk Games to the Age of Televised Sports,* Sixth Edition (Upper Saddle River, NJ: Pearson/Prentice Hall, 2009), 179.

The "Accidental Industry"

17. See Brian Ingrassia, *The Rise of the Gridiron University: Higher Education's Uneasy Alliance with Big-Time Football* (Lawrence, KS: University Press of Kansas, 2012), 8.

18. Taylor Branch, "The Shame of College Sports," *The Atlantic*, October 2011, accessed October 2, 2021, https://www.theatlantic.com/magazine/archive/2011/10/the-shame-of-college-sports/308643/; and Benjamin G. Rader, *American Sports*, 91.

19. Sean Gregory, "It's Time to Pay College Athletes," *Time*, September 16, 2013, 38.

20. Gregory, "It's Time," 38.

21. Smith, *Pay for Play*, 3. Smith cites a Harvard student publication from 1880 that revealed the practice.

22. See Michael Oriard, *King Football: Sport and Spectacle in the Golden Age of Radio and Newsreels, Movies and Magazines, the Weekly and the Daily Press* (Chapel Hill: University of North Carolina Press, 2001).

23. Eliott J. Gorn and Warren Goldstein, *A Brief History of American Sports* (Urbana, IL: University of Illinois Press, 2004), 231.

24. Allen L. Sack and Ellen J. Staurowsky, *College Athletes for Hire: The Evolution and Legacy of the NCAA's Amateur Myth* (Westport, CT: Praeger Publishers, 1998), 24.

25. Watterson, *College Football*, 152; and Smith, *The Myth of the Amateur*, 12.

26. Lane Demas, "The Test of Time: Revisiting Stagg's University and College Football Historiography," *Journal of Sport History* 39, no. 1 (Spring 2012): 115.

27. Rader, *American Sports*, 180.

28. Watterson, *College Football*, 157.

29. Kurt E. Kemper, *College Football and American Culture in the Cold War Era* (Urbana, IL: University of Illinois Press, 2009), 15.

30. Daniel E. Lazaroff, "The NCAA in Its Second Century: Defender of Amateurism or Antitrust Recidivist," *Oregon Law Review* 86 (No. 2, 2007): 329–336.

31. Smith, *Pay for Play*, 68–69.

32. Rader, *American Sports*, 192.

33. Unattributed, "Dubuque Head Bars Athletic Contests," *New York Times*, May 31, 1925, accessed March 24, 2021, https://www.nytimes.com/1925/05/31/archives/dubuque-head-bars-athletic-contests-president-wettstone-declares.html.

34. Unattributed, "Harvard Creates Board of Sports Director," *Chicago Tribune*, January 14, 1926, 21, accessed July 5, 2020, www.newpapers.com/image/363670215.

35. Unattributed, "Criticism of College Athletic Is Severe," *Lincoln Journal Star* (Nebraska), February 5, 1930, 12, accessed June 16, 2021, https://www.newspapers.com/image/66422007.

36. Unattributed, AP, "'Big Time Football is Crooked, Players Are Paid,' Creighton U. President Charges in Article," *Quad-City Times* (Davenport, Iowa), March 4, 1934, 17, accessed April 23, 2021, https://www.newspapers.com/image/301280446.

37. Unattributed, "Athletic Systems Assailed: Says Pressure and Business Interest Cause of Trouble," *Fort Madison Evening Democrat* (Iowa), December 1937, 2,

accessed January 15, 2021, https://newspaperarchive.com/fort-madison-evening-democrat-dec-28-1937-p-2/.

38. "Football Most Costly Sport," *St. Joseph Gazette*, October 31, 1932, accessed on Apr 20, 2021, https://www.newspapers.com/image/560767532.

39. Oriard, *King Football*, 8.

40. Oriard, *King Football*, 114.

41. Oriard, *King Football*, 106, 108.

42. Watterson, *College Football*, 157.

43. Reed Harris, *King Football: The Vulgarization of the American College* (New York: The Vanguard Press, 1932), 8.

44. Unattributed, "Dr. Allen Sees Sports Purge As Only Hope," *The Ogden Standard-Examiner*, January 26, 1941, accessed January 4, 2021.

45. Richard O. Davies, *Sports in American Life: A History* (Chichester: Wiley-Blackwell, 2012), 214.

46. Oriard, *King Football*, 116; and Kemper, *College Football and American Culture*, 13–14.

47. Branch, "The Shame."

48. Oriard, *King Football*, 81; Thalberg, I. (Producer), & Wood, S. (Director) (1935). *A Night at the Opera* [Motion Picture]. United States: MGM.

49. Kathleen M. O'Toole, "John L. Griffith and the Commercialization of College Sports on Radio in the 1930s," *Journal of Sport History* 40, no. 2 (Summer 2013), 241–257, 247.

50. Sanderson and Siegfried, "Why American."

51. Branch, "The Shame"; for a lively account of the emergence of televised college football, see Keith Dunnavant, *The Fifty-Year Seduction: How Television Manipulated College Football from the Birth of the Modern NCAA to the Creation of the BCS* (New York, NY: Thomas Dunne Books, 2004, 5ff.

52. Branch, "The Shame."

53. Mike McIntire, "The College Sports Tax Dodge," *New York Times*, December 31, 2017, 10A.

54. Walter Byers, *Unsportsmanlike Conduct: Exploiting College Athletes* (Ann Arbor, MI: University of Michigan Press, 1995), 99.

55. Byers, *Unsportsmanlike Conduct*, 169.

56. Watterson, *College Football*, 334–6.

57. Branch, "The Shame."

58. Mary H. Tolbert and D. Kent Meyers, "The Lasting Impact of NCAA vs Bd. of The University of Oklahoma," *Oklahoma Bar Journal*, October 18, 2018, https://www.okbar.org/barjournal/oct2018/obj8926tolbertmeyers/, accessed March 11, 2021.

59. Branch, "The Shame."

60. Howard P. Chudacoff, *Changing the Playbook: How Power, Profit, and Politics Transformed College Sports* (Urbana: U of Illinois, 2015), 128.

61. Joe Drape, "As N.C.A.A. Field Comes Together, Integrity is on the Bubble," *New York Times*, March 10, 2018, accessed March 24, 2021, https://www.nytimes.com/2018/03/10/sports/ncaabasketball/ncaa-tournament-selection-committee.html.

62. Dan Wolken, "No. 1 Gonzaga Has One Glass Ceiling to Shatter and It Better Happen Soon," *USA Today*, October 28, 2021, 1C.

63. Steven Conn, "Singing the Team-Spirit Blues," *Chronicle of Higher Education*, January 1, 2011, accessed October 11, 2021, https://www.chronicle.com/articl/singing-the-team-spirit-blues/.

64. Chip Scroggins, "U Budget Concerns Signal New College Era," *Star Tribune*, April 9, 2020, C1.

65. Dan Wolken, "Alliance Will Dictate Future of College Sports," *USA Today*, August 25, 2021, 2C.

66. Byers, *Unsportsmanlike Conduct*, 5.

67. McIntire, "The College Sports Tax Dodge," 10A.

68. Loretta8, "Friendly Reminder: The NCAA Invented the Term 'Student-Athlete' To Get Our of Paying Worker's Comp," Northwestern University SB Nation, January 28, 2014, https://www.insidenu.com/2014/1/28/5355988/ncaa-student-athlete-kain-colter-union-workers-comp, accessed January 15, 2022.

69. Sack and Staurowsky, *College Athletes for Hire*, 80.

70. Branch, "The Shame"; and Emily Langer, "Football Paralysis Led to More Spinal Cord Research, *Star Tribune*, March 13, 2022, A2.

71. Steve Rushin, "Morality Players," *Sports Illustrated*, March 18, 2013, 64.

72. Branch, "The Shame."

73. Byers, Unsportsmanlike Conduct, 347.

74. Gregory, "It's Time," 38.

CHAPTER TWO

The Big Gamble:
Peddling College on the Front Porch of D-I Sports

> Professor Quincy Adams Wagstaff (Groucho Marx) to the faculty of Huxley College:
> "And I say to you, gentlemen, that this college is a failure. The trouble is we're neglecting football for education. . . . Where would this college be without football? Have we got a stadium?"
> "Yes."
> "Have we got a college?"
> "Yes."
> "Well, we can't support both. So tomorrow we start tearing down the college."
> "Professor, where will the students sleep?"
> "Where they always sleep—in the classroom."
> —*Horse Feathers* (1932)[1]

The plot of *Horse Feathers*, if that really matters in that scattershot joke fest of a Marx brothers' film, is the hiring of professional ringers to win a college football game. However, the film keenly satirizes the built-in contradictions of college sports with Wagstaff's final line above.

The increased costs of intercollegiate sports have not resulted in tearing down colleges, but there is a direct correlation between the exploding expenditures of athletic departments, the rising costs of higher education, and scrimping on academic budgets. To subsidize D-I sports, administrators must increase tuition and student fees as well as cut the number of tenure-track professorships. From 2000 to 2020, in-state tuition and fees went up by 212 percent at public universities and 144 percent at private schools.[2] Students are being asked to underwrite intercollegiate sports; at the same time, collective student debt in the last quarter of 2020 rose to the highest levels in history: approximately $1.7 trillion for 45 million borrowers.[3]

In the late nineteenth century, on-campus games were a way for colleges to encourage more students to matriculate. Supply exceeded demand at the new land-grant universities, and football, basketball, and baseball became a way of luring young men to their campuses for "camaraderie and recognition."[4] Historians Elliott J. Gorn and Warren Goldstein observe,

> College football, as a consuming phenomenon in institutions of higher learning, stood at the center of the cultural transformation of the late nineteenth and twentieth centuries. It assisted in the redefinition of American middle- and upper-class masculinity; it helped reorganize American colleges and universities into institutions controlled by alumni in the service of class socialization and character-building at the expense of academics.[5]

The popularity of college football soon eclipsed any intentional or unintentional didactic purposes of sport for the average student. As the games became more competitive and publicized in the press, teams such as Yale, Harvard, and Pitt began to recruit top high school players. Other students' opportunities to play at the best schools dwindled. Rosters were full of sought-after players, who were often paid under the table. The huge expenditures on D-I college sports today are made on a miniscule part of the student body, relegating most students to spectating rather than participating. Instead, the revelry surrounding big football and basketball games has become an important sales pitch to potential students.

Sports and the University's "Front Porch"
College leaders recognized early on that football was a way to promote their schools, and winning became paramount. The better the team, the bigger the advertisement. At the turn of the century, Harvard President Charles Eliot lamented, "Colleges are presenting themselves to the public, educated and uneducated alike, as places of mere physical sport and not as educational training institutions."[6] After World War I, print media and radio expanded coverage of games, and college football began to make money.[7] What many colleges began to do—in the parlance of marketing departments today—is "brand" their product as a place that

produced winning football teams and a school that prospective students wanted to attend for the fun and games. "[D-I] athletics is a common good," argued University of Virginia athletic director Craig Littlepage several years ago, "bringing people together, developing relationships, unifying the institution, bringing fantastic exposure."[8] That would be all well and good if the huge expenditures on sports entertainment did not marginalize academic objectives.

In the 1920s, Southern Methodist University (SMU) decided to embark on the path that brought Notre Dame, USC, and Michigan, among others, to national football prominence. Symbolic of SMU's new emphasis on football was the postponement of building a new library in favor of a new football stadium. Michael Oriard pinpoints this shift in educational priorities: "As the Mustang football team dazzled New York sportswriters and fans with its 'aerial circus' passing attack over the early 1930s, ultimately claiming the top ranking in 1935 and a trip to the Rose Bowl, faculty salaries dropped while the football coach's rose to several times that of a full professor."[9] The formula was set—and not only at SMU—that the contracts of top college football coaches would dwarf the average college professor's salary.

The success of the Notre Dame and SMU football teams after World War I put their relatively unknown schools on the map, and others wanted to follow. Success on the gridiron became a huge publicity stunt; for some schools, it became more important than touting a school as a top-notch academic institution. The 1929 Carnegie Foundation report chastised NCAA football for its detrimental impact on college education, finding that a vast majority of colleges were breaking amateur and eligibility rules because football had become such a big marketing tool:

> The athlete is the most available publicity material the college has. A great scientific discovery will make good press material for a few days, but nothing to compare [sic] to that of the performance of a first-class athlete.... A college wants students, it wants popularity, and above all it wants money and always more money.[10]

The Carnegie Foundation's indictment of college football rings true today. Division I schools spend millions on men's basketball and football teams as a recruiting tool—the so-called "front porch" of the university house—to entice students to enroll. It is a huge gamble, but most college administrators do not question the premise of wagering general funds and student fees on fielding winning teams; the message to their athletic departments is to win or get fired. Everyone involved in running sports programs mouths the importance of academic excellence and graduation rates, but winning is the only real way to make the investment worthwhile.

Although many university presidents began as professors, they have become steeped in the business rather than the academic model of higher education. Almost to a person, they are fully on board with the current system and see sports as the best way to get prospective students to matriculate. They have fully accepted that the packaging on the outside is as (or more) important than the product inside. When the University of Minnesota hired Ben Johnson to coach the men's basketball team in 2021, University President Joan Gabel said, "Athletics is such an inviting 'front porch' for so much of the great work we do here at the university. Few programs are more visible or closely followed than Gopher men's basketball." Again, the message to prospective students is loud and clear: Choose Minnesota because of its winning basketball team, not because of its excellent pre-law or pre-med programs. Diverting some of the athletic budget to recruiting top students and faculty would be a more honest and effective use of the taxpayers' and students' money.[11]

Some schools have de-emphasized big sports programs and promoted themselves as leading academic institutions. Princeton, Harvard, and Yale were among the most followed football programs before World War II, but in the 1960s, the Ivy League decided to return to its core educational mission. That strategy has served these elite academic schools and their alumni well; there is little doubt that an Ivy League degree is a huge advantage for job applicants. Top students who go to Kansas or Kentucky because they have good basketball teams or to Alabama or Oklahoma because they have winning football teams will likely come up short in competition with the Ivy Leaguers after graduation.

Aside from the deficits that most D-I schools run to field winning teams year after year, the sports-as-front-porch strategy is a peculiar way to sell an institution of higher learning. Dave Brandon, the Domino's Pizza CEO who was the athletic director at Michigan from 2010 to 2014, said that his main job was to "build the brand"—the brand being winning sports teams.[12] Elson Floyd, a former president of Washington State University, saw no alternative to sports as the best advertisement for universities. "Like it or not," he said, "football serves as the front door to institutions. . . . The reputation of a school is predicated on athletics. Football is first. Basketball is second. If you have a successful football program, it will support all the other revenue and non-revenue sports."[13]

Richard Brodhead became president of Duke University in 2004. Duke is considered one of the best academic institutions in the country, but a decade later, he said that it was "foolish" and "disheartening" that prospective students cite the men's basketball team as the "primary reason they applied to attend Duke." They want to be "Dukies." Brodhead quickly found out that the most important figure on campus was Coach Mike Krzyzewski, or "Coach K," as he is affectionately known to his legion of fans. Longtime Duke anthropology professor Orin Starn says that Duke basketball rests on a high altar: "Big-time sports have become a modern tribal religion for college students . . . [causing a] strain of anti-intellectualism." Hired in 1969, Notre Dame philosophy professor Gary Gutting witnessed the increased importance of football to a school that already had a long history of great teams. "When colleges commit so much to a non-intellectual, even an anti-intellectual endeavor," Gutting contended, "they joined hands with the forces that want to marginalize intellectual endeavors."[14]

Decades ago, there were still some university presidents who thought differently, but any candidate for the job today who suggested shifting money from the athletic budget to academics would be disqualified. Seattle University, which made it to the NCAA basketball final in 1958 with future NBA Hall of Famer Elgin Baylor, dropped D-I sports in 1980 in favor of the National Association of Intercollegiate Athletics (NAIA). Father William Sullivan, Seattle University's president, posed this rhetorical question: "Should an institution like Seattle be placing such a large amount of money into subsidizing a program for a handful of students—one that in many ways contaminates the educational ideals of a university?" The money saved from D-I sports went to intramural sports for all students and minority scholarships. In addition, alumni increased their giving.[15] Father Sullivan's vision did not last long. In 2009, Seattle University went D-I again, spending millions on sports every year in the process. The Seattle Redhawk basketball team has posted mediocre records; admissions have remained constant. Athletic facilities that used to be available to the entire student body are now often reserved for D-I teams.[16]

Former University of Michigan President James J. Duderstadt understood the paradox of presenting athletics as the face of the school: "The popularity of Michigan athletics is a double-edged sword," he said. "While it certainly creates great visibility for the university—after each Rose Bowl or Final Four appearance, the number of applications for admission surges—it also poses a significant threat to the institution."[17]

No losing football or basketball team presents an inviting front porch, so the NCAA has expanded the postseason football and basketball games to make sure that more schools can claim success. Except for the handful of heavyweights who play in the best bowl games every year or have a realistic shot at making a deep run in March Madness, the bar is set low for what might be considered a winning season.

Regular season championships are barely noticed. As one Ohio State Buckeye football fan put it, "League titles don't count for much anymore; it's the national championship or you lose."[18] The same is true for conference basketball tournaments, except for the winners that get an automatic bid to March Madness. Athletic directors and coaches boast about playing in any bowl game, but it is worth noting that in 2021–22, 88 out of the 130 D-I football programs made it to a bowl game, some as prestigious as the Cheez-It Bowl and the Famous Idaho Potato Bowl. Not many campuses get excited about their teams playing in these lowly bowl games. Nevertheless, these days, even teams with records under .500 can get a bowl bid.

Basketball teams that have a slim chance of winning a single game in March Madness sit around in front of a television camera on Selection Sunday and go bananas when they hear their school's name as having made the sixty-eight-team field (of more than 350 D-I teams). The bottom feeders are likely to get whipped in their first tournament game. As of 2021, fifteen and sixteen seeds in the tournament had a record of 10–274, a dismal .036 winning percentage. Nonetheless, athletic directors put up banners in their arenas for just *making* the tournament. One has to hand it to athletic departments for convincing the public that just playing in a bad bowl game or getting one of the great many March Madness bids constitutes a successful season.

Most prospective college students do not pick a D-I school because of their success on the field of play, although there is some evidence that school enrollments initially rise as a result of a winning season. Winning ball games does not guarantee long-term success for a university, however, in enrollment and academic reputation.[19] It may even hurt the latter; do colleges really want to be known for sports first, with academic excellence a distant second? Do college presidents want to boast that increased enrollment is due to a winning football or basketball team, and not to the excellence of their faculty and academic programs? The answer to both questions seems to be an emphatic yes.

The University of Nevada Las Vegas (UNLV) was a basketball powerhouse in the 1970s and 1980s under Coach Jerry Tarkanian, who did not care about his players' performance in the classroom. Ultimately, Tarkanian was charged with numerous NCAA violations and left to coach in the NBA. The Runnin' Rebels have had mostly mediocre records since.

No one would say that Tarkanian's run elevated UNLV to elite academic status or even to a go-to school in the West. In 1984, UNLV hired a new president to rein in the emphasis on D-I sports. "I have been single-minded in my commitment to build the academic reputation of the university," Robert Maxson said. "Sports are extracurricular activity. They are not central to the mission of this institution."[20]

As already noted, SMU fielded great football teams before and after World War II, until repeated boosters' payments to players forced the NCAA to ban the Mustangs from competition in 1987. SMU is a very good school academically, but the football scandal sullied its reputation. Southern Methodist boosters made a bad bet when they helped pay players. In fact, SMU's alumni donations did not grow even when the Mustangs were winning, because it was common knowledge what the boosters were doing. After SMU got the "death penalty," overall donations to the university dropped precipitously.[21]

In 1984, quarterback Doug Flutie led underdog Boston College to an improbable last-second victory over heavily favored Miami, and the school's admission applications shot up due to that one win. At the same time, Boston College's reputation as a good "party school" got a boost too. The so-called "Flutie Factor" encouraged other schools to increase athletic budgets to field winning football and men's basketball programs. It made no difference that the Flutie Factor was a fleeting phenomenon. Since then, Eagles football has fallen on relatively hard times, with mediocre records year after year.[22]

In 2006, business magnate T. Boone Pickens, who lost his scholarship to Texas A&M University when he was cut from the basketball team, gave Oklahoma State football $165 million. "What I keep coming back to," he said, "is we're in the Big 12, and it's a tough conference. I want us to be competitive.[23] Student enrollment went up fourfold and annual giving to the school increased.[24] It is not known whether any of the money was used to hire more faculty to teach all those new students. Schools also see a significant increase in applications when their teams make a run in March Madness. After mid-major George Mason University made it to the Final Four in 2006, applications jumped. Similarly, Butler University made two straight Final Fours in 2010 and 2011, and applications to the school increased 43 percent.[25]

The problem with this formula for attracting students is that no one can ensure that their teams will win and continue to win. And investment in D-I athletic programs certainly does not increase the absolute numbers of students going to college. The arms race to field winning teams merely attracts students to the winners, evidently leaving the losers behind, regardless of their academic standing and whether a school has the field of study that a prospective student wants.[26]

Naturally, for every winning team, there has to be a losing one; recruiting is a zero-sum competition for a finite number of prospective students. Furthermore, serious questions should arise about the branding of schools as sports juggernauts rather than as high-level intellectual institutions. It is a Faustian bargain. Winning teams certainly did nothing to enhance the academic reputation of Boston College, Butler, or Oklahoma State. Even if one is rightfully skeptical of the validity of *U.S. News and World Report* annual rankings of universities, Oklahoma State never cracks the top 150 as a top academic school, regardless of how its football team performs.

Alan Sanderson and John Siegfried call attention to the ephemeral nature of the big gamble on college teams as a recruitment tool:

> Student recruitment remains one of the ostensible rationales for hosting commercialized intercollegiate sports, although there is little evidence that the boost to enrollment for schools with winning teams is either substantial or enduring. Moreover, most of the (limited) effect is simply to rearrange students among institutions rather than stimulate overall college attendance. In any event, one has to wonder whether students (or the institutions) are well served by marketing that conflates the quality of education offered with the win–loss records of their sports teams.[27]

The NCAA's Bad Business Practices

College coaches are hired and fired on an objective bottom line of wins and losses. Although athletic directors are charged with squeezing the most money possible from their revenue-producing sports programs (if they have any), the definition of what constitutes their success is less clear. "College sports is a business," observes B. David Ridpath, an associate professor of sports administration at Ohio University, "but it is a poorly, poorly run business because most everybody is losing money. And it's continually being subsidized through budget transfers, student fees, and everything."[28] Dave Brandon, a former Michigan athletic director, concurs. "If anybody looked at the business model of the big-time college athletics, they would say this is the dumbest business in the history of the world. You just don't have the revenue to support the costs. And costs continue to go up."[29] The University of Florida athletic department lost about $36 million in 2021.[30] If running their budgets in the red constituted failure, one would expect more pink slips for athletic directors.

The Covid pandemic was the latest hit to athletic department coffers, but the NCAA was already leaking oil. Attendance is down at most college football and basketball games.[31] In the late 2010s, for example, the University of Minnesota saw a small increase in fans going to its football games, but men's basketball was in a downward spiral. One would expect the "state of hockey" to support the Gopher pucksters, but from 2013 to 2019, attendance at men's games was down an average of more than 4,000 fans.[32]

In the wake of the pandemic and immense revenue shortfalls in 2020, athletic departments have begun to cut non-revenue sports. Stanford planned to close eleven sports programs, including women's fencing and men's rowing and wrestling, for a savings of $70 million across three years. Alumni protests and new outside funding sources led to their reinstatement.[33]

In 2021, the University of Minnesota regents had to authorize the Gopher athletic department to procure up to a $50 million loan to cover its losses due to the pandemic. Minnesota only needed to take out a $21.5 million loan.[34] In early 2022, Minnesota's athletic director Mark Coyle got a two-year extension and a raise of about $25,000 to nearly $1 million a year, with hundreds of thousands of dollars in incentives.

Coyle cut three men's programs—tennis, indoor track and field, and gymnastics. Given the Gophers' recent mediocre records in football, men's and women's basketball, and men's hockey (a big deal in Minnesota), as well as the athletic department's annual deficits, one wonders what it would take for someone like Coyle to be fired instead of getting a pay raise. Of course, Coyle points to the relatively high grade-point average of Gopher athletes as a measure of his success, but if non-athletes received a four-year scholarship, dedicated dorms, posh lounging areas and food courts, personal academic tutors, supervised study halls, and soft courses of study, their GPAs might improve as well.[35]

Few university leaders today openly question whether sports are the best way to promote their universities, even though most athletic departments lose millions of dollars every year. One former University of Michigan president admitted, "Nine of ten people don't know what you are saying when you talk about research universities. But you say 'Michigan' and they understand those striped helmets running under the banner."[36] After Northwestern won the Big Ten football title in 1995, applications to the school went up 21 percent, but it has maintained its high admission qualifications as well as a fine academic reputation. Northwestern does not need good football and basketball teams to attract top students, and they attract athletes with stellar academic credentials. There are not many excellent scholars who are also D-I-caliber athletes—Stanford, Rice, Vanderbilt, California Berkeley, and Northwestern, to name a few top academic schools, snatch them up.[37]

Defenders of the system argue that donors would not contribute at all to their universities if not for the opportunity to bolster their team's chances of landing the best recruits. Michael Oriard found that "giving to athletics [comes] at the expense of academics."[38] The scramble for money is an insidious diminution of the educational mission and in no way contributes to the integration of pampered athletes into the student body as a whole. Fostering an intellectual climate on campus is an afterthought. In 2017, journalist Jason Gay wrote sarcastically, "Football is the only way for a modern university to be truly great. Yeah, yeah, yeah—there are admission standards, classes, research, and maybe even Nobel Prizes and stuff, but those are pretty boring."[39]

Richard W. Conklin, a former vice president of Notre Dame, is adamant that spending on D-I sports does not boost donor contributions:

> Repeat after me. There is no empirical evidence demonstrating a correlation between athletic department achievement and [alumni] fundraising success. A number of researchers have explored this putative relationship, and they all have concluded that it does

not exist. The myth persists, however, aided by anecdotal evidence from sports reporters who apparently spend more time in bars than in development [fund-raising] offices.[40]

Campus Ball and Beer

Intercollegiate athletic competitions have been an important part of the college experience for a long time, and they are a big lure to schools today. Division I schools are unabashed about promoting game days as one reason to come to their campuses.

In the 1920s, college football became a big draw for fans and a staple of campus life at some schools. Noted journalist Paul Gallico observed that football had a particularly strong pull for spectators, like the 125,000 people who showed up for the 1930 Army-Notre Dame game at Soldier Field in Chicago. "When football becomes a near-tragic race against time," he wrote, "there is nothing like it for thrill or excitement or suspense. The game exerts its magic, and you forget that it is just football."[41]

Providing entertaining sports on campus today has become, for many schools, part of their hospitality business, somewhat akin to a very expensive four-year stay at an all-inclusive resort. When admissions offices take prospective students on tours, they show them the nice digs at residence halls, the extravagant food courts, the athletic club-like recreation facilities, and luxurious student centers. They are rarely shown a class session.[42] The pep rallies, drinking, and carousing—all the extracurriculars associated with college sports—are part of selling schools on student life outside of the classroom.

As the competition for new students and revenues increased in intensity in the 1990s, universities began to focus on what they dubbed the new "three R's"—student recruitment and retention, and renewal of alumni donations. The subtle message was that the old three "R's"— actually learning—were not the main objective. Some schools put the success of their sports teams into recruiting guidebooks as a reason to matriculate. College administrators invite students to come for the revelry (another "R") at athletic contests—or the "beer and circus," as sports historian Murray Sperber called it. In the University of Arkansas guidebook, one Razorback student is quoted as saying, "I'm a true Razorback fan!" Another student confesses, "My family loves the Razorbacks passionately." The guidebook suggests that students come to Arkansas for the game-day festivities, although that is hardly a good reason to pick one school over another, unless over-the-top partying is worth $100,000 or more in tuition over four years.[43]

Beer—the cheaper the better—has become intimately linked to the promise of college sports bacchanal. One student from Indiana University said that he and his buddies liked to go to bars rather than to the arena for basketball games. "Drinking with your [fraternity] brothers is a big part of watching a game," he said, "and a whole lot better than cheering when dumb-ass cheerleaders tell you to."[44]

In the 1980s, Miller Lite and Bud Light competed to slake the thirst of college sports fans. Bud Light introduced Spuds MacKenzie to shill its suds, specifically targeting college campuses. The cute little dog was a hit. In one ad, he was even linked with the hated Islamic leader of Iran. "Posters of the Ayatollah Partyollah," wrote a *Los Angeles Times* journalist, "in which he often appears surrounded by beautiful young women, are now the best-selling pin-ups in the country."[45]

One of the most visible examples of the importance of college football to campus life is the enormous Texas A&M game day "Bonfire," a tradition dating back more than one hundred years. According to an A&M website, "Bonfire became a symbol of the deep and unique camaraderie that is the Aggie Spirit." During construction of the enormous bonfire structure in 1999, it collapsed, killing twelve and injuring twenty-seven students.[46] Texas A&M decided to go ahead with its big game against Texas a week later. The football show had to go on. The Aggies no longer officially sponsor Bonfire, but since 2003, students have taken the big burn off campus.

Danger stemming from praying at the altar of college athletics takes other forms as well. The partying surrounding college athletic events often becomes criminal when exultant or enraged students riot after a win or a loss in a big game. After Michigan State lost in the 1999 NCAA basketball tournament, Spartan fans vandalized stores and overturned cars on the streets of East Lansing. Noted *New York Times* sportswriter Robert Lipsyte wrote, "Sports was clearly some kind of excuse, a permission to go mad. Alcohol was a fuel, and this is the Bud Light generation to which beer, breasts, and ball games are inextricably bound."[47]

College leaders are either indifferent to on-campus binge drinking centered around the gameday experience or powerless to stop it. Many alumni coming back "home" to their alma mater for games do not abide by rules banning alcohol on campus. A University of Mississippi promotional piece pushed the slogan "Party, party, party" with the tagline,

"We may lose a game, but we never lose a party." One Rebel student observed alumni getting as stinky drunk as students: "Husbands bring their wives, and you see forty-year-olds passed out on the floor! It gets a bit ridiculous."[48] The sidewalk in front of the dozens of bars near the University of Nebraska football stadium has the distinction of having been dubbed "the most puked-upon stretch of concrete in the United States." The annual Florida-Georgia football game in Jacksonville claims to be "The World's Largest Outdoor Cocktail Party."[49] It is not a good sign that bars on some college campuses, such as Iowa State, are called "The Library."

Other big-time party schools are Florida State and Ohio State, whose home games turn into weekend-long campus carnivals. *The Princeton Review* ranks the home of the Seminoles near the bottom on the quality of undergraduate education. In 2010, Ohio State canceled classes on Thursday afternoon in anticipation of the night game.[50] For a Saturday home game, many Buckeye fans skip Friday classes to start drinking and continue to imbibe until early the next morning, something cheekily dubbed "kegs and eggs."[51] After celebrating a win or drowning in beer over a loss, there is not much studying going on Sunday for Monday's so-called "hangover" classes. One senior at Ohio State observed, "This school treats the average [undergraduate] student like shit. And so we blow off our classes and party on High Street. *Go Bucks*. I've had a great four years of partying and following the Bucks but an awful four years of course work."[52]

In 1998, former University of Wisconsin Chancellor and United States Secretary of Health and Services Donna Shalala suggested that universities cut off the connection between alcohol and athletic contests. "No bringing alcohol to the site of an event. No turning a blind eye to underage drinking at tailgate parties—and on campus. And no alcohol sponsorship of intercollegiate sporting events."[53] The reader can conclude how far that idea went. One journalist with expertise in medical issues found that "the highest risk campuses . . . [those with] big sports programs, fraternities, and sororities . . . go that way for two reasons: They attracted binge drinkers and they turned non-drinkers into binge drinkers."[54]

College Kids and Gambling

Betting on D-I sports has also become a big part of the college party scene, and university administrators know it. A 1990 study estimated that nearly a quarter of college students (the vast majority male) bet on games at least once a week.[55] One US district attorney investigating a Northwestern University gambling operation quipped, "If I had to design a place to groom gamblers, I would design a college.... College students have access to credit cards, access to athletes, and access to computers."[56]

Betting on college football and basketball games is ubiquitous now, as most anyone can do it on a cell phone, but the NCAA sticks its collective head in the sand regarding the staggering amount of wagering on its "amateur" games. This is yet another way that the organization obfuscates its role in what is seen by moralists as an unseemly practice. Much like the association of alcohol with the college sports scene, gambling is more or less harmless if not overdone or done to the point of addiction. In any event, jaundiced gamblers have this wry motto: "Good coaches win. Great coaches cover [the betting spread]."

Only in the last few years have sports announcers dared to acknowledge that if, for example, a college football score is 45–3 at the end of the game, that someone was paying attention to an attempted field goal (alluding, of course, to the over and under total or to the point spread). It used to be an unwritten rule that TV broadcasters did not mention the betting lines, but sports aficionados were aware of one who did: Brent Musburger would regularly make cryptic comments about a meaningless (to the outcome) score at the end of a blowout college game. It was no surprise that he joined a streaming network for gambling news and analysis.

In 2018, ESPN's Scott Van Pelt and his sidekick "Stanford Steve" began a segment on Sports Center called "Bad Beats," a reference to a wager that looks like gold until the very end of the game, then turns into a loser because of some quirky, improbable plays. Most of the "bad beats" are college games. *New York Post* columnist Justin Terranova asked Van Pelt if the network had tried to stop the popular weekly bit: "There was very little pushback. I basically told the bosses all along that I'm going to do this.... If anything, Bad Beats is a cautionary tale [about gambling]."[57]

The NCAA downplays the gambling on college sports, but athletic directors schedule games at any time on any day of the week, regardless of whether it interferes with the players' scheduled classes for the players and the student fans. During the basketball season these days, there is a D-I game almost every night of the week. Every Saturday during the basketball season, there are more than thirty televised college games. As long as there is some game being played somewhere between two bad college teams, gamblers get action, television networks get viewers, and the money pours into the NCAA and athletic departments. The networks know that bettors will bet on and are therefore likely to watch all or part of any game, regardless of its importance in the standings. The NCAA has even allowed Friday games in the fall, a traditionally dry night for college football in deference to the Friday night lights of high school contests. Television networks also determine the starting times for football games. Obviously, the TV tail is wagging the college dog.

The NCAA's decision to play games at any time of the week to fill television slots puts the organization squarely complicit in keeping the networks and gamblers happy. The Mid-American Conference (MAC) has played football games on Tuesdays and Wednesdays for years. Thankful bettors call it "MACtion."

The Athletic "Arms Race"

Relying on winning men's basketball and football programs to boost admissions is like playing roulette. The losers playing the wheel will always outnumber the winners. Robert Mulcahy, the athletic director at Rutgers from 1998 to 2008, put the gamble this way: "Everyone acknowledges that winning football and basketball programs can generate millions of dollars of revenue for their schools."[58] The key word here is "can." Most don't.

The so-called "arms race," the competition between schools to build bigger and better facilities for their athletes and hire the best (and most expensive) coaches, increases the amount of the wager every year. In the 1950s, Texas A&M put other schools on notice that it would dedicate big money to recruiting players. The university built a special dorm complex for athletes that included a swimming pool and TV room. The University of Kentucky joined in the high-stakes competition by refurbishing a private mansion into what looked like a ski lodge for its basketball players, appropriately called the "Joe B. Hall Wildcat Lodge" after the famed coach. The Atlantic Coast Conference (ACC) commissioner complained that it looked like a "rich man's club," so the NCAA forced Kentucky to make the place "less luxurious," as NCAA head Walter Byers put it. Kentucky got around any sanction by allowing a few non-athlete students to live there.[59] The huge investments in recruiting enticements did not always pan out. After building a posh dorm spa for its football players in 1969, Kansas State posted a miserable .327 winning percentage for the next ten years.[60]

Spending on intercollegiate sports is out of control. In 2007, Texas erected an $8 million scoreboard dubbed the "Godzillatron." The school had to install an air conditioner to keep the 134-foot-wide behemoth from overheating.[61] As of 2017, twenty-seven universities spent more than $100 million annually on intercollegiate sports, with the University of Texas at Austin leading the way at more than $171 million. All but five made money for their universities. All of the schools are in the Power Five conferences (ACC, Big Ten, Big 12, Pac-12, and SEC).[62] Former Texas athletic director DeLoss Dodds said, "Football is the train that drives everything and pays for everything. It just is. Everything begins and ends with football."[63] Maybe for Texas. In 2010–11, only 22 of 120 of the big football programs broke even or made money.[64]

Minneapolis *Star Tribune* sports columnist Chip Scoggins recently exposed profligate spending at the University of Minnesota: "In 2012, the Gophers athletic department reported $83.6 million in expenses. In 2019, that figure swelled to $129.5 million. They spend more on facilities, salaries, recruiting, equipment, team travel—basically everything, because they had the money."[65] In 2017, Minnesota spent $166 million on a new athletes' village for players, which the athletic department also viewed as a recruiting tool. The official name of the building—the "Land 'O Lakes Center for Excellence"—reveals the corporate connection to big-time college sports. The name also disguised that the facility was for D-I athletes only, and that its primary purpose was not academic but athletic excellence. Minnesota athletic director Mark Coyle admitted that the real aim of the glistening new facility was to recruit and retain players: "If I was an 18-year-old kid, I'd say 'Wow'. It's going to be neat and going have an impact an [sic] all of our programs and our student-athletes."[66]

Schools now pay up to $200,000 on basketball court designs as a means of advertising during television games. Florida International University features palm fronds, the nation's capital is etched on George Washington's court, and Oregon's hardwood has the silhouette of a pine forest. Marketing agent Maddie Stoehr sees no problem promoting a school through sports. "It's free advertising—to have millions of viewers see top athletes performing on a court," she claims. "We try to encourage universities to stand out as much as possible, something that will pop and look good on the screen, while also getting the community excited in person."[67] Given that most D-I sports programs run in the red, court designs are hardly "free advertising."

Examples abound of schools that have lost the big gamble to go D-I. Florida Atlantic University made the leap up in 2001. From 2005 to 2013, the football team had a paltry .379 winning percentage. Attendance was sparse, and the team took to playing unwinnable "money games" with Alabama and Auburn—guarantees to cut into the athletic department's deficit.[68] When Mark Becker was hired as president of Georgia State in 2009, he made a statement that was typical of administrators' belief in the vital importance of intercollegiate sports to a university, and their willingness to bet university money on winning teams: "Great research universities tend to have great athletic programs." Evidently, he was ignorant of the lack of marquee D-I sports teams at Cal Tech, MIT, the University of Chicago, and the Ivy League schools, among others. University of Oregon professor Nathan Tublitz, who once led the Coalition on Intercollegiate Athletics (a partnership of faculty senates), stated the obvious: "Schools without teams don't have any problem getting applications."[69]

Becker wagered that a winning NCAA sports program at Georgia State would increase exposure, student enrollment, and generous donations from sports boosters and other university supporters. "As a striving institution," Becker contended, "taking a risk is something people embrace." The Panthers lost the gamble. In 2013 and 2014, Georgia State won one football game, and about 10,000 fans squeezed into the 70,000-seat Georgia Dome for a typical home game. Bill Curry, the embattled Georgia State coach, lamented that "in America, and especially in sports, you're not allowed an intelligent timeline. You've got to take one that launches you so you're on [ESPN's] GameDay sooner." He added that the efforts of smaller schools like Georgia State to compete at the NCAA's top levels might be "fundamentally flawed."[70] At least Curry was honest. The NCAA feigns a commitment to competitiveness on an even playing field, but although they both have D-I football teams, Georgia State will not be playing Alabama for a national football championship any time soon. From 2010 to 2019, Georgia State's win–loss record was 36–83.

Most college sports programs are losers in the big arms race. Unlike Alabama in football or Duke in men's basketball, not every school can consistently field winning teams. There will always be schools like Georgia State that cannot compete because there are not enough top-flight athletes to go around. Yet, more and more universities are plunking down big money on sports; from 2010 to 2015, public universities used an average of more than $10.3 million in subsidies and student fees for athletic programs. Student fees in that time period increased by 10 percent. A *Huffington Post/Chronicle of Higher Education* study found that subsidies are highest at such schools as Georgia State and Miami University, where ticket and other revenue is lowest.[71]

Student Fees and the "Mid-Major" Dilemma

Few D-I men's basketball and football teams cover the costs of the other sports. In 2012, only 22 of the 227 public universities playing D-I sports were self-sufficient—that is, the athletic department needed no financial support from the institution or student fees. Of the 338 total D-I universities, both public and private, only 23 athletic programs made money in 2013. In 2020, the NCAA reported that 25 D-I athletic departments turned a profit. All of those had elite D-I football teams. Athletic departments in the rest of the schools tap their students to pay for intercollegiate athletics, and the costs are going up. According to a 2013 finding by the non-profit American Institutes of Research, "athletic subsidies per athlete at public schools with top-tier football teams spiked 61 percent from 2005 to 2010. Meanwhile, per-student academic spending rose just 23 percent."[72]

College presidents and boards of trustees are largely mute on the subject of student subsidies for D-I athletic programs. Joel Maxcy, a Drexel University economist, says, "There's no one to put the brakes on them. There's no one to say, 'No, this is not a sound investment.'"[73] Faculties might make this case, but they have no power to restructure intercollegiate sports.

Even the few athletic programs that are flush with money tap student fees in the arms race for recruits and winning teams. Anyone touring the athletes' apartments, locker rooms, workout facilities, training tables, and study halls would gasp at the extravagance. According to a 2014 *Washington Post* study of thirty-two schools in the Power Five conferences, students paid a combined $125.5 million in student fees that went to athletics.[74]

Jeff Smith, a business professor at the University of South Carolina-Upstate, has studied student athletic fees at hundreds of schools. He figured that college students borrow almost $4 billion annually just to cover the fees they pay for athletics. Studies show that Black students incur the most debt to attend college. Virginia student Paige Taul worked for $8.25 an hour at the university bookstore, meaning she had to work about eighty hours to pay her student fees that went to athletics. "Wow," she exclaimed. "That doesn't seem fair." Because she was working, she didn't have time to go to games. David Catt, a former golfer at Kansas University, agreed, "It's a huge problem in higher education. You think you're paying for a degree, and you wind up as a piggy bank for a semi-professional sports team."[75]

As difficult as it is to make the case that the financial risk of trying to field winning sports teams pays off for the majority of D-I schools, the case is impossible to make for "mid-major" schools such as those in the MAC. Mid-majors also spend a great deal of money on the endeavor, but they don't pull in nearly the same television, attendance, and booster revenues. In 1996–97, Miami University's athletic department lost $6 million. The football team was the biggest loser at $2.2 million. Title IX requires public schools to issue the same number of scholarships to female athletes as to male athletes, and in that same year, women's sports cost Miami about $2 million.[76]

There is no way that an athletic director at a mid-major D-I school can make intercollegiate sports profitable. Miami is typical of a university that has to subsidize its athletic department with millions of dollars. In 2019, three of the top ten salaries at Miami University went to football, men's basketball, and men's hockey coaches. There were no women on the top ten list.[77]

In 2010, Miami head football coach Mike Haywood took home $300,000. The University of Pittsburgh hired him away from Oxford but fired him within a month for a domestic assault charge. Chuck Martin arrived in 2014, and although Miami has had only a few winning records under his tenure, Martin's salary grew to $532,000 in 2019—almost $400,000 more than Ohio Governor Mike DeWine. Martin's salary was north of $10,000 more than that of the university president, Greg Crawford.[78]

Miami paid another $1 million for Martin's assistants, making an outlay of at least a million and a half to pay for the football coaches who direct eighty-five football players. The head men's basketball coach at Miami had an even sweeter deal at almost $369,000. The coach and his four or five assistants only have to keep track of fifteen guys. No other division in the university comes close to that per capita outlay for mentoring individual students. The average salary for an assistant professor

Chapter Two

at Miami, most of whom teach and advise well over a hundred students a year, is just more than $67,000.[79]

The MAC is one of the mid-major conferences that is a springboard for winning coaches to move to a top D-I school. Louisiana State's new football coach Brian Kelly, late of Notre Dame (where he was making $3 million a year), was lured away in 2022 with a $9 million a year deal—about $6 million more than he had made with the Irish. In 2006, Kelly made $185,000 at Central Michigan (about $254,000 in 2021 dollars).[80] In 2017, Western Michigan's P. J. Fleck left for Minnesota, where, in 2021, he was awarded a new seven-year contract for about $5 million annually—not a bad return on his investment for coaching in the MAC. The list of Miami football coaches includes Woody Hayes, Ara Parseghian, John Pont, Bo Schembechler, and Randy Walker, all of whom made their names after leaving Oxford.

If he *were* producing consistent championship teams, is there any doubt that Chuck Martin would leave Miami for a multimillion-dollar deal someplace else? Coaches follow the money, and many of them don't seem to have any loyalty to their players or universities. Jackie Sherrill, a former Texas A&M football coach and athletic director, said, "If you equate it [the college carousel] to college education, it's insane. If you equate it to business, it makes sense."[81] On the contrary, neither the educational nor the business model of D-I sports makes sense.

Adjuncts and visiting professors with PhDs make less than most high school teachers.[82] The problem is that athletic directors and coaches are paid far too much. College administrators, who also deposit much higher paychecks than most professors, perpetuate the spurious argument that they must pay "market value" to find qualified people to fill these positions. There are a lot of coaches who would take a fraction of Martin's salary to put a losing team on the field (his record from 2014 to 2019 was 30–45). Miami's senior vice president of finance and business services, David Creamer, who makes more than $376,000 annually, shrugs off these coaches' salaries as meeting the market rate, as though they were essential to the mission of the university. "Unfortunately, football coaches are paid more than presidents today," Creamer says. "So, while it may seem to be a little out of step, it is a reality then when you use, again, market to determine what the compensation would be."[83] This market logic also dictates paying adjunct professors about one-tenth of Martin's salary. The market is not allowed to operate for paying D-I athletes.

In 2015, Miami University student government vice president Nathan Lombardi led a task force to evaluate the chunk of student fees that went to intercollegiate athletics.[84] The effort to cut the subsidies went nowhere: Miami student fees dedicated for D-I sports went up to more than $1,000 annually. In a 2014 poll of students from six MAC schools, almost half of the students wanted a reduction in fees for athletics, and 73 percent reported that sports was "unimportant" in their school choice.[85]

Administrators still recite the fiction that winning athletic programs are a cost-effective way to market a school. "We had over 4,000 at a football game this year [2014]," said Miami University athletic director David Sayler. "So, I just think it's a rallying point for them and a chance to participate in something that, if we're winning and doing things the right way, we'll bring a lot of pride and support to the institution." In fact, the Miami student body is mostly indifferent to its teams. Miami's Yager Stadium holds more than 24,000 people. Several thousand fans in the stands, many from the surrounding communities, are hardly a number to justify the costs. Furthermore, under Sayler's watch, Miami's men's sports teams have had desultory records, and the athletic department has been forced to buy back its own tickets to boost virtual attendance.[86] Even the hockey team, which was a powerhouse in the mid-2010s and regularly sold out, has fallen on hard times, winning less than a third of its games from 2018 to 2020. There are far more empty seats than filled ones for Miami basketball games.

More than fifty years ago, a University of Toledo history professor wrote then NCAA executive director Walter Byers, "I think they [the students] are absolutely correct in objecting to the policy of so many universities, which force them to buy athletic tickets [through student fees] which they don't want in order to support armies of mercenary athletes and right-wing autocratic coaches."[87] In the early 1980s, the NCAA required all D-I football schools to have a requisite number of seats in the stadium. Six schools in the MAC were forced to build new venues if they wanted to play with the big boys. These mid-major programs fell deeper into debt to their universities simply because their football programs sapped millions of dollars. In 2021, the Miami University athletic director claimed that football made money. Still, when asked about it, the university's financial head said, "That has never been the case."[88]

In 2011, the outlay for sports at each of the twelve MAC schools averaged more than $23 million, climbing 29 percent from 2006 to 2011. Three-fourths of the budget was made up in subsidies, most from student fees. By the end of the 2010s, student fees for intercollegiate sports at the biggest public schools in Ohio amounted to $135 million.[89]

Carol Cartwright, former president at Kent State, said in 2012 that "we fund intercollegiate athletics through a student fee. That's been historic in the Mid-American Conference for more than 50 years. There are no secrets about it."[90] On the contrary, many students have no idea that they are subsidizing athletic departments. Another study of 3,500 students from MAC schools revealed that 40 percent "either didn't know or were highly uncertain about whether they paid athletics fees. Many said they were willing to pay fees for student centers or healthcare, but in general did not support paying fees for athletics."[91] In 2019, Miami University subsidized its athletic department to the tune of more than $17 million in student fees and more than $7 million in institutional support.[92]

In early 2013, the Drake Group, an oversight group made up of college faculty and scholars, polled some 4,000 students from the twelve schools in the MAC about what they knew of the money they paid to subsidize intercollegiate sports. Miami's 16,000 students plunked down $950 annually—more than half of their total student fees. About 40 percent of the students polled had no idea that so much of their fees went to sports. "Ridiculous," commented one student, reflecting the views of many. "I pay a ridiculous amount for events I don't attend.... I'm here to learn, not to watch sports.... My feelings with this news stretch no shorter than outrage." University of Akron President Luis Proenza downplayed any problem with student subsidies for D-I sports: "I would say to most people, 'Don't get too worried about it, and enjoy what it does bring to our campuses, our society. It's a tremendous learning opportunity for student athletes. For many of them, it's a ticket to a higher education.'"[93]

Creamer defended the system by claiming that Miami's smaller student body relative to schools like Ohio State and Cincinnati necessitated syphoning more money to support athletics from student fees. In fact, however, Miami's student population is much larger than many D-I schools like Duke and Gonzaga that have revenue-producing basketball programs. Miami has not been able to create a tradition of winning, a fact about which students are indifferent. Alluding to the dismal attendance at sporting events in 2015, a representative of Miami's student organizations said, "You can't force a cultural change on campus."[94] One wonders at the spendthrift ways of the Miami University athletic department, which sends the football and men's basketball team to overnight at a nearby hotel before home games, paid for in part by student fees.

For its part, Eastern Michigan, another team in the MAC, lost tens of millions of dollars on sports in the 2010s. About 85 percent of the athletic department's revenues came from general operating costs and student fees. "The board [of trustees] has this belief that football is the window to the university," laments one Eastern Michigan accounting professor. "If we just put the resources into football, we will really help enrollment. I think they are wrong. We are stuck." The university president, a big football booster, would not talk to Gilbert M. Gaul, the author of the report on Eastern Michigan.[95]

Several decades ago, the University of Buffalo made the decision to enter the costly world of D-I sports by joining the MAC. Buffalo's president William Greiner justified the move: "You do [big-time] athletics because . . . it is certainly a major contribution to the total quality of student life and the visibility of your institution." Buffalo's spending on sports had a direct impact on undermining undergraduate education. *The Princeton Review* ratings of colleges and universities in 1999–2000 put Buffalo at the bottom of student satisfaction with their professors and classes.[96] The canard is alive and well that intercollegiate sports are an important part of the college experience for most students.

"Bodybag Games"

Mid-major football teams get handsome payouts every year for playing patsy to the Ohio States and Alabamas, with virtually no chance of winning. In 2018, Alabama whipped Louisiana Lafayette by 42 points, and they gave a similar drubbing to Southern Mississippi in 2019. In 2018, Ohio State invited Tulane to Columbus for a 43-point shellacking. So much for former NCAA President Mark Emmert's claim to promote a "level playing field," because the turf in Tuscaloosa and Columbus seems slightly tilted in favor of the home team.

In the last few years, teams from the Historically Black Colleges and Universities (HBCUs) have served as fall guys for the NCAA powerhouses. In 2015, Howard University lost to Boston College, 76–0; Grambling lost to Cal, 73–14; and Southern University lost to Georgia by 42 points. Southern spends $9 million on sports, Georgia $100 million. Mark Nagel, a professor of sports and entertainment management at the University of South Carolina, said of these Faustian deals, "From a financial standpoint, they're definitely worth it for HBCUs. . . . It's a large paycheck, and the players usually like the opportunity to play on television or in front of 80,000 people. At the same time, it is an automatic loss, and there's always risk of injury when another team's players are so much stronger and faster. It does raise the question, 'Is this what we're really trying to foster when we talk about sportsmanship and college sports?'"[97]

Journalist Joe Nocera documented some of the games that HBCUs played against powerhouse football teams in 2016. The payday was big for the HBCUs: Howard got $350,000 to get hammered by Maryland, 52–13, and the same amount from Rutgers to take a 52–14 loss. Southeastern Louisiana State cashed in $385,000 from Oklahoma State to lose 61–7. Texas A&M gave Prairie View A&M $450,000 to suffer a 67–0 shellacking.[98]

These mismatches between the top D-I teams and the sure losers are known as "bodybag games." The collateral damage in these mismatches can be devastating. It is one thing to pit David against Goliath in basketball or some other non-contact sport, but the size of big-time college football players dwarfs HBCU players. Nocera writes that the cost of athletics to these small schools is such that "they feel they have no choice but to use their players as sacrificial lambs in guarantee games." From 2011 to 2015, the average score for these games was 55–8. Howard Head Coach Gary Harrell said that he likes the games "just because of the excitement and the exposure." Nonetheless, after losing to Boston College in 2015, Harrell admitted that his team was "decimated with injuries the rest of the year."[99]

The MAC is another conference that the big boys go to for non-conference football games, although MAC teams are relatively more competitive and demand more money. In 2018, Kent State finished 2-10, including taking it on the chin from Penn State 63-10. The next season, the Golden Flashes earned $4.5 million to lose at Arizona State (30-7), Auburn (55-16), and Wisconsin (48-0). That blood money covered about ten to fifteen percent of Kent State's athletic budget. Kent State athletic director Joel Nielsen says that big away football games are a good way to sell the school. "It's an opportunity for not only (the players) as individuals but also our program and our university," he claims. "It's a university strategy also to brand ourselves and get our brand out there." Kent State would not allow *USA Today* to talk to its players about how they felt about those blowout football games.[100] In 2019, Ohio State slaughtered the Miami Redhawks by 71 points.

Covering Athletic Department Debt from the Academic Budget

When television contracts entered the picture in the 1950s, revenues and coaches' salaries exploded, and universities saw an opportunity to promote their schools widely through sports. Walter Byers said that television exposure "enshrined the Power Coach [sic] and made him the controlling force in deciding colleges' policies." Byers saw a direct correlation between TV money, increased interest in NCAA sports, and the decline in the importance of academics. "Even as the money flowed and the popularity of intercollegiate sports increased," he observed, "destructive forces were subverting the academic standards and administrative integrity of colleges across the country."[101]

The disparity in money spent on athletes and non-athletes is eye-popping. For example, the University of Texas spent $262,728 on each football player in 2012, compared to $20,903 on each non-athlete. During DeLoss Dodds' thirty-three years as Texas athletic director (1981–2013), the football budget went from $2 million to $110 million.[102]

As of 2014, more than a dozen universities had long-term athletic debts in excess of $150 million. The University of California, Berkeley athletic department posted a deficit of $22 million in 2016, adding to the highest long-term debt of any college sports program. That same year, Cal's debt service amounted to nearly $18 million. Cal's football and men's basketball teams made money, but bigger and better new athletic facilities were at least partially responsible for this shortfall. Athletic departments, such as Alabama, which owes $225 million, or Illinois, in the hole for a cool $260 million, run these deficits on expected TV revenues. If those TV dollars should decline, these schools will be in big fiscal trouble. Cal physics professor Bob Jacobsen, a faculty representative for athletics, said that servicing the debt on athletic budget shortfalls cuts directly into academic programs: "Not only does athletics have a problem on account of debt service, but it's also taking up a chunk of our available borrowing."[103]

Athletic directors and their financial enablers in university administrations are not forthcoming with the raw numbers about how much sports programs cost their schools. Walter Byers warned about the way "accounting variables in college athletics make it difficult if not impossible to know whether a big-time sport pays for itself, much less whether it generates net receipts to finance the deficit [non-revenue] sports."[104] "Economists who have attempted to make sense of athletic budgets," writes one sports scholar, "confess that there is no way to determine actual bottom lines."[105] In recent years, public universities have had to come clean about the costs of D-I athletics. In fiscal year 2016–17, for example, 63 percent of Kent State University's athletic budget of $29.5 million came from the academic side—tuition, student fees, and state subsidies. The percentage was similar for other MAC schools.[106]

While the quest for bigger and better athletic facilities continues unabated, students are shepherded into bigger and bigger classes, increasingly taught by underpaid graduate students, adjunct professors, and lecturers. According to the American Association of University Professors (AAUP), tenure-track and tenured professors have shrunk to a paltry 25 percent of all faculty.[107] Robert Mulcahy III admitted, "Universities . . . are under constant pressure from the media, trustees, and donors to produce winning programs at the expense of student athletes' academic achievement."[108]

Murray Sperber was one of the first scholars to show that spending on college sports has a direct, detrimental impact on the classroom. Sperber, who has done several thorough studies of the NCAA, pulls no punches in castigating athletic programs for siphoning off money from educational budgets. "Money that could go to academic programs annually disappears down the athletic department financial hole. . . . One inescapable conclusion appears: *College Sports MegaInc. is the most dysfunctional business in America.* [italics Sperber's]"[109] Professor Howard Schein from the University of Illinois also contends that the supposed increase in the donations for a school's academic side because of winning teams is a myth. "The public hears about the millions that universities rake in from the NCAA basketball tournaments and bowl games," Schein said, "and people conclude that higher education doesn't need their tax dollars or private contributions. They believe that universities are doing great from their big-time college sports teams. . . . At Illinois, it couldn't be further from the truth, and that's also the situation at most other schools."[110] It doesn't help university leaders lobbying state legislatures for more funding when the football and men's basketball coaches' salaries are in the hundreds of thousands, or even millions annually.

The Delta Cost Project funded by the non-profit American Institutes for Research revealed that between 2005 and 2010, "public universities competing in NCAA Division-I sports spend as much as six times more per athlete than they spend to educate students. . . [and] spending by athletic departments rose more than twice as fast as academic spending on a per-student basis." A common misconception is that most of the athletic budgets go to scholarships for athletes. By far, the biggest piece of the pie goes to athletic departments, coaches' salaries, and facilities; about half of athletic departments' budgets across all subdivisions goes to coaches' salaries. As of 2019, less than a fifth of sports budgets at D-I schools went to athletic scholarships, and few of those were full rides.[111]

The NCAA has turned a deaf ear to criticisms that the organization has pushed higher education to the sidelines. In 1993–94, Duke spent $4 million on 550 athletes; in that same academic year, 5,900 Duke students had to split $400,000 in merit scholarships.[112] A 2013 study of median per capita spending on athletes and other college students revealed a startling disparity. Spending per student at Big Ten schools was $19,225, while spending per athlete was a whopping $116,667. Most football and men's basketball players make money for Big Ten schools, but their tuition voucher to attend classes does not compensate them fairly.[113]

In 2012, the Knight Commission, a group of reform-minded administrators, trustees, and former athletes, surveyed ninety-seven of the public schools in the Football Bowl Series (FBS). From 2005 to 2009, spending on athletics grew by 50 percent to more than $90,000 per athlete, while academic spending went up by 22 percent to about $15,000 per student.[114]

The trend to spend more and more on athletes continues. In 2012, the FBS schools spent $91,000 on each athlete and only $13,000 on non-athletes.[115] A 2014 AAUP study confirmed that athletic programs were getting more than their fair share of university finances:

> Even as their spending on instruction, research and public service declined or stayed flat, most colleges and universities rapidly increased their spending on sports. . . . Increasingly, institutions of higher education have lost their focus on the academic activities at the core of their mission.

The report not only found this disparate spending true for D-I schools but for D-II, D-III, and community colleges as well. From 2004 to 2011, spending on sports increased by 24.8 percent at all public four-year colleges, while outlays for academics remained flat. The study also revealed that the number of low-paid adjunct professors increased while tenure-track positions declined. Hires of higher-paid administrators to run the universities also rose.[116]

It is clear from the increase in the proportion of college budgets spent on sports and the decrease in monies spent on academics that many universities prioritize their athletic departments. In the last three decades, public football coaches' salaries have increased 750 percent, twenty times that of college professors. In 2017, Minnesota football coach P. J. Fleck got a healthy $18 million contract ($3.6 million annually). That would have paid the in-state tuition for about 1,300 students or seventy-five surgeons at the university hospital (average pay $245,000). Athletic Director Mark Coyle made $850,000.[117]

There is nothing wrong with having some fun at a sporting event. And no one cares if the beer and circus show surrounds pro games. But does it belong as an essential part of the college experience, especially given today's exorbitant tuition costs? The amount of money that students pay to go to college—often going into deep debt to do it—is hardly worth the revelry associated with on-campus athletic contests. Faculty and serious students scratch their heads at what some universities have become. As one Emory University woman asked rhetorically, "What kind of dumb-ass chooses their college on the basis of its sports teams and boozing? Does anyone actually say yes to these questions?"[118] Sadly, some indeed do, and college administrators are complicit in erecting and maintaining a front porch that has nothing to do with the academic mission of their houses.

Notes

1. Mankiewicz, H. (Producer), & McLeod, N. (Director) (1932). *Horse Feathers* [Motion Picture]. United States: Paramount Pictures.

2. Briana Boyington and Emma Kerr, "20 Years of Tuition Growth at National Universities," *USA Today*, September 17, 2020, accessed May 20, 2021, https://www.usnews.com/education/best-colleges/paying-for-college/articles/2017-09-20/see-20-years-of-tuition-growth-at-national-universities.

3. Stephen Roll, Jason Jabbari, and Michal Grinstein-Weiss, "Student Debt Forgiveness Would Impact Nearly Every Aspect of People's Lives," Brooking Institution, May 18, 2021, accessed May 20, 2021, https://www.brookings.edu/blog/up-front/2021/05/18/student-debt-forgiveness-would-impact-nearly-every-aspect-of-peoples-lives/.

4. Sanderson and Siegfried, "Why American."

5. Gorn and Goldstein, *A Brief History*, 169.

6. Rader, *American Sports*, 95.

7. For the best analysis of the media and the growth of college football see Michael Oriard's seminal work, *King Football*.

8. Will Hobson and Steven Rich, "Why Students Foot the Bill for College Sports, and How Some Are Fighting Back," *Washington Post,* November 30, 2015, accessed December 1, 2015, https://www.washingtonpost.com/sports/why-students-foot-the-bill.

9. Oriard, *King Football*, 82.

10. Gregory, "It's Time to Pay," 38.

11. Marcus Fuller, "Gophers Hand the Ball to U Alum Johnson," *Star Tribune*, March 23, 2021, A1.

12. Jeff Benedict and Armen Keteyian, *The System, The Glory and Scandal of Big-Time College Football* (New York: Doubleday, 2013), 45.

13. Benedict and Keteyian, *The System*, 185.

14. Bill Morris, "A Tent City for Fun and Profit," *New York Times*, February 24, 2013, S1; and Laura Pappano, "How Big-Time Sports Ate College Life," *New York Times Education Life*, January 22, 2012, 24.

15. Murray Sperber, *College Sports Inc.: The Athletic Department vs The University* (New York: Henry Holt and Company, 1990), 141–2.

16. Scott Hanson, "After Return to D-I Athletics, Seattle U's Journey Back to Prominence is Still Only 'Two-Thirds' Done, *Seattle Times,* April 7, 2019, accessed July 3, 2022, https://www.seattletimes.com/sports/seattle-university/seattle-university-returned-to-division-i-athletics-more-than-a-decade-ago-but-the-journey-back-to-prominence-is-only-two-thirds-done/.

17. Duderstadt, *Intercollegiate Athletics*, 8.

18. Murray Sperber, *Beer and Circus: How Big-Time Sports is Crippling Undergraduate Education* (New York: Henry Holt and Co., 2001), 202.

19. Sanderson and Siegfried, "Why American."

20. William Rhoden, "Colleges; As Glitz Wore Out, the Coach Wore Thin," *New York Times*, July 2, 1991, 9B.

21. Sperber, *Beer and Circus*, 259.

22. Sean Silverthorne, "The Flutie Effect," *Forbes*, April 29, 2013, accessed June 15, 2021, https://www.forbes.com/sites/hbsworkingknowledge/2013/04/29/the-flutie-effect-how-athletic-success-boosts-college-applications/?sh=4b6d26456e96; and Michael Oriard, *Bowled Over*, 247.

23. Rader, *American Sports*, 294-5.

24. Benedict and Keteyian, *The System*, 158, 161.

25. Gregory, "It's Time to Pay," 38.

26. Sanderson and Siegfried, "Why American."

27. Sanderson and Siegfried, "Why American."

28. Laura Bischoff and Jeremy P. Kelley, "Students Pay Big for NCAA Sports," *Dayton Daily News*, March 28, 2015, accessed April 3, 2015.

29. Benedict and Keteyian, *The System*, 2.

30. Edgar Thompson, "UF Athletics Report $36 Million Loss, but SEC Affiliation Offsets Pandemic's Impact," *Orlando Sentinel*, February 10, 2022, accessed March

Chapter Two

15, 2022, https://www.orlandosentinel.com/sports/florida-gators/os-sp-gators-36-million-lost-pandemic-0211-20220210-2lj7fyd4gnfg3lmh6cwwqmbjc4-story.html.

31. Dennis Dodd, "College Football Attendance Declines for Seventh Straight to Lowest Average Since 1981," CBS Sports, February 24, 2022, accessed July 31, 2023, https://www.cbssports.com/college-football/news/college-football-attendance-declines-for-seventh-straight-season-to-lowest-average-since-1981/.

32. Sid Hartman, "Ticket Sales Already Were in a Tough Spot," *Star Tribune*, April 17, 2020, C2.

33. Juliet Macur and Billy Witz, "Stanford, Facing Pressure, Reverses Plan to Cut 11 Sports, *New York Times*, May 18, 2021, accessed January 21, 2022, https://www.nytimes.com/2021/05/18/sports/stanford-sports-reinstated.html.

34. Marcus Fuller, "Q&A: Gophers Athletic Director Mark Coyle Finding His Footing Amid Seismic Changes in College Sports," *Star Tribune*, August 26, 2021, accessed August 26, 2021, https://www.Star Tribune.com/mark-coyle-gophers-athletic-director-21-5-loss-st-thomas-q-and-a/60009100.

35. Joe Christiansen, "U's Coyle Receives Two-year Extension," *Star Tribune*, February 5, 2022, C2.

36. Pappano, "How Big-Time Sports," 25.

37. Demas, "The Test of Time," 112.

38. Michael Oriard, *Bowled Over: Big-Time College Football from the Sixties to the BCS Era* (Chapel Hill, NC: University of North Carolina Press, 2009), 249.

39. Jason Gay, "Please Hire Me to Coach!" *The Wall Street Journal*, December 7, 2017, S1.

40. Sperber, *Beer and Circus*, 256.

41. Oriard, *King Football*, 166.

42. When the author's daughter came for her campus visit to Miami University, this was the tour she received. When the Covid epidemic hit, adjunct and visiting professors were among the first Miami employees to be fired.

43. Sperber, *Beer and Circus*, 46.

44. Sperber, *Beer and Circus*, 194.

45. Sperber, *Beer and Circus*, 50.

46. Texas A&M, "Remembering Bonfire," https://bonfire.tamu.edu/, accessed April 13, 2021.

47. Sperber, *Beer and Circus*, 148, 153.

48. Sperber, *Beer and Circus*, 148, 153.

49. Sperber, *Beer and Circus*, 171.

50. Conn, "Singing the Team-Spirit Blues."

51. Sperber, *Beer and Circus*, 171.

52. Sperber, *Beer and Circus*, 68, 98, 111.

53. Sperber, *Beer and Circus*, 182.

54. Sperber, *Beer and Circus*, 186.

55. Sperber, *Beer and Circus*, 207.

56. Dick Vitale, *Campus Chaos: Why the Game I Love Is Breaking My Heart* (Indianapolis: TimeOut Publishing, 2000), 71.

57. Justin Terranova, "My Show," *New York Post*, May 17, 2018, accessed December 5, 2021, https://nypost.com/2018/05/17/espn-anchor-talks-bad-beats-changes-in-sports-betting/.

58. Robert E. Mulcahy III, *An Athletic Director's Story and the Future of College Sports in America* (New Brunswick, NJ: Rutgers University Press, 2020), 70.

59. Byers, *Unsportsmanlike Conduct*, 101.

60. Byers, *Unsportsmanlike Conduct*, 102.

61. Rader, *American Sports*, 294.

62. Steven Kutz, "These Public Universities Spent More than $100 million on Sports Last Year, Market Watch, July 29, 2017, accessed March 3, 2021, https://www.marketwatch.com/story/over-30-public-universities-spent-more-than-100-million-on-sports-last-year-2017-07-10.

63. Gilbert M. Gaul, *Billion-Dollar Ball: A Journey Though the Big-Money Culture of College Football* (New York: Viking, 2015), xii.

64. Benedict and Keteyian, *The System*, 2.

65. Chip Scoggins, "Feeding Football is Pragmatic Play," *Star Tribune*, December 15, 2020, C1.

66. Jason Gonzalez, "Progress is Turning Heads at Athletic Department Gem," *Star Tribune*, August 2, 2016, C2.

67. Scott Gleeson, "Geographic Shift: College Court Designs Go Bold with Local Ties," *USA Today*, February 27, 2020, S1.

68. Gaul, *Billion-Dollar Ball*, xvii.

69. Brad Wolverton, Ben Hallman, Shane Shifflett, and Sandhya Kambhampati, "The $10-Billion Sports Tab: How College Students Are Funding the Athletics Arms Race," *Huffington Post*, accessed April 12, 2022, http://projects.huffingtonpost.com/ncaa/sports-at-any-cost.

70. Wolverton, Hallman, Shifflett, and Kambhampati, "The $10-Billion Sports Tab."

71. Wolverton, Hallman, Shifflett, and Kambhampati, "The $10-Billion Sports Tab."

72. Sean Gregory, "The Real March Madness? Soaring Athletic Bills Catch Students Off Guard," *Time*, March 25, 2013, 60; and Bill Morris, "To Love, or Hate, Notre Dame," *New York Times*, January 6, 2013, SP5; and Kathy Johnson Bowles, "Should Institutions Support Sports Programs That Don't Make Money," *Inside Higher Ed*, December 15, 2021, accessed January 15, 2022, https://www.insidehighered.com/blogs/just-explain-it-me/should-institutions-support-sports-programs-don%E2%80%99t-make-money.

73. Wolverton, Hallman, Shifflett, and Kambhampati, "The $10-Billion Sports Tab."

74. Hobson and Rich, "Why Students Foot the Bill."

75. Hobson and Rich, "Why Students Foot the Bill."

76. Mike Gruss, "Miami Athletics Losing Money," *The Miami Student*, March 28, 1998, 1.

77. Rachel Berry, "How Much Do Miami's Highest Employees Make," *Miami Student*, December 3, 2019, 3.

78. Berry, "How Much," 3.

79. https://www.payscale.com/research/US/Employer=Miami_University/Salary, accessed June 18, 2020.

80. Steve Berkowitz, "$370 Million and Four College Coaches Deals," *USA Today*, December 1, 2021, 7C.

81. Alan Blinder, "On College Coaching Carousel, Rewards Soar," *New York Times*, December 5, 2021, 1.

82. Unattributed, "How Much Does a High School Teacher Make?" *U.S. News and World Report*, 2020, accessed February 11, 2021, https://money.usnews.com/careers/best-jobs/high-school-teacher/salary; and Colleen Flaherty, "Barely Getting By," *Inside Higher Ed*, April 20, 2020, accessed February 11, 2021, https://www.insidehighered.com/news/2020/04/20/new-report-says-many-adjuncts-make-less-3500-course-and-25000-year.

83. Berry, "How Much," 3.

84. Bischoff and Kelley, "Students Pay Big."

85. Bischoff and Kelley, "Students Pay Big."

86. Bischoff and Kelley, "Students Pay Big."

87. Byers, *Unsportsmanlike Conduct*, 225.

88. Interview with David Saylor, August 12, 2021; and interview with David Creamer, August 19, 2021.

89. Gregory, "The Real March Madness?" 60.

90. John P. Evans, et al., "Institutional Experience with Academic Reform: A Panel Discussion," *Journal of Intercollegiate Sport* no. 5 (2012), 110.

91. Wolverton, Hallman, Shifflett, and Kambhampati, "The $10-Billion Sports Tab."

92. Max Filby, "Ohio Wants to Prevent College Students from Paying More Fees," *Dayton Daily News*, April 19, 2019, accessed July 6, 2022, https://www.daytondailynews.com/news/local/ohio-public-universities-subsidize-athletics-181m/gKjLUnU5nHbzhQmsXGOriO/.

93. Gregory, "The Real March Madness?" 60.

94. Mary Schrott, "Fee Frustration: Students Pay $997 Yearly for Athletics," *The Miami Student*, April 7, 2015, 1.

95. Gaul, *Billion-Dollar Ball*, 212.

96. Sperber, *Beer and Circus*, 65, 67.

97. Jake New, "Pick on Somebody Your Own Size," *Insider Higher Ed*, October 7, 2015, accessed April 3, 2020, https://www.insidehighered.com/news/2015/10/07/hbcu-football-teams-playing-big-teams-means-big-losses-and-worse.

98. Joe Nocera, "Historically Black Schools Pay the Price for a Football Paycheck," *The New York Times*, September 19, 2016, D1.

99. Nocera, "Historically Black Schools Pay."

100. Chris Bumbaca, "Kent State Will Earn $4M, Likely Lose," *USA Today*, August 29, 2019, 4C.

101. Byers, *Unsportsmanlike Conduct*, 133, 147.

102. Gaul, *Billion-Dollar Ball*, 6.

103. Eben Novy-Williams, "College Football's Top Teams are Built on Crippling Debt, January 4, 2017, *Bloomberg News*, accessed February 21, 2022, https://www.bloomberg.com/news/features/2017-01-04/college-football-s-top-teams-are-built-on-crippling-debt.

104. Byers, *Unsportsmanlike Conduct*, 221.

105. Davies, *Sports in American Life*, 209.

106. Rich Exner, "Inside the Sports Budgets at Akron, Kent State, Cleveland State, and other Ohio Schools," April 30, 2018. Cleveland.com, accessed July 17, 2023, https://www.cleveland.com/sports/erry-2018/04/75b2bda3ed/money_in_ohio_college_sports.html.

107. Colleen Flaherty, "A Non-Tenure-Track Profession?" *Inside Higher Ed*, October 12, 2018, accessed January 8, 2022, https://www.insidehighered.com/news/2018/10/12/about-three-quarters-all-faculty-positions-are-tenure-track-according-new-aaup.

108. Mulcahy III, *An Athletic Director's Story*, 176.

109. Sperber, *Beer and Circus*, 221.

110. Sperber, *Beer and Circus*, 221.

111. Mary Beth Marklein, "Athletics Get More Dollars Than Academics," *USA Today*, January 16, 2013, 3A.

112. Łukash Miniowski and Tomasz Jacheć, "Illusory Facets of Sport: The Case of the Duke University Basketball Team," *Physical Culture and Sport Studies and Research* 75 (October 2017), 48.

113. Sheldon Anderson, editorial in *The Miami Student*, January 22, 2013.

114. Pappano, "How Big-Time Sports," 24.

115. Benedict and Keteyian, *The System*, 2.

116. Tamar Lewin, "Colleges Increasing Spending on Sports Faster than on Academics, Report Finds," *New York Times*, April 7, 2014, A12.

117. Joe Tamborino letter to the *Star Tribune*, January 2017, A8.

118. Sperber, *Beer and Circus*, 57–59.

CHAPTER THREE

You Play, We Profit
The Exploitation of College Athletes

> "[Red] Grange has no right to capitalize upon his athletic fame; his fame belongs to Illinois, not to him."
>
> —Illinois coach Robert Zuppke on his star running back leaving the university in 1925 to play for the Chicago Bears[1]

The founders of intercollegiate athletics meant well in their attempt to build strong bodies and minds through participation in team sports, and many in the entertainment business of college sports today are similarly principled. But the Grand Poohbahs at the NCAA headquarters in Indianapolis and their accomplices running D-I sports should not be surprised that NFL Hall of Famer Jim Brown, an alumnus of Syracuse University, would chastise them with these harsh words: "The NCAA is probably the most reprehensible organization God ever created."[2] NCAA rules prohibit giving needy college players airfare to fly home for a family funeral. Yet, in 2006, the NCAA top brass chartered private jets for nearly $1 million. Coaches at elite football and basketball schools also have access to private jets. Rick Johnson, a lawyer who has litigated on behalf of college players, asks the obvious question: "What kind of non-profit organization leases private jets?"[3]

Furthermore, most of the big-money college sports teams are associated with public universities, and athletic departments run at a loss. Taxpayers should wonder how their hard-earned dollars are being squandered. For example, in 1991, the *Washington Post* exposed a University of Michigan scheme to use "a federal research grant to cover some travel and entertainment expenses for its contingent to attend the Rose Bowl game in Pasadena."[4] Eight years later, the University of Wisconsin took an entourage of more than 830 people to the Rose Bowl. NCAA rules prohibited players' parents from getting on the "gravy plane," but spouses of athletic department employees could board. Some stayed at a posh Beverly Hills hotel. The school overspent its Rose Bowl stipend by $300,000. What is standard practice for college football programs astounded one travel manager at a major corporation: "They could have done this [trip] for about a fifth of the cost and still stayed at nice hotels and eaten well. And that's with all the extra people—I've never seen so many free-loaders on a trip before, and it appears completely unjustified. . . . These athletic department administrators could give lessons to drunken sailors on how to throw money around."[5] This extravagance occurred at a time during which state legislators around the country had begun getting stingier about funding their respective states' public institutions of higher learning.

On the one hand, the big moneymakers in college sports today take their ideological cue from the British amateurs of yesteryear—the upper classes who played their lawn games of tennis, golf, and cricket just for sport, not cash. That class of Brits could afford to do so; the country club set already had a lot of money in the bank, so it was easy for them to decry "playing for pay." On the other hand, the NCAA models the worst inequities of the American free market system by running a monopoly that fights against the rights of its workers (players). The NCAA bureaucrats, athletic departments, and coaches don't want their "student-athletes" corrupted by the hundreds of millions of dollars that the organization gleans every year. "Total exploitation," Jim Brown called it. "The kind of money they [the NCAA and athletic departments] make, the kind of life they live. It's embarrassing."[6] In 2021, the "nonprofit" NCAA netted more than $1.15 billion, up from $1.12 billion two years earlier, before the Covid pandemic prompted the cancellation of March Madness.[7]

The NCAA is "Non-Profit" for Athletes Only

It is a paradox that in the United States, the proud country of capitalism, free markets, commercialism, and individualism, the NCAA is the last big-money sports organization to shun the tag "professional." Since its inception, the NCAA has been swimming upstream against paying players. American games—baseball, football, and basketball—have had pros from the start, with many playing in college games.

The NCAA has the word *collegiate* in its name, but *corporate* would be more apt. In the late nineteenth century, famed Yale University football coach Walter Camp linked the free market to college sports. "American business has found in American college football the epitomization [sic] of present day business methods," he observed."[8] He could have been talking about the NCAA structure today. It is no secret that the NCAA—the gatekeeper of "pure" amateur sports—is running a for-profit system. NCAA revenues have exploded in the last fifty years.[9] The combined business of men's college basketball and football generated more than $16 billion in 2017—this in association with institutions whose primary purpose is to educate students and advance knowledge, not to entertain the public.[10]

The "market" argument for paying athletic directors and coaches the handsome "going rate" doesn't seem to merit paying college players who make millions for their schools. But that is a trademark of American capitalism too; many businesses try to keep wages as low as legally possible. Since its inception, the NCAA monopoly has denied players the right to profit from their skills in the free market.

Basketball and football players coming from poor families have been hard-pressed to begin their earning careers. In the mid-1970s, high schoolers Moses Malone and Darryl Dawkins joined the pro ranks right out of college, but today, college players must play a season before the NBA will draft them. In 1999, former NBA coach Sam Mitchell, then an NBA player with the Minnesota Timberwolves, said that he never watches March Madness. "You give coaches millions of dollars. You give schools millions. And then a kid who's got nothing gets $20 to buy a pizza or call home, and it's a violation. When I hear [about] the 'purity and sanctity of college basketball' . . . that's bull."[11]

The NCAA has hoodwinked the public into believing that its system is a purely amateur, non-profit organization. Historians Elliott Gorn and Warren Goldstein point out that "fans have always complained that 'greed has ruined our games,' or that 'players used to be grateful for the chance to play'. . . . The history of American sports reveals that motives were never pure; there were no 'good old days' when people played only for the honor of their town or the love of the game."[12]

Except for franchise owners, professional basketball and football players command most of the profits from their respective teams' enterprises. Managers in the front office and coaches on the field usually make a fraction of the average player's salary, especially in the NBA and MLB. This is the way it should be, because players have rare skills that only a handful of people in the world possess. Unlike managers or coaches, they are not easily replaced. The NCAA has it reversed; the players get no cash, but management is awash in money. Recent proposals for modest payments to players will not change that imbalance.

We are asked to overlook the handsome six-figure salaries that D-I management pays itself, as well as the multimillion-dollar salaries top coaches pull down. Boards of trustees, boosters, and college administrators are all in with this business model of intercollegiate sports. The demarcation between amateur and professional applies only to players, who do not get a significant piece of the NCAA's multibillion-dollar revenue base. "The NCAA wants to get their labor for free," said University of Minnesota regent Michael Hsu in 2019. "But there's a point where there's a moral problem with that."[13]

College athletes are fully aware that they are not reaping the educational or financial rewards of D-I sports. Most players can't even choose a course of study that might benefit them after graduation. Not many study engineering, pre-med, or other challenging and time-consuming majors. The bottom academic line for D-I athletic programs is not future employment opportunities for their players but assurance that they remain eligible. After players' use up their allotted years on the playing field, graduation is optional. Considering that the average dropout rate for all students from their first to second year in college is about 71 percent nationally, it is remarkable that virtually no top football or men's basketball star has been declared academically ineligible in recent years. It is not because they are all "A" students.

In 2017, former football players Shawne Alston of West Virginia and Martin Jenkins of Clemson brought a class-action lawsuit against the NCAA, questioning the limits on compensation for college athletes. In a deposition, Morgan Burke, Purdue University's athletic director from 1993 to 2016, said that athletes got their fair share of the revenues. "In his opinion, student-athletes already are provided with everything that they need to be successful . . . [meaning] what student-athletes need to be successful academically and athletically." Burke worried that if athletes got even more benefits and cash payments, big Purdue boosters would cut back on their donations.[14]

Unscrupulous sports equipment representatives, agents, boosters, and coaches are tempted to meet players' demands for a piece of the action. Based on a fifty-fifty split of the profits between management and players in pro leagues, the National Bureau of Economic Research estimates that a top quarterback such as Clemson's Trevor Lawrence would have made up to $2.4 million in 2020 and that a marquee wide receiver could make $1.3 million.[15] As an "amateur" at Clemson, Lawrence's tuition, room, and board amounted to about $55,000 a year. Hsu argued that there were already inequities in the worth of a student-athlete's scholarship. Northwestern scholarships cost $70,385, Minnesota's cost $25,269, and Illinois' cost $29,000. "[Northwestern quarterback] Clayton Thorson was the highest paid quarterback in the NCAA in 2017," Hsu said. "Because his full cost of attendance was more than [every other school]."[16] Although Wildcat football has had a resurgence, this disparity in the value of a Northwestern degree brings to mind the fans' chant when the team could barely win a game in the 1970s: "That's all right, that's okay. You'll be working for us someday."

It is incorrect to call college athletes indentured servants; they are free to play or not to play and to leave their servitude without having to buy themselves out. However, there is no question that their services are underpaid and exploited. Journalists Joe Nocera and Ben Strauss point out that, unlike any other entertainment business, until recently, college players were banned from marketing themselves. For example, "[Auburn quarterback] Cam Newton compliantly wore at least fifteen corporate logos—one on his jersey, four on his helmet visor, one on each wristband, one on his pants, six on his shoes, and one on the headband he wears under helmet—as part of Auburn's $10.6 million deal with Under Armour."[17] After the University of Connecticut won the NCAA championship in 2014, Shabazz Napier pointed out that the university could sell game jerseys to fans but players could not.[18] In 2015, LSU star running back Leonard Fournette tried to sell his own jersey, but the NCAA said "no"—that jersey was not for personal sale.

Florida State quarterback Charlie Ward, who led the Seminoles to a national championship in 1993, was one of the first players to call for a change to the rules to cash in on his celebrity. That effort went nowhere, but for more than a decade, UCLA basketball player Ed O'Bannon fought the NCAA for the right to market his name, image, and likeness (NIL). The NCAA enlisted its full legal team to fight O'Bannon's right to sell his own likeness on video games or to at least get a piece of the NCAA's profits. The NCAA won the case, essentially denying O'Bannon his first amendment right to free speech and the basic free market principles of the American economy. In 2021, the courts reversed the decision and allowed players to market their NIL.

Chapter Three

The NCAA's marketing team is relentless in selling its product and keeping the profits. The organization has patented more than seventy trademarks, including twenty for its men's basketball tournament, such as "March Madness," "Final Four," "Elite Eight," and "The Big Dance." Sports bars are prohibited from using any of these slogans to attract customers. "Frozen Four" (ice hockey) and "College World Series" (baseball) are other terms on the NCAA's exclusive use list. "For the NCAA," says Christopher Schulte, a trademark lawyer, "it comes down to guarding its brand and ensuring the organization gets its share of licensing revenue from ticketing sales, merchandise, and advertising."[19]

Unlike college football and basketball players, who have to play for one year and three years, respectively, tennis, golf, and track and field athletes, among others, can go pro whenever they want. Music, art, and theater majors can also peddle their artistic talents for a payday. Alluding to the NBA's and NFL's restrictions on drafting younger players, Sanderson and Siegfried argue, "One need not be excessively cynical to assume that universities like the rule because it guarantees them a steady supply of talent at a low, capped price."[20] Incredibly, in 2013, the NCAA told Gopher wrestler Joel Bauman, who had a sideline as a rapper, to stop grappling because it was illegal for him to make money on his music under his own name. Bauman quit the team.[21]

Even cheerleaders at NCAA games can sign endorsement deals. Jamie Andries from the University of Oklahoma made thousands from sponsorships with Crocs, L'Oréal, American Eagle, and Lokai. She hired an agent to promote her deals. "Coming to OU for college was a big milestone for me," Andries said, "but it has given me so many amazing opportunities, like being able to cheer for the Sooners. . . . I was like, 'Wow, I get to cheer, and I get to have this sort of side job that I get to focus on, and I get to make some money that I can save up for myself to use after college." Until recently, the players she cheered for didn't have the same NIL opportunities.[22]

There will be no less fan interest in NCAA football and men's basketball because players can now also sell their NIL. Broadcaster Jim Nantz, who has called more than thirty NCAA men's basketball tournaments, is nostalgic about the collegiate atmosphere and amateur tradition (for players). "Any time you factor in the enthusiasm that comes with college sports, it comes with a whole new level," Nantz says. "It is less corporate; it's more of an unharnessed, kidlike atmosphere." The NCAA execs sitting in their luxury boxes at college games have fought hard to sustain that myth—and to keep money (like the NIL) out of their pure, "non-profit" system.[23]

The NCAA's High Paid Top Brass

Division-I men's basketball and football programs are run like many big corporations, with exorbitantly paid CEOs (athletic directors and head coaches), bloated and over-compensated middle management (athletic departments and assistant coaches), and poorly paid workers (players). While college athletes hardly suffer the horrible conditions in which factory workers toiled in the nineteenth century, their economic exploitation is similar. Further, much like laboring in factories in the Gilded Age, playing college football today is a dangerous endeavor. Get hurt and you are out of a job—or worse, you've suffered life-changing injuries.

It is common knowledge that most of the financial benefits of steady economic growth in the United States in the past several decades have gone to those in the upper income levels. That's the nature of business. It is up to workers' organizations to demand their fair share and for politicians to decide whether those efforts need legislative support. College sports—ostensibly as part of a higher mission of educating students for the good of society—should not tolerate the same economic inequities. And unlike workers in the free market, the NCAA's monopoly makes it virtually impossible for players to bargain for any share of the profits, let alone a fair one.

The proliferation of athletic department employees confirms that D-I universities are running a huge entertainment industry. In the early 2010s, the University of Texas athletic department had 400 people on its payroll.[24] The Miami University athletic department has sixteen people listed in "senior administration" and more than forty others in offices ranging from "communications" to "marketing and fan engagement" to "human performance and wellness." Ohio State is typical of the numbers connected to a top D-I football program, with about a dozen coaches and twenty-five other related positions, from the Director of High School Relations to the Director of Student Well Being.

In a 2015–2016 investigation, *Washington Post* journalist Will Hobson documented that over the space of a decade, payrolls for administrators at Power Five conference schools jumped 69 percent, while the number of teams they oversee didn't significantly change. At UCLA, the athletic director tripled his salary to $920,000. The number of administrators in the Michigan athletic department making $100,000 or more rose to thirty-four. "Everybody's got a director of operations," acknowledged one athletic director. Only 17 percent of D-I athletic budgets went to scholarships for the athletes. The rest went to athletic department employees, coaches, and facilities.[25]

The NCAA's 430-page rules and regulations handbook ensures the hiring of academic and compliance officers; Miami University has six of the latter. Miami men's basketball has a director of basketball operations and five coaches to handle a squad of fifteen players. The women's basketball team has its own director of basketball operations but only four coaches. The baseball team has four coaches, the women's softball team three; they share a director of baseball and softball. The football team has a director of football operations and eleven coaches.[26]

As the pile of cash in D-I television contracts has grown, the gap between the salaries of NCAA administrators and coaches on the one hand and D-I men's basketball and football players' non-fungible scholarship stipends on the other has steadily increased to indefensible proportions. It *is* embarrassing, as Jim Brown charged. Karl Marx would say that these athletes are in no way receiving the value of their labor. Like the robber barons of the Industrial Age, NCAA nabobs have monopolized college sports and fended off any and all antitrust suits, all the while lining their pockets as the athletes who make the spectacles profitable get a nonrefundable scholarship. The NCAA's men who own the means of production have few unique talents, unlike the skilled players they administer. When Walter Byers proposed to the NCAA Council that players "share" in the revenues, he was met with icy silence.[27] The organization saw no reason to take money out of its own pockets.

Bigger salaries in higher education exist in the administration and athletic departments. Business school professors can sometimes hit hundreds of thousands in annual salaries too. Here is a sample of the presidents' and professors' salaries at big D-I schools and mid-majors: as of 2020, Georgia State president Mark Becker's total pay was more than $2.8 million; Ohio State president Michael Drake took in more than $1.4 million; Eric Kaler at Minnesota north of $700,000; and Miami University's Gregory Crawford $629,000.[28] According to the AAUP's 2016–17 Report, the average salary of all full professors in the

United States was $102,402.²⁹ The average salary for a full professor at four-year public schools was $130,000, compared with $92,000 for an associate professor and $80,000 for assistants (the average salaries are skewed upward because faculty in business schools make about twice that of professors in colleges of arts and sciences, fine arts, and education). Instructors and lecturers, who teach more than half of the credit hours at many universities today, make between $61,000 and $63,000.³⁰ Adjunct professors take home less than that, in some cases with no benefits.

Employees at the top of the NCAA system pay themselves handsomely too. From 1987 to 1995, full-time salaried NCAA employees increased from 127 to 229, and today there are some 500 people working at the Indianapolis office.³¹ In 2018, the non-profit organization doled out $2.3 million in base pay to President Mark Emmert; he made another $400,000 on miscellaneous income. His chief operating officer's base salary was $1.1 million. Eight other employees received more than a half million.³² The top ten moneymakers at the NCAA make a collective $8 million annually. The organization spends "$44.8 million a year in 'administrative' costs and another $58.4 million for sundry business expenses," writes *Washington Post* columnist Sally Jenkins. "Then there is the whopping $23 million devoted to 'governance committees' and an annual convention. That's $126 million—for what? For double-talk and book-cooking."³³

The NCAA's well-compensated bureaucrats have no interest in changing a system that pays them so well. Famed Georgetown basketball coach John Thompson once told a group of athletic directors, "All you administrators preach education, but you vote money. When it's time to make rules, you vote for the rules that will make everybody the most money."³⁴

The NCAA spends hundreds of millions of dollars every year to maintain the status quo—to make sure that the money stays in its pockets, not in the players'. In 2013, there were fifteen pending lawsuits against the NCAA.³⁵ From 2002 to 2011, the NCAA spent $69.1 million in legal fees.³⁶ The NCAA's lobbying budget nearly doubled between 2014 and 2019, and during the same period, the organization forked out a whopping $184.4 million to outside legal firms to defend itself from any wrongdoing.³⁷

In a remarkable statement for a leader who claims to be an educator first and foremost, Emmert reasoned, "If you are not getting sued, you are not doing anything."³⁸ The NCAA argues that the many lawsuits they have to fight just go with the territory of being a multibillion-dollar business, and that criminal behavior happens within any institution. An educational system should be held to a higher ethical standard. Any school administrator or teacher would be immediately sacked and prosecuted for misusing funds, bribing parents, hiding sexual assaults, fixing grades, and other infractions regularly committed by athletic department employees. Most enterprises with this kind of sordid reputation would rightly go out of business.

By far, though, the best paydays are to be had by D-I college coaches. The practice of paying some coaches much more than professors is hardly new. In 1905, Harvard football coach Bill Reid made almost two times the average full professor's salary.³⁹ Notre Dame's Knute Rockne was one of the first high-profile football coaches to cash in on his celebrity. Endorsements and public speaking gigs made him a well-paid national figure. A year before he died in a plane crash, Rockne said that college football needed to be "more commercial." He strayed from the educational mission of the university, using unfair recruiting practices and showing indifference to his players' studies. "It was he, more than anyone else," writes historian Richard O. Davies, "who established the template for future generations of big-time college coaches."⁴⁰

Basketball coaches got into the money too. In 1928, Duquesne University was paying Charles "Chick" Davies an annual salary of $1,500. From the time he was hired in 1924 to 1932, Davies got a more than 170 percent raise at a time when universities were struggling through the Great Depression.⁴¹ Nonetheless, after World War II, many football and basketball coaches often taught classes in the physical education department and did not make much more than a full professor. Alabama head football coach Bear Bryant's salary in 1957 was $57,000, a sizable one for the time, especially at a Southern school.⁴²

If there is any question about the priorities of D-I schools, it is revealed in the huge increase in coaches' salaries in the last few decades. Duke University professor Charles Clotfelter found that from 1985 to 2010, average salaries at public universities rose 32 percent for full professors, 90 percent for presidents, and 650 percent for football coaches.⁴³ This is a far cry from the day when coaches like UCLA's John Wooden felt a duty to their school rather than to their pocketbook. Wooden made $33,500 in 1975, his last year with the Bruins. He refused to make any shoe (product endorsement) deals. "I didn't sign," Wooden said, "because I didn't think that money belonged to me."[44]

Wooden's principled stance was a naïve idea in the eyes of former coaches like UNLV's Jerry Tarkanian and North Carolina State coach Jim Valvano, and for other D-I coaches today, whose salaries average around a half million dollars annually. In the mid-1980s, Valvano made more than $800,000 a year on his coaching salary and business deals, but he had to resign his position because of numerous NCAA violations. In the 1990s, Arizona's Lute Olson had a package of more than $1 million annually. Kentucky's Rick Pitino, another habitual rules violator, totaled twice that.[45]

Some D-I coaches are now pulling down the same kind of multimillion-dollar salaries as CEOs at large corporations, making hundreds of times more than their lowest-paid employees. The biggest jump in salaries has come in the last two decades. Major college football coach's salaries increased 70 percent from 2006 to 2013, to an average of $1.64 million.[46] The average salary of the ten highest paid college football coaches in 2013 was $4.1 million.[47] Seventy-seven college football coaches took in more than $1 million in 2017. Alabama's Nick Saban's total compensation topped the list at $11.1 million.[48]

In 1990, the average salary for an incoming tenure-track history professor at public and private schools was less than $30,000.[49] In 2015-16, the average pay for a full professor in history at public and private four-year schools was less than $90,000. That change across time equals about a $2,400 raise annually.[50] In contrast, Syracuse head coach Jim Boeheim made $300,000 in 1990. In 2020, he was making $2.84 million—a nice pay bump of more than $2.5 million.[51] In 1990, Ohio State football coach John Cooper made $400,000. Three decades later, head coach Ryan Day took home $6.6 million.[52]

As of 2015, fourteen D-I basketball coaches made more than $3 million, and seventy-seven D-I football coaches made more than $1 million.[53] In 2017, Texas A&M gave Jimbo Fisher a ten-year, $75 million contract to coach football. It would take a typical full professor about 750 years to make that amount. *Wall Street Journal* columnist Jason Gay joked that he would take half of Fisher's pay to coach A&M, leaving $37.5 million left over to "add hot tubs and panic rooms to the corporate boxes. You could build a practice facility with a butler, an IMAX theater, and a wine cellar. . . [or] give it to some of your underpaid professors and teaching assistants on campus. Ha! Just kidding! Nobody cares about those underpaid professors and teaching assistants."[54]

In 2009, Clemson's head football coach Dabo Swinney's total compensation was $816,850. Ten years later, he made $9.3 million, which is approximately the cost of 100 university professors. Swinney mentors about eighty-five football players every year—not for educational purposes but to ready them for a pro career. In the same time span, a hundred professors would teach at least a thousand students annually and advise many more.

Even military service teams try to hide the embarrassingly high salaries paid to their coaches. In 2017, US Secretary of Defense James Mattis made $207,800 while overseeing a department funded at $639 billion, with 1.3 million active service members. This was public knowledge. The military academies, however, refused to divulge their coaches' salaries. It is safe to say that the head football and basketball coaches made more than Mattis. The Navy athletic department said that Congress had passed laws to exempt military academies from public disclosures and that it would "not release confidential data of this manner." Navy did reveal, however, that football coach Ken Niumatalolo made $2 million a year to run a program of about 100 players and coaches.[55] Even national defense does not take priority over college sports.

Nick Saban has a convoluted defense of the current system that pays coaches so handsomely at the players' and university's expense. In response to a question about the advent of players selling their NIL, the Alabama coach said:

> I'm all for the players, but I'm for all players and all sports. I think there's a lot of folks out there that see college football—college athletics—as a big business; it's revenue producing. Wayne [Huizenga] paid so much for the [Miami] Dolphins, he made so much money every year, he sold it for a lot more than he bought it for, and that's business. In college, we revenue produce. We have 21 sports—I don't know how many hundreds of student-athletes we have on scholarship—and most of those sports create no revenue. But the parts that create revenue make it possible for all of these sports to exist. We reinvest all the resources, all of the income, we reinvest in the programs. I hear people say all the time, 'Well, you make a lot of money.' Yeah, but I create a lot of value.[56]

Saban's focus on subsidizing other non-revenue Alabama sports rather than the educational mission of his school brings to mind the famous fundraising plea from former University of Oklahoma president George L. Cross in 1950: "We're trying to build a university our football team can be proud of."[57]

Assistant football coaches also reap the benefits of this explosion in salaries. In 2009, Tennessee gave Monte Kiffin a $1 million contract (with benefits), making him the first football assistant to reach that figure. Now there are more than twenty assistant football coaches who make more than $1 million. As of 2018, three were making more than $2 million.[58] In late 2021, Fleck fired offensive coordinator Mike Sanford Jr. and rehired his previous Gopher coordinator Kirk Ciarrocca for $625,000 annually.[59]

Women's basketball coaches are paid less because, supposedly, "the market" will not bear it. If college sports were truly a non-profit part of institutions of higher education, that argument would not hold. After the University of Connecticut won the 2015 NCAA men's basketball tournament, Coach Kevin Ollie was given a raise to $3 million a year. Nonetheless, highly successful UConn women's coach, Geno Auriemma, whose Huskies had won ten national titles to that point, was asked whether he was concerned about Ollie making a million more than he did. "Not at all." Auriemma reasoned. "That's where the market is. . . . It's what the market will bear for those guys, and I'm all for it. Sometimes there is a cap [on coaches' salaries], but that's not workable. This is America. Anyone should be able to make all they can. . . . I don't ever use that Title IX crap about what I should get paid."[60]

Highest Paid State Employees: College Coaches

In 2003, former Michigan president James J. Duderstadt observed that "Joe Paterno, Bobby Bowden, and Steve Spurrier in football, or Mike Krzyzewski and Bobby Knight in basketball transcend their teams, their institutions, and even the sport itself."[61] With the exception of Krzyzewski, the other coaches were employed by public institutions. Public service is not paid like top jobs in the private sector (the president of the United States makes $400,000 annually), except when it comes to the salaries of some D-I coaches.

Top coaches' salaries dwarf those of other state employees. The highest public salary in forty states is either a college football or men's basketball coach.[62] Minnesota's head football coach Tim Brewster made a million dollars in 2009. A decade later, his successor, P. J. Fleck, cashed an annual salary of $3.6 million. The governor of Minnesota made $128,000. Nick Saban made $8.9 million in salary in 2019, compared to the governor's $120,000.[63] In one week, Saban pulled in over $50,000 more than the Alabama governor's total compensation. Saban's salary was more than 360 times what his players received in a tuition voucher. The chancellor of Alabama's University System said that Saban's contract was "the best financial investment this university has ever made."[64] That might be true in the sense that Crimson Tide football is highly profitable, but Alabama is nowhere to be found in any rankings of the top 100 research universities in the country; *U.S. News & World Report* ranks Alabama 153rd out of 399 schools.[65]

The ratio of Clemson's Dabo Swinney's salary to the South Carolina governor's is even greater ($9.3 million to $106,000). Similar huge salary disparities exist between the governors and football coaches in Florida (University of Florida), Michigan (University of Michigan), and Texas (University of Texas).[66] Football and men's basketball coaches can also make up to a million in bonuses if their teams reach a certain round in the national championships. They can cash in on endorsements, radio and TV shows, and other extraneous income sources.

The Pandemic: Profits Over People

If there was ever any question about whether D-I sports is a big business, the Covid pandemic that hit in 2020 revealed the truth when, for monetary reasons, the games had to go on—even if it put peoples' lives in jeopardy. At first, some conferences canceled their football seasons, but others, such as the SEC and ACC, decided to play. Apparently, the billions of dollars in losses were just too great to bear, the health of the players being of secondary importance; soon, other conferences decided to play as well. Somehow, everyone involved in an NCAA game, from the players and coaches to the referees and scorekeepers, jumped the line of testing for the virus—this at a time when Covid tests were hard to come by for all other Americans—and were able to test daily.

Not everyone was blind to the callousness. Kim Mulkey, the women's head basketball coach at Baylor, warned of the risks of going ahead with the season when she said, "The almighty dollar is more important than the health and welfare of me, the players, or anybody else."[67] In order to preserve the marquee sports programs in the darkest days of the pandemic athletic departments cut some 350 non-revenue sports such as men's gymnastics and track and field.[68]

The budget crunch during the pandemic also prompted universities to fire a great many visiting and adjunct professors, those who actually carry the load of teaching students. At the same time, however, there were no mass layoffs of administrators or coaches in athletic departments.

The canceling of football and men's basketball games threatened to bring down the entire NCAA edifice, so some universities took out big loans to bridge the budget gaps. The Power Five schools' sports revenue fell by some $1.7 billion during the fiscal year 2021. Tom McMillan, the head of the LEAD1 Association, which represents FBS athletic directors, stated the obvious: "Debt service will obviously be a cost that will impact. You wonder whether, in the aggregate, the debt service incurred will exceed the economies incurred."[69]

When some conferences, such as the SEC, ACC, and Big Twelve, went ahead and played football anyway—virus or no virus—other conferences reconsidered the risks and rewards and decided to play too. Even without ticket-buying fans in the stands, the TV revenue was just too tantalizing to ignore. The pressure on conference commissioners was immense. Ohio State athletic director Gene Smith, making $1.6 million a year, expressed his anger with Big Ten Commissioner Kevin Warren for canceling the 2020 football season (it was, in fact, the Big Ten presidents who made that decision). Athletics at Ohio State made $230 million in 2019, of which $185 million came from football games. Yes, the show had to go on; even at the time during which the pandemic was running wild and there were not yet effective vaccines available, the danger of the virus to coaches, players, referees, and all other personnel on the field was of secondary consideration. Legislators from six of the states in the Big Ten urged Warren to let the kids play. They argued that the decision was not fair to those players who wanted to go on to the NFL, once again showing the priority of sports over students' health and academics. Even President Donald Trump put pressure on Warren. Covid cases shot up that fall, in part because of game-day gatherings around the TV (going to the games was off). Buckeye revelers, for example, told one reporter that "it was as though the party animals had been released from their cages." In one week of the season, almost half of the D-I football games were canceled because of infected players.⁷⁰

As the country struggled to battle the pandemic and the number of Covid-related deaths climbed into the hundreds of thousands, the need for rapid testing became even more evident, yet the limited number of tests available had to be reserved for EMTs and other "front-line" workers in the nation's economy. Most Americans could not test as often as they would have liked—if they could test at all. Still, somehow, everyone associated with D-I football and men's basketball programs was able to get tested regularly. The average student as well as their professors (let alone many essential workers) received no such treatment. That few, if any, college administrators criticized the testing priorities was yet another transparent revelation of the importance they placed on sports.

The decision to have student athletes play unmasked the NCAA's naked greed. Was playing the games despite the pandemic worth it? The answer for the NCAA, with the increased number of viewers for its TV games, was an unequivocal "yes."

Like the television networks, the gambling business was loath to lose revenue during the pandemic. Betting on college sports is a huge enterprise. It wasn't always so. After World War I, guardians of proper American bourgeois values cast drinking, sex, and gambling as corrupting influences. Prohibition banned the bottle, the Hays Code of 1934 ensured that bare bodies were covered in the movies, and gambling on sports, until recently, was prohibited in every state except Nevada. Gambling was one of those sins connected with strip clubs and speakeasies. It is no longer a hellbent transgression. In 2012, police in south Florida uncovered an operation to wager on youth football games. More than $100,000 was bet on a pee wee title game.⁷¹

Casinos don't rely on sports betting for a big share of their profits; instead, they view it as a "loss leader" to lure gamblers into the building, where they lose more money on games like blackjack and slot machines, which are more heavily skewed in the casino's favor. When betting online, one can place wagers from his or her living room. Back in 2013, before the advent of widespread legal online gambling, it was estimated that between $60 and $70 billion was illegally wagered on college football annually. The FBI figured that $2.5 billion was illegally wagered on March Madness alone.⁷² With about $8.5 billion in legal betting on the March Madness games these days, it is no wonder that—global pandemic or not—the games had to go on. Sports fans demanded it, and the NCAA obliged.[73]

Conference Musical Chairs

The big D-I athletic departments are relentless in their quest for bigger and bigger profits. Schools switch conferences like a game of musical chairs, none of them wanting to be left out of the money-making circle. With hundreds of millions of dollars at stake, athletic departments look for business mergers with teams anywhere in the country, dollar signs blinding conference bureaucrats and athletic departments to the importance of educational connections and historic geographic rivalries. Athletes' studies are secondary considerations as conference games are played farther and farther away from their campuses.

With only fourteen football and basketball conference members, and only seven in men's ice hockey, the Big Ten's storied history no longer matters to those who control it. Minnesota's men's hockey team plays in the Big Ten, while the women's team competes in the seven-team Western Collegiate Hockey Association. Go figure.[74] In the early 2010s, the Big Twelve lost Nebraska to the Big Ten and Texas A&M and Missouri to the SEC, setting up such classic gridiron matchups as Indiana against Nebraska and A&M versus Vanderbilt. Gone are Nebraska's annual games with neighboring Oklahoma and A&M's showdowns with the Texas Longhorns. Minnesota started playing Michigan in football in 1892, but they no longer play for the "Brown Jug" every year, replacing it with such red-hot rivalries as the Gophers against Rutgers.

College teams have gone down the (supposedly) gilded highway to faraway conferences. Travel expenses for away games are of no consideration. Miami University's men's hockey team plays in the National Collegiate Hockey Conference with such geographic rivals as the University of North Dakota and the University of Nebraska-Omaha. Butler University in Indianapolis now plays in the Big East, and Notre Dame's football and basketball teams compete in the Atlantic Coast Conference—who knew that South Bend was on the East Coast? Meanwhile, it makes seemingly perfect sense for Notre Dame's men's ice hockey team to continue to skate in the Big Ten.

The University of St. Thomas (MN) recently left D-III for D-I sports, and although as a "mid-major" the athletic department will run millions of dollars in the red for making this move, it actually boasts about the fact that the school will no longer have nearby road trips, replaced by costly long plane rides to distant away games. As a Tommie athletic department brochure put it, "Road trips in previous years often involved bus rides across the Twin Cities; a 'long' road trip usually meant northwest Minnesota. . . St. Thomas teams now travel coast to coast. The first year of road trips included visits to 28 states like Alaska, California, Texas, Florida, Ohio, Missouri, Michigan, New York, and the Carolinas." What the writer of the description in the brochure conveniently left out is that the exorbitant costs of all this long-distance travel will be covered by regular student fees and money from the university's general budget. As one journalist put it, "[St. Thomas will] have to develop those resources to start to compete in their league and with everybody."[75] No mid-major has these resources to balance the athletic budget.

These moves from conference to conference are yet another big gamble for universities. The poster child for a switch gone wrong is Rutgers, which, along with Maryland, was welcomed into the Big Ten in 2014. At the time, Scarlet Knights' athletic director Tim Pernetti gushed, "It's a transformative day for Rutgers University." Rutgers and Maryland eyed the Big Ten's huge TV revenues, while the conference hoped to tap into the big East Coast market. Never mind that the matchups between the Boilermakers and the Scarlet Knights, or the Gophers and the Terrapins, might not capture much interest.[76] The Rutgers athletic department predicted that the Scarlet Knights new football rival would be Penn State.[77] It's been more than eight years since Rutgers hopped conferences, but no sports fan today will claim that a Knights-Nittany Lions game is a must-see event.

The Rutgers athletic department also enlisted "ambassadors" (young coeds) to escort prospective recruits about campus, a recipe for indiscretion. Still, the new athletic director, Patrick Hobbs, waxed optimistic: "Our teams and student-athletes have enjoyed a great deal of success in the Big Ten"—pointing to winning wrestling, lacrosse, and women's soccer programs. The big money-maker sports did not do so well. The football team posted a 2–10 record in 2016, 0–9 in Big Ten play. The basketball team won four games in the Big Ten. In 2021, the football team improved to 5–8, and 2–7 in the Big Ten. The basketball team went 12–8 in the conference. The athletic department responded by upping the ante on student fees by two percent, evidently to improve Rutgers' winning records.[78]

The Rutgers athletic department has lost about $20 million annually since 2006. As of 2017, the combined debt was bigger than the shortfalls at all of the other Big Ten schools combined. To keep the athletic program afloat, the university bank loaned the department $10.5 million, which would cost $18 million to repay, and shifted "$11 million in student fees and $17.1 million from its general fund to cover the athletic shortfall." Something had to give at a university whose tuition ranked among the highest nationally. Unfortunately for all of the students attending college for an education, that amounted to a great deal more spending on athletics to the detriment of academics. By 2017, just three years after the university made its much-ballyhooed move to the Big Ten, low-paid contract instructors taught nearly a third of the courses at Rutgers.[79]

The allure of revenues from big TV deals also prompted the University of Maryland to jump ship from the ACC to the Big Ten. The Big Ten (television) Network was launched in 2007, which saw conference revenues increase from $126.9 million in 2006 to $217.7 million in 2008. An internal report in 2011 claimed that Maryland's intercollegiate teams would face a $17.2 million deficit by 2017 if the school did not join the Big Ten. The study also projected that Maryland would have to spend nearly $73,000 on every student athlete, not nearly enough to compete with ACC powerhouses Florida State ($128,700 per athlete) and the University of Miami ($116,914).[80] So what choice did Maryland have but to leave?

In 2021, the Big Twelve was rocked when Texas and Oklahoma decided to join the SEC, which was by this time the best college football conference in the country. The Longhorn and Sooner top brass salivated at the prospect of playing big football games against Bama, Georgia, LSU, and Florida. Texas and Oklahoma had to wait until 2025 to make the move, however. If they left before then, the two schools would have to make a payment of approximately $80 million each to get out of the Big Twelve's conference media deal—as well as be liable for other revenue losses to the conference.[81] The meaning in traditional geographic rivalries is evaporating. Indiana football coach Tom Allen commented, "The landscape is changing. West Virginia is in the Big 12. It doesn't make any sense to me. I was raised when everything was regional. Those barriers are kind of breaking down."[82]

Obviously, when athletic directors take their schools to another conference, they are following the money rather than seeking associations with more prestigious academic institutions. Conferences used to cooperate on educational matters and were proud of their academic reputations. For example, according to its website:

> [The Big Ten Academic Alliance] is the nation's preeminent model for effective collaboration among research universities. . . . [T]hese world-class institutions have advanced their academic mission, generated unique opportunities for students and faculty, and served the common good by sharing expertise, leveraging campus resources, and collaborating on innovative programs.[83]

Big Ten athletic directors apparently did not consider academic standards and educational cooperation when they welcomed in Penn State (1990), Nebraska (2011), Maryland (2014), and Rutgers (2014). In fact, the Big Ten already had outstanding research institutions, such as Minnesota, Wisconsin, Northwestern, Michigan, and Ohio State. Expansion to the new schools arguably lowered the conference's overall academic standing, which was of little importance to the businesspersons calling the shots in D-I sports. In 2022, UCLA and USC rocked the PAC-12 by announcing that they were joining the Big Ten, a corporate merger that left their long-time West Coast partners in the lurch.

Notes

1. Oriard, *King Football*, 235.
2. Pat McManamon, "Jim Brown Rips 'Reprehensible' NCAA," May 3, 2014, accessed November 16, 2020, https://www.espn.com/college-sports/story/_/id/10877754/jim-brown-calls-ncaa-most-reprehensible-organization-god-ever-created.
3. Branch, "The Shame."
4. John R. Thelin, "Academics and Athletics: A Part and Apart in the American Campus," *Journal of Intercollegiate Sport* no. 1 (2008), 74.
5. Sperber, *Beer and Circus*, 223.
6. McManamon, "Jim Brown Rips 'Reprehensible' NCAA."
7. Unattributed, *Star Tribune*, February 3, 2022, C5.
8. Gorn and Goldstein, *A Brief History*, 158–9.
9. Sanderson and Siegfried, "Why American."
10. Richard M. Mikulski, review of Howard P. Chudacoff, *Changing the Playbook: How Power, Profit, and Politics Changes College Sports*, *Journal of Sport History* 44, no. 3 (Fall 2017), 492–3.
11. Sheldon Anderson editorial in the *Miami Student*, 1999; for the salaries paid to D-I administrators, see also Kenneth Shropshire and Collin D. Williams, *The*

Miseducation of the Student Athlete: How to Fix College Sports (Philadelphia, PA: Wharton School Press, 2017).

12. Gorn and Goldstein, *A Brief History*, 253.
13. Chip Scroggins, "U Regent: NCAA is Living in Dark Ages," *Star Tribune*, March 3, 2019, C11.
14. Steve Berkowitz, "Do College Athletes Get Enough?" *USA Today*, April 18, 2017, 6C.
15. Tom Huddleston, Jr., "College Football Stars Could Be Earning as Much as $2.4 million per year, based on NCAA Revenues," *NBC News*, September 2, 2020, accessed December 4, 2020, https://www.cnbc.com/2020/09/02/how-much-college-athletes-could-be-earning-study.html.
16. Scroggins, "U Regent."
17. Joe Nocera and Ben Strauss, "Here's How the NCAA Hurts College Athletes," *Fortune*, February 27, 2016; see also Nocera and Strauss, *Indentured*, 213.
18. Marc Tracy, "Waiting for Student Athletes to Become Student Activists," *New York Times*, April 9, 2019, B9.
19. Austen Macalus, "March Madn . . . Wait, Is it Legal the Say That?" *Star Tribune*, March 26, 2019, B3.
20. Sanderson and Siegfried, "Why American."
21. Scroggins, "U Regent."
22. Tess DeMeyer, "The College Athletes Who Are Allowed to Make Big Bucks: Cheerleaders, *New York Times*, November 29, 2020, accessed May 26, 2021, https://www.nytimes.com/2020/11/29/sports/the-college-athletes-who-are-allowed-to-make-big-bucks-cheerleaders.html?action=click&module=Editors%20Picks&pgtype=Homepage.
23. Sid Hartman, "For Nantz, Final Four Retains Special Aura," *Star Tribune*, April 7, 2019, C2.
24. Gaul, *Billion-Dollar Ball,* 30.
25. Sally Jenkins, "The Financial Burden on NCAA Sports Wears Wingtips, not Sneakers." *Washington Post*, 2 Apr. 2021, https://www.washingtonpost.com/sports/2021/04/02/ncaa-women-basketball-tournament-cost-burden/, accessed April 2021.
26. Miami University Athletic Department, https://miamiredhawks.com/staff-directory, accessed March 31, 2020.
27. Byers, *Unsportsmanlike Conduct*, 369.
28. Dan Bauman, Tyler Davis, and Brian O'Leary, "Executive Compensation at Public and Private Colleges," *The Chronicle of Higher Education*, July 17, 2020, accessed November 25, 2020, https://www.chronicle.com/article/executive-compensation-at-public-and-private-colleges/?cid=FEATUREDNAV&cid2=gen_login_refresh#id=table_public_2019.
29. "Professor Salaried from Around the World," American Association of University Professors 2016/2017 Report, accessed April 29, 2020, https://academicpositions.com/career-advice/professor-salaries-from-around-the-world.

30. "Average salaries by rank, 4-year public," *Chronicle of Higher Education* Data, 2018–2019 academic year, accessed November 25, 2020, https://data.chronicle.com/category/sector/1/faculty-salaries/.

31. Byers, *Unsportsmanlike Conduct,* 367; and Bruce Weber, "Walter Byers, Ex-N.C.A.A. Leader Who Rued Corruption, Dies at 93," *New York Times,* May 27, 2015, accessed November 2, 2021, https://www.nytimes.com/2015/05/28/sports/walter-byers-ex-ncaa-leader-who-rued-corruption-dies-at-93.html.

32. Steve Berkowitz, "NCAA President Mark Emmert Credited with $2.7 million in Total Pay for 2018 Calendar Year," *USA Today,* June 2, 2020.

33. Jenkins, "The Financial Burden."

34. John Thompson, Jr., "Let's Drop the Charade and Pay College Athletes," *New York Times,* November 24, 2021, accessed March 24, 2021, https://www.nytimes.com/2020/11/12/opinion/sunday/ncaa-sports-paying-college-players.html?searchResultPosition=1. This opinion piece was adapted from his autobiography, *New York Times,* November. 12, 2020.

35. Rachel George, "Challenging the NCAA," *USA Today,* April 26, 2013, 13C.

36. George, "Challenging the NCAA."

37. Steve Berkowitz, "NCAA President Mark Emmert Credited with $2.7 million in total pay for 2018 Calendar Year," *USA Today,* June 2, 2020.

38. George, "Challenging the NCAA," 13C.

39. Branch, "The Shame."

40. Davies, *Sports in American Life,* 130, 133.

41. Kemper, *College Football and American Culture,* 39.

42. Davies, *Sports in American Life,* 212.

43. Bill Morris, "A Tent City for Fun and Profit," *New York Times,* February 24, 2013, SP1; and Laura Pappano, "How Big-Time Sports," 24.

44. Byers, *Unsportsmanlike Conduct,* 9.

45. Byers, *Unsportsmanlike Conduct,* 9.

46. Gregory, "It's Time to Pay"; and unattributed, "Coaches Compensation," *USA Today,* November 20, 2014, 8C.

47. Sanderson and Siegfried, "Why American."

48. Sanderson and Siegfried, "Why American."

49. "Faculty Salaries Rise in 1991-92." *Perspectives on History,* November 1, 1992, accessed January 8, 2022, https://www.historians.org/publications-and-directories/perspectives-on-history/november-1992/faculty-salaries-rise-in-1991-92.

50. Scott Jaschik, "What You Teach is What You Earn," *Inside Higher Ed,* March 28, 2016, accessed January 8, 2022, https://www.insidehighered.com/news/2016/03/28/study-finds-continued-large-gaps-faculty-salaries-based-discipline.

51. Jake Elman, "What is Jim Boeheim's Salary Coaching Syracuse's Men's Basketball Team?" *Sportscasting,* March 19, 2021, accessed February 10, 2021, https://www.sportscasting.com/jim-boeheims-salary-coaching-syracuses-mens-basketball-team.

52. Sperber, *College Sports Inc.,* 154; and Hayleigh Colombo, "Here's how Ryan Day's Pay Compares to Nick Saban, Dabo Swinney and Jim Harbaugh," *Columbus*

Business First, October 24, 2021, accessed January 10, 2022, https://www.bizjournals.com/columbus/news/2021/10/24/ryan-day-salary-ranking-2021.html.

53. Ihsan Taylor, "Sports: 'The Grind', 'Billion-Dollar Ball', and More," *New York Times Book Review*, December 6, 2015, 65; and Sanderson and Siegfried, "Why American."

54. Jason Gay, "Please Hire Me to Coach!" *The Wall Street Journal*, December 7, 2017, S1.

55. Unattributed, "Military Academies Hush on Sports Finance," *USA Today*, November 9, 2017, 1A.

56. Alan Blinder, "The Saban Way: Always Winning and Never Standing Pat," *New York Times*, August 30, 2021, D6.

57. Daniel A. Nathan, "'I'm Against It!' The Marx Brothers' *Horse Feathers* as Cultural Critique: Or, Why Big-Time College Football Gives Me a Haddock," in Ron Briley, et al., eds, *All-Stars and Movie Stars: Sports in Film and History* (Lexington: University of Kentucky Press, 2008), 40–54, 46–47.

58. Branch, "The Shame of College Sports"; and "Best-paid Assistant Coaches," *USA Today*, December 6, 2018, 4C.

59. Randy Johnson, "Ciarrocca's Two-year Deal Worth $625K Per Season," *Star Tribune*, December 8, 2021, C4.

60. Erik Brady, "Auriemma Doesn't Begrudge Ollie," *USA Today*, April 2, 2015, 4C.

61. Duderstadt, *Intercollegiate Athletics*, 153.

62. John D. Hollis, "California Lets Athletes Share in the Bounty," *USA Today*, October 4, 2019, 7A.

63. Unattributed, "Special Report: Coaches' Salaries, *USA Today*, November 10, 2009, 5C; and unattributed, "Governors vs. Football Coaches," *USA Today*, October 24, 2019, 4C.

64. *New York Times Book Review*, December 6, 2015, 65; Sanderson and Siegfried, "Why American."

65. Unattributed, "2020 Best National University Rankings," *U.S. News and World Report*, https://www.usnews.com/best-colleges/rankings/national-universities, accessed June 10, 2020.

66. Tom Schad and Steve Berkowitz, "College Football Coaches vs. Governors: Who Makes More Money," *USA Today*, October 23, 2019, accessed April 15, 2020, https://www.usatoday.com/story/sports/ncaaf/2019/10/23/college-football-coaches-vs-governors-who-makes-more-money/4008753002/.

67. Steve Gardner, "Baylor Women's Coach Kim Mulkey Blames 'Almighty Dollar' for College Basketball's COVID Problems," *USA Today*, January 17, 2021, accessed June 16, 2021, https://www.usatoday.com/story/sports/ncaaw/big12/2021/01/17/kim-mulkey-ncaa-values-almighty-dollar-more-than-players-health/4197521001/m.

68. Ken Powell and Steve Sviggum, "Financial, Title IX Realities Drove U Decision," *Star Tribune*, December 26, 2020, A7.

Chapter Three

69. Steve Berkowitz, "Colleges Absorbed Pandemic Losses," *USA Today*, October 20, 2021, 3C.

70. Bruce Schoenfeld, "Was the College Football Season Worth It?" *New York Times*, December. 30, 2020, accessed January 11, 2022, https://www.nytimes.com/2020/12/30/magazine/college-football-pandemic.html?referringSource=articleShare.

71. Uncredited, "Massive Gambling Operation Found," *Star Tribune*, October 31, 2012, C2.

72. Gillian Spear, "Think Sports Gambling Isn't Big Money? Wanna Bet?" *NBC News*, July 15, 2013, accessed November 30, 2020, https://www.nbcnews.com/news/us-news/think-sports-gambling-isnt-big-money-wanna-bet-flna6C10634316.

73. Nancy Armour, "College Basketball Gets a Much-needed Do-over with March Madness, *USA Today*, March 18, 2019, accessed October 28, 2020, https://www.usatoday.com/story/sports/columnist/nancy-armour/2019/03/18/college-basketball-march-madness/3195546002/.

74. Author's note: My brother Randy used to ride me because I couldn't remember which college team was in which conference. Now with midwestern schools such as Butler, Creighton, DePaul, Xavier, and Marquette in the Big East Conference, and Notre Dame, Pittsburgh, and Louisville in the Atlantic Coast Conference, he has stopped.

75. Marcus Fuller, "Q&A: Gophers Athletic Director Mark Coyle Finding His Footing Amid Seismic Changes in College Sports," *Star Tribune*, August 26, 2021, accessed August 26, 2021, https://www.Star Tribune.com/mark-coyle-gophers-athletic-director-21-5-loss-st-thomas-q-and-a/60009100.

76. Michael Powell, "After Years of Disgrace, Rutgers Drifts in Money Pit," *New York Times*, March 12, 2017, SP1.

77. Mulcahy III, *An Athletic Director's Story*, 95.

78. Powell, "After Years of Disgrace."

79. Powell, "After Years of Disgrace."

80. Mike Kaszuba, "Big Ten is Bringing in Big Money as a TV Star," *Star Tribune*, January 20, 2012, A1.

81. Unattributed, "Texas, Oklahoma Formally Submit Request to Join SEC," *Star Tribune*, July 28, 2021, C11.

82. Randy Johnson, "Beefier SEC Grabs Big Ten by the Ears," *Star Tribune*, July 24, 2021, C4.

83. Big 10 Academic Alliance website, https://www.btaa.org/about, accessed November 24, 2020.

CHAPTER FOUR

The D-I Rap Sheet:
Point Shavers, Sexual Predators, Escorts, and Cheats

> "Nine out of 10 schools are cheating. The other one is in last place."
>
> —Former UNLV basketball coach Jerry Tarkanian[1]

In 1992, Jerry Tarkanian's luck ran out, and he was fired as the head coach of men's basketball at UNLV for repeated NCAA rule violations. Tarkanian's prolonged court battles with the NCAA over his alleged misdeeds was one of the reasons longtime NCAA head Walter Byers wrote an exposé of the sham of amateurism in major college sports and the fallacy of the "student-athlete," a term Byers himself had coined years before. Tarkanian was indifferent to his players' work in the classroom. Byers observed that "He [Tarkanian] looks like the winner to me; UNLV clearly was the loser."[2] Byers was right. In 1998, Tark the Shark countersued and won a settlement of $2.5 million from the NCAA. Since then, the Runnin' Rebels have returned to mediocrity.

Byers disagreed with Tarkanian about the number of cheaters in D-I sports, estimating that only about a third of the big programs were breaking the rules, which is still hardly a ringing endorsement of the system.[3] In fact, in the 1990s, the NCAA imposed sanctions on more than half of D-I athletic programs.[4] Longtime Nebraska football coach Bob Devaney reflected the cynical attitude of many other coaches when he said, "I don't expect to win enough games to be put on NCAA probation. I just want to win enough to warrant an investigation.[5]

Some of the most egregious NCAA rule violations have come to light in the last few decades, including criminal investigations. Obviously, many guilty parties have not been exposed. Nonetheless, the sheer volume of known NCAA scandals should hit college administrators in their olfactory nerves—something stinks in the locker room.

Chapter Four

These abuses primarily stem from men's sports programs. Few scandals have hit women's sports. Women athletes are better able to balance their sports and studies because they are not under the illusion that they will make life-changing money by playing professionally. The average WNBA salary in 2020, for example, was $116,000, and women's athletic careers have a statute of physical limitations that is typically even shorter than men's.[6]

Cheating Pays

For any fan who reads the sports section of the newspaper every day, the list of D-I wrongdoers might illicit a shrug and a "What's new?" College sports scandals, including illegal payments to players, recruiting violations, player felonies, and coaching infractions, are regular news. It is a sordid saga of dark money, hookers, rape, point shaving, cheating, and coverups.

Schools have been breaking the amateur rules since the beginning of intercollegiate sports. When college football became more profitable after World War I and the pressure on coaches to win increased, compensating players became commonplace. One way for schools to get around the NCAA's prohibition on paying athletes outright was to give them phantom jobs. Other conferences criticized the SEC when it began to allow athletic scholarships in 1935, but every big conference was using phony work, hidden payments from alumni and boosters, and "loans" to subsidize players.[7]

Booster clubs were often the conduit for these pay-for-no-work schemes. In the 1930s, one Northwestern lineman said that, in addition to a "job" as a night watchman at the football stadium, "he had received payments to help him with expenses, though he never knew who provided this assistance."[8] Ohio State football players labored as pages at the state legislature in Columbus. While at Ohio State, the great track-and-field star Jesse Owens ran an elevator at the state capitol to earn money; evidently, he actually showed up to push the buttons.[9] In the mid-1950s, the Columbus Chamber of Commerce was doling out about $75,000 to Ohio State athletes every year, mostly for jobs with no work.[10]

In the late 1940s, Minnesota Gopher football star and future NFL Hall of Fame Coach Bud Grant was employed at Investors Diversified Services in Minneapolis. His only duty there was to pick up a monthly paycheck. Grant's little bonus and other suspected payments struck columnist Sid Hartman of the *Minneapolis Tribune* as a great deal for the

The D-I Rap Sheet

newspaper. "We would increase the press run for Sunday by 30,000," Hartman said, "if the Gophers won on Saturday."[11] The NCAA banned these phony jobs for a time, but it now permits the practice again if there is documentation that the player actually does some work and with the stipulation that the pay is in line with the average wage rate. Nevertheless, it is and always has been hard to stop boosters from slipping players an envelope full of some extra cash.

Athletic programs have also lured players by giving their fathers a spot on the coaching staff. Academically prestigious Cal-Berkeley participated in such a ploy in the 1950s. Another famous case was LSU's hiring of Press Maravich in 1966 to get his sought-after son "Pistol" Pete to play for the Tigers. Kansas head basketball coach Larry Brown coincidently gave Ed Manning an assistant coaching job at the same time Brown was courting prize recruit Danny Manning, who ended up helping the Jayhawks win the NCAA title in 1988. Milt Wagner found his way onto John Calipari's Louisville staff in 2000, and Wagner's blue chip son, Dajuan, soon followed to play for the Cardinals. Another Kansas head coach, Bill Self, gave Ronnie Chalmers a spot as director of basketball operations, with son Mario Chalmers coming to the Jayhawks in a package deal. Like Manning, Chalmers led Kansas to another championship in 2008. These are but a few cases of the widespread practice.[12]

It has historically not only been dads who got plum jobs but also recruits' former coaches and mentors. In 2010, the NCAA passed a rule against employing any "individual associated with a prospective Student-Athlete [sic]." Once again, the NCAA, in its feeble effort to take the moral high road, was restricting the free market. "The line between hiring legitimate candidates for employment with a basketball program and providing a recruiting inducement," the NCAA declared in defending the new rule, "is being blurred by the hiring of individuals whose primary value to an institution is in their ties to specific prospective student-athletes."[13] In the business world, hiring friends and family is a standard and legal practice.

This scheme continues transparently, as Purdue's head basketball coach Matt Painter admits, "Yes, I would consider adding a player if I had to hire his coach. It depends on the quality of the player and the quality of the person who would be the coach." In 2017, Missouri head coach Cuonzo Martin hired Michael Porter Sr. as an assistant coach, knowing that, as a bonus, Porter Jr., a 6'10" McDonald's All-American, would come to Columbia. "First of all, we made it clear at every opportunity that this job offer had to be about me," Porter Sr. claimed. "I was not going to be pressuring my son to go someplace so I could have a job. It did not go down like that."[14] How could a father say anything else?

Obviously, it is easier to cheat by simply sneaking money into a recruit's or player's pocket. In 1929, the Big Ten booted out Iowa for keeping a slush fund to pay football players, but the Hawkeyes got back in the next year because they threatened to go public with the incriminating evidence they had on other schools who were running the same game.[15] In a highly publicized case in the early 1930s, Columbia University student Reed Harris was briefly expelled for chastising the administration for its shady football program. In *King Football: The Vulgarization of the American College* (1932), published in the same year that *Horse Feathers* appeared, Harris's indictment of college football holds true nearly a century later:

> [To have a winning football team] alumni, faculty, and trustees of the colleges will lie, cheat, and steal, unofficially. Officially, they know nothing of the sordid business behind the gigantic spectacles which are college football games. . . . Coaches are hired at outrageous salaries, players are bought and paid for, elaborate training staffs are maintained to keep the gridiron warriors in the peak of condition, special quarters are constructed to house these privileged mugs, and money is beautifully wasted there and everywhere.[16]

Journalist Ted Benson defended paying players, ridiculing the Carnegie Foundation, a critic of college sports, for "hold[ing] up its collective palsied hands in horror at the thought that Joe Zilch, son of a miner, receives all of fifteen simoleons a week during the football season plus his room and some plain unfrilled chow. . . . Players at Michigan," he continued, "[were] going hungry because they were underpaid."[17]

After World War II, college football was rife with illegal payments to players and academic fraud to keep players eligible. In 1953, it came out that Michigan State had forked over about $50,000 to compensate its football players. Boosters of schools in the Pacific Coast Conference—Southern Cal, Washington, UCLA, and California—were also found to have regularly funneled cash to players.[18] Ohio State, Cal, Washington, USC, and UCLA were banned from the 1957 Rose Bowl for paying players. Auburn, Florida, and Texas A&M also landed on probation. Sports journalist Francis Wallace called the players pawns in a patently professional system. "[Their] gridiron labor is sold by the college at tremendous profit." Wallace blamed "well-meaning college administrations which demand both big-time profits and 'classic amateurism.'"[19]

As college football attendance jumped and television revenues boomed in the 1950s, the temptation to swindle increased. Almost fifteen million fans went to games in 1956; that number had doubled by 1971. Television revenues went from more than $2 million in 1959 to $12 million a decade later. In 1956, UCLA was reprimanded for a football slush fund run by the Westwood Club and the Bruin Bench. Southern Cal was implicated that same year. The NCAA acted swiftly but, as usual, weakly, limiting recruiting visits, booster activities, letters of intent, and scholarships.[20]

The beat of the cheats went on. Even that paragon of sportsmanship and gentlemanly behavior, UCLA's revered basketball coach, John Wooden, had his secret bag man. The *Los Angeles Times* found that booster Sam Gilbert "arranged and paid for abortions for the players' friends, and helped players get discounts on cars, stereos, and airline tickets."[21]

Rules Meant to Be Broken

Some of the NCAA's "amateur" rules are ludicrous. The 430-page *NCAA Division I Manual* comprises so many nitpicky rules that infractions, from the petty to the serious, are inevitable. The NCAA's laws are like the American tax code, replete with loopholes that entice people to fudge their payments to the government, knowing full well that the IRS can only audit a small fraction of federal tax returns. Similarly, even when the NCAA finds wrongdoing in a particular school's athletic program, the offending school can simply impose light sanctions on itself and thereby duck the NCAA's harsher (albeit still weak) penalties. The NCAA has its version of capital punishment, but throughout the entire history of the association, only three D-I athletic programs have (temporarily) been given the axe, including Kentucky men's basketball in 1952 and SMU football in 1987. In short, NCAA penalties are no deterrent to cheating.

But in addition to penalties that don't disincentivize widespread cheating, the NCAA guidelines contain rules that strike one as incredibly petty. For example, boosters are forbidden from buying a meal for a student athlete, but the same booster is in no way prohibited from donating to an athletic facility. Todd Berry, the executive director of the American Football Coaches Association, recalls, "We saw what happened in the 1970s and where you've got some boosters saying, 'I can't afford to buy an NFL team, but I can afford to buy a college team,' and they're puffing out their chest right now like they're the wheeler-dealer and they could have significant control over a program."[22] Big spenders get tax deductions for season ticket seats, "charitable deductions," and "preferred seating plans." Alabama has at least 26,000 people on a waiting list for season football tickets.[23] In February 2019, ticket outlet SeatGeek.com was selling a single ticket to the Duke–North Carolina basketball game in Durham for more than $3,000. Super Bowl tickets a few weeks earlier averaged $4,656.[24] Once again, the prestige and big money in college sports is just too tantalizing for the profiteers to ignore.

Sometimes the motives for subsidizing players are innocent enough, though they violate the NCAA's amateur rules even still. Some coaches just want to help their players. For example, in 1955, Ohio State football coach Woody Hayes told *Sports Illustrated* that he occasionally gave cash to poor players. Thereafter the Buckeyes were put on probation and the football team was barred from going to the next Rose Bowl.[25] Until recently, the NCAA would not allow any exceptions to the rule that players got only free tuition, books, room, and board. After university mess halls were closed, hungry players were out of luck. University of Connecticut guard Shabazz Napier, who helped the Huskies win two NCAA basketball championships in 2011 and 2014, recalled at the time that "there are hungry nights that I go to bed, and I'm starving."[26] It is no wonder that well-meaning coaches are tempted to break the rules and slip a few sawbucks to cash-strapped players, just as Hayes did a half-century ago.

Without legitimate pay for play, some collegians turned to rigging games for gamblers. In the late 1940s, three Kentucky basketball players from Coach Adolph Rupp's two championship teams were indicted for point shaving (the practice of beating the point spread while still winning the game). Rupp didn't believe it. "Gamblers couldn't touch my boys with a ten-foot pole," he claimed, but then had to eat crow when two of the players admitted to the scheme.[27]

One of the most notorious cases of gamblers taking advantage of needy students was the City College of New York point-shaving scandal of the early 1950s. "At various times, CCNY's entire starting five, poor, working-class kids all took money to shave points," writes historian Nelson George. "Just as [coach Nat] Holman had compromised the academic integrity of his school for victories, the players worked in a gray area where they gave up cheap points or missed easy shots, yet still tried to win."[28] This is not, however, just a practice of some bygone era. In 1994, Arizona State and Northwestern basketball players were involved in point-shaving scandals. *New York Times* columnist Robert Lipsyte wrote that the sordid affair "nullified Northwestern University's bet that the million it spent [on intercollegiate athletics] would pay off in national happy news, increased enrollment, and alumni donations."[29] The practice was endemic enough to make it into the movie *Diner* (1982), when Boogie (Mickey Roarke) makes a $2,000 lock bet on a basketball game, informing a friend that he knew that points were being shaved. Boogie lost.

The NCAA's Puny Punishments

Some might argue that the NCAA has cleaned up its act in the past few decades. If anything, though, the depth and breadth of scandals have worsened; dozens of D-I schools have been implicated in cheating, criminal cases, and academic fraud. In just one decade—the 1980s—almost half of the D-I football programs incurred some NCAA sanctions.[30] The NCAA accepts this high level of wrongdoing without ever taking a long hard look at whether the whole system is beyond redemption. According to *Inside Higher Education*, from 2005 to 2015, "More than a quarter of all Division-I colleges, 43 percent of all universities that play in the high-profile Football Bowl Subdivision and more than half the members of the Power Five conferences committed major violations of National Collegiate Athletic Association rules. . . . Of the 351 colleges and universities in Division I, 96 were found guilty of such infractions. Sixteen institutions were censured more than once, and two—the University of Oklahoma and West Virginia University—were punished three times each."[31]

The following are among the big football and/or men's basketball powers that have violated more serious NCAA rules in recent years, ranging from players' unethical conduct, criminal offenses, improper cash payments and financial aid, to academic fraud: Arizona State, Baylor, Boise State, Brigham Young, Florida State, Georgetown,

Chapter Four

Indiana, Iowa State, LSU, Ohio State, Oklahoma State, Purdue, SMU, Syracuse, Temple, TCU, Arizona, Alabama, Florida, Georgia, Iowa, Kansas, Miami (FL), Michigan, Nebraska, Minnesota, North Carolina, Oregon, USC, and Tennessee.[32] Additionally, four national championship football coaches have been implicated in major rules violations: Urban Meyer, Ed Orgeron, Les Miles, and the late Bobby Bowdon.

Southern Methodist is the only big NCAA football school to have received the death penalty for repeated rules breaking. From 1975 to 1984, the NCAA put SMU on probation seven times. None of those slaps on the wrist mattered. By the mid-1980s, the illegal payments to players had reached $400,000 annually.[33] In 1985, the university's Board of Governors, which knew about the payments, decided to continue them. "After much discussion and much agonizing," recalled board chairman and eventual Texas governor Bill Clements, "we chose a phase-out system. We did it reluctantly and uncomfortably but feeling that this approach would be in the best interests of SMU, the Dallas community, the players, and their families." Finally, in 1987, the hammer from the NCAA came down and the SMU football program was shuttered for two years.[34]

SMU was not the only Texas school in hot water with the NCAA in the mid-1980s for illegal payments, although the penalties, as usual, were hardly deterrents for future infractions. The University of Texas received a two-year probation and was banned from postseason bowl games. Baylor was also slapped with two years on probation, and TCU got three years. One Rice University representative on the NCAA Council said, tongue-in-cheek, that NCAA rules should be changed to allow "fifteen dollars per month for incidental expenses and one new Trans Am sports car."[35] The Southwest Conference meetings were "a joke," recalled the Texas faculty representative. "They'd say, let's keep [NCAA head] Walter Byers from learning about this. We had cases [of NCAA rules breaking] proven beyond any doubt and nothing was done."[36]

Plenty of schools in the Big Eight Conference (now the Big Twelve) also ignored the rules. In 1973, Oklahoma received a two-year probation, in part for the suspiciously nice cars parked outside the football players' dorms. Hardly, however, did probation stop the chicanery. Indeed, Oklahoma went on to lead the Big Eight in infractions in the 1980s. Sooner linebacker Brian Bosworth said that Coach Barry Switzer provided an apartment and cars for players to use. Bosworth also alleged that some players, with Switzer's knowledge, used cocaine at the apartment and were even high on game days.[37] Switzer denied it, but in the late 1980s his players were charged in connection with an on-campus shooting, a gang rape, and drug peddling.[38]

In 1995, Nebraska running back Lawrence Phillips assaulted his girlfriend, but his hearing was conveniently delayed until after the season had ended. The Cornhuskers ultimately penalized Phillips with community service and mandated that he go to class (of all things). About the same time, two of Phillips's teammates were brought up on second-degree murder charges.[39] Athletic departments are cagier now about how they deal with such criminal accusations. Players are advised to get a lawyer before talking to police.[40]

In the late 1990s, agents were paying Steve Spurrier's Florida Gator football players. Spurrier displayed outrage over the uncovering of the practice, but he took no responsibility for it and stayed on as "the Head Ball Coach." Allegations surfaced that some of the players on Michigan's "Fab Five" basketball team had also taken money to play. Coach Steve Fisher was shown the door, but he landed on his feet at San Diego State. In 1994, Bobby Bowden's Florida State players got shopping sprees at a Foot Locker shoe store, prompting wags to call FSU "Free Shoes U." Bowden suffered no penalties.[41]

Perennial football championship contender Alabama has been under scrutiny too. In the early 2000s, the NCAA found that twenty-two football players had received free textbooks as part of their scholarships, which they had sold to fellow students. The NCAA's penalties were as laughable as the petty offenses—vacating twenty-one Crimson Tide victories and putting them on probation for three years.[42] In 2013, it came to light that Alabama tackle D. J. Fluker had received illegal cash payments in excess of $45,000. Coach Nick Saban would not answer any questions about the money, sending reporters off to ask the school's compliance department about it, and thus maintaining his plausible deniability—the tired old "I know nothing about it" routine.[43]

One study found that only about a quarter of Alabama football players who had committed minor crimes were kicked off the team. In 2013, several Alabama football players beat up and robbed a fellow student, their victim landing in the hospital. This case was serious enough that Saban tossed the offending players from the program, and they pled guilty to the charges. Despite direct requests from the victim, however, no one on the Alabama football staff would agree to talk to him, including Saban.[44]

Other football programs were suspicious of Saban, wondering how, year after year, he managed to get the best recruiting class. Saban was a good football coach because he was a stickler for details, and he was careful that these indiscretions did not happen again. He had more than forty people on his staff who were dedicated exclusively to the football program (of Alabama's some 370 employees listed on the athletic department roster). Alabama players start their day at 6:15 a.m. In addition to the four or five hours spent on the practice field, lifting weights, and watching film, Alabama's players are sometimes accompanied to class and counseled on their courses from the time they get up to the time they go to bed around 10 p.m.[45] No hanky-panky for the Crimson Tide. The proportion of Bama football players to their handlers is about two to one.

For their part, the NCAA would argue that strict oversight has reduced scandals to a trickle, but do the facts add up to that conclusion? In early 2022, Louisville showed basketball coach Chris Mack to the door "for failing to follow university guidelines in his handling of an extortion attempt by a fired assistant coach."[46] In March 2022, LSU fired head basketball coach Will Wade right before the NCAA tournament in order to avert tougher NCAA sanctions. Back in 2019, the university had suspended Wade for various violations, including making a recruit a "strong-ass offer"—meaning cash. Louisiana State reinstated Wade but subsequently fired him after more allegations were revealed and he refused to cooperate with the investigation.[47] The NCAA charged LSU with offering jobs and $300,000 in cash to family members of recruits.[48] One way for universities to avoid expensive buyouts is to do internal investigations and find the coach guilty of infractions, thus nullifying the contract.[49]

The Oklahoma State and University of Miami Cases

Oklahoma State was another serial offender, one with a long rap sheet of NCAA violations stretching back to the 1950s, when the school was known as Oklahoma A&M. Oklahoma A&M was unofficially tagged as a "jock school" that openly made payments to players. The school was already in the news in 1951 for a vicious cheap shot by one of its players on Black running back Johnny Bright from Drake, breaking his jaw.[50]

In 2013, *Sports Illustrated* did an exposé on the rapid rise of Oklahoma State football in the 2000s. Les Miles ran the program from 2001 to 2004. The magazine interviewed sixty-four Cowboy players, most of whom did not graduate. Corruption permeated the entire program: a bonus system to pay players for on-field performance, money for faux jobs, academic fraud to keep players eligible, recreational drug use, and a "hostess" group to escort recruits, sometimes with sexual favors. The latter practice had been going on for a long time in college sports, with recruits meeting such coquettish coeds as the Clemson's Bengal Babes, Florida's Gator Getters, or Miami's Hurricane Honeys. "The idea was to get [recruits] to think if they came [to Oklahoma State] it was gonna be like that all the time," recalled one player, "with all these girls wanting to have sex with you."[51] Cowboy athletic director Mike Holder was either derelict in his duty or untruthful when he acted surprised by the findings, saying, "It's very disconcerting to hear about all these things that are alleged to have happened. But there's nothing more important to us than playing by the rules."[52]

If the priority of the Oklahoma State athletic administration was to produce graduates with meaningful degrees, it would not have steered its players into easy courses for which tutors completed the "student athletes'" assignments. Evidently, Holder was unaware of that practice too. Fath' Carter, who played for Oklahoma State from 2000 to 2003, allowed, "The goal was not to educate but to get [the best players] the passing grades they need to keep playing. . . That's the only thing it was about."[53]

In 2020, Oklahoma State breached yet another of the NCAA rules when it was discovered that an assistant men's basketball coach was taking bribes from financial advisors to get him to provide access to Cowboy basketball players. In response to the uncovering of the rules violations, the NCAA's infractions committee handed down one of its typically light penalties—a $10,000 fine and a reduction in scholarships and recruiting visits. It didn't seem to hurt the Cowboys much; Oklahoma State posted a 21–9 record in 2020–21. The committee had originally banned the school from postseason play but then decided to rescind the decision. As for the Cowboys, they made it to the second round of the NCAA tournament.[54]

Notably, even Oklahoma State's case pales in comparison to the serious infractions piled up at the University of Miami. So brazen were Hurricane football players that they became the butt of jokes about the perks they received, their flaunting of the law, and their lack of any interest in receiving an education, with the Miami Hurricane 1980–84 football cohort boasting a graduation rate of 24 percent.[55]

Chapter Four

Miami players had a favorite strip joint that they dubbed "The Office," a place where drugs, alcohol, and sex were all on tap. In the early 1990s, an academic advisor in the athletic department stole more than $125,000 from federal Pell Grant monies intended for needy students and proceeded to dole it out to football players. According to a leaked memo from the athletic department, "[stiffer academic standards] could mean that our department could become another Rice or Northwestern—what a thought!"—alluding to the high academic reputations of those schools that fielded only middling teams.[56]

In 1995, *Sports Illustrated* reporter Alexander Wolff wrote an open letter to Miami President Tad Foote, imploring him to follow the University of Chicago's example in 1939 and get rid of the football program:

> For all its victories, Miami football has been worse in more ways over a longer period of time than any other intercollegiate athletic program in memory. Scan the list of abuses that beset college sports, and your football team can claim, going back to 1980, at least one entry in virtually every category: improper benefits; recruiting violations; boosters run amok; academic cheating; use of steroids and recreational drugs; suppressed or ignored positive tests for drugs; player run-ins with other students as well as with campus and off-campus police; the discharge of weapons and the degradation of women in the football dorm; credit-card fraud and telephone credit-card fraud. . . . The illegal acts with which your Hurricanes have been charged run the gamut from disorderly conduct and shoplifting to drunken driving, burglary, arson, assault, and sexual battery. Surely you read the exhaustive and chilling piece about your football program in *The Miami Herald* of May 18. That paper's reporters did the math: No fewer than one of every seven scholarship players on last season's team has been arrested while enrolled at your university.[57]

In 2000, Rutgers hired head coach Greg Schiano away from Miami. Reflecting on the momentous hire, Rutgers athletic director Robert Mulcahy III said with no trace of sarcasm, "Greg shared my commitment to values, academics, and the holistic development of our student athletes. . . as well as winning."[58]

The D-I Rap Sheet

As the 2000s rolled along, Miami continued to pile more citations onto its long rap sheet. In 2011, Hurricane booster Nevin Shapiro admitted that he had given at least $170,000 to Miami players from 2002 to 2010, as well as millions of dollars in "extra benefits," including prostitutes and "endless champagne-soaked nights partying on his multimillion-dollar yacht or in South Beach clubs, all with the knowledge or direct participation of at least seven Miami coaches."[59]

In 2011, it was revealed that Auburn players also had received cash and perks of a sexual nature during some of their recruiting visits.[60] Commenting on Auburn's indiscretions, Shapiro, Miami's racketeer, boasted that "[the media] are making a big deal about an Auburn coach giving a player $400. That wouldn't even cover the valet for the first 10 guys I'd bring into a club—without the tip." The NCAA, with the supposedly reform-minded Mark Emmert in command, botched the investigation into Miami sports, eliciting more Shapiro sarcasm: "I thought I was dealing with the FBI. Instead, I was dealing with a bunch of clowns. I gave the NCAA the body, the evidence on a platter, and they found a way to screw it up." Emmert declined to speak with *Sports Illustrated* about the Shapiro affair, but he and the NCAA had let Miami off easy in part because the 'Canes had preemptively declared thirteen players ineligible and self-imposed a two-year ban on postseason play.[61]

The Hurricanes eventually lost some recruiting privileges, as well as nine football and three basketball scholarships over three seasons. The football program suffered a bit but finished a respectable 8–5 in 2015 and 9–4 in 2016, winning a bowl game and finishing twentieth in the final AP poll. Not bad for a program that should have received the death penalty. The basketball team fared even better, posting a 27–8 record in 2015–16 and making the Sweet Sixteen in March Madness. After the Hurricane affair blew over, the NCAA executive committee gave Emmert a vote of confidence.[62]

The NCAA's Role Models

Many male athletes at big D-I schools draw lessons from corruption among the administrators of their sports. Martin Luther King once said that "intelligence plus character—that is the goal of true education." Sports in a school setting are supposed to teach teamwork, sacrifice, and sportsmanship. It can also foster discipline, honesty, and integrity. Division I sports do not always engender these character traits.

Early on, intercollegiate athletics in America emulated the edifying mission of English soccer and rugby—the idea that sport could make gentlemen out of ruffians—a "muscular Christian" of morality and masculinity. The connection between higher education and sports in New England universities derived from the English model of private schools, where sports were called on to make men out of boys and upstanding, fair-minded citizens out of original sinners.[63]

The British purveyors of the amateur sporting ideal came from the upper classes, and they used games to teach proper behavior to the rowdy and unlawful working classes. Amateurs were "misters," while professional players were "menials." To put it simply, sports became a means of trying to get the masses to play by societal rules, on the playing field and off. In American college sports, working-class lads could use sports to overcome their socioeconomic status and escape from their modest backgrounds.[64]

College sports were supposed to teach good sportsmanship, camaraderie, and high morals. Dr. Luther Gulick, the head of the YMCA Training Institute where basketball pioneer James Naismith taught, adapted the British notion of "muscular Christianity" to the American spirit. "[Gulick] sought to harmonize Protestant spirituality, late nineteenth-century science, and athletic endeavor," writes historian Yago Colás. "He also designed the YMCA's logo, the inverted red triangle whose three sides—symbolizing the physical, mental, and spiritual dimensions of the human being—join to form a single whole." Naismith echoed Gulick's hope that sports would instill good behavior: "Games have been called the laboratory for the development of moral attributes."[65]

In the late nineteenth century, Harvard president Charles Eliot recognized that trying to win games by using "tricks, surprises, and habitual violations of the rules" was teaching immorality and unethical behavior.[66] At the turn of the century, the Harvard faculty called for an end to the school's football program, citing the numerous serious injuries to the players. But Eliot was more worried about endemic corruption. "Death and injuries are not the strongest argument against football," he said. "That cheating and brutality are profitable is the main evil."[67]

The idea that sports builds character has deep roots in American schools. During the Cold War, there were many critics of universities that downplayed sports as something un-American and symbolic of the decline of the mettle of its men. The Ivy Leaguers were denigrated as weak-muscled, pasty-faced, and doughy-bodied—hardly the strong men needed to take on the dangerous Reds. President John F. Kennedy declared, "Except for war, there is nothing in American life which trains a boy better for life than football. There can be no substitute for football."[68] Paul Dietzel, the legendary LSU football coach, once said, "You can learn more character on the two-yard line than anywhere else in life."[69] Many people swallow these dubious axioms as absolute truth.

University educators always put moral, upstanding character building into their mission statements. If there is one academic institution that seemed to be the very model of purity, it was West Point, whose honor code reads, "A Cadet will not lie, cheat or steal, nor tolerate those who do." In 1951, about half of the Army football team was kicked out of the academy for academic cheating. Even the son of famed head coach Red Blaik was implicated in the scandal. At the same time, William & Mary, another respected teacher of football men, was exposed for rampant academic fraud.[70]

The lesson for athletes at D-I football and basketball programs today is that cheating is the best way to get ahead. Dave Meggyesy from the Syracuse Orange, in *Out of Their League*, decried the cheating, violence, and exploitation of college football players. Texas Longhorn Gary Shaw wrote *Meat on the Hoof*, in which he accused head football coach Darrell Royal of taking away scholarships from players who did not perform, forcing players to play hurt, and steering players into softball courses—or into tough ones if Royal wanted to coerce certain players to quit the program. Indeed, at that time, many big D-I football programs doled out scholarships on a year-to-year basis, thereby allowing coaches to cull out players who did not perform or got injured.[71]

In the summer of 2018, Maryland football coach D.J. Durkin and others on his staff were suspended following the death of offensive lineman Jordan McNair after a team practice. Several players said that Durkin had created a "toxic" atmosphere of verbal abuse and humiliation. Durkin was fired in October, with two years left on his five-year, $12.5 million dollar contract.[72]

With these kinds of role models, it is no surprise that D-I athletes score low on the good behavior scale. For years, the NCAA has tried to maintain sportsmanship and propriety in college games by penalizing taunting and excessive celebrations on the field.

Chapter Four

Football, above all, encourages kids to hit hard and punish their opponent by running the ball down their throats. It is not a recipe for gentlemanly conduct off the gridiron. One college president on the executive committee of the NCAA's President's Commission cited a "frightening study that suggests athletes lag behind other students in 'ethics and moral reasoning.'"[73] Case in point: at the end of the 2020 Armed Forces Bowl, a melee erupted between Tulsa and Mississippi State. One Bulldog player kicked a prone Tulsa player in the head, then later praised himself and joked about it on social media.[74]

Athletes commit a far greater number of crimes and cheat at a higher rate than the rest of the student body. Sociologists and psychologists likely have their theories as to why athletes are more prone to offend, but privilege and entitlement might be one place to start. Too many coaches ignore all manner of bad behavior on the part of their players in order to field a winning team. Buzz Bissinger, the author of *Friday Night Lights* (1990), sees a lack of moral guidance for elite athletes at all levels. "On the playing field, every single mistake a player makes is pointed out and criticized until corrected," Bissinger says. "By design, on the field of real life, the athlete rarely faces similar accountability. Issues that most of us deal with every day ... have no place in the athletic realm, except when a public relations staffer thinks it's a good idea."[75]

During the 2022 ACC basketball tournament, Syracuse's Buddy Boeheim, son of coach Jim Boeheim, slugged a Florida State player in the stomach. Video replay caught the sucker punch, but Coach Boeheim denied that the blow had been intentional.[76] An impulsive act from a young player is one thing but an obvious cover-up from the coach is another.

Shortly before he died in 2020, famed Georgetown basketball coach John Thompson charged D-I leaders with failing to teach anything about integrity and honesty, the ethics that are supposed to come from playing team sports:

> The NCAA is also teaching young athletes that the way to succeed in life is to break rules, not follow them. We are abdicating our responsibility to act on the rules we make and corrupting the educational mission that universities are supposed to have. It seems that the NCAA is making players into thieves. It feels like entrapment. ... If I were coaching right now, I would cheat, too. I would

pay for players, because if I didn't, I would lose to the cheaters and get fired. The NCAA has almost given coaches no other choice but to cheat if they want to compete for championships.[77]

Campus Criminals

Pay for play, sexual favors for recruits and players, and academic scandals are bad enough, but the high rate of felony assaults committed by D-I athletes is the most troubling corruption of higher education. It's a case of the studious athlete Dr. Jekyll in the classroom and the deviant Mr. Hyde on the street.

In the late 1990s, athletes comprised 3.3 percent of the male college student population, but that tiny cohort committed 19 percent of campus sexual assaults and 37 percent of domestic violence cases.[78] Studies consistently show that football and basketball players are much more likely to be charged with sexual assault than other men on campus; one of the studies found that they were implicated 38 percent more times.[79]

Even more troubling is that these types of cases are vastly underreported and that most universities do not comply with requests for this information. "[This] is a sad commentary on the culture of secrecy and image obsession that permeates higher education," says Florida University Professor Frank LoMonte. "People in higher education have come to regard their institutions as a brand and will do anything to protect the brand, even if that means putting people on campus at risk."[80]

Since the mid-1980s, sexual assault accusations have come against players from BYU, Nebraska, Notre Dame, Wisconsin, Kansas State, Arizona, Miami (FL), USC, Montana, Baylor, Florida State, and Minnesota, among others.[81] Some schools have either been indifferent to allegations of sexual assault or have tried to hide the evidence. Of course, coaches and athletic departments try to cover up their players' misdeeds. In 2012, a first-year student at Florida State University reported a rape. She named the alleged perpetrator as Jameis Winston, the football team's star quarterback. The university knew about the allegation but allowed Winston to finish out the season, for which he won the Heisman Trophy. The prosecutor declined to take the case to court for lack of evidence, and the entire ordeal was kept hush-hush for more than a year before the news media identified Winston as the alleged perpetrator. The prosecutor admitted that the investigation was cursory, and the *New York Times* reported that there was "virtually no investigation at all, either by the police or the university." Winston's DNA was not solicited. When the story broke in late 2013, the university cooperated with the *Times* at first but then abruptly stopped talking to reporters, citing privacy laws.[82]

In 2016, Baylor fired football coach Art Briles after nineteen of his players had been accused of sexual assault in the previous five years. The NCAA did nothing about the allegations because it had no rules regarding a university's handling of reports of sexual violence.[83] The NCAA said that the players' "abhorrent conduct" and Baylor's "moral and ethical failings . . . did not constitute violations of NCAA legislation."[84] The NCAA hit Baylor with weak sanctions and probation for preventing investigations into the assaults. In that same year, Liberty University saw no problem in hiring former Baylor athletic director Ian McCaw as its new athletic director, even though McCaw had been pushed out of Baylor after numerous scandals, including the cover-up of players' sexual assaults. "You look at what Baylor was able to do during his tenure," said Liberty President Jerry Falwell, Jr., "it fits perfectly with where we see our sports programs going."[85]

In September 2016, ten members of the University of Minnesota football team were accused of lining up at an on-campus party for serial sex with a drunk and incoherent woman. The county attorney could not prove a crime, although he called it deplorable behavior.[86] Gopher coach Tracy Claeys "claimed that FERPA [Family Educational Rights and Privacy Act] forbade him from disclosing the number of student-athletes that the U had recommended for expulsion." The university eventually expelled four players, although no criminal charges were brought. FERPA has been used to hide other sports-related misdeeds. "One Ohio court even classified e-mails between a football coach and a booster suspected of offering cars to a recruit as 'education records,'" writes LoMonte, an expert on federal privacy laws.[87]

According to LoMonte, universities and the NCAA are just hiding behind the law to protect their brands:

> FERPA has in fact never been enforced against any educational institution in its nearly 43-year history—that's right, not a single college or school has been found to be a violator and fined a nickel. Yet college attorneys continually cite the statute's theoretically ruinous financial penalties to justify withholding records that the

public has a right to see.... If the Minnesota football case does not awaken Congress to the overdue need to rewrite this disastrously broken statute, then somebody needs to check for a pulse.[88]

In 2006, a hired stripper erroneously accused three Duke lacrosse players of gang rape. The incident happened while other students were on spring break, but the lacrosse team had to stay in Durham to practice. To make up for missing the fun in the sun, the Duke lacrosse coach handed out $10,000 in cash to team members—their meal money for the week. Bacchanalia followed, including hiring the dancer. While the players had committed no crimes, the spotlight shown brightly on an elite group of rich scholarship athletes who took their privilege and entitlement to another lascivious level.[89]

The Penn State Coverup

One of the most heinous and most widely publicized cases of sexual assault was committed over many years at Penn State, not by a player but by one of head football coach Joe Paterno's trusted assistants, Jerry Sandusky, who had a predilection for young boys. After rumors about Sandusky's behavior swirled in the late 1990s, he retired, but he still had access to Penn State facilities. Even after a grad student witnessed Sandusky assaulting a youngster in a locker room shower and Sandusky was barred from bringing boys to State College, Sandusky was allowed to run a summer football camp on a regional Penn State campus. "Jerry Sandusky admitted to my face, he admitted it," said an outraged mother of one victim. "He admitted that he lathered up my son. They were naked and he bear-hugged him."[90]

Paterno acknowledged that he had "backed away" when he first heard about the allegations against Sandusky. When the much beloved Paterno was fired, students rioted, as their counterparts in Bloomington had when their hallowed Hoosier coach Bobby Knight got the axe. Paterno had 111 victories vacated, a penalty which nobody cares about.[91]

In a *USA Today* article titled "Call for Athletics' Oversight Gains Urgency," University of Virginia President John Casteen, the head of the Association of Governing Boards of Universities and Colleges (AGB), spoke of a turning point in the operation of NCAA sports: "Our take on this as Penn State evolved as a national issue—we started working before any of that was in the press—but here was a case that would make a political impetus to do something." In another statement, the

Chapter Four

AGB promised serious reforms. "The impact at Penn State extends far beyond the reputational damage to its own athletics program or to the university," the AGB claimed. "It was instead a painful reminder that all boards need to be well informed and clearly establish the appropriate role of athletics in relation to the core values and academic mission of their institutions."[92] It is not clear what was meant by "the appropriate role of athletics," but no change ensued.

The courts sentenced Sandusky to spend the rest of his life in prison. As usual, the NCAA took no drastic action. For its shameful conduct surrounding the Sandusky scandal, the Nittany Lions were barred from postseason bowl games for four years, were placed on a five-year probation, lost forty scholarships, and incurred a $60 million fine.[93] The team has since rebounded nicely. Since Paterno left the program in 2012, Penn State football has declined some but still managed to win roughly 70 percent of its games.

The example of administrators, coaches, and players flouting the rules and committing criminal acts also carries over into the behavior of college fans. Students regularly riot when their school wins an NCAA men's basketball or football title. At the height of the Covid crisis in January 2021, thousands of Alabama students celebrating the Tide's football championship on the streets of Tuscaloosa paid no mind to masking or social distancing. And woe to those who blow the whistle on their teams and beloved celebrity coaches. When Indiana fired Bobby Knight, student protests turned violent. In the early 1990s, Auburn defensive end Eric Ramsey recorded conversations with head coach Pat Dye and his assistants promising cash payments and other perks. Dye was fired and rabid Tiger fans deluged Ramsey with death threats and then jeers when he walked across the stage to receive his degree.[94]

College sports fans have exhibited behaviors that do not belong anywhere, let alone on a university campus. Oregon native basketball player Kevin Love chose UCLA over playing in his home state. Before the Bruins were to play Oregon in early 2008, Love received several threatening messages from rabid Ducks' fans. One read, "If you guys win, we'll come to your house and kill your family." Another was more graphic: "We'll find your hotel room and blow your fucking head off with a shotgun." When Love took the floor, Oregon's infamous student fan club—the "Pit Crew"—met him with homophobic slurs. Fans threw popcorn and cups at Love's family, gave them the "bird," and called them "whores." After reneging on a commitment to play at Illinois, when Indiana guard Eric Gordon played in Champagne, the Illini faithful yelled, "Fuck you, Gordon," and someone threw a drink at his mother.[95]

One of the worst cases of despicable behavior happened when the University of Arizona's Steve Kerr played a game at Arizona State in 1988. Some Arizona State fans taunted Kerr with the chant "PLO, PLO," a reference to the assassination of Kerr's father Malcolm in Beirut four years earlier, when he was president of American University there. "When I heard it, I just dropped the ball and started shaking," Steve Kerr recalled. "I sat down for a minute. I admit they got to me. I had tears in my eyes. For one thing, it brought back memories of my dad. But, for another thing, it was just sad that people would do something like that."[96]

Sports are supposed to be fun, not a life-or-death contest for some deranged fans. College students—the leaders of tomorrow—shouldn't be exhibiting this kind of mob behavior. But then, they take their cues from the unethical behavior of many of those who run the NCAA system.

The NCAA would like us to think that these scandals are infrequent, anomalous occurrences, but despite the growth of compliance sections in the organization and member schools, the list of rulebreakers goes on and on. The next chapter puts the spotlight on the corrupt carpetbagger coaches, whose indiscretions, if they win, are of no consequence. They profess dedication to their players' education and the university, but everyone knows that, for most D-I coaches, if a higher salary beckons, they will fly off in a private jet to that new gig.

Notes

1. George Will, "The Real March Madness," *Star Tribune*, March 29, 2020, OP4.
2. Byers, *Unsportsmanlike Conduct*, 1.
3. Byers, *Unsportsmanlike Conduct*, 1.
4. Duderstadt, *Intercollegiate Athletics*, 7.
5. "Good Husker Quotes," Huskerboard.com, accessed February 11, 2022, https://www.huskerboard.com/index.php?/topic/26243-good-husker-quotes/#comment-321009.
6. Jabari Young, "WNBA agrees to 53% pay raise, maternity benefits for players in new collective bargaining agreement", CNBC News, January 14, 2020, accessed March 24, 2020, https://www.cnbc.com/2020/01/14/wnba-agrees-to-53percent-pay-raise-maternity-benefits-for-players-in-new-collective-bargaining-agreemet.html.

Chapter Four

7. Ronald A. Smith, *The Myth of the Amateur: A History of College Athletic Scholarships* (Austin, TX: University of Texas Press, 2021), 93.
8. Watterson, *College Football*, 186.
9. Rader, *American Sports*, 192.
10. Kemper, *College Football*, 51.
11. Sid Hartman, *Sid! The Legends, the Inside Scoops and the Close Personal Friends* (Stillwater: Voyageur Press, 1997), 55, 58.
12. Myron Metcalf, "The Art of the Package Deal in College Basketball," ESPN, May 19, 2017, accessed April 21, 2021, https://www.espn.com/mens-college-basketball/story/_/id/19408831/the-art-package-deals-coach-father-son-college-basketball.
13. Metcalf, "The Art of the Package Deal."
14. Metcalf, "The Art of the Package Deal."
15. Watterson, *College Football*, 164.
16. Harris, *King Football*, 16–17, 29–30.
17. Oriard, *King Football*, 246.
18. Davies, *Sports in American Life*, 206.
19. Oriard, *King Football*, 119.
20. Watterson, *College Football*, 281–2, 285–6.
21. Sperber, *College Sports, Inc.*, 270.
22. Dan Wolken, "College Football Starts Season Under a Dark Cloud," *USA Today*, September 3, 2021, 1C.
23. Gaul, *Billion-Dollar Bill*, 45–51. Michigan officials declined to speak to Gaul.
24. *Sports Illustrated*, February 19, 2019, accessed January 15, 2022, https://www.si.com/college/2019/02/19/duke-unc-ticket-prices-acc-rivalry-game-over-4000-zion-williamson.
25. James E. Odenkirk, "The Eighth Wonder of the World: Ohio State University's Rejection of a Rose Bowl Bid in 1961," *Journal of Sport History* 34, no. 3 (Fall 2007), 389–395.
26. Marc Tracy, "Waiting for Student Athletes to Become Student Activists," *New York Times*, April 9, 2019, B9.
27. Davies, *Sports in American Life*, 136-7.
28. Nelson George, *Elevating the Game: Black Men and Basketball* (New York: Harper Collins, 1992), 79.
29. Sperber, *Beer and Circus*, 211.
30. Watterson, *College Football*, 381.
31. Doug Lederman, "The Rule Breakers," *Inside Higher Ed*, January 11, 2016, accessed December 11, 2020, https://www.insidehighered.com/news/2016/01/11/96-division-i-colleges-violated-major-ncaa-rules-last-decade,.
32. Lederman, "The Rule Breakers."
33. Davies, *Sports in American Life*, 216.
34. Paul Weingarten, "Governor 'Sorry' for SMU Scandal," *Chicago Tribune*, March 12, 1987, accessed December 16, 2020, https://www.chicagotribune.com/news/ct-xpm-1987-03-12-8701190899-story.html#:~:text=The%20scandal%2D%2Ddubbed%20",and%20limited%20the%201988%20one.

35. Byers, *Unsportsmanlike Conduct*, 171.
36. Byers, *Unsportsmanlike Conduct*, 122–3.
37. Benedict and Keteyian, *The System*, 314.
38. Watterson, *College Football*, 375, 377–8.
39. Watterson, *College Football*, 372, 375, 377–8.
40. Benedict and Keteyian, *The System*, 166.
41. Mike Dame, "Coach Spurrier: 'We're Playing Free Shoes U,'" *Orlando Sentinel*, November 20, 1994, accessed June 29, 2022, https://www.orlandosentinel.com/news/os-xpm-1994-11-21-9411210175-story.html.
42. Alex Callos, "The Most Dubious Programs in College Football, February 28, 2012, accessed January 15, 2021, https://bleacherreport.com/articles/1084562-the-8-most-dubious-programs-in-college-football; and Unattributed, "Alabama's Long History of Unpunished NCAA Violations under Nick Saban, December 9, 2018, accessed January 16, 2021, https://mgoblog.com/mgoboard/alabama%27s-long-history-unpunished-ncaa-violations-under-nick-saban.
43. Unattributed, "D.J. Fluker, 4 Others Named in Report," ESPN, accessed March 25, 2021, https://www.espn.com/college-football/story/_/id/9663355/dj-fluker-five-sec-players-received-extra-benefits-college-according-report.
44. Benedict and Keteyian, *The System*, 306–309.
45. Benedict and Keteyian, *The System*, 383.
46. Unattributed, "Louisville Dumps Mack," *Star Tribune*, January 27, 2022, C4.
47. Billy Witz, "L.S.U. Fires Coach After N.C.A.A. Accuses Him of Violations," *New York Times*, March 13, 2022, 29.
48. Billy Witz, "A Messy Season for L.S.U., Down to the Bitter End," *New York Times*, March 20, 2022, 32.
49. Dan Wolken, "Nebraska Mess Shows Why Athletes Need a Union," *USA Today*, August 23, 2021, 6C.
50. Watterson, *College Football*, 273–4.
51. *Sports Illustrated* Special Report, "The Dirty Game: How You Go from Very Bad to Very Good Very Fast," *Sports Illustrated*, September 10, 2013, 33, 39; and Rader, *American Sports*, 284.
52. *Sports Illustrated* Special Report, "The Dirty Game," 33.
53. *Sports Illustrated* Special Report, "The Dirty Game," 36.
54. NCAA, "Oklahoma State University Public Infractions Decision, June 5, 2020, accessed March 25, 2021, https://ncaaorg.s3.amazonaws.com/infractions/decisions/Jun2020D1INF_OklahomaStatePublicDecision.pdf.
55. Sperber, *College Sports Inc.*, 304.
56. Alexander Wolff, "Broken Beyond Repair," *Sports Illustrated*, June 12, 1995, accessed December 18, 2020, https://vault.si.com/vault/1995/06/12/broken-beyond-repair-an-open-letter-to-the-president-of-miami-urges-him-to-dismantle-his-vaunted-football-program-to-salvage-his-schools-reputation.
57. Wolff, "Broken Beyond Repair."
58. Mulcahy III, *An Athletic Director's Story*, 113.
59. See Benedict and Keteylan, *The System*. p. 211.

Chapter Four

60. Phil Taylor, "How Low Can You Go?" *Sports Illustrated*, April 11, 2011, 84.

61. Pete Thamel and Alexander Wolff, "The Institution Has Lost Control," *Sports Illustrated*, June 17, 2013, 60–69.

62. Associated Press, *The Gazette*, February 23, 2013, accessed June 29, 2022. https://www.thegazette.com/sports/emmert-gets-vote-of-confidence-from-ncaa/.

63. Owen Mann, "The Cultural Bond? Cricket and the Imperial Mission," *The International Journal of the History of Sport* 27 (no. 13, September 2010): 2192. The British often equated sport with the fitness of its soldiers, the willingness to sacrifice individual goals for the good of the team, and adherence to rules. When the Germans shelled Belgian towns, killed civilians, and used poison gas, some British attributed this lack of sportsmanship to the German authorities' disdain of the British team sports. What balderdash.

64. Oriard, *King Football*, 231, 236.

65. Yago Colás, "Our Myth of Creation: The Politics of Narrating Basketball's Origin," *Journal of Sport History* 43, no. 1 (Spring 2016): 43.

66. Davies, *Sports in American Life*, 55.

67. Branch, "The Shame."

68. Kemper, *College Football*, 25.

69. Christopher J. Walsh, *Where Football is King: A History of the SEC* (Lanham, MD: Taylor Trade Publishing, 2006), 100.

70. Davies, *Sports in American Life*, 206; and Watterson, *College Football*, 223.

71. Watterson, *College Football*, 301-2.

72. Ralph D. Russo, "Terps Coach Put on Leave as Program Analyzed," *Star Tribune*, August 13, 2018, C5.

73. George Vecsey, "Schultz Was Caught by 'System,'" *New York Times*, May 12, 1993, B7.

74. Tyler Horka, "Mississippi State WR Malik Heath Jokes on Instagram About Kicking Tulsa Player in Brawl," *Clarion Ledger*, January 1, 2021, accessed June 29, 2022, https://www.clarionledger.com/story/sports/college/mississippi-state/2020/12/31/mississippi-state-football-wide-receiver-malik-heath-jokes-kicking-tulsa-player-brawl/4104733001/.

75. Buzz Bissinger, "The Boys in the Clubhouse," *New York Times*, October 19, 2014, SR 7.

76. Mike Curtis, "Jim Boeheim Defends Buddy Boeheim, Says Punch to Florida State Player was 'Inadvertent,'" Syracuse.com, March 9, 2022, accessed April 15, 2022, https://www.syracuse.com/orangebasketball/2022/03/jim-boeheim-defends-buddy-boeheim-says-punch-was-inadvertent.html#:~:text=Syracuse%20coach%20Jim%20Boeheim%20said,was%20inadvertent%2C%20but%20that's%20OK..

77. John Thompson, Jr., *New York Times*, November 12, 2020, (essay adapted from his autobiography), accessed March 24, 2021, https://www.nytimes.com/2020/11/12/opinion/sunday/ncaa-sports-paying-college-players.html?searchResultPosition=1.

78. Kathy Redmond, "And Justice for All," *New York Times*, October 19, 1997, 30.

79. Sperber, *College Sports, Inc.*, 272.

80. Kenny Jacoby, "College Athletes More Likely to Be Disciplined for Sex Assault," *USA Today*, December 16, 2019, accessed December 16, 2020, https://

www.usatoday.com/in-depth/news/investigations/2019/12/12/ncaa-athletes-more-likely-disciplined-sex-assault/4379153002/.

81. Benedict and Keteyian, *The System*, 58-65.

82. Walt Bogdanich, "A Top Player Accused, and a Flawed Rape Inquiry," *New York Times*, April 16, 2014, A1.

83. Jessica Luther, "Clearing Baylor Puts Women at Risk," *Los Angeles Times*, August 21, 2021, D4.

84. Stephen Hawkins, "NCAA Hands Baylor Probation, Fine in Sex Assault Scandal," *Star Tribune*, August 12, 2021, accessed August 13, 2021, https://www.startribune.com/ncaa-hands-baylor-probation-fine-in-sex-assault-scandal/600086911/.

85. Unattributed, "Liberty Names Former Baylor AD McCaw New Athletic Director, *Sports Illustrated*, November 28, 2016, accessed January 15, 2022, https://www.si.com/college/2016/11/28/ap-liberty-ad.

86. Josh Verges, "Judge Dismisses Gophers Football Players' Lawsuit Over 2016 Sexual Assault Case, *Twin Cities Pioneer Press*, June 25, 2019, accessed April 11, 2020, https://www.twincities.com/2019/06/25/judge-dismisses-gophers-football-players-lawsuit-over-2016-sexual-misconduct-case/.

87. Frank LoMonte, "Train Wreck of a Privacy Law Made Matters Worse," *Star Tribune*, December 20, 2016, A9.

88. From LoMonte, "Train Wreck." LoMonte is a lawyer and executive director of the Student Press Law Center.

89. Caitlin Flanagan, "Nothing to Cheer About," *New York Times*, April 24, 2014, accessed April 14, 2020, https://www.nytimes.com/2014/04/27/books/review/the-price-of-silence-by-william-d-cohan.html; see William D. Cohan, *The Price of Silence: The Duke Lacrosse Scandal, the Power of the Elite, and the Corruption of Our Great Universities* (New York: Scribner, 2014).

90. "Penn State Sex Scandal: Jerry Sandusky Ran Boys Camps for Years, November 8, 2011, *Los Angeles Times*, accessed December 16, 2020, https://latimesblogs.latimes.com/nationnow/2011/11/sandusky-penn-state-.html.

91. Ronald A. Smith, *Wounded Lions: Joe Paterno, Jerry Sandusky, and the Crises in Penn State Athletics* (Urbana: University of Illinois Press, 2016), 170–181.

92. Unattributed, "Call for Athletics Oversight Gains Urgency," *USA Today*, October 10, 2012, 9C.

93. Pete Thamel, "Sanctions Decimate the Nittany Lions Now and for Years to Come," *New York Times*, July 23, 2012, accessed January 12, 2021, https://www.nytimes.com/2012/07/24/sports/ncaafootball/penn-state-penalties-include-60-million-fine-and-bowl-ban.html.

94. Watterson, *College Football*, 380.

95. Grant Wahl, "Over the Top," *Sports Illustrated*, March 3, 2008, 40–45.

96. Tracy Dodds, "Arizona St. Apologizes to Kerr: Arizona Guard Was Target of Taunts Before Game," *Los Angeles Times*, March 1, 1988, accessed May 23, 2022, https://www.latimes.com/archives/la-xpm-1988-03-01-sp-257-story.html.

CHAPTER FIVE

Take the Money and Run:
Carpetbagger Coaches and Recruiting Ruses

"[College football is] one of the last strongholds of genuine old-fashioned hypocrisy... the leader (among sports) in the field of double-dealing, deception, sham, cant, humbug, and organized hypocrisy."

—Sportswriter Paul Gallico, in the late 1930s[1]

There is a common denominator in the case of NCAA rules violations, especially the illegal payments and perks for college recruits and players: it is a very good investment for coaches. Players come and go, but successful coaches are the faces of their teams. During the Covid pandemic in the fall of 2020, Nick Saban came down with the virus, meaning that he would have to miss the big intra-state battle with Auburn. "The Iron Bowl will be without its biggest star," lamented the Associated Press.[2]

When coaches do get caught for breaking the rules, they are not the ones who suffer. Athletic directors rarely get the boot for infractions. When unscrupulous coaches commit serious NCAA infractions, they either receive an admonishment from the administration or simply leave the university and their players behind and look for a new job. Some are fired, but if the coach in question has posted a winning record, he is virtually guaranteed to find work at another university or in the pros. The players, program, and school are expendable.

Good college professors will tell you that their top priority is the well-being of their students. Any faculty member who broke academic rules, misused or stole university funds, covered up students' crimes, or swore at students in class would be fired, disgraced, and unemployable at another school. Rightfully so. For such indiscretions, coaches—professors' colleagues on the sidelines—suffer no such consequences.

Chapter Five

Rulebreaking coaches are notoriously indifferent to the academic mission of higher education, but they have little trouble keeping or finding new jobs mentoring athletes. NCAA investigations into a coach's cheating can drag on for many years, leaving players at his former school in limbo. No professor acting this way would ever get a second chance, let alone a third or fourth one.

The Long List of Infamous Rules Violators

As long as coaches and athletic directors oversee winning teams and stay out of prison, toothless NCAA infractions are a small risk to take. This has long been the case, as Michael Oriard points out:

> Rogue programs such as those at Maryland and Auburn [in the 1950s] nonetheless taught a lesson not lost on their competitors: do whatever it takes to build a winning team, accept your wrist-slapping by the NCAA if you got caught, then enjoy the fruits of championship football. Men such as Bear Bryant developed the corollary for coaches; do whatever it takes to win at one school in order to move on to the next, should the first be caught cheating.[3]

The great Bear Bryant had brushes with NCAA investigators at Kentucky and Texas A&M in the mid-1950s before landing the head job at Alabama in 1958. When the Aggies faced significant penalties for illegal payments to players, Bryant, incredibly, asked the NCAA infractions committee if alumni were allowed to give cash to his players. When he got a flat "no," Bryant gave up his appeal, saying, "Well, I guess I don't have anything to argue about."[4] Bryant then moved on to the Crimson Tide, where the rules violations on the coach's resume were no deterrent to his hiring. NCAA executive director Walter Byers was unequivocal in his denunciation of the revered coach: "Paul had played the game to win. Damn the rules, full speed ahead! And the NCAA honored him for the results."[5]

The men who have been directly or indirectly involved in scandals in the last three decades reads like a who's who list of highly sought-after coaches—past and current. Among the most notable habitual rulebreakers are Ron Meyer, Eddie Sutton, Larry Brown, Pete Carroll, Ed Orgeron, Rick Pitino, Mike Leach, Les Miles, Urban Meyer, Jim Calhoun, Roy Williams, John Calipari, Bill Self, Steve Fisher, Kelvin Sampson, and Bruce Pearl. Although they committed infractions, most of them either kept their jobs or blew town for another lucrative coaching position.

Southern Methodist's infractions resulted in the death penalty for their football program, but SMU Coach Ron Meyer left in 1981 before the NCAA could catch him. He took off to coach the New England Patriots. Southern Methodist leaders knew of the illegal payments and continued them, even as the team was under investigation.

In 1988, the NCAA found out about a package containing $1,000 that was addressed to Claud Mills, the father of Kentucky star basketball player Chris Mills. For the infraction, the NCAA imposed on the Wildcat program a three-year probation and a two-year postseason ban; in addition, the Wildcats could not appear on TV for the 1989–90 season.[6] Head coach Eddie Sutton and assistant coach Dwane Casey were implicated in the scandal, but the case was never proven. While Mills was barred from playing for Kentucky, Sutton happily moved on to a successful coaching career at Oklahoma State. When the smoke settled, it was Assistant Coach Casey who took the hit for the infractions, getting a five-year ban, which the NCAA later lifted. He went to Japan to coach until the Seattle Supersonics hired him as an assistant coach.[7]

Jerry Tarkanian took UNLV to the 1990 NCAA basketball title. Most of his players were students in name only, and he committed a string of NCAA infractions. The NCAA banned UNLV from postseason play in 1992, and Tarkanian announced that he was leaving the school. Fresno State ignored Tarkanian's previous misdeeds, and he was hired to coach the Bulldogs in 1995.

Until recently, athletic departments were barred from making small payments to players for such things as buying snacks after the dining halls closed. While University of Connecticut (UConn) star guard Shabazz Napier often went to bed on an empty stomach, his coach Jim Calhoun was raking in about $2.5 million annually—and he was also cheating to win. In 2011, Calhoun was sanctioned for recruiting violations; the NCAA charged him with "failing to create an atmosphere of compliance within his program." He retired a year later.[8] His successor, Kevin Ollie, also managed to get himself fired in 2018 for "failing to monitor his staff, not promoting an atmosphere of compliance, and allegedly providing false or misleading statements to NCAA investigators."[9] Liking what they saw in Calhoun's record, and clearly unconcerned with the atmosphere he had fostered at UConn, the University of St. Joseph's (in Connecticut) went calling for Calhoun to coach their

D-III basketball team in 2018. In 2022, Ollie won a court case against UConn for $11 million for wrongful termination of his contract. He now works with top high school prospects who skip college to train for the pros.

Football coach Les Miles also committed a series of misdeeds, but he denied having any knowledge of the many infractions committed under his leadership at Oklahoma State. He left the Cowboy football program in 2004 and landed the head coaching job at LSU. He got into trouble there too. The law firm Husch Blackwell investigated Miles for Title IX issues at LSU, which detailed inappropriate behavior that included "texting female students, taking them to his condo alone, making them feel uncomfortable, and, on at least one occasion, kissing a student and suggesting they go to a hotel after telling her he could help her career." The law firm's 148-page report further alleged that Miles "tried to sexualize the staff of student workers in the football program by, for instance, allegedly demanding that he wanted blondes with big breasts, and 'pretty girls.'" Miles was fired in 2016 before these allegations came out. Kansas hired him for the 2019 season but then terminated his contract in 2021, by then having learned of Miles's behavior at LSU. Even still, he received a $1.99 million buyout of his contract.[10]

None of the University of Miami head coaches suffered for the football program that ran amok in the 1980s and 1990s. Howard Schellenberger (1979–1984) ended up at Louisville in 1985. Jimmy Johnson (1984–1988) took off for the Dallas Cowboys. His successor, Dennis Erickson (1989–1994), left for the Seattle Seahawks; during his tenure in the NFL, he was tagged for driving drunk at twice the legal limit. Erickson's assistant Gregg Smith was charged with reckless driving under the influence, and Ed Orgeron settled a civil suit against him for a saloon brawl.[11] Larry Coker, the 'Canes coach in the early 2000s, was fired in 2006—not because of Miami's violations but for disappointing records. Coker found a head coaching job at the University of Texas San Antonio.

Rick Neuheisel was the head football coach at the University of Washington from 1999 to 2002. He was fired for lying about his involvement in a minor—albeit illegal—gambling pool. He later received a $4.5 million settlement for wrongful termination. More serious was the criminal behavior of at least a dozen of the players on Neuheisel's 2000 Rose Bowl-winning team. Some of the punishments were meted out after the season was over. One of the safeties beat up his wife and was allowed to play with an outstanding warrant for his arrest. A linebacker was under investigation for shooting and robbing a drug dealer, and a tight end was suspected of rape. Another player was charged with assaulting a police officer but got out of jail without posting bail and continued to play. The outrageous abuses during Neuheisel's reign at Washington proved to be no drag on his college coaching career. In 2008, he landed the lucrative head coaching job at UCLA.[12]

Within five decades, peripatetic basketball coach Larry Brown headed ten different NBA teams and three D-I squads. Although his winning records during those stints were impressive, playing by the rules and loyalty to a school were not Brown's priorities; he left behind scandals at every college program he ran. While at UCLA, Brown made under-the-table payments to his players and used ineligible players in a run to the 1980 NCAA title game. Brown left Westwood for Lawrence, where Kansas won the championship in 1988, a victory tainted when the NCAA slapped the Jayhawks with a three-year probation for recruiting violations. Kansas was banned from the 1989 tournament—the first time a champion was denied the chance to defend its title.[13]

By then, however, Brown had ditched Lawrence for the NBA. A *New York Times* headline read, "In Troubled Times, Larry Brown Skips Town Again." In addition to winning championships, Brown's main objective in coaching college students was clear. "Every kid I recruited for college felt they had an opportunity to play in the NBA," Brown said, "and I liked them to have these expectations. So they give themselves, their trust, to you from day one, hoping to reach that goal."[14]

Although Brown paid little attention to his players' performance in the classroom, he was a winner, and SMU came calling in 2012. A year later, Brown went after McDonald's All-American Keith Frazier from Kimball High School in Texas. In their quest to land the coveted kid, Brown and SMU ignored Frazier's shortcomings as a high school student. When Southern Methodist's faculty committee recommended denying him admission, the administration at SMU simply altered his transcript. In this incident, assistant coach Ulric Maligi was Brown's fall guy, as it was *allegedly* Maligi who had asked Frazier's high school to change his grades. In a statement on Frazier's questionable admission to the university, "an SMU spokesman said in an email that the university's coaching staff asked about [Frazier's] grades only because 'we care about the potential of our student-athletes to be academically successful.'"[15]

Chapter Five

When the grade-fixing scandal emerged, SMU was barred from postseason play, Brown was suspended for nine games, and Frazier left the team.[16] Brown saw it as a lost opportunity to shore up his Mustangs, and Frazier was just another player who got away. "I think I invested more time in that kid than my family," Brown lamented. "It's a tragedy now in college sports—kids leave." As journalist Michael Powell frankly put it, "That is not the tragedy."[17]

Frazier ended up at North Texas State and finished up his career at UTEP, where he was a graduate student.[18] His dreams of playing in the NBA died in west Texas, as he went undrafted in 2018. SMU was put on probation for three years and lost nine scholarships during that time. For his part, Brown shipped out to coach an Italian team but was fired after one year.

Yet another repeat offender is Kelvin Sampson. The head basketball coach at Oklahoma from 1994 to 2006, Sampson was also president of the National Association of Basketball Coaches, which has an ethics committee. Evidently, Sampson did not take that part of the job seriously; when the NCAA discovered that he had committed numerous recruiting violations at Oklahoma, he was fired. Indiana immediately snatched him up, but he ended up doing the same thing in Bloomington, with the Hoosiers ushering him out the door in 2008. At this point, the NCAA effectively banned him from coaching for five years. Not to be deterred by Sampson's documented record of cheating, the University of Houston gave him another shot in 2014. In an unfortunate choice of words, Sampson said, "I wanted to invest in a program where I could fix something."[19]

Former Florida and Ohio State football coach Urban Meyer didn't care what his players did off the field as long as they stayed eligible and out of jail. He led the Gators to two national championships in 2006 and 2008. The latter roster had 121 players, 41 of whom were arrested during their years at Florida. Twelve players were arrested for "felonies or violent misdemeanors, including aggravated stalking, aggravated assault, domestic violence, and burglary."[20] Tight end Aaron Hernandez and three other Florida players were questioned in a shooting incident in 2007. Hernandez was connected to a double homicide in Boston in 2012, and a shooting and another murder in 2013. He hung himself in jail in 2017.[21]

Quarterback Cam Newton, a Meyer recruit, was accused of stealing another Florida student's laptop computer and then throwing it out a window when the police showed up.²² That turned out to be no problem for Newton, who transferred from Florida to Auburn, where he helped the Tigers win the 2010 national championship, in part because Auburn forked over $180,000 to Newton's father in a pay-to-play scheme. As the Tigers were primed for a run at the national championship late in the 2010 season, news of the illegal payments came out, and Auburn suspended its star quarterback. Auburn's season was dashed until investigators could find no proof that Auburn coaches or administrators knew of Newton's father's shakedown and, even more improbably, no proof that Newton himself was aware. Newton was reinstated just in time to play in the SEC championship and steer Auburn to a win in the national championship game against Oregon.²³ It is not clear what Newton's major was at Florida or Auburn, how he did in class, or whether he came close to earning a degree, but, apparently, such information is irrelevant in the dog-eat-dog, win-at-all-cost world of NCAA D-I sports.

Meyer took no responsibility for his players' behavior, stating flatly that "relating or blaming these serious charges to the University of Florida, myself, or our staff is wrong and irresponsible." Meyer's wife also stuck her nose into the matter, laying the blame on those players who engaged in criminal activities. "When will we start holding individuals accountable for their own decisions/actions and stop blaming everyone else," she asked.²⁴ A fair question, but when a coach is running a system that prioritizes winning over academics and athletes' performance on the field over character and integrity off it, should the leader not be held at all accountable?

Before Meyer got to Ohio State, the football program had embarrassed itself with repeated scandals, not the least of which when revered Coach Woody Hayes coldcocked Clemson noseguard Charlie Bauman during the 1978 Gator Bowl. Bauman intercepted a Buckeye pass at the end of the game, costing Ohio State a chance at a game-winning field goal. "You SOB," Hayes was heard yelling, "I just lost my job!" That wasn't the first time Hayes had punched a player. Glen Mason, one of Hayes's assistant coaches, recalled, "I think if you spent four years at Ohio State and Woody didn't hit you, you felt cheated."²⁵

In the early 2000s, Buckeye boosters slipped star running back Maurice Clarett tens of thousands of dollars (his real worth to the program was a lot more because Ohio State won the 2003 national title). It was also revealed that Clarett had been given special treatment from professors and had falsified a police report claiming that someone had stolen $10,000 worth of property and cash from him. He was later convicted of robbery and carrying an AK-47 in his car. Clarett got a three-and-a-half-year stay at a correctional institution, which is longer than he lasted at The Ohio State University.[26] Thankfully, Clarett has turned his life around, having started up mental health clinics for kids.

Buckeye head coach Jim Tressel had long bid adieu to Maurice Clarett when "Tattoo-gate"—the free tattoos and other perks given to Buckeye players under Tressel's blind eye—led to his dismissal in 2011. Tressel knew about his players getting cash, phantom jobs, discounts on cars, and free tattoos but lied to investigators to keep his players on the field. The NCAA slapped the program with a three-year probation, vacated wins, excluded the Buckeyes from a 2012 bowl game, banned booster Robert DiGerinimo from Buckeye athletics for ten years, and suspended Tressel from coaching for five years. Despite all of this, a University of Akron search committee found nothing on Tressel's curriculum vitae that prevented them from hiring him as the vice president of strategic engagement in 2012, a $200,000 position that was created just for him.[27] The Board of Trustees at Youngstown State also liked Tressel's record, so much so that they hired him as president in 2014. So much for the notion that coaches are role models for their players. The message is that cheating pays.

Meanwhile, Urban Meyer maintained the Buckeye football program's tradition of excellence on the field and ignominy off it. In 2018, he was suspended for three games for having covered up a domestic abuse case against his receivers coach Zach Smith, something Meyer had heard about before. When Smith was a graduate assistant for Meyer at Florida in 2009, Smith had been arrested for the same charge.[28]

Meyer's tarnished record did not, however, affect his job opportunities. In early 2021, the NFL's Jacksonville Jaguars made him head coach, a position he would manage to keep for all of one season, compiling a 2–11 record. Once with the Jaguars, Meyer hired strength coach Chris Doyle, who had allegedly made racist comments while at the University of Iowa. Meyer fired Doyle a few days after hiring him. In contradiction to the many misdeeds committed under his watch at previous jobs, Meyer was apparently chastened, saying, "We are responsible for all aspects of our program and, in retrospect, should have given greater consideration to how his [Doyle's] appointment may have affected all involved."[29]

Coaches' physical abuse of players has gone unpunished as well. The late Mike Leach was able to dodge multiple accusations of abusing players, parlaying winning records into a long and profitable career in college football. Leach was the head coach at Texas Tech in 2009, when one of his wide receivers, Adam James, suffered a concussion. Leach put him in a practice field shed for two hours as a sort of punishment. An investigation into Leach's coaching methods found other similar incidents, but Leach denied any wrongdoing. Although the media and Red Raider boosters supported Leach, he was suspended for the Alamo Bowl. Leach was eventually fired, but the James affair had no bearing on his marketability. Washington State athletic director Bill Moos liked Leach's resume, so he hired him for $2.25 million a year. Even at Washington State, however, allegations of the mistreatment of players continued to follow Leach. A member of the Cougar squad accused Leach and his assistant coaches of verbally abusing certain players by referring to them in derogatory terms, such as "coward, pussy, [and] bitch." No matter. Mississippi State liked Leach's style too, and in 2020 Starkville hired him away from Spokane.[30] It is hard to imagine any other college job—from administration to faculty to staff—for which someone accused of abusing a student (guilty or not) would be actively recruited by another school.

In his 2020 autobiography, longtime Georgetown basketball coach John Thompson pulled no punches in censuring the cheaters:

> Everybody within college basketball knows which schools are buying players—illegally offering cash or other gifts to players or their families to persuade them to attend and play at their schools. The whole system is filthy with it, well beyond the few schools publicly named by the NCAA. Since the NCAA won't hold everyone accountable, paying players might as well be legal. Schools that don't pay for players have an extremely hard time competing for championships, and coaches who don't cheat can barely hold on to their jobs, because their losses against the cheaters are counted against them.[31]

The disloyalty of coaches to their universities and their scholar-athletes is revealed these days in the merry-go-round of coaching jobs after the regular football season is over but *before* their teams play in bowl games. Coaches leave their boys hanging out to dry even as they are signing on the dotted line for a few extra million to move on to another team. In late 2021, two coaches bolted from high-profile football programs for more greenbacks: Notre Dame's Brian Kelly went to LSU, and Lincoln Riley left Oklahoma for USC, flying on a private jet to confirm his commitment to the Trojans. Riley had an easy time recruiting players to Norman—the land of such educators as Barry Switzer and Bob Stoops and top scholars such as cocaine-snorting Brian Bosworth and running back Joe Mixon, who was seen on tape punching out a woman in 2014. Southern Cal, despite its academic reputation, has not been above providing special perks for football and basketball players. The Reggie Bush affair, in which he got cash payments to play, among others, showed that the school does not take NCAA rules seriously.[32] Likewise, there is no doubt that Kelly will have an easier time getting top players admitted to LSU. Aside from the $100 million he is getting from the school, Notre Dame's higher academic standards were probably a factor in Kelly's departure. Tiger football has never been a stickler for players getting "A" grades in the classroom. Kelly left the Fighting Irish shortly before its bowl game against Oklahoma State. Kelly showed his loyalty to his players by informing them in a text message that their captain was jumping ship.[33]

Before the Covid pandemic hit in 2020, players were not afforded the same opportunity to switch schools without sitting out a year. Players could appeal to play immediately, but the NCAA often denied these requests. For example, in 2018, the University of Pittsburgh fired Kevin Stallings, the basketball coach who had recruited guard Marcus Carr. Carr transferred to the University of Minnesota, but the NCAA would not let him play the next season. Stallings got a $9 million buyout.[34]

In 2018, the NCAA initiated what they called the "transfer portal"—a euphemism for athletes to look around for other places to play, much like coaches looking for other jobs. Coaches began to encourage opposing players to leave and come to a new program on the other side of the portal. The movement of players from team to team is mindful of the "tramp athletes" of late-nineteenth-century college football who played under aliases for various college teams. If athletes have to go through this portal process, why not have a transfer portal for coaches in which their past rulebreaking might prohibit them from taking new jobs?

Recruiting Chicanery

NCAA bylaws promise "minimizing the role of external influences on prospective student-athletes and their families and preventing excessive contact or pressure in the recruitment process."[35] Parents, apparel companies, boosters, and agents are fully aware of the multimillion-dollar earning potential of a star high school athlete and want to cash in on the product. Top prospects are also not naïve about their earning potential and find out early on that sports, not academics, are the pot of gold at the end of the rainbow. They are coddled from the moment someone sees their potential on the playing field.

The NCAA system is ripe for corruption in how high school athletes are recruited. College coaches' jobs depend on getting the best players, by hook or by crook. At least the professional sports leagues have drafts to ensure parity among the teams. The system may not be fair to pro players, who have to play for the team that drafted them or sit out a year, but at least the draft ensures some competitiveness.

Agents and coaches single out the best players at younger and younger ages. In one satirical episode on their 1990s TV show, "Mr. Show," comedians Bob Odenkirk and David Cross play recruiters going to kids' basketball games. The bit is funny but sadly too close to the truth. "There's one kid in particular I've had my eye on," says LaFonte (Chicago) University's recruiter Carter Blanchard (Cross) as he watches a little tyke dribbling a ball that is almost as big as he is. "Young Will Hawkins. He's five years old," says Blanchard. As little Will sits on a basketball, Blanchard tells him, "You're NBA material." Rival recruiter Ty Keenan (Odenkirk) from Indiana Basin Silt College advises Will, "*You* decide what's the route you're gonna take. You come to Indiana or freeze your butt off in Chicago." When Blanchard visits Will's parents, he says, "Here I come, bearing gifts" (an NCAA rules violation, of course). "I brought along some tokens of gratitude . . . some LaFonte slippers for Mom, you put those on your feet . . . for Dad, a LaFonte vest . . . for little Will, I got the little man the little LaFonte basketball. And for the family, homemade potato soup." Blanchard gets Will to sign a fourteen-year letter of intent. The recruiters take the process to its logical conclusion, trying to sign a one-year-old, and then trying to get a letter of intent from a gene-gifted fetus. Will Hawkins does not get the scholarship. The father is distraught, blaming his son for shooting too much: "You're a point guard. Eating too much chocolate."[36]

The skit is not that far-fetched. More than thirty years ago, Murray Sperber pointed out the incongruity of big-time sports on the college campus. "Athletes are the only group of students recruited for entertainment—not academic—purposes," he wrote, "and are the only students who go through school on grants based not on educational

Chapter Five

aptitude but on their talent and potential as commercial entertainers."[37] Ralph "Shug" Jordan, Auburn's football coach from 1951–76, anticipated Sperber: "A coach simply must resign himself to the fact that he is no longer involved with the educational process but with entertainment."[38]

The incentive is strong for coaches to sidestep the NCAA's recruiting rules; they have to win to keep their huge contracts. Good players give coaches good records, so landing the best recruits is top priority. In 2004, it was revealed that the University of Colorado regaled football recruits with "escorts," strippers, alcohol, and drugs. Nine women came forward with claims that Buffalo players or recruits had sexually assaulted them. Two women athletic trainers also charged an assistant coach with assault. Coach Gary Barnett was suspended over the incident, but the university fired him only after he and his team got trounced in the last three games of the 2005 season. The *New York Times* wrote, "He was able to weather repeated investigations because he continued to win games. But when he started to lose, his security vanished."[39]

In the early 2000s, football recruit Reggie Bush's parents took hundreds of thousands of dollars in bribes and a rent-free house in Malibu to send their son to USC. When the news of the illegal perks broke, Bush had to give up his 2005 Heisman Trophy. Southern Cal was put on probation for four years, received a two-year bowl ban, and lost thirty scholarships over three years. The Trojans, a perennial PAC-12 power, didn't win a conference championship for another nine years, the longest such streak USC has suffered since the 1920s.[40]

While USC's football fortunes tanked for nearly a decade, Coach Pete Carroll escaped scot-free, fleeing to the NFL's Seattle Seahawks. Carroll's assistant, who had recruited Bush, was none other than Ed Orgeron, who was hired away to Mississippi post-scandal, and from there to LSU, where he won the 2020 National Championship. While at Ole Miss, one of Orgeron's top high school recruits could barely read or write, so he was "parked" at the Hargrave Military Academy in Virginia, where he could bring up his GPA and be eligible to play college football. It is safe to say that Orgeron did not prioritize the student's future academic career over playing for the Rebels.[41]

After LSU won the NCAA football championship game in 2020, Cleveland Browns wide receiver and Tigers' alum Odell Beckham Jr. generously doled out $2,000 in cash to appreciative LSU players. It is not clear whether Orgeron, who made $4 million that year, got any of the loose change. LSU came down hard on Beckham Jr. for handing out the money, barring him from team facilities for two years. In order to preempt tougher NCAA sanctions, the university also admitted to illegal payments to the team from a booster's embezzled money. Nevertheless, Beckham and the booster got their money's worth—a coveted national title. There is no movement afoot from the NCAA to vacate LSU's championship, which means nothing to fans anyway. Who cares if the trophy case is missing a piece? The games were played, and LSU won.[42]

After posting a mediocre 3–5 record during the Covid-filled 2020–21 football season, LSU fired Orgeron, not for any violations but for having turned in a lousy record. A *New York Times* headline read, "For L.S.U., Not Winning Enough Is the Biggest Scandal." The article alluded to LSU players involved in sexual assaults and Orgeron's alleged lackluster support of issues of racial justice, but the bottom line was Orgeron's recent won–loss record.[43]

LSU imposed sanctions on itself to preclude harsher NCAA penalties. The school said that the football team would not accept a bid to play in a 2020–21 bowl game. That offer might have come from the Cheez-It Bowl, where, because of the pandemic, the Tigers could have played in an empty Camping World Stadium in Orlando, Florida, sans tents and campers.

Lane Kiffin was another assistant coach under Pete Carroll at USC when Reggie Bush and his family were cashing in. Kiffin left to run the Tennessee Vols program in 2009. Tennessee football recruiters enlisted young coeds—known as the "Orange Pride"—to lure prospects to Knoxville. "Our job," said one proud member, "was to flirt with them, to be honest." Kiffin's coaches helped two coeds go on a high school recruiting visit. Kiffin, to the fury of Vol fans, took off after one year to take the head job at USC. After having coddled Carroll for so many years, the USC athletic department was unconcerned about any blemish on the Kiffin name. Failing to win at USC, Kiffin was fired in 2013 and became an Alabama assistant under Nick Saban. Kiffin landed another head coaching job at Florida Atlantic in 2017, then proceeded to move up in 2020 to a better job at Ole Miss.[44]

In early 2022, Auburn's head basketball coach Bruce Pearl took his Tigers to the number one ranking in the country. A dozen years earlier, as the coach at Tennessee, Pearl had admitted to lying to NCAA investigators about his illegal recruiting practices but only after he was caught on photos. At the age of fifty, Pearl had an epiphany. "I learned that it's not okay to tell the truth most of the time," he confessed. "But you've got to tell the truth all of the time." That is not necessarily true in the world of NCAA sports, because if a coach wins, there is always another school like Auburn to offer a job. Auburn was a good fit for Pearl because the school also has a record of indifference to NCAA rules.[45] In the late 2010s, former Auburn and NBA player Chuck Person took almost $100,000 in bribes from a financial counselor to steer college players to Auburn.[46]

John Calipari has been particularly deft at taking advantage of the NCAA's weak oversight and anemic penalties. Scandals took him down at the University of Massachusetts and the University of Memphis, leaving both programs and their players in the lurch. Calipari now makes more than $9 million a year at Kentucky.[47] His team is little more than a one-season stop for blue chip recruits, and they know it. On NBA draft day, Calipari sits with his guys and their parents, proudly sending the nineteen-year-olds off to the pros without a meaningful college education anywhere in sight. Finishing one semester is mandatory for the young multimillionaires (two is optional); having to return to class at Kentucky is a booby prize for the undrafted Wildcats.

In 2017, a scandal broke out over money that assistant basketball coaches from Louisville, Auburn, Southern California, Creighton, Texas Christian, Oklahoma State, and Arizona had slipped to players through a Nike agent, as well as to the father of highly regarded Louisville recruit Brian Bowen II. An FBI investigation found that two Adidas employees and agent Christian Dawkins were giving money to college recruits, and were doing so with the knowledge of coaches, among them Sean Miller of Arizona and Will Wade of LSU. Eventually, ten players were implicated. Adidas got into the bidding war for Bowen as well. It came out at trial that Adidas had sent $100,000 to Bowen Sr. At the time, Louisville was already on probation, so one assistant coach told Dawkins, "We have to be very low key [about smuggling cash to the player and his parents]."[48]

Although a Louisville assistant testified to the payments in court, Rick Pitino denied knowing anything about it. "In my 40 years of coaching, this is the luckiest I've ever been [in landing Bowen II]," Pitino explained.[49] For his part, Dawkins saw it as a down payment for the player and the college team. "You pay $50K to make $5 million," he said. "I would think people in Silicon Valley would like those odds." He probably meant Las Vegas. *USA Today* columnist Christine Brennan called for the NCAA to impose the death penalty on Louisville: "Consider it a kind of lifetime achievement award for the egregious and ongoing transgressions of its men's basketball program under the legendary and notorious Rick Pitino."[50]

The FBI caught Wade and Miller on tape discussing the high cost of landing recruits, but both disavowed any knowledge of illegal payments. In 2018, Dawkins and the Adidas representatives were found guilty of wire fraud.[51] Book Richardson, a former Arizona assistant coach, pled guilty to federal bribery charges the next year. Arizona found five Level I violations in the basketball program and cited Miller's lack of institutional control. In 2021, Miller was ousted after twelve seasons with the Wildcats. LSU fired Will Wade in 2022.[52]

In 2010, *Sports Illustrated* cited a sports agent who exposed the cash and other favors that he and others had given to college players. Tone deaf Nick Saban, who pulled in more than $10 million a year, was outraged: "I hate to say this, but how are they [agents] any better than a pimp?" Retired LSU basketball coach Dale Brown turned the focus on coaches and administrators. "Look at the money we make off predominantly poor Black kids," he said candidly. "We're the whoremasters."[53]

In response to the Adidas scandal and other recruiting violations, the NCAA formed the (Condoleeza) Rice Commission. President Mark Emmert declared, "This is not a time for half-measures or incremental change." The NCAA's reaction was neither a half-measure nor incremental. A few players were suspended, but no university received a sanction.[54] The *New York Times* chastised the NCAA: "The college sports establishment has indicated no movement toward reforming its economic system that appeared to prompt the scheme: multimillion-dollar apparel sponsorships; huge financial incentives to win big; and amateurism rules that bar paying players."[55] The New York district attorney who prosecuted the case called the shoe deals the "dark underbelly of college basketball."[56]

From 2010 to 2014, the Louisville basketball program underwrote an extracurricular activity that brought strippers and "escorts" to the men's basketball dorm at least twenty times. Coach Rick Pitino had already gotten himself into trouble for allegedly having an affair with the wife of the basketball team's equipment manager and then paying for her abortion.[57]

In addition to the previously mentioned schools, using young women to flirt (or more) with prospective and current players has been a tried-and-true tactic for schools such as Tennessee, Louisville, Miami (FL), and Texas. Famous boxing promoter Don King ran a strip joint in Austin that Longhorn players, like Miami Hurricane players and their bawdy bar, also called "The Office." "Over the years," King boasted, "I've done more for recruiting at UT than [head football coach] Mack Brown."[58]

The bigwigs running the bowl games get in on the skin game too. John Junker was fired as CEO of the Fiesta Bowl for various fiscal indiscretions, among them using $1,200 in bowl money to cover a trip to a strip joint.

Pitino feigned ignorance of the knowledge of any strippers and escorts, but after the bribery scandal emerged, he was fired in October 2017.[59] In his memoir, *Pitino: My Story*, he denied knowing anything about what his subordinates were doing, and he did not take responsibility for his lack of oversight. He did acknowledge that "we are not getting shoe companies out of college sports."[60] In 2020, Pitino landed another gig, accepting the head coaching job at Iona University, a Catholic school. Successful there, St. John's University (another Catholic institution) hired him away in 2023.[61] Evidently Christian values were ignored.

Sometimes, college admission departments term academically challenged recruits "coach-admits." About half of the athletes at these schools rank in the bottom third academically. Even the Ivy League and other non-athletic scholarship schools skirt their strict admission rules for prospective athletes. In a study done in the late 1990s, William G. Bowen and Sarah A. Levin found that sports recruits at four Ivy League schools were almost four times as likely to be admitted to the university. At elite small liberal arts schools, "close to 45 percent of the places for males in each entering class (more than 30 percent of the female places) have been reserved in recent years for candidates whose chief distinction derives from achievement in a sport rather than from academic or scientific pursuits."[62]

The admissions scandal that broke in 2019, in which several celebrities were indicted, revealed further lack of oversight in athletic departments and the privilege that wealthy White kids receive in admissions to selective schools, even though many didn't even play. Rich parents paid William Singer, the central figure in the scam, about $25 million to bribe coaches and athletic department administrators to get their children into top colleges on athletic scholarships based on fabricated sports resumes. Donna Heinel, USC's senior associate athletic director, pocketed $1.3 million in the racket. One student got into USC as a phony punter/kicker even though his high school did not field a football team. Obviously, he did not make the Trojan roster. Parents of "rowers" made big bribes to get into USC, even if the landlubbing recruits did not know a scull from a skull. Trojan water polo and women's soccer coaches were also charged. Among the other schools implicated in the scandal were such elite academic institutions as Georgetown, Wake Forest, Stanford, and Yale.[63] Georgetown's tennis coach Gordon Ernst pled guilty to the scam, for which, as mentioned, he received more than $3 million in bribes.[64]

Some top high school players and their coaches and parents take advantage of the "pay-for-play" system. For example, Chris Mills and Shawn Kemp were among the most highly recruited high school basketball players in the late 1980s. Mills's player-host for his on-campus visit to Indiana University recalled the player's demands. "I have to have money," Mills told him. "I have to have a car. I have to live in my own place." The Hoosiers refused to pony up, so Mills went to Kentucky, which was more obliging. Kemp made similar demands. Indiana player Rick Callaway recalled, "He just wanted stuff. He kept saying, 'You all don't get nothing? I know you're lying.'" Kemp also went to Kentucky, where evidently Coach Eddie Sutton was handing out stuff. The loot Kemp got from Kentucky was not enough, however; he was caught pawning gold necklaces he stole from Sean Sutton, the head coach's son. Kemp left for a short stint at junior college and then moved to the NBA at age nineteen.

Some high school coaches are complicit in the shakedowns. Georgetown head coach John Thompson said that there were "a lot of high school coaches [who] have their hands out—a lot of them." It doesn't have to be this way. Some parents have integrity. According to Clark Kellogg's father, his son rejected a four-year, $100,000 cash deal from one school (Kentucky?) to attend Ohio State on a scholarship.[65] Such integrity is too often lacking.

Notes

1. Ira Berkow, "Sports of the Times; Old American Game," *New York Times*, March 7, 1987, 49.

2. Unattributed, "Saban Tests Positive," Associated Press, *Star Tribune*, November 26, 2020, C7.

Chapter Five

3. Oriard, *King Football*, 125.
4. Byers, *Unsportsmanlike Conduct*, 121.
5. Byers, *Unsportsmanlike Conduct*, 363.
6. Jack Pilgrim, "Sports Illustrated: How Former Wildcat Dwane Casey went From Center of Kentucky Probation to Elite NBA Coach," March 12, 2018, accessed May 23, 2020, https://kentuckysportsradio.com/basketball-2/sports-illustrated-how-former-wildcat-dwane-casey-went-from-center-of-kentucky-probation-to-elite-nba-coach/; and Jeff Borzello, "Former Oklahoma State, Kentucky Coach Eddie Sutton Dies at 84," May 23, 2020, ESPN, accessed December 10, 2020, https://www.espn.com/mens-college-basketball/story/_/id/29214667/former-oklahoma-state-kentucky-coach-eddie-sutton-dies-84.
7. "Woman Hit by Eddie Sutton in 2006 Car Crash Still Fighting to Sue," September 25, 2012, accessed December 10, 2020, https://www.koco.com/article/woman-hit-by-eddie-sutton-in-2006-car-crash-still-fighting-to-sue/4290161#; and *New York Times*, accessed December 10, 2020, https://www.nytimes.com/1989/05/20/sports/kentucky-s-basketball-program-and-2-players-heavily-penalized.html.
8. ESPN.com News Services, February 22, 2011, accessed December 15, 2020, https://www.espn.com/mens-college-basketball/news/story?id=6146656.
9. ESPN, "NCAA Upholds Penalty for Ex-UConn Coach Kevin Ollie, May 6, 2020, accessed December 15, 2020, https://www.espn.com/mens-college-basketball/story/_/id/29142679/ncaa-upholds-penalty-ex-uconn-coach-kevin-ollie.
10. Kyle Boone, "Kansas, Coach Les Miles Part Wars Amid Allegation of Misconduct from Time at LSU, March 9, 2021, CBS Sports, accessed March 9, 2021, https://www.cbssports.com/college-football/news/kansas-coach-les-miles-part-ways-amid-allegations-of-misconduct-from-time-at-lsu/; and "Miles is Out as Football Coach at Kansas," AP, *Star Tribune*, March 9, 2021, C7.
11. Wolff, "Broken Beyond Repair."
12. Nick Perry and Ken Armstrong, "The Disturbing Story Behind the Last Great UW Team—and How its Legacy Still Casts a Shadow on the Huskies," *The Seattle Times*, January 27, 2008, https://www.seattletimes.com/seattle-news/the-disturbing-story-behind-the-last-great-uw-team-8212-and-how-its-legacy-still-casts-a-shadow-on-the-huskies/, accessed February 15, 2022; and Jay M. Smith and Mary Willingham, *Cheated: The UNC Scandal, the Education of Athletes, and the Future of Big-Time College Sports* (Lincoln, NE: Potomac Books, 2015), 213.
13. Associated Press, "N.C.A.A. Acts Against Kansas," *The New York Times*, November 2, 1988, accessed April 15, 2021, https://www.nytimes.com/1988/11/02/sports/ncaa-acts-against-kansas.html.
14. Sperber, *College Sports, Inc.*, 159, 229.
15. Michael Powell, "The Tragedy of a Hall of Fame Coach and His Star Recruit," *New York Times*, March 6, 2016, 1.
16. Powell, "The Tragedy."
17. Powell, "The Tragedy."
18. Powell, "The Tragedy."

19. Jerry Brewer, "11 Years Ago, Kelvin Sampson was Effective Banned from the NCAA. Now, He's Restored Houston to Prominence—and Vice Versa, *Chicago Tribune*, March 14, 2019, accessed February 16, 2022, https://www.chicagotribune.com/sports/college/ct-spt-kelvin-sampson-ncaa-violations-penalty-20190314-story.html.

20. Greg Bishop, "Hernandez Among Many Arrested at Florida in the Meyer Years," *New York Times*, July 7, 2013, SP1.

21. Tadd Haislop, "Aaron Hernandez Timeline: From Murders and Trials to Prison Suicide," *The Sporting News*, January 18, 2020, accessed June 29, 2022, https://www.sportingnews.com/us/nfl/news/aaron-hernandez-timeline-murders-trials-prison-suicide/1886y82a8bgyx123qxcgg04lb5.

22. Bishop, "Hernandez Among Many."

23. Branch, "The Shame."

24. Bishop, "Hernandez Among Many."

25. Brian Bennett, "Woody Hayes' Last Game Coaching, December 30, 2013, accessed December 18, 2020, https://www.espn.com/college-football/bowls13/story/_/id/10215217/the-punch-ended-woody-hayes-career.

26. ESPN, "Timeline: The Rise and Fall of Maurice Clarett," August 9, 2006, accessed December 16, 2020, https://www.espn.com/nfl/news/story?id=2545204.

27. Benedict and Keteyian, *The System*, 111–118.

28. Bill Chappell, "Urban Meyer Will Retire as Ohio State's Football Coach, After Scandal-Marred Season," National Public Radio, December 4, 2018, accessed December 16, 2020, https://www.npr.org/2018/12/04/673222935/urban-meyer-will-retire-as-ohio-states-football-coach-after-scandal-marred-season; and David Ching, "Urban Meyer Clearly Ranks Among College Football Greats, But Scandals Complicate His Legacy, *Forbes*, December 4, 2018, accessed December 16, 2020, https://www.forbes.com/sites/davidching/2018/12/04/he-clearly-ranks-among-the-all-time-greats-but-off-field-scandals-complicate-urban-meyers-legacy/?sh=183735012784.

29. AP, "Jaguars Strength Coach Out," *Star Tribune*, February 24, 2021, C11.

30. Benedict and Keteyian, *The System*, 76, 334, 345.

31. John Thompson, Jr., *New York Times*.

32. See Anemona Hartocollis, "Former U.S.C. Official Pleads Guilty in College Admissions Scandal," *New York Times*, November 5, 2021, accessed March 5, 2022, https://www.nytimes.com/2021/11/05/us/usc-official-varsity-blues-guilty.html.

33. In 2021, LSU women filed a lawsuit against the football program for egregious violations of Title IX, prompting the Louisiana legislature to pass a law mandating reporting of such misbehavior. See Jason Gay, "How to Quit a College Football Job," *Wall Street Journal*, December 1, 2021, A14.

34. Jim Souhan, "NCAA Blows Decision on Gophers Marcus Carr, Associated Press, November 15, 2018, accessed January 15, 2022, https://apnews.com/article/04cbe332a5974dedb07d29014e39b11c.

35. 2018-19 NCAA Division I Manual, "Commitment to the Division I Collegiate Model," xi.

36. See "The Basketball Recruiters," *Mr. Show*, Season Two, Episode Five https://www.youtube.com/watch?v=7dR_Nb7fx0E

37. Sperber, *College Sports Inc.*, 1.

38. Sperber, *College Sports Inc.*, 156.

39. Lee Jenkins, "Losses Do to Barnett What Colorado Scandal Could Not," *New York Times*, December 9, 2005, accessed December 16, 2020, https://www.nytimes.com/2005/12/09/sports/ncaafootball/losses-do-to-barnett-what-colorado-scandal-could-not.html.

40. Ivan Maisel, "Welcome Back, Reggie Bush. You Never Should Have Left," ESPN, June 10, 2020, accessed December 15, 2020, https://www.espn.com/college-football/story/_/id/29292508/welcome-back-reggie-bush-never-left.

41. Charles McGrath, "Smells Like Team Spirit," *New York Times Education Life*, November 4, 2007, 37.

42. Unattributed, "LSU Bans Beckham," *Star Tribune*, October 12, 2020, C6.

43. Billy Witz, "For L.S.U., Not Winning Enough Is the Biggest Scandal," *New York Times*, October 19, 2021, B9.

44. Benedict and Keteyian, *The System*, 28.

45. Phil Taylor, "How Low Can You Go?" *Sports Illustrated*, April 11, 2011, 84.

46. Marc Tracy, "Former Auburn Assistant Pleads Guilty in Corruption Case," *The New York Times*, March 19, 2019, accessed April 15, 2021, https://www.nytimes.com/2019/03/19/sports/chuck-person.html.

47. Adam Zagoria, "John Calipari Signs Lifetime Contract at Kentucky Worth $86 Million," *Forbes*, June 13, 2019, accessed June 29, 2022, https://www.forbes.com/sites/adamzagoria/2019/06/13/john-calipari-signs-lifetime-contract-at-kentucky-worth-86-million/?sh=7ec90023e384.

48. Lindsay Schnell, "Indictments May Be Just Start of Scandal," *USA Today*, September 27, 2017, A1.

49. Marc Tracy and Adam Zagoria, "A Prized Recruit's Path to Stardom, Line with U.S. Prosecutors," *New York Times*, October 5, 2017, 1A; and Dan Wolken, "College Coaches Should Be Afraid," *USA Today*, September 27, 2017, C1.

50. Christine Brennan, "Cardinals Deserve to Get NCAA Death Penalty in Scandal," *USA Today*, October 5, 2017, 6C.

51. Patrick Reusse, "HBO Show on College Hoops Jolting," *Star Tribune*, April 19, 2020, C2; Michael Powell, "A 'Drop the Mic' Moment for a Man Who Paid College Basketball Recruits," *New York Times*, March 17, 2020, accessed April 20, 2020, https://www.nytimes.com/2020/03/17/sports/ncaabasketball/ncaa-christian-dawkins.html; and Marc Tracy, "Three Found Guilty in N.C.A.A. Basketball Recruiting Scheme," *New York Times*, October 25, 2018, B9.

52. Billy Witz, "A Messy Season for L.S.U., Down to the Bitter End," *New York Times*, March 20, 2022, 32.

53. Branch, "The Shame."

54. Billy Witz, "Who's on Trial in a Corruption Case? Not the Big Players," *New York Times*, April 23, 2019, B9.

55. Reusse, "HBO Show."; Michael Powell, "A 'Drop the Mic' Moment for a Man Who Paid College Basketball Recruits," *New York Times*, March 17, 2020, accessed April 20, 2020, https://www.nytimes.com/2020/03/17/sports/ncaabasketball/ncaa-christian-dawkins.html; and Marc Tracy, "Three Found Guilty in N.C.A.A. Basketball Recruiting Scheme," *New York Times*, October 25, 2018, B9.

56. Wolken, "College Coaches Should Be Afraid."

57. Nancy Armour, "Armour: Rick Pitino Has to Go as Details of Louisville Sex Parties Emerge," *USA Today*, October 15, 2015, accessed March 21, 2021, https://www.usatoday.com/story/sports/2015/10/20/rick-pitino-louisville-sex-parties-katina-powell/74267474/.

58. Benedict and Keteyian, *The System*, 55, 57.

59. Witz, "Who's on Trial?"

60. Danielle Lerner and Gentry Estes, "Pitino Tells All on Scandals, Kentucky, Future," *USA Today*, September 5, 2018, 3C.

61. Will, "The Real March Madness."

62. Benjamin DeMott, "Jocks and the Academy," *The New Review of Books*, May 12, 2005, 29–32.

63. A.J. Perez, "USC Caught in Admissions Scandal," *USA Today*, March 13, 2019, C1.

64. Anemone Hartocollis, "Guilty Pleas by Ex-Coach at University in Bribe Case," *New York Times*, September 16, 2021, A16.

65. Sperber, *College Sports, Inc.*, 250–3.

CHAPTER SIX

Good Ol' Boys' Club:
The NCAA's Fight Against Minorities and Women

"These are largely African American players that are being kept poor in order to enrich White athletic directors, coaches, and sports company executives.... There's no other marketplace in the country in which the people providing the labor should be compensated millions of dollars and are instead being given no salary."

—Connecticut Senator Chris Murphy, 2019[1]

For nearly a century, the NCAA fought to keep Black people and women out of intercollegiate sports. The organization's dismal track record on leveling the playing field for all students and its continued resistance to hiring minority and women administrators and coaches are further blemishes on intercollegiate sports. And while they have learned to give lip service to efforts to achieve equality, the NCAA and its members remain insincere about eradicating discrimination.

Higher education should have forged a more enlightened path, but college sports has mirrored the racism in the rest of the United States. As historian Donald Spivey writes, "The reality of intercollegiate sport in the years prior to World War II is far less magnanimous and noble when the experiences of African-American athletes are considered."[2]

Until well after World War II, most African Americans did not have a chance to go beyond high school unless it was to a Black college. On December 27, 1892, two North Carolina schools, Biddle University and Livingstone College, played the first intercollegiate football game between Black schools. Until then, sports in HBCUs were intramural because they had little extra money to fund sports. The Livingstone yearbook reads, "In 1892, several men ... decided to inaugurate football at Livingstone. To that end, an order was placed for one of the regulation footballs from Spalding's . . . each man chipping in and paying for it." The game was played in a cow pasture. Biddle won, 4–0.³

The NCAA Obliges Jim Crow

A few Black players made their way onto Northern football teams, but there was no way for them to play in the Jim Crow South. As football gained in popularity in the 1920s, segregated Southern schools took to football to negate, at least symbolically, the Confederacy's loss in the Civil War, to bring back pride to the downtrodden, largely impoverished, region.⁴ Alabama won the Rose Bowl in 1926, and the Crimson Tide appeared again in the game in 1927 and 1931. Georgia Tech beat Cal in the 1929 Rose Bowl (famous for Cal's Roy Riegals' wrong way run), and in a big victory for the South, Georgia beat the Yanks from Yale the next season.⁵

Southern schools would not breach the color line and refused to play against Black players. In 1916, Rutgers was scheduled to play Washington and Lee University, a small private school in Virginia. In keeping with the slave-owning history of its namesakes, Washington and Lee declared their team would not show up for the game if Rutgers let Paul Robeson play. Rutgers obliged, and kept Robeson, who went on to fame as an actor, singer, and political activist out of the game. The so-called "gentlemen's agreements" not to play Black players against Southern schools—hardly the definition of a true gentleman—even applied to African Americans playing against the Naval Academy in Maryland. In 1941, Harvard's lacrosse team bowed to Navy's demands that Lucien Alexis Jr. be taken out of the lineup.⁶

There are numerous examples of Northern teams acceding to the "gentlemen's agreements." In 1940, Leonard Bates did not travel with his NYU team to play Missouri in Columbia in deference to the Tigers' demand that they would not play against Blacks. Despite student protests, the NYU president and coaches kept Bates out. The next year, Bates was sidelined for four games against Southern teams.⁷ In 1947, Virginia told Harvard not to play the Crimson's Chester Pierce, but the team voted to have him play anyway. Once in Virginia, when Pierce was told he would have to stay in a segregated annex of a hotel, the whole of the Harvard team followed him into the annex through the "colored-only" entrance and stayed there as well.⁸

Well into the 1950s, teams from the South refused to allow their athletes to play against integrated teams. In 1955, Georgia Governor Marvin Griffin told Georgia's Board of Regents, "The South stands at Armageddon. The battle is joined. We cannot make the slightest concession to the enemy in this dark and lamentable hour of struggle." Griffin said that to cross the color line on the field would lead to integrating the classroom. "One break in the dike," he declared, "and the relentless enemy will rush in and destroy us."[9] Georgia Tech, with opposition from the Georgia governor, went ahead and played in the 1956 Sugar Bowl against the University of Pittsburgh, which had a Black player, Bobby Grier. Still, Mississippi State did not play in the NCAA basketball tournament in 1959, 1961, and 1962 because the school would not play against integrated teams.[10]

When Blacks did play against Whites, they were subjected to the same kind of taunts that Jackie Robinson got when he integrated Major League Baseball. Games were marred by brutal racist assaults. One of the worst occurred in a football game between Iowa State and Minnesota in 1923. Jack Trice, Iowa State's first Black player, died from intentional injuries suffered in the game. The night before it, Trice had made a note to himself: "The honor of my race, family and self are at stake. Everyone is expecting me to do big things, I will!"[11] Tragically, he is remembered in the history books because of his death on the field.

In 1951, an Oklahoma State player blindsided and broke the jaw of Drake's Johnny Bright, another Black player. The photographer for the *Des Moines Register* caught the vicious blow on film.[12] The hit was an intentional, racist act. In the run-up to the game, the *Stillwater News-Press* wrote that Bright was "a marked man." Bright could not stay with the team at the A&M dorms, so a local Black minister took him in. The buzz around campus was that Bright, as *Life* magazine reported, "would not be around at the end of the game." Rumor had it that A&M students were betting on whether the Aggie players would take him out, as the Aggie Coach J. B. Whitworth was exhorting his players to do. Bright suffered several deliberate hits, the last one ending his day on the field. He had to have his jaw wired shut and was out for the rest of the season.[13]

Black athletes, even when they were allowed to play at predominantly White Northern schools, faced bald-faced discrimination off the field as well. For example, before a game against Brigham Young University in 1969, Wyoming head football coach Lloyd Eaton told fourteen

Chapter Six

Wyoming football players that he would throw them off the team if they wore black armbands in protest against the segregated Mormon school, and in support of the campus's Black Student Alliance's stance against the Vietnam War and demands for civil rights. Eaton told them to go back to an HBCU like Grambling or Morgan State or return to picking cotton. The "Black Fourteen" did not play in the game, and most of them never played for Wyoming again.[14] During the BYU game, the stadium announcers declared, "Our coach has had to expel fourteen players, but we think he has done the right thing, so let's stand up and give him a cheer." The Wyoming fans obliged.[15]

Needless to say, it was difficult for Black players to integrate into predominantly White schools like Wyoming. Going far away from home to play sports is not an easy transition into college life for any eighteen-year-old, let alone a Black student in mid-twentieth-century America. When Southern schools finally began to integrate, Jake Gaither, the famed coach at Florida A&M—an HBCU—questioned whether going to a White school was the right choice for a Black athlete.

> [High school coaches] think it's the greatest thing in the world to send their players to a White college," he observed. "A boy's education doesn't confine itself to the football field. In order to get a well-rounded education, he's got to be integrated into every phase of university life. [At White schools], he's denied all the social activities of the university—can't join the fraternity and can't date the girl in the dormitory.... They complain about discrimination and a lack of a social life, but what did they expect?[16]

Gaither was right; sadly, many Black athletes feel the same social isolation today on predominantly White campuses.

The NCAA has been complicit in discriminating against Blacks. In 1951, it decreed that basketball teams could only play in either the NCAA or the NIT basketball tournament but not both. In the 1950s, the NCAA also tried to crush the basketball tournament hosted by the National Association of Intercollegiate Athletics (NAIA), which was more inclusive of teams with Black players. The NCAA did not want to alienate its Southern members by forcing them to play integrated teams. In 1957, the NCAA created a rival College Division Basketball Championship. A year later, the four HBCUs that were invited to the thirty-two-team tournament were put into a South Central regional to avoid playing any integrated team, thus ensuring that only one HBCU would make the tournament championships in Evansville, Indiana. According to historian Kurt E. Kemper, "the tournament committee conveniently located the two segregationist Southern schools in the field in the opposite bracket to ensure that the two halves of America's racial conscience could meet only in the championship, if at all."[17]

Frequently overlooked on the slow road to the integration of college basketball was the success of the University of San Francisco in the mid-1950s. With two famous Black players, future NBA Hall-of-Famers Bill Russell and K. C. Jones, leading the way, the Dons won two straight NCAA championships. Loyola Chicago, a predominantly White school, was the first major college team to play five Black players at one time, and the Ramblers won the 1963 title. Texas Western's championship victory over the all-White Kentucky basketball team in 1966 is most often remembered as the key milestone in the integration of college basketball, probably because of Kentucky's famous coach, Adolph Rupp, who had no Black players on his teams.

The Exploitation of Black Labor

College coaches as a whole have not been interested in the intellectual development of their Black athletes, in their case, even in terms of their roles on the field or the court. It was not very long ago that Black athletes were largely excluded from the football's "brain" positions—quarterback, center, and middle linebacker. Ohio State football coach Woody Hayes did not have a Black starting quarterback until Cornelius Greene came to Columbus in 1972 (and proceeded to lead the Buckeyes to three straight Big Ten titles and Rose Bowls). Greene lost just one Big Ten game in three years as the Buckeye quarterback, and in so doing, he smashed Hayes's perception of the mental limitations of Black folks.[18]

Hayes had won games for years without a Black quarterback, but as schools became more integrated and competition got tougher, coaches desperate to win began to recruit the best players in any position regardless of their ethnicity or, as noted, their preparation for academic work. To be clear, the racial integration of college sports did not happen because progressive educators wanted to give Black students a shot at a college degree but only because coaches couldn't compete without Black players on the field.

Southern schools, such as Mississippi and Georgia, were among the last to integrate their football teams, doing so in the 1960s. "The most powerful force for integration [of college football in the South] was not high-minded principle," observes Michael Oriard, "but the need to win football games, and integration, as future generations would learn, could mean recruiting ill-prepared young athletes with slight prospects of graduating. Opportunity and exploitation became deeply entangled."[19]

One Southern powerhouse, the University of Alabama, is known first and foremost for its football team. To this day Alabama and other Deep South schools see football as an intersectional battle, and victories against Northern teams as a way of sticking it to them. No matter that Southern states are at the bottom in just about every economic and educational ranking, the Crimson Tide football team gives Bama bragging rights. In the mid-1980s, Alabama president Joab Thomas made a halfhearted attempt to emphasize the academic side of things. In a half-time commercial, he held a book in one hand and a football in the other: "At the University of Alabama, we're going to make *this* [the book] as important as this [the football]."[20] Theatrics notwithstanding, Alabama's flagship university is not in the top 100 in any ranking.

Some scholars and pundits have foolishly compared the NCAA today to a plantation system and the work that Black players do to slavery. That charge was first made after World War II regarding White players, when the G.I. Bill enabled returning soldiers (the vast majority of whom were White) to enroll in school. In justifying dropping football, American University (Washington D.C.) President Paul F. Douglass declared, "A human slave market extends from the Atlantic to the Pacific and from Canada to Alabama. Day by day, young [White] men come to the auction block for sale to the highest bidder. The bidding is bitter, determined, and unscrupulous. The country is ridden with agents and scouts directed by coaches who receive their salaries higher than university presidents." Douglass said that the players "surrender their complete freedom to coaches, today's slave drivers."[21]

Even former NCAA executive director Walter Byers used that terminology nearly four decades ago in chastising the riches in college sports that were going to the managers instead of the workers. Byers once said:

> Today, the [decade-old] NCAA President's Commission is preoccupied with tightening a few loose bolts in a worn machine, firmly committed to the neoplantation [sic] belief that the enormous proceeds from college games belong to the overseers (the

administrators) and supervisors (coaches). The plantation workers performing in the arena may receive only those benefits authorized by the overseers."[22]

It is wrongheaded to equate slavery to the exploitation of Black players today. Noted journalist and author Taylor Branch is right: "College athletes are not slaves."[23] While the system is unfair to players, it is not slavery or indentured servitude. This misguided comparison of college athletes to the shackled masses 150 years ago constitutes a great disservice to the memory of those who suffered so horribly under that brutal, inhumane institution. College athletes are not chattel—whipped, chained, and sold to the highest bidder. They can choose to play or not to play, and they can decide their own future. Most D-I football and men's basketball players, although they are not paid a salary, live a comfy life with their own dorms, training tables, team trainers, doctors, and tutors to help them pass courses.

The coach–athlete relationship is not master–slave; it is more akin to an exploitation of labor by management in nineteenth-century industries in which workers had little recourse to make better wages or seek better and safer working conditions. Workers in those sweatshop times also had it much worse than college athletes at any level.

The tryouts that would-be NBA and NFL draftees go through do, however, give one pause. Football players attend combines where their "physicality" is measured in height, weight, arm length, wing spread, hand size, speed, and jumping ability—a practice that conjures up uneasy comparisons to the auction block.

Many White coaches are ignorant of the experiences and sensibilities of their Black players. Although many people these days are hypersensitive to statements they perceive as micro-aggressive, sexist, or racist, what Creighton head basketball coach Greg McDermott told his players after a loss to Xavier University in 2021 was deafening in its lack of historical awareness: "Guys, we got to stick together," McDermott told his players. "We need both feet in. I need everybody to stay on the plantation. I can't have anybody leave the plantation."[24]

The labor of D-I athletes—primarily African Americans in men's basketball and football—is exploited to enable the huge salaries of D-I coaches, athletic directors, and NCAA executives. Coaches like Nick Saban and Dabo Swinney made around $10 million a year while their players, until recent NIL deals, got a tuition coupon. Duke's full tuition is $56,000. In-state tuition at Alabama is $10,800, out-of-state $29,000. In other words, Saban made about 800 times what an in-state Alabaman is guaranteed for playing Crimson Tide football.[25]

Professional franchises share revenues between the owners, the front office, players, and coaches. With the exception of owners, stars on professional teams make much more on average than others in the organization. In the NCAA, the relationship is reversed. Marketing executive Sonny Vaccaro, the man behind Michael Jordan's "Air Jordan" Nike deal, says that "ninety percent of the NCAA revenue is produced by one percent of the athletes. Go to the skill positions. Ninety percent African Americans." He calls the NCAA a "fraud."[26]

The Power Five athletic departments depend on D-I football and men's basketball programs to help cover the deficits incurred by the rest of their athletic programs. The predominance of Black men in the two revenue-producing sports means that they subsidize sports such as women's volleyball, soccer, lacrosse, gymnastics, softball, rowing, and equestrian, and men's sports such as baseball, gymnastics, golf, lacrosse, and wrestling. Rowing and equestrian are not equal opportunity sports. Except for track and field and women's basketball, White athletes overwhelmingly dominate non-revenue sports. As of 2015, non-White women made up more than 26 percent of the college population but only 17.5 percent of the women athletes.[27]

In a study done by the Aspen Institute's Project Play, "children from families making more than $100,000 per year are twice as likely to play sports as those from families earning less than $25,000 per year." Given the huge amount of money parents must spend to place their kids on youth club teams, only relatively well-off families can afford the costs of high-level competition that might land their son or daughter a college scholarship, mostly in non-revenue sports. In 2018, *The Atlantic* journalist Saahil Desai wrote an article titled, "College Sports Are Affirmative Action for Rich White Students." The NCAA estimated that 61 percent of all student-athletes were White, most of them participating in such sports as golf, water polo, fencing, lacrosse, and sailing. None of the 232 D-I sailors were Black, and 85 percent of the lacrosse players and 90 percent of the ice hockey players were White. "It's curious to me that these elite universities are holding on to these policies," observes Harvard Professor Natasha Warikoo, "because I think they expose the contradictions of what universities do in admissions. They're blatantly privileging already privileged groups."[28]

Arizona State University sports historian Victoria L. Jackson ran track at the University of North Carolina, and she understands that her scholarship was subsidized by the moneymakers at UNC—men's basketball and football teams—which are overwhelmingly manned by Black players. Black men at UNC account for 2.8 percent of the undergraduate student body but 62 percent of the football and basketball player population; 45 percent finish a degree (compared to 74 percent for Black non-athletes). Jackson acknowledges her debt to Black athletes:

> Thanks to the labor of football and basketball players, I did not pay for college, took full advantage of attending one of the top public universities in the nation, and traveled to cool places on the school's dime. But for those [football and basketball players] who don't go on to make millions as pros after graduation—and the vast majority of Division I football players don't—the NCAA narrative simply doesn't apply. This divide correlates with race. Nonrevenue athletes are mostly White, while revenue-sport athletes are disproportionately Black. This is especially true at the most elite sports schools, the Power Five conferences.[29]

In *The Last Amateurs* (2000), highly regarded and prolific sportswriter John Feinstein praised the Patriot League for maintaining the academic integrity of its basketball programs, even if it resulted in losing seasons.[30] With the exception of Army and Navy, the other five members of the Patriot League at the time—Bucknell, Colgate, Holy Cross, Lafayette, and Lehigh—had an overwhelmingly White student body. All the schools in the Patriot League had high standards for admittance, including athletes. Although Feinstein does not go into the family finances of the players in the league, it is likely that they came from well-off households. The 2020–21 Lehigh women's basketball team had one Black player, as did Bucknell. Colgate had three, Lafayette five.

The Ivy League is the other D-I conference that does not give athletic scholarships, but it is easier for athletes to get into the Ivy League schools, where 65 percent of the players are White.[31] Harvard's annual survey of first-year students found that "nearly half of recruited athletes in the class of 2022 came from families making $250,000 per year or more, compared to only one-third of the entire class."[32]

Taylor Branch says that "the tragedy at the heart of college sports is not that some college athletes are getting paid, but that more of them are not."[33] He draws parallels between colonialism and the "well-meaning paternalists" who cared about the welfare of their subject peoples, as though the system benefitted the colonized in their long path to democracy, economic prosperity, and political independence.[34] There is no doubt that those who run the NCAA system have perpetrated the myth that D-I men's basketball and football is for the good of the "student-athlete." Everyone knows about the serious inequities in the NCAA system, and one wonders whether the authorities are willfully blind to any injustices, are paternalists who really believe in the myth, or simply don't care.

From the early 1970s to the mid-1980s, for example, only four Memphis State basketball players graduated. None were Black. The local leader of the NAACP charged that "athletes are allowed to take courses with no depth, that require no study, and lead to no degree." Murray Sperber called it the "hideaway curricula." In the early 1980s, under UNLV head coach Jerry Tarkanian, almost half of the credits taken by men's basketball players were in physical education and anthropology. Even top institutions like Princeton have developed soft offerings for athletes. One not-so-hard geology course offered there was dubbed "Rocks for Jocks."[35] Abolishing the current system will not hurt opportunities for minorities to get an education, as some argue.

Some defenders of the NCAA system argue that athletic scholarships open the door to a university education for Blacks, whose presence diversifies campuses. The latter might be true if the top-level athletes were treated like other students; instead, they are separated into special dorms and largely channeled into the same easy classes, which does little to integrate a campus. At many rural universities, a knee-jerk reaction to a Black person walking around campus is to assume that a person is an athlete. This assumption is too often correct. At a school like Miami University, a so-called "public ivy" that is overwhelmingly attended by relatively affluent White students, about one-third of the 2019 Miami football team was Black.[36]

Academically unprepared or indifferent athletes, regardless of race, take seats and scholarship money away from other students whose main goal is to get an education. Many of the latter do not have the financial wherewithal to attend college. According to *The Atlantic* journalist Jemele Hill, "Black men make up only 2.45% of the total undergraduate population of the 65 schools in the so-called Power Five athletic conferences. Yet Black men make up 55% of the football players in those conferences and 56% of basketball players."[37] In 2020, the Institute for Diversity and Ethics in Sport found that White athletes graduate at a rate 16.3 percent higher than their Black teammates. Another study in 2021 put the number at 15.6 percent.[38]

Exorbitant spending on intercollegiate sports undermines efforts to diversify campuses, especially as state legislatures have cut spending for public universities. Schools have had to increase tuition and fees to make up the difference. As one college president asked rhetorically, "Did declining state support force us to play Division I basketball? Did the legislature require us to build that nifty exercise facility?" Tighter budgets have resulted in fewer and less generous scholarships for minorities and needy students. Minorities have been saddled with the greatest debt. According to education historian Jonathan Zimmerman, "four out of five African Americans graduate college with debt; on average they carry 70 percent more than White students do."[39]

The Professional Pipe Dream

Impoverished Black athletes coming from poorer high schools often see sports as their only way out, but the playing field has rarely been a springboard to sustainable economic security. While the focus here is on NCAA D-I sports, the marriage of sports and education in secondary education has a long history too. The link between communities and their high school sports might be even more difficult to break, because many small towns rally around their teams, and game nights are big social events. The most visible example of this is Texas high school football, displayed in full glory in the 2004 movie *Friday Night Lights*. Sports and the remote promise of a full D-I athletic scholarship (let alone a pro career) are no replacement for a solid secondary education to learn academic or vocational skills. The high school sports hero, if he does not go off to college, is left with on-field memories and little else. There aren't even any serious organized sports programs for post-grads. Their athletic careers are over.

A sad example is Glades Central High School in Belle Glade, Florida, which has produced several NFL players. A muckraking book on the football team is aptly titled *Muck City*. Author Bryan Mealer calls it "a place so removed from modern society that some families had resorted to catching rainwater to survive." When former Glades receiver Jessie Lee Hester was drafted in the first round in 1985, it was discovered that Belle Glade had the highest per capita cases of AIDS in the world.

Chapter Six

Mealer writes that, for talented players, football is "like salvation itself." The rest are left behind.[40]

Young high school players are encouraged to think that they will make the big time. Every kid has dreams, but the chances of landing a pro contract for life-changing money are slim. Sports historian Benjamin Rader estimates that the odds of a high school athlete making it to the pros is about 1 in 15,000.[41] Only about 2 percent of high school athletes score an athletic scholarship.[42] Less than 2 percent of D-I athletes go on to play professionally, and only 5 percent of those players in the "revenue sports"—men's basketball and football.[43]

The Amateur Athletic Union (AAU) is an organization that sponsors elite youth teams that play all over the country to gain exposure for their players, with the dream of an NBA career clearly planted in their heads. The AAU even holds a national basketball championship for second-grade boys. "When you think about it, it is ludicrous," admits Dante Jackson, who runs an AAU team out of Tacoma, Washington. "But a lot of parents are into it. It is our mission to compete on the national level every year."[44] Parents spend tens of thousands of dollars to chase a free ride to college, or better yet, the big jackpot of a pro contract. It's a long shot, because only 1.2 percent of NCAA basketball players go to the NBA, and 1.6 percent of the football players make the NFL. A measly .08 percent of senior high school football players are drafted by the NFL, and only .03 percent of basketball players are drafted by the NBA.[45] The message to athletes should be to use their scholarship to get a good education and a marketable skill.

One long-time AAU basketball coach in Texas, Erven Davis, admitted that the "amateur" association is riddled with characters who dangle money in front of prospects and their parents: "It gets bad, man. People offering kids and parents all kinds of stuff—stuff that people get into trouble for."[46] One unscrupulous coach concocted a fictitious Bishop Sycamore High School of Columbus, Ohio, as a front for would-be college players. The school's website listed no address, and the school was not registered with the Ohio Department of Education. It didn't appear that there was any organized school or curriculum.[47] It was a "school" for athletes—without an education. The same can be said for many D-I universities.

Nevertheless, the promise of big money has encouraged ambitious entrepreneurs to form new leagues for teenagers with the express purpose of guiding them to the NBA. One such business is Overtime Elite, which has created a league with six teams playing in Atlanta and provides coaches, tutors, and facilities for youngsters to hone their skills. Florida State basketball coach Leonard Hamilton thinks that the young people playing in these types of leagues need a dose of reality. "Making the NBA is extremely hard," he notes. "How many of these kids are really going to get there? . . . There are 6,000 kids playing Division I basketball every year, and only about 30 kids have a chance to end up in the NBA."[48]

The average career in the four big pro sports in the United States—basketball, football, baseball, and hockey—lasts fewer than four years. Some of those who do make it to the show quickly lose their money on cars, parties, and mansions. Former NFL player Adewale Ogunleye recognized this problem and subsequently started partnerships with banks and athletes to promote "creating and preserving Black wealth."[49]

Evidently, the basketball and football players were not enrolled in business and finance courses, because a shocking number of NBA and NFL players end up bankrupt. *Sports Illustrated* studied the problem in 2009, finding that approximately three out of five NBA players go bankrupt within five years after retirement; almost 80 percent of NFL players are bankrupt or in some "financial stress" only two years after leaving the game.[50]

The NCAA sports system is doing players a disservice if it dupes them into thinking they will get a pro contract that will set them up for life. There are millions of doctors, teachers, lawyers, and businesspeople among many other college-educated professionals, but there are fewer than 500 slots on NBA teams and about 1,500 on NFL teams. Football players play an average of just longer than three years, and sadly, many are broke after their football careers end. The 1994 documentary film *Hoop Dreams,* about the dashed hopes of two Chicago-area high school basketball phenoms, is a cautionary tale about the long odds of making the pros.

Given the infinitesimal chances of making it to the big time, it is hard to argue that anyone in the entertainment business (of which college sports are a part) is a useful role model for young kids. Henry Louis Gates Jr., a noted professor of humanities at Harvard University, says that "an African American youngster has about as much chance of becoming a professional athlete as he or she does of winning the lottery. The tragedy for our people, however, is that few of us accept the truth.... The blind pursuit of attainment in sports is having a devastating effect our people." One national survey found that more than half of Black high school athletes think they can make the pros.[51]

Historian David Wiggins, the author of several important books on African American sports, agrees with Gates.

> [I am] hard pressed to see how the success of a handful of elite African American athletes can eliminate the myriad racial problems and inequality in the United States. In fact, I take the position of sportswriter Kevin Blackstone [sic], who makes the case that the 'games we love' have not been 'in the vanguard of social change' in the United States. The most famous racial advances in sport have typically followed rather than preceded major civil rights and social movements.[52]

Former basketball coaches John Thompson and John Chaney, who had benefited from players with marginal academic credentials, opposed Proposition 48—the minimum grade and standardized test requirements that the NCAA set in 1986 for athletes to get into college—on the basis that standardized tests were culturally biased against African Americans. Tennis great Arthur Ashe and sociologist Harry Edwards favored the benchmark academic standards, arguing that they would refocus athletes on school first, sports second. Sports offered kids a small window for success, Edwards argued.

> [The] single-minded pursuit of sport fame and fortune has spawned an institutionalized triple tragedy in Black society: the tragedy of thousands upon thousands of Black youths in obsessive pursuit of sports goals that the overwhelming majority of them will never attain; the tragedy of the personal and cultural underdevelopment that afflicts so many successful and unsuccessful Black sports aspirants; and the tragedy of cultural and institutional underdevelopment throughout Black society at least in some part as a consequence of the draining in talent potential toward sports and away from other vital areas of occupational and career emphasis, such as medicine, law, economics, politics, education, and technical fields.[53]

More recently, Edwards has said that given the failure of society to provide other avenues of success for African Americans, sports is the last "hook and handle" to lift them out of poverty and dead-end lives.[54] "The emphasis should be upon why society puts that racist emphasis upon Black sports achievement," Edwards now contends. "And secondly, why is Black achievement limited to sports in disproportionately high numbers, and not at least representative across the full spectrum of high-prestige occupational categories?"[55]

The NCAA's Fight Against Gender Equality

The NCAA's record on gender equality is also disappointing. A year before the passage of Title IX in 1972, girls comprised less than 7 percent of high school athletes. About 2 percent of college athletic budgets was dedicated to women's sports.[56] The men running intercollegiate sports did not willingly give women the chance to play. That took the congressional Title IX legislation, which forced athletic departments to treat women equally.

This is not to say, however, that US representatives and senators were necessarily more enlightened than NCAA bureaucrats. Just as civil rights legislation had passed in the mid-1960s in part because of Soviet criticism of Jim Crow, Title IX was driven by Soviet propaganda about the equal legal rights enjoyed by women in the USSR, as evidenced by the trouncing that American women took at the Olympic Games at the hands of Soviet athletes. Three years after the passage of Title IX, Senator Roman Hruska (R-Neb) sounded the alarm about what gender equity would do to big-time football programs: "Are we going to let Title IX kill the goose that lays the golden eggs in those colleges and universities with a major revenue-producing sport?"[57]

The NCAA also marginalized the AAU and, after Title IX passed, took on the Association of Intercollegiate Athletics for Women (AIAW). "The NCAA went to war with the AIAW in 1979 by leveraging its finances and prestige," Kemper writes, "offering athletic scholarships, championship events, and paid travel for participating teams to lure a membership of almost a thousand schools on the eve of their battle with the NCAA, most of them abandoned the AIAW for the NCAA, and by 1983 the AIAW ceased operations."[58]

Women did not immediately benefit from Title IX or the NCAA's takeover of their sports. A 1987 study found that "fewer championships in fewer divisions are available to women [under the NCAA] than were available in 1981–82, the last year of the AIAW." Women even lost control of their teams. In 1973, 92 percent of women's teams were coached by women, and women ran 95 percent of their athletic programs. By 1984, the number of women coaches had dropped to 53 percent and women ran only 14 percent of the athletic programs.[59] A decade later, 21 percent of women's athletic programs were headed by women—a modest increase.[60] Many athletic departments merged their separate women's and men's divisions, leaving more men governing and coaching women's sports.[61] In the fifty years since the Title IX legislation, the number of all women coaches at D-I schools has actually decreased by nearly half.[62]

The NCAA and athletic directors have been railing against Title IX ever since it passed, especially at mid-major D-I schools that spend millions to provide the mandated equal numbers of athletic scholarships for women at publicly funded schools. NCAA executive director Walter Byers predicted that Title IX might be the "possible doom of intercollegiate sports." In 1975, John Fuzak of the NCAA wrote to the Ford administration, "The HEW [Health, Education, and Welfare] concepts of Title IX as expressed could seriously damage if not destroy the major men's intercollegiate athletic programs."[63]

Nearly half a century later, some athletic departments are still not sincere about treating women athletes equally. Although progress has been made, the NCAA is still largely run by the good ol' boys' network who resent Title IX and loathe sharing profits derived from men's sports with women. Mid-major athletic departments run multimillion-dollar deficits because their football and men's basketball teams are not revenue producing. Except for a few basketball teams, women's sports do not make money for athletic departments.

The NCAA 2018–19 Division I Manual reads, "It is the responsibility of each member institution to comply with federal and state laws regarding gender equity."[64] Big schools like Michigan, Alabama, and Iowa have taken to recruiting women for their rowing teams just to get the same number of women and men on scholarship. Even Kansas State, a school with no suitable water course nearby, started a big rowing program. Kansas State's women's rowing coach lamented, "Winters can be horrendous. The amount of water time is minimal. You can't recruit people who have rowed before [in high school or in clubs]. We have no tank [indoor practice facility]. No real facilities."[65]

As an organization linked to institutions of higher education, it might be expected that the NCAA would be more sympathetic to issues of gender equity, but this is far from reality. This state of affairs came into full view during the 2021 NCAA men's and women's basketball tournaments. In that year's contests, the men had access to fully equipped workout gyms, while the women's workout rooms were furnished with a few light free weights. According to one journalist, "[The women also] received far less in their swag bag, and poorer food options.... The men were given even more reliable COVID tests." Noted *Washington Post* columnist Sally Jenkins pulled no punches, writing, "Sick and tired of the chiseling administrators with their million-dollar salaries and monstrous heaps of revenue who act like women's basketball players should be thankful for a uniform that isn't funded by a bake sale." Stanford head coach Tara VanDerveer concurred, "A lot of what we've seen this week is evidence of blatant sexism.... The message that is being sent to our female athletes is that you are not valued at the same level as your male counterparts."[66]

When the weight room discrepancy made the news, critics also pointed out that the men had sixty-eight teams in their tournament, the women only sixty-four, and that the NCAA paid for the men's National Invitational Tournament (NIT), but not the women's. The NCAA claims that the women's NCAA tournament yields "no net revenue," although nearly eighty companies sponsored TV ads for the 2021 tournament. The NCAA combines its TV revenues and keeps its accounting hidden from view. "Part of the issue," says financial analyst Daniel Rascher, "is that they blend the revenue from media deals. When you start pulling at threads, you find the NCAA has a highly flexible definition of 'costs', amid a tangle of revenue streams, unallocated funds, resources, and values-in-kind."[67]

Washington Post reporters Ben Strauss and Molly Hensley-Clancy claim that the NCAA has understated the value of the women's tournament by nearly $100 million. The women's contract is part of a $500 million ESPN package of twenty-four championships. The NCAA has said the women's event is worth just 15 percent of that deal, or about $75 million. But people in the industry, including some who worked on that pact, say the women's tourney actually accounts for one-third of the total revenue, or $167 million.[68]

After the weight room screw up, the NCAA hired the law firm Kaplan Hecker & Fink to study equity in D-I sports. One wonders if the NCAA expected to be exonerated and praised for its inquiry into how it might level the playing ground for men and women. Instead, the law firm's report was scathing: "With respect to women's basketball, the NCAA has not lived up to its stated commitment to 'diversity, inclusion and gender equity among its student-athletes, coaches, and administrators. . . . [The NCAA systems] are designed to maximize the value of and support to the Division I Men's Basketball Championship as the primary source of funding for the NCAA and its membership."[69] As a possible corrective, the firm suggested that the men's and women's tournaments take place at a common site for "cross-promotion of the events," estimating that this would raise the worth of the women's tourney to somewhere around $100 million by 2025, with the worth of the men's games coming in around ten times that.[70]

While women athletes have much better chances of playing D-I sports today than they did before the passing of Title IX, the NCAA and its members have resisted providing equal opportunities for women and minorities to land administrative and coaching jobs. Academic departments have made great strides in diversifying their faculty over the last few decades, although a PhD is usually required to get a job. An average doctoral program takes six years.[71] Faculties search diligently for candidates to make their faculties more diverse, even though in some fields there is a dearth of qualified candidates. The hiring process for tenure-track faculty usually takes several months from the time the administration gives the go-ahead to fill a position to the time the winning candidate accepts an offer. The nationwide searches thoroughly evaluate candidates for their teaching credentials and publication records. Except for occasional "spousal hires" to retain other valued faculty, familial and friendship ties have nothing to do with hires.

College football and men's basketball coaches are often hired within days of a job coming open. In these realms, the good ol' boys' network is alive and well, and nepotism runs rampant. The sons of Rick Pitino (Richard), Monte Kiffin (Lane), Eddie Sutton (Sean), John Thompson (John III), Bobby Bowden (Tommy), and Lou Holtz (Skip) readily come to mind. Revered coaches can even name their own successors. No academic department chair can just offer an open job to a son or daughter or to a good friend.[72] It is no wonder that the record of diversity hiring in athletic departments remains so dismal.

Keeping the White Male Power Structure

There is no excuse for not hiring women and minorities in college athletic administrations. Unlike the relatively small number of elite athletes at the college level, qualified women and minority administrators and coaches abound. An undergraduate degree is all that is required to run an athletic program, which means that current administrators either overlook qualified minority and female candidates or don't even bother to solicit their applications.

As of early 2022, there was one Black head coach in the NFL—this at a time when 70 percent of the players were Black.[73] The NCAA and its athletic departments are no different from the NFL and other big businesses that long have been, and still are, almost exclusively run by White males. A vast majority of FBS coaches are White, while most of their players are African American. Athletic department staff are also still overwhelmingly White and male. In short, it is White guys who decide who are amateurs and therefore eligible to play, as well as dictate the rules of the games and how players are to act on and off the field. These White male elites dictate class, racial, and gender relations through sports, securing their hold on political and economic power.[74]

In 2018, the Institute for Diversity and Ethics in Sports at Central Florida State University studied the personnel of university leadership positions in the FBS that were directly or indirectly connected to sports, including presidents, athletic directors, football coaches, and conference commissioners. The findings were damning: of the 395 leadership positions included in the study, Whites held 337, or about 85 percent. Whites held 62.5 percent of the assistant football coaching positions, while 54.2 percent of their players were Black. Richard Lapchick, the head of the institute and the report's lead author, described the progress in diversity hiring as "glacial."[75] If college administrators were serious about diversity, they would insist on change. Apparently, they are more comfortable hiring athletic directors and coaches who look like them.

The numbers speak for themselves. About 14 percent of Americans are Black. In 1989, 57 percent of D-I basketball players were Black, but only 9.1 percent of D-I schools had Black coaches. Only 4 of 175 D-I football coaches were Black, and 9 of 263 women's coaches.[76] Progress in this area, too, has grown at a snail's pace. In 2015, Black men made up fewer than 25 percent of D-I men's basketball coaches—this at a time when well more than half of the D-I male athletes were Black.[77] Of the 130 schools in the FBS, only 15 had Black head coaches in 2017. There were twenty-two coaching changes in that same year, but only three Black coaches were hired. White football coaches made up 89 percent of FBS coaches. Black offensive and defensive coordinators were similarly vastly under-represented.[78] As of late 2021, the Big Ten had five Black men's coaches but only two Black women's coaches. The Big East had six Black men's coaches, the ACC five, the SEC two, and the Big Twelve one. The PAC-12 had none. Overall, nineteen out of seventy-six full-time head coaches in the Power Five conferences were Black.[79]

In 2021, Minnesota athletic director Mark Coyle hired Ben Johnson, an African American, to coach men's basketball. Prior to that, in his five years on the job, all of Coyle's eleven head coaching hires were White. Given that Minnesota was the only Big Ten school that did not have a person of color as a president, athletic director, or head coach, Coyle was under some pressure to hire a Black coach.[80] Of course, there were qualified Black and women coaches who had been passed over in the past. The best coach in Minnesota might be Minnesota Lynx Coach Cheryl Reeve. She has the highest winning percentage of any coach in WNBA history and has won four championships. No woman, including Reeve, was even mentioned as a possible candidate for the Gopher men's basketball job.

Few women are trusted to run D-I athletic departments, even though almost half of all college athletes are women. "We're talking about sports programs that are balanced by gender, roughly," observes University of Pittsburgh's chancellor Patrick D. Gallagher, "so I don't see any reason why, in a world where we're half women and half men, we shouldn't see similar parity." As of 2019, Pitt's Heather Lyke was one of only four women who headed the athletic department of the sixty-five colleges in the five biggest conferences (6.2 percent).[81] In 2013, just more than 8 percent of all D-I athletic directors were women.[82] Six years later, that percentage had only climbed by a measly three points to 11 percent.[83]

Most of the D-II and D-III schools with female athletic directors do not have football programs. Those who justify this are the people who ask how a woman who has never played the sport can lead a big-time football program at the D-I level, as though playing a sport at a higher level is a prerequisite for the job. "We're trying to make a cultural shift—that's the big piece," says Pattie Phillips, the head of Women's Leaders in College Sports, "and those things don't happen overnight."

The organization has a roster of about 300 women who seek an athletic director or conference commissioner position. Sandy Barbour at Penn State had the only salary that approached $1 million in 2017–18; at least seventeen of her male counterparts made that or more.[84]

Studies on leadership have shown that women are generally more competent, while men are more confident. The *New York Times* blamed old prejudices that male administrators have about putting women in charge, in business or in sports: "When a woman doesn't lead well, it's evidence that women can't lead. When a man doesn't work out, he wasn't the right fit." Harvard conducted studies that refuted these biases, finding that teams that have men and women coaches do better than those with an all-male coaching staff. Furthermore, "women outscored men on 17 of the 19 capabilities that differentiate excellent leaders from average or poor ones."[85]

After March Madness in 2015, Sally Jenkins called out the NCAA for its hypocritical, self-righteous call for diversity and an end to discrimination. "In looking at their demographics and hiring practices," Jenkins wrote, "for a moment I mistook them for a litter of rare Chinese albino kittens." She pointed out that nearly 88 percent of the D-I athletic directors were White, and that 90 percent were men. Seventy percent of the assistant athletic directors were White, likely ensuring that the trend will continue in the future. The NCAA's record of hiring minorities and women was worse than that of every professional league, dead last for hiring minorities, and for women, tied for last with the NFL. Texas women's athletic director Chris Plonsky termed the record "dismal." As of 2015, all but one of the thirty D-I commissioners were White.[86]

Again, change has been slow. In 2018, White men held 77 percent of the athletic directorships of the 130 FBS schools.[87] Two years later, the Institute for Diversity and Ethics in Sport unsurprisingly found significant "underrepresentation" of women and people of color in leadership jobs in the FBS. The institute gave the universities an "F" in gender hiring and a "B-" for racial hiring.[88]

White men not only dominate the leadership positions in the NCAA and athletic departments but they are also overrepresented on women's coaching staffs. Before 1972, the few women's teams were mostly coached by women. The percentage of women coaches in all sports has been in decline for decades. When Title IX created more women's teams and well-paying coaching jobs, men gobbled them up. In 2013, there were no women coaches of a D-I men's basketball team.[89] The

Institute for Diversity and Ethics in Sports found that in 2015, men coached more than 60 percent of D-I women's basketball teams.[90]

Women have made little headway. As of 2019, 60 percent of all women's college teams were still coached by men, while women headed only 3 percent of the men's teams.[91] In 2021, there were no women coaching D-I football, baseball, or men's basketball and ice hockey teams.[92] Evidently, athletic directors think that women can't possibly control young men, are too emotional, or don't understand the games as well as men.

Even when Black men and women land coaching positions, athletic directors hold them to a higher standard. They are in the hot seat from the start. Penn State head football coach David Franklin acknowledges that Black coaches "feel like we carry an extra weight." In 2018, CBS Sports conducted an anonymous survey of FBS coaches: "Three of the nine coaches labeled as 'overrated' were Black: Franklin, [Florida State's Willie] Taggart, and Stanford's David Shaw." Shaw's Cardinals win nearly three-fourths of their games and have been to three Rose Bowls.[93] Taggert was fired after only two seasons at Florida State.

Defenders of the current D-I system argue that administrators have to hire the most qualified athletic directors and coaches. But what is the harm of making sure that women and minorities have an equal shot at those jobs? Hiring unqualified faculty could have a negative impact on the career paths of hundreds of students. There is a lot riding on expert mentoring of future doctors, scientists, economists, and lawyers; for some of these professions, decisions can mean life or death. If a coach does not quite get that blocking technique right or correct a flawed shooting motion, is that really crucial to the long-term future of most athletes? People forget that the NCAA is a sports organization.

The NCAA is now wrestling with the issue of transgender athletes competing in women's sports, challenging long-held notions of rigid, traditional gender roles. In addition to discrimination against minorities and women, college sports—especially football—have promoted a masculine character defined by hard work, toughness, and discipline. Wimpy domesticated boys need not apply. Football guys were the antithesis of the "sissy" or "powder puff youths" as Notre Dame coach Knute Rockne called them.[94]

In 2021, at least twenty-eight state legislatures initiated laws to ban transgender women from competing in women's sports. Nearly half of women in a *Politico* poll supported such a ban.[95] Because the cases are so rare, this is, as they say, a solution seeking a problem. Don't look to the NCAA for enlightenment on this subject. In fact, transgender athletes have to take testosterone suppression drugs for a year before they are allowed to compete in women's events.[96] Once more, one can expect that the organization will remain behind the times in the fair treatment of transgender athletes, just as it has been with minorities and women.

Notes

1. Dan Wolken, "States Lit Fuse for College Athletes," *USA Today*, November 12, 2019, 3C.

2. See Donald Spivey, *Racism, Activism, and Integrity in College Football: The Bates Must Play Movement* (Durham, NC: Carolina Academic Press, 2021).

3. Michael Hurd, *Black College Football, 1892-1992: One Hundred Years of History, Education, and Pride* (Virginia Beach, VA: Donning Publishers, 1993), 27-8.

4. See Richard Ian Kimball, "Football Culture at New South Universities: Lost Cause and Old South Memory, Modernity, and Martial Manhood," in Christian K. Anderson and Amber C. Fallucca, eds., *The History of American College Football: Institutional Policy, Culture, and Reform* (New York: Routledge, 2021), 37-63.

5. Oriard, *King Football*, 85.

6. Zoe L. Almeida and Devin B. Srivastava, "Reaching Across Harvard's 'Color Line,'" *The Harvard Crimson*, October 26, 2017, accessed June 29, 2022, https://www.thecrimson.com/article/2017/10/26/harvard-color-line-sports-athletics/.

7. Spivey, *Racism, Activism, and Integrity*, 15.

8. Watterson, *College Football*, 312-3.

9. Watterson, *College Football*, 316-7.

10. Victor Mather, "When Loyola-Chicago Broke a Racial Barrier 55 Years Ago," *New York Times*, March 29, 2018, accessed February 20, 2020, https://www.nytimes.com/2018/03/29/sports/loyola-chicago-1963-ncaa-tournament.html; see also Charles Martin, *Benching Jim Crow: The Rise and Fall of the Color Line in Southern College Sports, 1890-1980* (Urbana, IL: University of Illinois Press, 2010); and Lane Demas, *Integrating the Gridiron: Black Civil Rights and American College Football* (New Brunswick, NJ: Rutgers University Press, 2010), 72-74.

11. Watterson, *College Football*, 309.

12. Berry Tramel, "Johnny Bright Incident: Wilbanks Smith Speaks," *The Oklahoman*, April 20, 2006, accessed June 30, 2022, https://www.oklahoman.com/story/news/2006/04/20/johnny-bright-incident-wilbanks-smith-speaks/61889340007/.

13. Demas, *Integrating the Gridiron*, 59-61.

14. Watterson, *College Football*, 322-3; see also David K. Wiggins, "'The Future of College Athletics is at Stake': Black Athletes and Racial Turmoil on Three Predominantly White University Campuses, 1958-1972," *Journal of Sport History* (Winter 1988): 304-333.

15. Demas, *Integrating the Gridiron*, 118.

16. Hurd, *Black College Football*, 45.

Chapter Six

17. Kemper, *College Football*, 1.

18. S. Kaazim Naqvi, "O-H! I-O! Black Students, Black Athletes, and Ohio State Football, 1968-1976," *Journal of Sport History* 40, no. 1 (Spring 2013): 111–126.

19. Oriard, *King Football*, 313.

20. Gorn and Goldstein, *A Brief History*, 232.

21. Uncredited, "'Market' in Football is Charged," *The Lantern*, December 2, 1946, accessed March 22, 2021, https://osupublicationarchives.osu.edu/?a=d&d=LTN 19461202-01&e=-------en-20--1--txt-txIN.

22. Byers, *Unsportsmanlike Conduct*, 2–3.

23. Branch, "The Shame."

24. Victor Mather, "Creighton Suspends Basketball Coach Over 'Plantation' Pep Talk," *New York Times*, March 5, 2021, accessed March 23, 2021, https://www.nytimes.com/2021/03/05/sports/ncaabasketball/creighton-greg-mcdermott-plantation.html?auth=login-email&login=email.

25. "Undergraduate Tuition & Fees, Duke Financial Services: Bursar, accessed January 12, 2022, https://finance.duke.edu/bursar/TuitionFees/tuition; and University of Alabama, Student Aid: Cost of Attendance, accessed January 12, 2022, https://financialaid.ua.edu/cost/.

26. Branch, "The Shame."

27. Susan K. Cahn, *Coming on Strong: Gender and Sexuality in Women's Sport* (Urbana, IL: University of Illinois Press, 2015), 288.

28. Saahil Desai, "College Sports Are Affirmative Action for Rich White Students," *The Atlantic*, October 23, 2018, accessed March 22, 2022, https://www.theatlantic.com/education/archive/2018/10/college-sports-benefits-white-students/573688/.

29. Victoria L. Jackson, "A Jim Crow Divide in College Sports, *Chicago Tribune*, January 16, 2018, accessed April 29, 2020, https://www.chicagotribune.com/opinion/commentary/ct-perspec-college-sports-ncaa-black-athletes-exploited-0117-20180116-story.html.

30. See John Feinstein, *The Last Amateurs: Playing for Glory and Honor in Division I College Basketball* (Boston: Little, Brown, and Company, 2000).

31. Desai, "College Sports Are Affirmative Action."

32. Matthew Walsh, "College Sports: Affirmative Action for White People," *Brown Political Review*, December 10, 2019, accessed December 28, 2020, https://brownpoliticalreview.org/2019/12/college-sports-affirmative-action-for-white-people.

33. Branch, "The Shame."

34. Branch, "The Shame."

35. Sperber, *College Sports Inc.*, 282.

36. Miami Redhawks 2019 Football Roster, accessed March 15, 2021, https://miamiredhawks.com/sports/football/roster/2019.

37. Jemele Hill, "It's Time for Black Athletes to Leave White Colleges," *The Atlantic*, October 2019, accessed February 21, 2020, https://www.theatlantic.com/magazine/archive/2019/10/black-athletes-should-leave-white-colleges/596629/.

38. Unattributed, "Race Gap Widens," *Star Tribune*, December 23, 2020, S2.

39. Jonathan Zimmerman, "What is College Worth?" *New York Review of Books*, July 2, 2020, 36–37.

40. Jay Jennings, "Must Win," *New York Times Book Review*, December 30, 2012, 10.

41. Rader, *American Sports*, 330.

42. William Hageman, "Investing in Kids' Athletic Future Risky," *Star Tribune*, June 11, 2014, E1.

43. Nocera and Strauss, "Here's How."

44. Sean Gregory, "Final Four for the 4-Foot Set," *Time*, July 22, 2013, 46.

45. NCAA, "Estimated Probability of Competing Professional Athletics, April 8, 2020, accessed December 18, 2020, http://www.ncaa.org/about/resources/research/estimated-probability-competing-professional-athletics; and William J. Price, "What Are the Odds of Becoming a Professional Athlete?" *The Sports Digest*, U.S. Sports Academy, accessed December 18, 2020, http://www.thesportdigest.com/archive/article/what-are-odds-becoming-professional-athlete.

46. Powell, "The Tragedy."

47. Chris Bumbaca, "Director of Mysterious HS Football Team that Played on ESPN: No 'scam,'" *USA Today*, September 1, 2021, 5C.

48. Bruce Schoenfeld, "The Teenagers Getting Six Figures to Leave Their High Schools for Basketball," *New York Times Magazine*, December 5, 2021, 27–37.

49. Scooby Axson, "Ex-athletes Teach Financial Literacy to Students at HBCUs," *USA Today*, November 16, 2021, 1B.

50. Joe Christensen, "A $77 Million Warning to Athletes," *Star Tribune*, September 23, 2018, A1.

51. George H. Sage, "Racial Inequality and Sport," in D. Stanley Eitzen, *Sport in Contemporary Society: An Anthology* (New York: Macmillan, 2000), 283.

52. David K. Wiggins, "'The Color of My Writing': Reflections on Studying the Interconnection among Race, Sport, and American Culture," *Journal of Sport History* 43, no. 3 (Fall 2016), 315. The correct spelling is Blackistone.

53. Harry Edwards, "The Decline of the Black Athlete," in David K. Wiggins and Patrick B. Miller, *The Unlevel Playing Field: A Documentary History of the African American Experience in Sport* (Urbana, IL: University of Illinois Press, 2003), 435–437. 436.

54. Wiggins, "'The Color,'" 315.

55. Harry Edwards, "The Decline," 435–437, 440–1.

56. Susan Ware, *Title IX: A Brief History with Documents* (Long Grove, IL: Waveland Press, 2007), 1; and Smith, *Pay for Play*, 141–2.

57. Ware, *Title IX*, 5.

58. Kemper, *College Football*, 219–220.

59. Sperber, *College Sports Inc.*, 327–8; and Kelly Belanger, *Invisible Seasons: Title IX and the Fight for Equity in College Sports* (Syracuse, NY: Syracuse University Press, 2016), 6, 29.

60. Sack and Staurowsky, *College Athletes for Hire*, 124. When women were finally allowed to do track and field in the 1928 Olympic Games, women's sports organizations lost power to the IOC.

61. Cahn, *Coming on Strong*, 254, 255–261.

62. Alan Blinder, Jeré Longman, and Gillian R. Brassil, "Women's Basketball Battles Second-Class Treatment," *New York Times*, April 4, 2021, 26.

63. Sack and Staurowsky, *College Athletes for Hire*, 121.

64. NCAA 2018-19 Division I Manual, 2, accessed January 15, 2021, https://www.ncaapublications.com/p-4548-2018-2019-ncaa-division-ii-manual-august-version-available-august-2018.aspx.

65. Gaul, *Billion-Dollar Ball*, 176, 181; and Duderstadt, *Intercollegiate Athletics*, 169.

66. Jim Souhan, "Women Get Token Sliver of NCAA's Pie," *Star Tribune*, March 22, 2021, C1; and Alanis Thames, "Women Get Their Share of Madness at Long Last," *New York Times*, September 30, 2021, B9.

67. Sally Jenkins, "The NCAA's Shell Game is the Real Women's Basketball Scandal," *Washington Post*, March 25, 2021, accessed March 25, 2021, https://www.washingtonpost.com/sports/2021/03/25/ncaa-women-basketball-tournament-revenue/.

68. Jenkins, "The Financial Burden."

69. Unattributed, "Review Slams NCAA, Calls for Combining Final Fours," *Star Tribune*, August 4, 2021, C11.

70. Ralph D. Russo, Associated Press, *Star Tribune*, August 3, 2021, accessed January 12, 2022, https://www.startribune.com/report-drills-ncaa-on-equity-calls-for-combined-final-four/600084428/.

71. Ilana Kowarski, "How Long Does It Take to Get a Ph.D. Degree," *U.S. News and World Report*, August 12, 2019, accessed June 24, 2020, https://www.usnews.com/education/best-graduate-schools/articles/2019-08-12/how-long-does-it-take-to-get-a-phd-degree-and-should-you-get-one#:~:text=However%2C%20there%20are%20many%20types,D.

72. See John R. Thelin, "Academics and Athletics: A Part and Apart in the American Campus," *Journal of Intercollegiate Sport*, no. 1 (2008), 73–74.

73. Jeremy Engle, "Does the N.F.L. Have a Race Problem?" *New York Times*, February 9, 2022, accessed June 30, 2022, https://www.nytimes.com/2022/02/09/learning/does-the-nfl-have-a-race-problem.html.

74. Paul Myerberg, "Black College Football Coaches Still Lack in Numbers, Respect," *USA Today*, September 28, 2018, C1.

75. Associated Press, "FBS Programs Get a D in Diversity Hiring," *Star Tribune*, October 4, 2018, C3.

76. George, *Elevating the Game*, 219.

77. Sally Jenkins, "The NCAA's Diversity Madness," *The Washington Post Weekly*, April 12, 2015, 21.

78. Myerberg, "Black College Football Coaches."

79. Marcus Fuller, "Big Ten Schools Reverse Trend with More Black Men's Basketball Coaching Hires," *Star Tribune*, December 11, 2021, C1.

80. Jim Souhan, "Coach of Color Hire at U Overdue," *Star Tribune*, March 19, 2021, C1.

81. Alan Blinder, "Countable on One Hand: The Women Leading Power Five Athletic Departments," *New York Times*, September 13, 2019, accessed December 23, 2020, https://www.nytimes.com/2019/09/13/sports/countable-on-one-hand-the-women-leading-power-five-athletic-departments.html.

82. Nicole Auerbach, "No Crashing 'Glass Ceiling'," *USA Today*, November 12, 2013, 8C.

83. Carol Hutchins, Edniesha Curry, and Meredith Flaherty, "Where Are All the Women Coaches?" *New York Times*, December 31, 2019, accessed December 23, 2020, https://www.nytimes.com/2019/12/31/opinion/Women-coaching-sports-title-ix.html.

84. Blinder, "Countable on One Hand."

85. Hutchins, Curry, and Flaherty, "Where Are All the Women Coaches?"

86. Jenkins, "The NCAA's Diversity Madness."

87. Associated Press, "Study: White Men Still Dominate Leadership Positions in FBS, *USA Today*, October 3, 2018, accessed December 23, 2020, https://www.usatoday.com/story/sports/ncaaf/2018/10/03/study-white-men-still-dominate-leadership-positions-in-fbs/38035399/.

88. Unattributed, "Diversity Rises, Still Lacking," *Star Tribune*, January 7, 2021, C6.

89. Auerbach, "No Crashing 'Glass Ceiling'."

90. Jenkins, "The NCAA's Diversity Madness."

91. Hutchins, Curry, and Flaherty, "Where Are All the Women Coaches?"

92. Hutchins, Curry, and Flaherty, "Where Are All the Women Coaches?

93. Myerberg, "Black College Football Coaches."

94. Oriard, *King Football*, 333.

95. Lindsay Crouse, "So You Want to 'Save Women's Sports'?" *New York Times*, March 28, 2021, 6.

96. NCAA Media Center, "Board of Governors Updates Transgender Participation Policy," January 19, 2022, accessed June 20, 2022, https://www.ncaa.org/news/2022/1/19/media-center-board-of-governors-updates-transgender-participation-policy.aspx.

CHAPTER SEVEN

No Contest:
Sports Rout Academics

"He lives here? I thought he just flew in for games."

—Student on seeing football star (played by Forrest Whitaker) on campus in the movie *Fast Times at Ridgemont High* (1982)[1]

Jokes abound about the smarts of college athletes. Former Florida and Ohio State football coach Urban Meyer supposedly poked fun at one of his dimmer players: "He doesn't know the meaning of the word fear. In fact, I just saw his grades, and he doesn't know the meaning of a lot of words."[2] Or, how many freshman football players does it take to change a light bulb? "None. That's a second-year course." These barbs are unkind, but sadly, with all the messages that athletes get about making the pros rather than making the grades, they ring all too true.

Under the heading "The Commitment to Amateurism," the NCAA's 2018–19 D-I Handbook reads, "Member institutions shall conduct their athletics programs for students who choose to participate in intercollegiate athletics as a part of their educational experience and in accordance with NCAA bylaws, thus maintaining a line of demarcation between student-athletes who participate in the Collegiate Model [sic] and athletes competing in the professional model."[3]

Athletes' academic progress is written right into the NCAA mission statement, but the definition of success for NCAA employees is to bring more and more money into the organization. For athletic departments, the bottom line is determined by wins, losses, and profits. In the final analysis, athletic department employees are not judged on their athletes' grade point averages and graduation rates, although they publicly promote the latter (if they are high enough). Running programs "in accordance with NCAA bylaws" is impossible when athletic department jobs depend on getting the best players on the field.

Chapter Seven

Many people working in college athletic departments are hardworking, well-meaning, honest people who really believe in the NCAA's high-minded words. Although they are certainly aware of the fiscal incongruities in the system, they are committed to the success of their athletes, including as students and citizens. However, as noted repeatedly, athletic departments operate under a system heavily weighted against prioritizing education as their core mission. In 2012, William E. Kirwan, chancellor of the University of Maryland system, issued this clear indictment of D-I sports: "We've reached the point where big-time intercollegiate athletics is undermining the integrity of our institutions, diverting presidents and institutions from their main purpose."[4]

For decades, reformers have suggested shortening football and basketball seasons so that athletes can concentrate more on their studies. The NCAA and athletic directors have ignored that idea, adding increasingly more games to get the cash register ringing more often.

Players are not to blame for the NCAA's crooked system, either. There are hundreds of players like Minnesota Gopher 2020 All-American running back Mohamed Ibrahim, whose dedication to his team and his studies made him the very model of an "amateur" intercollegiate sports athlete, but he, too, was constantly undermined as a student by the imperative to win games. "I am extremely grateful for all the individual success that I have been fortunate to accomplish during my four years as a Gopher," Ibrahim said, "however, I would not be able to accomplish any of it without my teammates and my coaches. . . . Football is the ultimate team game, and any honor I receive is shared with everyone in the program. With that said, I am looking forward to coming back and make more memories in 2021—which also will include getting my degree."[5]

When devout members of the NCAA congregation want to shore up their belief that the work they do uplifts "student-athletes," they hold up exceptions to the rule like Ibrahim. The pious bureaucrats put the blame for scandals on a few sinners who break the NCAA's commandments, not on the corrupt and contradictory legal and moral strictures of the system they maintain. There is a wide and deep chasm between the rhetoric of university leaders and the reality of what goes on in D-I sports—one that is impossible to bridge. The money in college sports is just too big, as is the prestige that comes with a championship team.

As Bear Bryant put it, "Fifty thousand people don't come to watch an English class."[6]

The teaching of a sense of morality, sportsmanship, and comradeship that Ibrahim lauds is a luxury that D-I athletic departments cannot afford to prioritize. Losers are fired whether or not they try to do right by their players. The big money in D-I sports corrupts both those who are charged with educating athletes and the athletes themselves. At the 1988 NCAA convention, Georgetown coach John Thompson told the group, "If you think that I am up here because our kids graduate from school," he said, "You're foolish. I am up here because I win."[7] "College sports has a lot of hypocrisy," Thompson once said. "I believe it is time for the NCAA to stop pretending that education is its top priority and pay college athletes."[8]

What "Higher Education"?

Gaming the academic system is the most blatant corruption in higher education.

The practice of shepherding unprepared athletes through easy majors and classes goes way back. In the old days, when male professors dominated faculties, athletic advisors had no problem finding sympathetic teachers who liked giving players passing grades. In the 1920s, USC created a junior college, abolished until 1947, for football players who did not have the credentials to get into the main university. The University of Minnesota had a similar "General College" after World War II, a proxy college shut down until 2005, after numerous academic scandals involving athletes.[9] Other schools followed this model, if not with separate colleges but with majors created primarily for men's basketball and football players. "Believe me," said Walter Byers, "there is a course, a grade, and a degree out there for everyone."[10]

Nonetheless, in the mid-2010s, the graduation rate for D-I men's basketball and football was about 50 percent.[11] In most cases, the major with which top athletes finish is not one geared to a career or even a good job; rather, it is one chosen to maintain eligibility. A 2008 *USA Today* special report found that 83 percent of the schools in the survey had "at least one sports team [that] had a quarter or more of its juniors and seniors pursuing the same major. These majors tend to be the less rigorous programs, such as watered-down social science, general studies, and physical education." Funneling athletes into these easy courses is known as 'clustering' and gives athletes more opportunities to cheat on exams.[12] After graduating from Kansas State, defensive lineman Steven Cline wised up to the value of his athletic scholarship: "What did I really go to college for? Crap classes you won't use the rest of your life? Social science is nothing specific... I was majoring in football."[13]

Business, economics, physics, chemistry, and math professors, for example, tend to grade according to hard and fast objective measures. In these courses, in-class exams are harder to crib. A student's "effort" might make a difference for some professors, but answers on a math or chemistry test are either right or wrong. Players avoid courses with such rigorous testing, lest they become ineligible. Jerry Tarkanian's Runnin' Rebels basketball team was a prime example. Two UNLV psychology professors got a hold of the transcripts of ninety-three athletes, including those of the entire basketball team. The basketball players retained their eligibility based on junior college grades made before they came to university; the basketball players' average GPA in UNLV courses was 1.96, a D+. The courses they took at UNLV were not exactly challenging either. Almost a third of the athletes' courses were taken in the Physical Education Department. "Deprived of the P.E. credits," the two professors looking into the matter noted, "most of the basketball players and some of the football players would likely be ineligible to play."[14]

Minnesota's General College—a sort of remedial community college run by the parent university—provided a place for unprepared male athletes to find easy-to-pass courses. Even still, so few students managed to graduate from the college that the university closed it in 2005. For its part, Michigan offered a sports management major that functioned much like Minnesota's General College. When the university shored up the academic requirements for the major, athletes gravitated instead toward a general studies program. In the early 2010s, for example, more than half of Baylor's football players were enrolled in general studies.[15] According to University of North Carolina historian Jay M. Smith and athletic tutor Mary Willingham, "When confronted with questions about these suspect practices, faculty and administrators at Michigan—with a few notable exceptions—clammed up, ran away, or offered Pollyannaish assurances that all was well."[16]

Frank Howard coached Clemson football for more than a quarter century. He was a proponent of higher academic standards for incoming recruits, but he knew that his job depended on winning. The problem was, at least for Howard, that Clemson's admission standards were just too high. "Every year there are five or six football players in South Carolina who cannot predict a 1.6 (GPA), and they end up going to the University of Georgia, Auburn University, and the University of Alabama. They pretty consistently beat us." And if he failed to beat these rivals, Howard said, his days at Clemson were numbered.[17]

The NCAA's tortured efforts to establish academic standards in the 1980s came apart at the seams, and inevitably, many athletes who were either unprepared to do college-level work or had no interest at all in doing it were accepted. In the late 2000s, the NCAA changed the eligibility requirements for recruits by allowing even lower SAT scores.

The recruitment of not-ready-for-college athletes in the long run hurt all athletes but disproportionately affected members of the Black community. When the group who became known as the "Black Fourteen" was thrown off the Wyoming team for wanting to wear black armbands in a 1969 game against BYU, "one of the black players told [Wyoming head football coach] Lloyd Eaton that he had come to Wyoming to get an education, Eaton corrected him, 'Son, you're wrong, you came here to play Cowboy football.'"[18] No doubt many coaches today still think that way, even if they still can't say it out loud.

Former NCAA President Mark Emmert once said, "[Universities are] providing athletes with world-class educations and world-class opportunities."[19] One must question his definition of a "world-class education," because no D-I coach is going to suggest that players take courses that they might not pass. In 2014, a Pittsburgh *Post-Gazette* study of twenty-five big college football programs identified the most popular majors for athletes: "fitness studies . . . gender studies, communications, interdisciplinary studies, and sociology." Unlike the humanities and hard sciences, where professors are likely to have tougher grade criteria, it is no secret that the "studies" majors are worked by professors with liberal inclinations to give their students a break on grades.[20] Athletic academic advisors are fully aware of that. Even at an elite school like Cal-Berkeley, interdisciplinary studies is a favorite major among athletes.[21] Not many athletes are found in "writing" majors such as English, history, and languages, where evaluation is usually an essay test rather than a multiple-choice exam, a corrected copy of which can be kept on file at the athletic department. Sciences, too, are off limits, not only because grading is more objective but because attending labs, which are usually held in the afternoon, conflicts with practice times.

Chapter Seven

Today, athletic departments have a bevy of compliance officers whose job it is to try to keep players in line. It is more difficult now to determine which professors are willing to go along with giving out easy grades, but academic advisors still root them out. Several academic advisors at D-I schools told me that athletes choose their own majors, but that they rarely pursue a major in one of the hard sciences, for example. All but one of the eighteen football players recruited to Michigan in 2004 ended up in general studies. One defensive lineman said that an academic advisor chose most of his classes and gave him help writing papers. The advisor, if she wanted to keep her job, could not afford to let the player fail.[22] One Miami University basketball player said that he was advised against majoring in business because it would interfere with practice times and games.

When challenged about the academic failings of their male athletes, athletic directors go to great pains to point out that athletes graduate at a higher rate than non-athletes. In so doing, however, they are aggregating women athletes into the numbers, thereby disguising the lower achievement levels of men's football, basketball, baseball, and hockey players.[23] Few women athletes are fooled by the lure of a big pro contract, and they know that their future depends on how they do in the classroom. For example, in 2022, Miami University boasted a 3.23 grade point average for all of its athletes, women included, but it did not publicize the grade point average of the men in its major sports that year.[24]

Miami's athletic director denied that there were any go-to majors for athletes, or even that advisors steer them into certain courses of study.[25] A Miami academic advisor did, however, acknowledge that the average GPA of men's basketball and football players hovered around 2.80, and that some of their most popular majors are family social work, sports leadership and management, and kinesiology. Additionally, there are no restrictions on how many online courses athletes can take for credit—such courses are notorious for their lack of rigor. The advisor went on to indicate that a player is allowed to miss six classes in a semester course that meets three times a week. Many professors have stricter attendance requirements, so it is unclear how or even if those missed classes are made up. He also said that with the mid-week games, first-year players need time to adapt to keeping up with their schoolwork.[26]

An academic advisor from the University of Oklahoma said that the GPA for football players was in the C+ range and was slightly higher for male basketball players. He also said that players can choose their own major, but if they end up struggling with that major, advisors are on hand to suggest another one. Players might, he said, miss four to six classes per semester—two or three in any one course—but that there were no limits on taking online courses.[27]

A Temple University academic advisor was candid and honest about the emphasis on winning and keeping players eligible at his school. According to him, among the most popular majors for all athletes were business, media production, advertising, and criminal justice, and thanks to having the luxury of traveling to and from games on charter flights, football and basketball players didn't miss much class time; those who do try to work it out with professors. Frankly, he liked the idea of separating sports from the academic side of the university, saying it would help him sleep better at night.[28]

Athletic departments are reluctant to reveal what classes their male athletes take, except when they want to highlight the few of them enrolled in rigorous majors, such as engineering or economics. For example, in 2011, *Sport Illustrated* did a piece on Stanford's star quarterback Andrew Luck, who majored in architecture, and Florida State's Myron Rolle, a Rhodes scholar. Per the *SI* reporter, "College football is still played by actual college students, though saying that usually elicits eye rolls. But even the hardened cynic would have a hard time disputing the fact that the sport's biggest name in 2011 [Stanford's Andrew Luck]—a Heisman frontrunner and projected No. 1 draft pick—takes his course reading as seriously as he does his hot reads."[29] These cases are, as noted, the exception.

The Athletes' Advantage

The University of St. Thomas (MN) jumped from D-III to D-I in 2021, and an athletic department flyer boasted that "out of 505 student athletes, 270 hold a cumulative GPA of 3.5 or better." Nothing is known about the cumulative GPA of the other 235 athletes or the difference between the GPAs of males and females. Apparently, the athletic department at St. Thomas asks anyone concerned to forget whatever they have learned in statistics class about the validity of a sample. Without a control group of non-athlete students on full or partial scholarship—those who function without the special academic, dietary, and health support systems that athletes enjoy—there is no way to judge the relative success of athletes in the classroom. Some of the information is confidential, making it difficult to research exactly what courses athletes are taking.

The comparison of the classroom performance of athletes to nonathletes also does not take into consideration that most players have a full four-year or partial scholarship and personal tutors. Many regular students have to work on the side to make ends meet. Timewise, playing sports can be akin to a full-time job, but unlike other students, athletes get priority in class registration. This is a particularly unfair perk that can crowd out opportunities for other students to get into desired (or even necessary for their major) courses. In 2007, Texas spent $450,000 on "tutoring and advising football players."[30] It is almost impossible to fail in the athlete's academic cocoon. The University of Arizona's star basketball player Channing Frye's case is typical; in the 2000s, he said that an assistant coach helped him pick his courses and told him which instructors to avoid.[31]

Most academic tutors make honest efforts to offer athletes a meaningful, well-rounded course of study, but if athletes are ineligible because a tutor has steered them into a tough major and difficult courses with unforgiving professors, tutors lose their job too. Some athletes' handlers—called "class checkers"—drive around in golf carts to make sure their charges go to class. Oklahoma calls this practice getting a player "eyeballed into class."[32]

Academic advisors crib athletes for exams and "polish up" papers, if not write them outright. Nike mogul Phil Knight gave the University of Oregon $42 million (of his $300 million in total donations) for an academic support center called the "Taj Mahal of academic services." Oregon students call it "The Jock Box."[33] An Oregon biology professor points to the academic coddling of Duck athletes: "The administration trumpets the fact that these student athletes are graduating at the rate of the [regular] student body. I say to them, the rest of the student body doesn't get all of those perks. It's a sham. The athletes are living in a different parallel universe."[34]

Every year, the *Wall Street Journal* issues the "College Football Grid of Shame," in which Power Five teams' wins and losses are combined with "how athletes are doing in the classroom, (and) how much the university subsidizes athletics at the expense of the general student body." As expected, the likes of Kansas, Ohio State, Tennessee, Michigan, and

Michigan State end up on the "embarrassing" side of the academic grid. "The PAC-12 [with such top academic schools as Stanford, Cal, and USC]," writes the *WSJ*, "has the distinction of being the only conference with more than 75% of its teams in embarrassing territory on the 2021 grid." Surprisingly, Alabama checks in on the high end.[35]

How do we explain the Crimson Tide's ranking? The Tide can recruit from the cream of the high school football crop and can afford to pass on players with a checkered past or questionable academic credentials. More importantly, football programs such as Alabama and Clemson (the latter school has a much better academic reputation) hire an army of administrators and academic advisors to keep their players in courses they can pass (and earn A's in), as well as to watch them closely to make sure that they are doing their course work. Handlers ensure that players are not getting into trouble outside of the playing field and the classroom. The NCAA's handbook is followed to the letter. Most Tide and Tigers players set their sights on the NFL, and they behave well because they are reminded over and over that a misstep can blow their chance at a big pro contract.

The NCAA knows that it is virtually impossible to adhere to all of its anachronistic, nit-picky academic rules, and that enforcement of them is spotty at best. Even for those athletic programs that sincerely try to graduate their athletes, keeping them eligible to play remains the primary objective. According to legend, one college basketball coach advised a player who got four F's and one D, "Son, looks to me like you're spending too much time on one subject."[36]

No Sheepskin in the Game

Stephon Marbury was a high school hardcourt phenom who played for one year at Georgia Tech (1995–96) before turning pro. His high school coach, Bobby Hartstein, minced no words about what the academics meant to prospective pro basketball players: "It would be wonderful to think that all these kids are there for their educations, but they're not. A lot of them are there to play basketball. And under what fair system does the minority get wealthy and the workers get nothing?"[37]

The unfortunate reality is that many athletes choose a college without considering its academic standards. The Northwesterns, Stanfords, and Notre Dames might make that pitch to a recruit, but it is an afterthought for the Alabamas, Oklahomas, and Floridas. If a college player is unhappy with his situation on the team, he can transfer to another athletic program. Few likely make the change to pursue a particular course of study at a school with a better academic reputation.

Top recruits and their families are fully aware that most athletic programs are indifferent to academics. In 2013, a group of Kentucky basketball moms signed a contract for a reality show to follow them around as they championed their sons' basketball aspirations, ostensibly for a college scholarship, but with the brass ring of big NBA money as their main goal. The mothers spent thousands of their hard-earned money paying for basketball expenses. Michelle Green was a prime candidate for reality TV; she was obnoxious and confrontational to the point that she had been thrown out of a gym. "I'm an animal," Green admitted. "I heckle everybody—the parents, the players, the referees." So much for modeling the behavior that will make athletes good teammates and dedicated, respectful students. One mother moved her son around to three different high schools to further his basketball career but not for academic reasons. She would not let her daughters play sports to save money for her son's traveling teams. The player's wisdom far surpassed his mother's. "I don't want my children to go through what I've had to go through," he said.[38]

Ben Simmons played basketball for LSU in 2015–16 before leaving for the NBA. The academic side of LSU did not figure in his decision to play for the Tigers. "I don't think it really matters what school you pick," Simmons said. "Sometimes, maybe with a few players, but for me I believe if you're good enough, you're going to go [to the NBA]."[39] At least he was being honest about the importance of a college education to most would-be pros.

The NCAA's D-I football and men's basketball teams comprise a de facto minor league for the NFL and NBA at no expense to the pro teams. Top college teams even hold special practices for NBA scouts to attend. College coaches ask them what they would like to see in a practice, and the coaches comply by scrimmaging more than usual. UNLV basketball coach Dave Rice stated the obvious:

> We have to all come to grips with the fact that literally just about every kid comes to college thinking they may not be in college for four years and are going to put their names in the NBA draft. You're coming here to help us win basketball games, but at the

same time it's equally important for us for you to be able to maximize your pro potential while you're here."⁴⁰

Sharmeen Obaid-Chinoy co-directed the HBO documentary *Student-Athlete* (2018). "We don't prepare players for Plan B," she said. "We don't give them any life skills beyond the dreams we've sold them."⁴¹ Getting a legitimate college degree should be Plan A, because a tiny minority of college athletes play professionally. Even if they do, most do not make life-changing money, and an athlete's career is brief.

Although football players can't go to the NFL until after their junior year in college, more and more third-years decide to abandon their teams and studies after the regular season and opt out of playing in a bowl game to avoid an injury that will hurt their draft status. And every bowl season, there are always a handful of players who are tossed off the team for breaking team rules. These days, professional gamblers wait until the last minute before making bets on bowl games to see who will show up on the field.

Some players simply leave school before graduating to prepare for the NFL or NBA draft. In late summer 2020, Minnesota Gopher wide receiver Rashod Bateman decided not to play before the Big Ten subsequently canceled the season. Bateman signed with an agent, but then he decided to play after all when the Big Ten restarted games. The NCAA allowed him to return, but late that fall, Bateman left the Gophers again. In 2021, highly regarded first-year forward Jalen Johnson abruptly left the Duke basketball team to make sure he was healthy for NBA tryouts. "I have nothing but love for the Brotherhood and thank my teammates and everyone associated with the program," Johnson said. "Duke will always have a special place in my heart."⁴² Obviously he equated Duke with the court and not the classroom.

In early 2022, Minnesota Gopher hockey goalie Jack LaFontaine, the reigning Mike Richter Award winner as the best college goalie, suddenly abandoned his team to turn pro. The Minneapolis *Star Tribune* called it a "stunning move." LaFontaine tried to explain his departure from his college mates and their shared goal of a national championship. "The main piece to our season was to win a national championship. And for us as a team," he said, "we're going to be losing a lot of guys to the Olympics, and now I'm leaving. We have a lot of good players in that room that are going to get opportunities."⁴³ Now even women basketball players are leaving college for the pros. In 2021, Texas Longhorn center Charli Collier decided to forego her senior year and enter the WNBA draft.

The profit-making professional leagues do not have to make excuses—at least on the fiscal side—for their multibillion-dollar businesses. That's the free market. The "non-profit" NCAA, which ostensibly contributes to players' education, does. The many hours that D-I athletes spend on training, practice, and games amount to a full-time job. Michigan grad Allen Jackson, who won a 1951 Rose Bowl with the Wolverines, called it fiction that athletic departments prioritized academics over winning games. "I can see the benefits of big-time football are either grossly exaggerated or completely imaginary, and it seems to me the enormous amount of time I spent on the gridiron was wasted." He said he spent about half the time on his classes for a history major as he spent on football. He equated it with the professional game.[44]

More than fifty years later, defensive back Richard Sherman played at Stanford before going to the NFL. Stanford is one of the most prestigious schools in the country. "Show me how you're gonna get all your work done," Sherman said, "when after you get out at 7:30 or so, you got a test the next day, you're dead tired from practice, and you still have to study just as hard as everybody else every day and get all of the same work done."[45] Former Georgia running back Richard Samuel, who got a degree in sports management, candidly admitted that he was an athlete first, student second: "In the fall, we would spend way more time on sports than academics."[46]

Bobby Knight, the hard-driving former Indiana coach, was aptly nicknamed "The General"—a George Patton-type tough guy who was not one to ease up on the length of practices or game film study so his players could prepare for exams. NBA Hall of Famer Isiah Thomas played for Knight at Indiana. "When you go to college, you're not a student-athlete but an athlete-student," said Thomas. "Your main purpose was not to be Einstein but to be a ball player, to generate some money, put people in the stands. Eight or ten hours of your days are filled with basketball."[47]

Many athletes at the D-I level try hard to balance the demands of their sports with their academic requirements. Games and practice times make that difficult, even at elite institutions. In 2014, one Ivy League athlete teared up when relating his experience with D-I sports: "Look, I'm not getting anything close to an Ivy League education.

I'm just trying to attend as many of my classes as possible and to pass my courses."[48]

Division-I athletes can also forget about enhancing their employment resumé by doing work outside of the classroom. More than 60 percent of undergrads do an internship, and about one in ten study abroad. It has become an important educational experience for many undergraduates.[49] Scholarship D-I athletes cannot miss a season to work for a company or do an overseas semester; "red shirting" means sitting out of games while working out and practicing with the team.

CBS Sports surveyed more than 400 PAC-12 D-I athletes and found that they devote about fifty hours to their sport every week. Of those surveyed, 54 percent said they didn't have enough time to prepare for exams, and four out of five had to miss a class because of practice or a game. The study flatly concluded that "while student-athletes feel they have the resources at their disposal to succeed academically, they don't have the time to do so."[50]

In 1991, the NCAA attempted to limit practice times, but it did so by making rules that were virtually impossible to enforce. Furthermore, instead of reducing the number of games played, the NCAA lengthened the season, apparently finding it hard to resist making ever more revenue. Ohio State played nine or ten football games in the first few decades after World War II. Today, the Buckeyes play at least fourteen games. The College Football Playoffs will expand from four to twelve teams in 2024. From the 1950s to the 1970s, Duke played about twenty-five basketball games a year. Today, the team plays about ten more than that. And a deep run in the NCAA basketball tournament can bring that number up to nearly forty games. Some D-I baseball teams play sixty games in a season.

Decades ago, the NCAA and its member schools paid attention to class times and final exam schedules to ensure that games did not conflict. The profit motive now trumps any consideration of the athlete's academic commitments. Television schedules dictate when games are played, even if it means that a conference championship or bowl game interferes with classes or final exams. If a team makes it to the NCAA basketball finals, players can miss three weeks of classes. Michigan State law professor emeritus Robert McCormick is a big fan of the Spartan basketball team, which regularly goes deep into the NCAA basketball tournament. But in a piece for the *Washington Law Review* titled "The Myth of the Student-Athlete: The College Athlete as Employee,"

McCormick asks, "Have they [players in the tournament] taken a class in a month? How could they? . . . They can't possibly be in class. The idea that these guys are primarily students is farcical."[51] March Madness distracts regular students as well. One study found that colleges with teams in the tournament saw a 6 percent drop in the number of library articles viewed by students. On the day after a close tournament game, library use dropped by almost 20 percent.[52]

During the Covid pandemic, the NCAA held its 2021 basketball tournament in a bubble in one metropolitan area. In other words, there was no way for any of the quarantined players to attend classes on campus during the contests. No one, from NCAA bureaucrats to coaches to commentators, uttered one word about how academics would fit into this pandemic-modified schedule. Lynn Holzman, the vice president of NCAA women's basketball, also failed to mention players missing classes in her announcement of the tournament structure: "We appreciate the historical significance of moving the entire championship to one region and want to acknowledge the work by the Women's Basketball Committee and staff, our hosts, local organizers, and ESPN that has allowed us to make plans for a successful 2021 championship. . . . Our No. 1 priority is to focus on creating and implementing safety controls in an environment for student-athletes."[53]

For his part, Mark Emmert was wholly unapologetic, claiming that "our championships are one of the primary tools we have to enhance the student-athlete experience." Given the number of classes a player misses in the tournament, Emmert should have left off the "student" and just made it the "athlete experience."[54] And the "one-and-done" freshman basketball players who participate in March Madness don't have to show up for a single class in the spring semester. If the NCAA were an honest institution, it would call players "obligatory students."

Playing D-I sports is a year-round commitment. The so-called "off season" has become a vestige of the past. The NCAA has steadily loosened rules on coaches' supervision of off-season workouts. Even if the practices are not mandatory, a strong "suggestion" that players show up for weight training or some other workout related to their sport is enough to coerce them to oblige. Many players have to hang around campus to take summer term classes to remain eligible. They are virtually guaranteed a passing grade in these cherry-picked, softy summer courses.[55]

For those players who miss classes due to practices and games, professors are asked to make extra accommodations, such as doing one-on-one meetings, providing lecture notes and PowerPoints to the absentee athletes, and creating and grading make-up exams. Athletic department tutors regularly prod professors for extra updates on how their players are doing in class, another special perk that is not afforded to non-athletes.

More Game Days on Class Days

The NCAA Rules Book reads, "The time required of student-athletes for participation in intercollegiate athletics shall be regulated to minimize interference with their academic pursuits." With the proliferation of cable sports stations, such as ESPN, ESPN2, and ESPN-U (devoted solely to college sports), and conference stations, such as the Big Ten Network, D-I athletic schedules are now determined by open dates on the TV schedule. Athletic departments no longer care if games interfere with players' classes or exams. The NCAA does not try to compete with the NFL on Sundays or during Monday Night Football. Several years ago, the NFL began playing games on Thursday nights. That left Tuesday, Wednesday, and Friday as empty football nights.

In the early 2000s, ESPN offered the Mid-American Conference (MAC) a contract to play middle-of-the-week games, and cashed-strapped athletic departments at schools like Miami University leapt at the opportunity. Not only did the school score more than $800,000 in TV money annually in the 13-year contract the MAC signed in 2014, but also national exposure of about a million viewers per game. "In the sport of college football, you have 130 teams playing on basically the same day," MAC commissioner Jon Steinbrecher said. "We have a couple of days where we're the only games in the country. We're not competing against the NFL, we're not competing against other college properties. It's given us a chance to elevate and build a national brand, which is challenging to do."[56]

The MAC, like most mid-majors, is indifferent to its own fan base, giving no thought to the impact of mid-week games on academics for players and fans alike. In 2016—from the beginning of November to Thanksgiving at the end of the month—only two of the eighteen MAC football games were played on Saturday, when attendance is much higher. In 2018, only one of the sixty-eight home games that was not played on Saturday drew a higher number of fans. "We're playing Akron on a Tuesday night," Ross Simon, Miami Redhawk student radio broadcaster, remembered. "It must have been 35 degrees, and not only is it freezing cold, but it's pouring rain. It was me, my co-commentator, our engineer, and I'm pretty sure that we were the only students in the stadium. It was the middle of midterm season. And the east side of the stadium is exclusively for students, so that whole side of the stadium is completely barren." The Miami athletic department claimed that attendance was 12,000. Simon countered, "There is *no way* there were 12,000 people at that game."[57]

MAC football teams typically travel to road games the day before and return the night of the game or the day after, which somehow does not "minimize interference with their academic pursuits," as the NCAA mandates. Redhawk teams even stay overnight in an off-campus hotel before a home game. One football player told a Miami professor that he missed the day after a midweek game because he was too tired and beat up. Years ago, the professor had a Miami defensive back in a weekly Tuesday night senior seminar, a required class to complete his history major. Because of the midweek MAC games, the athlete had to miss several classes that could not be made up. The professor couldn't ask the other ten students to come together at another time to replicate the discussion for the football player. This situation probably would not arise today, because athletic departments make sure that their players finish their classes by early afternoon. The Miami athletic director said that football players do not miss any classes due to the mid-week games.[58]

The MAC football schedule followed the lead of its basketball teams, which have played games in the middle of the week for decades. In the 2019–20 season, the Redhawk men's basketball team played seventeen regular season games on Fridays, Saturdays, Sundays, and Mondays. Fifteen games were played in the middle of the week.

In the 2010s, the NCAA began to schedule football games on Friday, which was traditionally high school football night across most of the country. William Friday, the former head of the North Carolina university system, led two of the three Knight Foundation studies of NCAA sports. He said that if North Carolina had a game on a Thursday or Friday, "we shut down the university at 3 o'clock to accommodate the crowds."[59] Whatever classes the students had in the late afternoon or evening—for which they or their parents paid a lot of money—are sacrificed to the sacred pigskin and TV money. In 2011, Boston College canceled afternoon classes before a football game against Florida State that ESPN was broadcasting that night. A senior BC student wrote an angry editorial to the student newspaper questioning the school's priorities. In effect, she was paying for classes that the school did not provide. "We are the national role model," a university spokesman responded. "We are the school everyone calls to say, 'Where do you find the balance?'"[60] It's not clear what the spokesman meant by achieving "balance" when classes are canceled before games.

Coaches are careful not to say out loud what everyone knows—that the athlete's performance on the field comes first. No athletic director is swayed by a losing coach's argument that he graduated players. One Miami University football player said that when he was recruited, an assistant coach held up two fingers and told him, "Academics come first." Holding up one finger, the coach said, "And football comes second." Obviously, the assistant did not want to be caught uttering out loud the words "football comes first." That duplicity does a disservice to the athlete, who is served up a course of study that will keep him eligible but unprepared for a job after his football career is over. Miami, a relatively highly regarded academic school, is not Alabama, where many of its football players go on to the pros.

Athletic Departments vs Faculty

There is a cold war between D-I university faculties today, whose tenure track ranks have been thinned and for whom pay raises have been skimpy, and athletic departments, which have grown rapidly in terms of size and employees' average salaries. It used to be that educating students was a university's first budget priority for hiring and retaining excellent, permanent faculty. In their attempts to rein in runaway college sports programs, faculties have been pitted against athletic departments. Many faculty members consider coaches dumb jocks, while coaches see tenured professors as eggheads who just sit on their rear ends, write, pontificate, teach a couple of classes a week with summers off, and have permanent jobs regardless of their performance.[61]

The mutual animosity between professors and athletic departments goes way back. More than a century ago, famed football coach Pop Warner derided those who wanted to read a "series of scholarly essays from the professor of dead languages" rather than a briefing from the football coach.[62] In 1957, the Ohio State faculty issued a report suggesting that the faculty exercise greater control over the football program, and to raise the grade point average for athletes' eligibility to coincide with the Big Ten's, which was a D+. At least Coach Woody Hayes was honest when he responded that his players had to prioritize football over academics. "You don't attract the kind of crowds it takes to fill these arenas unless you pay a lot of attention to your job—and the job, to some extent, of these boys is football." Once, Hayes tried to pressure a professor, William Appleman Williams, to change the failing grade of a Buckeyes star halfback. Williams, who later became a highly regarded diplomatic historian, refused. Hayes threatened the untenured professor: "Well, you better goddam well believe that I'll change your job, *Instructor* Williams [sic]."[63]

As the actual Cold War years progressed, this contentiousness took on a political hue, with coaches and athletic directors charging professors of holding leftist, elitist views when they dared question the school's priorities. Many athletic leaders saw collegiate sports, especially football, as a training ground for the future leaders of the country. Chester LaRoche, the head of the National Football Association in the late 1950s and early 1960s, criticized the University of Chicago and other schools for dropping football, and charged that their student bodies were now full of "beatniks, leftists, and undesirables." In 1958, one television broadcaster said on air that those colleges without football were "hotbeds of communism." As for the Ivy League's deemphasis of football, one critic called it a "[surrender to] over-stimulated introverts and pinkish weaklings."[64]

Faculty committees used to have some say over intercollegiate sports. For example, in the 1950s, the University of Minnesota faculty was hesitant to commit the Big Ten football champion to the Rose Bowl game because it would interfere with the players' studies. It is unthinkable today that a faculty could exert its power as Ohio State professors did in 1960, when they declined a bid for Woody Hayes' Buckeyes to go to the Rose Bowl. These days, Division-I faculty athletic committees are regarded simply as nuisances, with no power to shift priorities from sports to academics.

Dean Smith, John Wooden, and Bobby Knight are consensus hall-of-fame coaches, and each one has a reputation for running a clean program and emphasizing their players' education. Unfortunately, each one of their programs had its darker side. Smith was part of UNC's infamous fake "paper course" scandal. Sam Gilbert was the notorious

UCLA booster who gave Wooden's recruits and players perks of all kinds, including clothes, cars, and plane tickets. According to the *Los Angeles Times*, "Gilbert held dinners at his home, provided UCLA players with advice, counsel, and much, much more.... [He was] a one-man clearing house who has enabled players and their families to receive goods and services usually at big discounts and sometimes at no cost."[65] Knight called out Wooden for cheating. "I don't mind saying it," Knight said. "I don't respect Wooden, because he allowed Sam Gilbert to do whatever it took to recruit kids."[66]

Knight, hardly a paragon of virtue, should have kept his mouth shut. No teacher would be kept on if they made a statement like the one Knight gave to a television reporter, which equated the pressure on top college basketball coaches to win with what women feel when being sexually assaulted. "If rape is inevitable," he said, "relax and enjoy it."[67] Knight's history of physical abuse of players and his childish behavior—like throwing a chair on the court to protest a referee's call—finally got him fired, but Texas Tech saw no problem with his record and hired him in the wake of his departure from Bloomington.

Professors, like coaches, are university employees and are held to a high standard of behavior. Berating and cursing a student in class or physically assaulting them results in immediate dismissal and little chance of future employment in higher education. In 2012, someone sent the Rutgers athletic department a video tape of its basketball coach, Mike Rice Jr., throwing balls at players and belittling them verbally, including homophobic slurs. Rice was fired, and the athletic director was let go too, replaced by Julie Hermann for the tidy sum of half a million dollars a year, even though Rutgers sports was running huge deficits. That was another bad choice. While Hermann was the volleyball coach at Tennessee, she had called some of her players "whores, alcoholics, and learning disabled." Hermann was out, as was the Red Knights' football coach Kyle Flood, who tried to get a failing grade changed for a player in his academically challenging "dance appreciation" class. Seven of Flood's players had been arrested for charges ranging from armed burglary to assault on another student, and another sixteen players were busted for using marijuana, which Flood and his staff covered up.[68]

Former Texas football coach Mack Brown, who went on to coach North Carolina, was blunt in his indictment of hypocrisy in big-time sports. "When you hear presidents and athletic directors talk about character and academics and integrity," he said, "none of that really matters. The truth is, nobody has ever been fired for those things. They get fired for losing."[69]

Faculty and college coaches work at cross purposes. Educators want their students to develop analytical and critical thinking skills. The increase in practice times and the proliferation of coaches on the sidelines and in the press box, as well as their bagful of time-outs, have already minimized the importance of teaching players to think. The shift to hierarchical lines of authority began in the late nineteenth century, when paid coaches took over running football teams from the players. After World War II, changes allowing for platoons on defense, offense, and special teams took more of the imagination out of the football players' game. Players simply have to improvise less now, which has increased the need for more coaches to teach each specialty squad. With more players on the field, they have become anonymous numbers, except for the backfield and receivers.

Today, college coaches control every minute part of the game. In non-broadcast contests, each basketball coach has six timeouts per game. That's twelve stoppages of play. Televised games have additional timeouts. In addition, interminable replays toward the end of the game give coaches virtual timeouts and extra opportunities to impose their will.

Coaches no longer trust players to call plays or manage the game on the playing field. Famed UCLA basketball coach John Wooden used to sit passively on the bench during games, rarely getting up to instruct players. Asked why, he said that he hoped he had adequately prepared his players during practices to head into games and figure things out on their own.[70] Coaches these days run around on the sidelines frantically calling time outs, telling players what to do, sometimes swearing at them, and berating referees, questioning their calls and exhorting them to rule otherwise. During these tirades, strings of expletives are likely to fly from their mouths, this with nary a blink of an eye from their university bosses. Some football coaches bombard referees with the nastiest of swear words, hardly modeling good sportsmanship. Again, a professor—technically coaches' university colleagues—would be fired on the spot for such aggressive behavior in the classroom or anywhere else on campus, let alone for cussing out a student.

Cultivating or Concussing the Brain

Another incongruity in college sports is the effort to impart wisdom to players in the classroom on the one hand, while risking damage to their brains on the football field on the other. In the late nineteenth century, university presidents like Harvard's Charles Eliot recognized the contradiction of educating youngsters at the same time they were incurring serious injury and even death on the field. Eliot was also concerned with misdeeds off the field that have plagued college sports since: "The evils of the intercollegiate sports . . . [sic] continue without real redress and diminution. In particular, the game of football grows worse and worse as regards to foul and violent play, and the number and gravity of injuries which the players suffer. It has become perfectly clear that the game as now played is unfit for college use." Eliot charged that the spectacle was akin to a "prize fight, cockfight, bullfight."[71] Eliot reacted to the proposal for more officials on the playing field to call penalties on players for illegal and injurious tactics. "The sufficient answer to this suggestion," wrote Eliot, "is that a game which needs to be so watched is not fit for genuine sportsmen."[72]

Eighteen college football players died in 1905. Eliot advocated for a suspension of the games, prompting President Theodore Roosevelt to write to Eliot, "I do not agree with you that the game should be stopped. I further think that one reason why [football abuses] are not remedied is that so many of our people whose voices would be potent in reforming the game, try to abolish it instead."[73] Reforms such as legalizing the forward pass were made but didn't stop serious injuries.

It is common knowledge that football can be a debilitating, even deadly, sport. In 1923, the *New York Times* reported that eighteen players had died from football, the same number of tragic deaths that had prompted the meeting with President Roosevelt in 1905. Twenty players died in 1927, and eighteen in 1928. Eight more died in 1931.[74]

From 1910 to 1950, more than 500 college and high school football players died of injuries sustained on the field of play.[75] In 1936, Bob Considine wrote an article in *Good Housekeeping* titled "Death on the Gridiron," which was a denunciation of the game and a plea for parents to think twice about letting their sons play football. "Somewhere between the point he caught the ball and the goal which rules of the game command him to attain," Considine wrote, "he will be brutally hit by one or more tacklers and thrown heavily upon the unyielding ground.

Chapter Seven

The crash may crush the very framework of his body, or in the ensuing pile-on he may be kicked in the temple or the spine."[76]

Famed football coach Bear Bryant was notorious for his brutal practices that weeded out the weak of body and mind. Tough guys "gut it out" and "play with pain." In those days, even giving water to players was a sign of weakness. When he was at Kentucky in the late 1940s and early 1950s, Bryant was said to have ended the kid-glove treatment of Wildcat players by "the horsey set"—referring to Kentucky's supposedly effeminate, upper-class racehorse owners and their doughy-bodied sons.[77]

If you play football, you will get hurt, perhaps even seriously or permanently. Efforts to tamp down the violence today through targeting penalties and concussion protocols have not mitigated the rate of injuries. What does the sport teach? Football is the most macho of college sports, and it has always called on players to show their manhood. It is an ultra-competitive, masculine, cutthroat culture of "knocking heads," "ringing someone's bell," and "pancaking." Putting a key opponent out of the game is not seen as unsportsmanlike. Games between elite D-I teams and patsy mid-major football programs are, as noted, cynically known as "bodybag games."

Every college football game today has numerous injury timeouts, and at least one replay to determine whether a targeting penalty is warranted—a hit to the head of a defenseless player. If the player is hurt badly, fans, players, and coaches wait in silence as the kid with a neck injury and possible paralysis is immobilized on a stretcher and carted off to the hospital. Nonetheless, the game has a visceral appeal to spectators, akin to the picnickers who sat on the bluffs above Bull Run to watch that early battle in the Civil War. As long as spectators are not the ones getting hit, it's a guilty pleasure to watch players cream each other. Big collisions bring a cringe and an "oooo"—but fans want more. In 2017, *The Washington Post* published a poll showing that "nine out of 10 sports fans say NFL injuries are a problem, but 74 percent are still football fans."[78]

The irony of playing football in an educational setting cannot be lost on all those associated with universities. Boxing is another sport in which the objective is to inflict physical pain. After numerous serious injuries, the NCAA got rid of the sport in 1960. There is no comparable movement to ban college football, even though concussions are a growing problem in the sport.⁷⁹ Players are much bigger and faster today, increasing the velocity at which they hit each other's heads. Violent collisions have increased, as coaches implore their players to hit harder and harder. The day after a game, players are expected to go into the classroom with a clear head, having done their homework the night before. The NCAA has fought lawsuits charging the organization with not protecting players from head injuries.

Research has definitively shown that football concussions can lead to chronic traumatic encephalopathy (CTE), amyotrophic lateral sclerosis (ALS), Parkinson's, and early dementia.⁸⁰ College administrators know that repeated blows to the head increase the chance of a player developing CTE. National Football League players are about four times likelier than the average person to die of Alzheimer's or ALS.⁸¹ Three players from the 1972 Miami Dolphins, which had a perfect season that year, died of CTE. But, as Bear Bryant used to tell his players, winning football only came to those who "paid the price."⁸² It is an increasingly high price to pay.

In 2019, Connecticut Senator Chris Murphy said, "The whole thing [college football] looks more professional than professional sports, and yet the kids were ending up poor with brain damage. . . . It's a scandal sitting right in front of our eyes."⁸³ "The reality is that this game destroys people's brains," charged noted sports broadcaster Bob Costas. He said that more and more parents would not let their boys play football. "The whole thing could collapse like a house of cards," Costas predicted, "if people actually begin connecting the dots."⁸⁴

Football is the boxing of the last century—a sport for disadvantaged kids. More and more affluent White parents are steering their boys away from football, and the sport is increasingly manned by poor Black youngsters. Former NFL player Michael Oriard asks, "What happens if football players become like boxers, from lower economic classes [and] racially marginalized groups?"⁸⁵ Sports journalist Tony Kornheiser predicted that the game would eventually become "only the province of the poor, who want it for economic reasons to get up and out."⁸⁶

Football also asks D-I offensive linemen and middle guards to bulk up to well over 300 pounds, hardly a healthy body type. Obesity plagues former players with heart problems, diabetes, sleep apnea, and hypertension. A study in the *American Journal of Medicine* "found that for every 10 pounds football players gained from high school to college, or from college to the professional level, the risk of heart disease rose 14 percent compared with players whose weight changed little during the same time."[87] For many college players, football is not good for the body or the mind.

Few Seniors for "Senior Night"

The NCAA depends on the pro leagues to make rules about how long athletes must play college basketball and football. Eighteen-year-olds can join the United States military but cannot play NBA basketball or NFL football. In 2007, the NBA declared that it would not sign a player until he was 19 years old or had played at least one year of college ball. The NFL mandated that no player can be signed until three years after having graduated from high school. The NHL and MLB have no such restrictions, nor do the Professional Golfers' Association or Major League Soccer. Players joining the Association of Tennis Professionals must be 15 or older.

Players who have used up their eligibility are recognized at the last home game of the basketball season. "Senior Night" has become an embarrassment at many D-I schools, because so few players make it that far. Marquee D-I basketball players don't even have to stay enrolled in college for two legitimate semesters, the "one-and-done" players making a mockery of the NCAA's student-athlete model. "Academic success, including graduation"—as the NCAA says is the objective for student-athletes—does not factor into the decision-making process of potential pro basketball players. The result is that the blue chip player need only pass a few meaningless classes in the fall semester to stay eligible for the rest of the basketball season, including the NCAA basketball tournament in the spring. If drafted by an NBA team, the player has no obligation to ever again darken the halls of the Ivory Tower.

The coup de grace for wannabe-pro college basketball players is the NBA draft. On draft night, one-and-dones sit with basketball coaches and wait to see which NBA team's jersey they will don and how many millions they will make. The NBA has tiered guaranteed contracts for players selected in the first round. In 2019, a historic high of eighty-six underclassmen opted for the NBA draft, only about half of whom were selected.[88]

For a time, some coaches resisted going down the one-and-done route, but refusal to do so makes it difficult for them to put together a championship-caliber team. A few mid-major schools, such as Butler and Davidson, have made deep runs in the tournament with upperclassmen, but these cases are rare. Longtime Michigan State coach Tom Izzo accepts one-and-dones, but he does not want a whole squad comprised of them. "I don't think I'd enjoy my job that way," he says. "It's like a factory. Nobody has any ties to the place."[89]

Duke University is a highly respected academic institution, and for years, Coach Mike Krzyzewski tried to get by without the one-and-dones. Coach K could have done the right thing and emulate Butler or Davidson, but he ultimately decided that winning NCAA championships was more important than his players graduating. Krzyzewski made a good financial decision by taking any top recruit, even in those cases when he knew that the player would only wear the Blue Devil jersey for a single season. Indeed, Krzyzewski banked tens of millions of dollars utilizing one-and-dones, such as 2019 first-round draft pick Zion Williamson.

Krzyzewski pointed to D-I football as a model of what the big basketball powers should do with hoops. "Collegiate NCAA football, they run it big-time. We don't do it. We don't do it. It's sad."[90] In other words, he is arguing that the big basketball conferences should take money and power away from the NCAA, run their own tournament, and make their own television deals. Academics do not enter into the conversation.

The NCAA does not want to hear any criticisms about its obvious indifference to the education of its athletes. As John Thelin observed, "As the scholarship on college sports gets better, the educational and ethical problems of college sports get worse."[91] In 2008, NCAA President Myles Brand, who as president of Indiana University had famously fired Bobby Knight, created the NCAA Scholarly Colloquium on Sport, a two-day conference of sports historians and journalists to convene before the NCAA's annual meeting. Brand had a PhD in philosophy and, unlike his successor, Mark Emmert, was sincerely interested in promoting the intellectual side of the student-athlete. Brand intended the colloquium to encourage serious research, and the *Journal of Intercollegiate Sports* published the papers written by the attendees. The first president of the group, Scott Kretchmar, was professor emeritus of philosophy from Penn State.

Dave Wiggins, a noted scholar of sports history from George Mason University, headed the colloquium until Emmert ended it in 2013; the gathered scholars were critical of the NCAA system and keen to expose the irreconcilable goals of big-time college sports and the core mission of higher education.⁹² The 2013 program chair, Ellen Staurowsky of Drexel University, said she was not sure why the NCAA pulled the plug on the colloquium, but when she listed some of the studies that the participants had produced, it was obvious that the NCAA leaders were not happy to have had their hypocrisy laid bare. "We had scholars looking at all kinds of things—" she said, "the pay rates of coaches of women's programs compared to men's programs, compensation packages for big-time coaches, whether or not the investment that campuses make in stadiums is worth it." At a news conference, Emmert was asked about quashing the colloquium and replied, "At the end of the day, I'm an academic, and nobody in this room values research more than me [sic]. There are lots of subjects around which we need good, thoughtful, objective research. We just need to deploy research in the effective way to get the best return on investment we can." The NCAA's chief operating officer, Jim Isch, in justifying ending the seminar, claimed that the colloquium was not reaching a wide enough audience.⁹³ On the contrary, the problem for the NCAA was that scholars were doing a good job of documenting its misdeeds, and was worried that too many people were becoming aware of the depths of the organization's corruption.

Notes

1. Azoff, I. (Producer), & Heckering, A. (Director) (1982). *Fast Times at Ridgemont High* [Motion Picture]. United States: Universal Pictures.

2. Mike Hall, "Having Fun with Sporting Sayings," *The Topeka Capital-Journal*, June 18, 2019, accessed December 22, 2022, https://www.cjonlin.com/story/opinion/columns/2019/06/18/mike-hall-having-fun-with-sporting-sayings/4881938007/.

3. NCAA Publications.com, "2018-2019 NCAA Division I Manual," accessed August 29, 2020, https://www.ncaapublications.com/p-4547-2018-2019-ncaa-division-i-manual-august-version-available-august-2018.aspx.

4. Bill Morris, "A Tent City for Fun and Profit," *New York Times*, February 24, 2013, S1. Kirwin was a co-director of the 2010 Knight Commission.

5. Randy Johnson, "Gophers Ibrahim to Return Next Year," *Star Tribune*, December 29, 2020, C5.

6. John R. Gerdy, *Air Ball: American Education's Failed Experiment with Elite Athletics* (Oxford, MS: University Press of Mississippi, 2006), 6–7.

7. Sperber, *College Sports Inc.*, 351.

8. John Thompson, Jr., essay adapted from his autobiography, *New York Times*, November 12, 2020, accessed March 24, 2021, https://www.nytimes.com/2020/11/12/opinion/sunday/ncaa-sports-paying-college-players.html?searchResultPosition=1.

9. Bob Collins, "Whatever Happened To: General College," *NPR News*, March 31, 2008, accessed October 21, 2021, https://blogs.mprnews.org/newscut/2008/03/_as_of_july_1/.

10. Chudacoff, *Changing the Playbook*, 150.
11. *New York Times Education Life*, February 8, 2015, 4.
12. Unattributed, "Majoring in Football," *USA Today*, November 20, 2008, 12A.
13. "Majoring in Football," *USA Today*, November 20, 2008, 12A.
14. Byers, *Unsportsmanlike Conduct*, 308.
15. Gaul, *Billion-Dollar Ball*, 107. One semester at Miami this author noticed a lot of really big guys going into a classroom across from my office. I glanced in to see an elderly colleague teaching Western Civilization, a course that fulfilled a university requirement. The professor was in his last couple of years of teaching, and was essentially mailing it in, giving students at least a "C". After he retired, I taught the exact same course, but I give only essay exams. I am a fair but tough grader, but evidently the academic advisors in the athletic department had a red flag by my name, because I had only one football player in the class. Maybe the class was too early in the morning for the players. Similarly, few male athletes appear in my sports history class, although it is an elective for the sports management major, a popular course of study for them. At many D-I schools it is a relatively recent major created in part for athletes.
16. Jay M. Smith and Mary Willingham, *Cheated: The UNC Scandal, the Education of Athletes, and the Future of Big-Time College Sports* (Lincoln, NE: Potomac Books, 2015), 222.
17. Byers, *Unsportsmanlike Conduct*, 159.
18. Watterson, *College Football*, 323–4; and Demas, *Integrating the Gridiron*, 102ff.
19. Steve Berkowitz, "NCAA President Credited with $2.7 Million in Total Pay for 2018 Calendar Year," *USA Today*, June 2, 2020, accessed June 30, 2021, https://www.usatoday.com/story/sports/2020/06/02/mark-emmert-total-pay-2018-calendar-year/3123547001/; and Smith and Willingham, *Cheated*, xvi.
20. Ben Strauss, "Football Major, Basketball Minor?" *New York Times Education Life*, February 8, 2015, accessed January 21, 2022, https://www.nytimes.com/2015/02/08/education/edlife/football-major-basketball-minor.html?searchResultPosition=149.
21. Interview with University of California, Berkeley academic advisor, September 29, 2021.
22. Smith and Willingham, *Cheated*, 223.
23. Mulcahy III, *An Athletic Director's Story*, 71; and Jaime Schulz, "The Test Time: Revisiting *Stagg's University* and College Historiography," *Journal of Sport History* 39, no. 1 (Spring 2012), 117. Even noted sports historian Jaime Schulz cites athletes' higher graduation rates without discussing the support system afforded to other students. She writes, ". . . the fact remains that white and black athletes today continue to graduate at *higher* rates than white and black students overall."
24. "Miami Finishes Fall Semester with 3.23 GPA," Miami Redhawks Website, December 12, 2022, accessed November 22, 2023, https://miamiredhawks.com/news/2022/12/19/general-miami-athletics-finishes-fall-semester-with-3-23-gpa.
25. Interview with Miami University athletic director, August 12, 2021.

26. Interview with a Miami University academic advisor, August 18, 2021.
27. Interview with a University of Oklahoma academic advisor, September 14, 2021.
28. Interview with Temple University academic advisor, September 29, 2021.
29. Schulz, "The Test Time," 116.
30. Gaul, *Billion-Dollar Ball*, 29.
31. John Morrow, "The Undergraduate Experience," *New York Times Education Life*, April 24, 2005, accessed July 2, 2020, https://www.nytimes.com/2005/04/24/us/education/the-undergraduate-experience-survival-of-the-fittest.html.
32. Sperber, *College Sports Inc.*, 280.
33. Gaul, *Billion-Dollar Ball*, 118–9, 124.
34. Gaul, *Billion-Dollar Ball*, 124.
35. Laine Higgins and Brian McGill, "College Football's 2021 Grid of Shame," *Wall Street Journal*, September 4–5, 2021, A16.
36. Texas A&M Men's Basketball, accessed June 29, 2021, https://texags.com/forums/7/topics/598735.
37. Harvey Araton, "College 101: There's No Business Like the Pro Business," *New York Times*, 1995, S25.
38. Nate Taylor, "Real Hoops Moms of Kentucky," *New York Times*, December 10, 2013, B11.
39. Marc Tracy, "Colleges Cut to the Chase, Holding Practices Just for N.B.A. Scouts," *New York Times*, October 21, 2015, B16.
40. Tracy, "Colleges Cut to the Chase."
41. Dan Wolken, "New Film Opens Eyes on Amateurism's Flaws," *USA Today*, October 1, 2018, 6C.
42. Megan Ryan, "U Receiver Bateman Leaves Team Once Again," *Star Tribune*, November 26, 2020, C1; and unattributed, "Top Freshman Done with Duke," *Star Tribune*, February 15, 2021, C5.
43. Randy Johnson, "LaFontaine Signs with Carolina," *Star Tribune*, January 10, 2022, C1; and Megan Ryan, "From College to the Pros Overnight," *Star Tribune*, January 11, 2022, C2.
44. Watterson, *College Football*, 251.
45. Steve Cameron, "The NCAA Brings in $1 Billion a Year—Here's Why it Refuses to Pay Its College Athletes," March 26, 2019, accessed April 8, 2015, https://www.businessinsider.com/ncaa-college-athletes-march-madness-basketball-football-sports-not-paid-2019-3.
46. Gregory, "It's Time to Pay."
47. George, *Elevating the Game*, 202.
48. Michael M Rooke-Ley, "Letter to the Editor," *New York Times*, February 4, 2015.
49. NAFSA: Association of International Educators, "Trends in U.S. Study Abroad," accessed January 5, 2021, https://www.nafsa.org/policy-and-advocacy/policy-resources/trends-us-study-abroad.
50. Cameron, "The NCAA Brings in $1 Billion a Year."

51. Michael Rosenberg, "Workers' Comp," *Sports Illustrated*, April 7, 2014, 64.
52. Bill Morris, "A Tent City for Fun and Profit," *New York Times*, February 24, 2013, S1; and Laura Pappano, "How Big-Time Sports Ate College Life," *New York Times Education Life*, January 22, 2012, 24.
53. Doug Feinberg, "San Antonio Area Will Play Host to Entire Women's Tournament," *Star Tribune*, February 6, 2021, C4.
54. Branch, "The Shame."
55. Jake New, "A Self-Fulfilling Prophecy," *Insider Higher Ed*, February 18, 2015, accessed June 30, 2022, https://www.insidehighered.com/news/2015/02/18/athletes-take-easier-courses-fit-teammates-study-asserts.
56. Rodger Sherman, "How the Rise of MACtion Forever Changed MAC Fandom," November 19, 2019, accessed April 9, 2020, https://www.theringer.com/2019/11/19/20972679/mac-midweek-games-maction-television-networks-fan-experience.
57. Sherman, "How the Rise."
58. Interview with Miami University athletic director, August 12, 2021.
59. Branch, "The Shame."
60. Pappano, "How Big-Time," 25.
61. See Chris Baucom and Christopher D. Lantz, "Faculty Attitudes Toward Male Division II Student-Athletes," *Journal of Sport Behavior* 24, no. 3, (September 2001): 265–276.
62. Oriard. *King Football,* 333.
63. Kemper, *College Football*, 54, 57.
64. Kemper, *College Football*, 28–29.
65. Chris Dufresne, "The Dark Side of the UCLA Basketball Dynasty," *Los Angeles Times*, June 8, 2010, accessed January 11, 2021, https://www.latimes.com/archives/la-xpm-2010-jun-08-la-sp-0609-wooden-gilbert-20100609-story.html.
66. Kyle Boone, "Bob Knight Slams Legendary Coach John Wooden, Says UCLA Cheated in Recruiting," *CBS Sports*, November 8, 2017, accessed January 11, 2021, https://www.youtube.com/watch?v=LahroOzvPVA.
67. Sperber, *Beer and Circus*, 24.
68. Michael Powell, "After Years of Disgrace, Rutgers Drifts in Money Pit," *New York Times*, March 12, 2017, SP1.
69. Gaul, *Billion Dollar Ball,* 1.
70. Seth Davis, "Revisiting the Remarkable Legacy of John Wooden, the Greatest Coach of Them All," *Sports Illustrated*, March 8, 2017, accessed July 6, 2022, https://www.si.com/college/2017/03/08/john-wooden-greatest-basketball-coaches.
71. Davies, *Sports in American Life*, 55.
72. Davies, *Sports in American Life*, 55.
73. Judy Battista, "Oval Office Quarterback," *New York Times Book Review*, August 14, 2011, 13.
74. Watterson, *College Football*, 171, 178.
75. Davies, *Sports in American Life*, 59.
76. Oriard, *King Football*, 173–4.

Chapter Seven

77. Oriard, *King Football*, 156.

78. Adam Kilgore and Scott Clement, "Poll: Nine in 10 Sports Fans Say NFL Injuries are a Problem, but 74 are Still Football Fans," *Washington Post*, September 6, 2017, accessed February 14, 2022, https://www.washingtonpost.com/sports/poll-nfl-remains-as-popular-as-ever-despite-head-injuries-other-concerns/2017/09/06/238bef8a-9265-11e7-8754-d478688d23b4_story.html.

79. College baseball is another sport in which coaches can ruin a pitcher's arm by throwing him too many innings, but at least they do not suffer concussions. The incentive to win at all cost is just too great. For example, Chicago Cubs pitcher Kerry Woods' career was shortened with arm trouble; the 175 pitches he threw in both ends of a doubleheader in college probably did not help. Another Cubs pitching phenom Mark Prior also threw too many innings in college, which probably ended his career prematurely.

80. See James Dunn, "If You Can't Play Football This Year, You Caught a Break," *Star Tribune*, September 20, 2020, A11.

81. Billy Witz, "A Football Family Watches, With Mixed Emotions," *New York Times*, January 12, 2020, S3.

82. Kemper, *College Football*, 21.

83. Dan Wolken, "States Lit Fuse for College Athletes," *USA Today*, November 12, 2019, 3C.

84. Tom Schad, "Journalists Question the Future of Football," *USA Today*, November 9, 2017, C3.

85. Aaron Baker, review of "League of Denial" (2013), *Journal of Sport History* 43, no. 1 (Spring 2016): 102–3. 103.

86. Tom Schad, "Journalists Question."

87. Ken Belson, "The NFL's Other Scourge: Obesity," *New York Times*, January 20, 2019, S1.

88. Pete Thamel, "Coach K on Lack of Vision in College Hoops," *Yahoo Sports*, February 5, 2020, accessed March 25, 2021, https://sports.yahoo.com/coach-k-on-college-hoops-i-wish-the-whole-thing-would-change-084051665.html.

89. Michael Rosenberg, "Fun and Done," *Sports Illustrated*, March 5, 2012, 13–14.

90. Pete Thamel, "Coach K on Lack."

91. Smith, *Pay for Play*, 208.

92. Paul Steinbach, "Authors React to Cancellation of NCAA Colloquium," *Athletic Business*, March 2013, accessed August 5, 2021, https://www.athleticbusiness.com/scholars-react-to-cancellation-of-ncaa-colloquium.html; and author interview with Dave Wiggins, December 3, 21.

93. Steinbach, "Authors React."

CHAPTER EIGHT

Cheating to Make the Grade:
Keeping Athletes Eligible

"I never graduated from Iowa, but I was only there for two terms—Truman's and Eisenhower's."

—Hall of Fame Hawkeye and Detroit Lions
defensive tackle Alex Karras[1]

This chapter covers a few of the most notorious academic scandals that have occurred in big-time college sports. The frequency of cheating to keep athletes eligible is an indictment of the entire D-I system.

Universities ostensibly teach students to be law-abiding, fair-minded citizens, but nearly a century ago, the Carnegie Foundation found a direct correlation between the moral shortcomings of big-time college sports and academic fraud: "The tragedy is that the cynicism that stems from the abuse in athletics infects the rest of student life, from promoting academic dishonesty to the loss of individual ideals. We find it disturbing that students who admit to cheating often excuse their conduct as being set by college examples such as athletic dishonesty."[2]

Pulling strings for the athlete has been common practice since the start of intercollegiate competition. In 1902, a handful of broad-shouldered, hefty lads showed up for the Princeton entrance exam. One would-be football player had been recruited by Charles Patterson, a Princeton booster. "You are a long way from college," the professor commented, after seeing the beefy boy's test. The young man responded, "Well, Professor, at the top of my paper, I wrote my weight—205 pounds. I guess I'll pass all right. Patterson said I would."[3]

For decades, university administrators have sold their institutions to prospective students with winning sports teams while at the same time adamantly claiming that academics are the top priority. Football put

Chapter Eight

Notre Dame on the national map in the 1920s. Famed Irish football coach Knute Rockne's best player was George Gipp, who led the team to a 9–0 record in 1919. However, Gipp's off-the-field antics and lack of attention to his studies riled the university faculty and administration, so they tossed him out of school. Rumors of his transfer to Michigan or Army prompted alumni and the South Bend business community, which had come to like the profits they realized from Saturday football games, to demand that the administration allow Gipp to play his senior year. With Gipp back in the lineup until the last two games of the season, Notre Dame went undefeated again. It was a happy ending for the Irish boosters and the town's businesses, but not so much for Gipp, who died of the flu at the end of the year.[4]

In 1952, *Life* magazine published a photo of four toothless Irish players, implying that they had more brawn than brains. Notre Dame officials took affront at the image and demanded an apology. *Life* obliged, and published photos of the same jocks-turned-scholars in suits and ties.[5]

Army was another marquee football team at mid-century, in its case one with the military's traditional image of running a squeaky-clean, honest, and disciplined program. College football fans were shocked by a huge academic cheating scandal at West Point in the early 1950s. Army football players, possibly with assistance from their coaches, developed a network of sharing questions and answers to quizzes and exams. More than thirty Army players were tossed out of the school, including quarterback Bob Blaik, the son of head coach Red Blaik.[6]

To this day, it is inevitable that some athletes who are completely unprepared to do college coursework are admitted to a university and somehow remain eligible to play. In 1973, the NCAA allowed any incoming athlete to compete if his or her high school grade point average was a C-, regardless of which courses comprised that GPA. The organization also ended the obligation to give athletes a four-year scholarship, which gave coaches more control over their players, on and off the field. Players could be shown the door even after a year if they did not perform well.[7]

In 1982, it came out that three-year Creighton University basketball player Kevin Ross could not read. "They promised me an education," Ross said, "but they used me by putting me in these bonehead courses. I stayed eligible by taking three required courses and such courses as theory of basketball, theory of ceramics. I made Ds in the required courses and As in the others."[8] In 1989, standout Washington Redskin defensive lineman Dexter Manley tearfully testified before the United States Senate Subcommittee on Education, Arts, and Humanities that he had been "functionally illiterate" while at Oklahoma State. Senator Barbara Mikulski (D) of Maryland responded to his testimony with a shot at the university and the NCAA: "You didn't fail, sir. The system failed you."[9] Manley and Ross bear some responsibility for their shortcomings in the classroom, but the system facilitated negligence of their academics. They could play their sports without really going to school.[10]

In the 1980s, a University of Georgia English instructor revealed that administrators had changed the grades she had given to certain football players so that they would remain eligible to play in the 1982 Sugar Bowl. The school's lawyer defended the action with this startling, if forthright, statement: "We may not make a university student out of him [a football player], but if we can teach him to read and write, maybe he can work at the post office rather than as a garbage man when he gets through with his athletic career."[11] An African American in the development office saw racial overtones in the whole affair, calling the instructor a "bigot" for not passing the Black players. Georgia president Fred Davison saw no need to raise academic standards for Bulldog players and thereby "unilaterally disarm" its athletic programs in the cutthroat competition of intercollegiate athletics.[12]

From the late 1970s to the early 2000s, basketball coach Jim Harrick had a string of academic fraud cases at Pepperdine, UCLA, Rhode Island, and Georgia. His son taught a course in the strategy of basketball at Georgia, in which he gave Bulldog players high grades to keep their GPAs in the eligible range. No wrong was proven.[13] There was also no definitive confirmation that someone took Derrick Rose's SAT to get him into Memphis to play basketball, but his coach John Calipari had several other rules infractions on his resume, including academic fraud, so he skipped off to coach the Kentucky Wildcats. When Michigan President James J. Duderstadt was the provost, he overrode the admissions department's rejection of basketball recruits Rumeal Robinson and Terry Mills. Duderstadt's intervention paid off with an NCAA championship for the Wolverines in 1989.[14]

Other academic scandals hounded college sports throughout the 1980s. Half of the PAC-10 schools were on probation for academic fraud. Arizona State, UCLA, USC, and Oregon State were found to have provided football players with unearned credits, phony transcripts, and

Chapter Eight

other machinations to keep athletes eligible.[15] Only one in five players in major D-I basketball programs graduated. If transfers and those who left the university "in good academic standing" were included, Bobby Knight's purported 100 percent graduation rate would be closer to 65 percent. Penn State football coach Joe Paterno recognized that even those athletes who did graduate were not taking meaningful courses. "We're getting so wrapped up in percentages," he said, "that we may be more concerned with the graduation rate than quality education."[16]

Chris Washburn got into North Carolina State with a combined 470 on his SAT, and some of his university grades were changed so he could remain eligible. He had a cup of coffee in the NBA, was drummed out of the league for drug use, and ended up penniless and homeless.[17] Cases like Washburn's prompted the NCAA to pass Proposition 48 in 1986, increasing the minimum academic performance for incoming athletes—a 2.0 GPA in high school or a combined 700 on the SAT. That made little difference. In a 1989 survey of Black athletes at D-I schools, only 31 percent said that their coaches pushed them to do well in the classroom; 44 percent thought that they would go on to a pro basketball or football career.[18]

According to the *Washington Post*, four Georgetown players on the 1999–2000 basketball team got into the university without meeting any of the criteria for the SAT, high school GPA, or required pre-college courses. The controversy surrounded the Hoyas' well-respected coach, John Thompson, one of the relatively few Black college coaches, about whether his highly successful program benefitted Black players in the long run (John Chaney at Temple, another Black coach, faced similar criticism because few of his players graduated). One of Thompson's players, Michael Graham, never graduated from high school but passed an equivalency test to get into Georgetown. Graham ended up leaving after helping the Hoyas win the 1984 NCAA championship. Commenting on the situation at Georgetown, Father John Brooks, president at Holy Cross at the time, questioned all such programs that recruited players who had little chance of graduating: "Some defend it, some don't. Some will tell you that [former coach] John Thompson did great things for the school, put it on the map, made it a lot of money. My answer is always the same, 'At what cost?' I would say it was too high in terms of academic integrity."[19]

In the late 1990s, Brooks sat on a panel with Thompson and legendary North Carolina coach Dean Smith. When asked about players leaving college early for the pros, Brooks "told them that I agreed with them [the players] a hundred percent. They [the coaches] were all stunned. And then I said, 'Because what you people are doing has very little to do with education." Both Thompson and Smith were livid.[20]

Tutors and Phony Courses

Much of the academic fraud can be traced back to the system of providing athletes with special tutors. Tutors can mask the amount of help they are giving athletes on papers, group projects, and take-home tests. At most schools, the money for the academic advising department comes in part from the fees that all enrolled students are required to pay. Lynne M. Tronsdal, former assistant vice president for student retention at Arizona, observed, "If we could do for the non-student-athlete what we do for the student athlete, we would have a retention rate that is incredible." According to Tronsdal, if an athlete has trouble writing, he or she will get a special writing tutor. "They work with professors on the athlete's grades," she adds, "and if the grade isn't good enough, they'll help petition the grade."[21]

Even with the extra help, the graduation rate for those male students under Arizona basketball Coach Lute Olson was pathetic. From 1995 to 2004, only two scholarship players graduated. Olson's success on the court was the result of running a minor league team for the NBA; nine of his players left early for the pro draft—this before the practice became commonplace.[22] In the 1990s, only a third of University of Florida basketball players graduated, despite having tutors to guide them through simple courses for simple majors.[23]

In addition to the outright criminal behavior of its athletes, the University of Miami has been guilty of nearly every violation in the NCAA's big 400+ page rulebook. In the last thirty years, the school has failed to hold its football and basketball players to a minimum of academic standards. "There was definitely cheating that took place." recalls one Miami athletic tutor. "There were female tutors who would offer sexual favors to the athletes in return for doing a paper. Miami was big for that."[24]

In 2010, a female tutor at the University of Missouri accused a football player of assault. The prosecutor in the case found that "too many tutors were having sex with athletes, and really filthy conversations were going on between players and girls. It was a sexually charged environment. It was a joke—the whole tutoring situation." The player was found guilty of assault. Two days after he was sent to prison, his head coach Gary Pinkel was arrested for drunk driving. It is no wonder that the prosecutor blamed the university for creating a toxic environment.[25]

In recent years, online courses have become a popular way of handing out credits to players who do not have to show up to scheduled classes. However, well before the advent of online education, similar "correspondence" courses were used and abused by unscrupulous athletic departments. In the late 1970s, it came out at Arizona State that the Sun Angels booster club was giving cash and other perks to players, many of whom stayed eligible by taking correspondence courses from dubiously accredited schools, as well as by getting credit from extension courses for which they had done little or no work. At the time, Coach Frank Kush told an advisor in the athletic department, "My job was to get our players eligible or I would be fired."[26]

In one Associated Press survey, twenty-seven of forty-six Power Five schools had no limits on the number of online courses a student could take. Star LSU quarterback Joe Burrow, who transferred from Ohio State, took all of his grad courses online. "I don't go to class," he admitted. Ohio State quarterback Justin Fields, who started at the University of Georgia, liked his online courses too: "Usually the assignments are all due the same day so that makes it easier for me." Illinois athletes take about 20 percent of their courses online. Oklahoma State's Marilyn Middlebrooks, the associate athletic director for academic affairs, sees no problem with this practice: "I get very heated when people make criticisms of online classes. It's simply another delivery system to help students get through schools. . . . It's worked beautifully for us." But Brian Russell, the associate athletic director for academic services and student-athlete development at Illinois, is aware that administrators see this an easy way to cheat—"a red flag and high-alert area" for tutors to do the players' work.[27]

In the 1970s, USC football was hit with a similar academic scandal for finding easy courses and professors willing to inflate players' grades. About half of the Trojans football team graduated, but only 30 percent of its Black players graduated. One USC professor found that Black players were sent into "invented" courses, such as "Special Problems in Speech Communication." Head Coach John Robinson said, "If I were to suddenly say, 'we close the doors [to unqualified athletes],' that's almost a racial move. Our team turns White. That's one thing that happens."

Former UCLA coach Dick Vermeil, who left the college game to join the pro ranks, downplayed the academic scandals in college football. "There's a lot worse things than fixing a kid's grades," he said. "They hire and fire football coaches on the basis of wins and losses. They don't give tenure like with a chemistry teacher. If the chemistry teacher were evaluated on 12 weekends, on the basis of wins and losses, he'd probably find a way to make sure the students got a little better grades too." At least Vermeil was being honest about the bottom line for coaches and that mentoring athletes to get a meaningful degree was not job one.[28]

In 1999, University of Minnesota tutor Jan Gangelhoff revealed that, from 1993 to 1998, she had written some 400 papers for at least twenty of Gopher coach Clem Haskins' basketball players, for which Haskins gave her a bonus of $3,000. Minnesota should have hired better tutors, because the graduation rates of Gopher basketball players were among the worst in the Big Ten. Guard Russ Archambault said, "In the two years I was there, I never did a thing."[29] In the wake of the scandal, Haskins lost his job, and the team was docked scholarships and placed on probation for four years. Haskins' victories were "vacated"—scrubbed from the record book. When the Gophers whipped Michigan State 81–56 on December 29, 2020, the Minneapolis *Star Tribune* referenced Minnesota's history with the Spartans: "The Gophers matched their biggest margin of victory ever in the series; the 1997 Final Four team won 68–43 in East Lansing, though that result has been vacated."[30]

That NCAA penalty is laughable—asking sports fans to have collective amnesia. In the late 2010s, it came out that Florida State football players were committing academic fraud. In response, the NCAA vacated twelve Seminole victories, denying legendary coach Bobby Bowden of any chance of overtaking Penn State coach Joe Paterno's all-time D-I victory record.[31] Paterno himself was fired after one of his assistants—Jerry Sandusky—was charged with sexually abusing young boys—with the famed (and now defamed) coach's indirect knowledge. Ironically, Paterno saw all his wins from 1998 to 2011 "vacated" as well.

The Tarheel Academic Scandal

So-called "paper" courses—latter-day correspondence courses—have become favorites of athletic department academic advisors these days. Such courses have no written work or exams in the classroom, where the athlete is on his own. Paper courses require only term papers and

Chapter Eight

take-home tests, on which tutors are allowed to give players all the help they need to get passing grades. What tutor at Alabama or Clemson is going to allow a football player to hand in an "F" paper or fail a take-home exam? Certainly not one who wants to keep their job.

Perhaps the topper of all the many cases of academic fraud was the paper course scandal perpetuated at North Carolina. The scam began in the late 1980s with the creation of phony independent studies courses and then gravitated to the Department of African and Afro-American Studies, led by Chair Julius Nyang'oro, who developed courses that required neither attendance nor the completion of a single paper. All the students enrolled in these courses received a passing grade. According to University of North Carolina historian Jay M. Smith and athletic tutor Mary Willingham, "The Nyang'oro course menu served well one of its initial purposes: to provide athletes easy grades that kept them eligible and academically on track."[32] The *New York Times* reported that North Carolina "found that over the last two decades, some 3,000 students, about half of them athletes, took courses that sometimes did not meet or require any work." Players always got high enough grades to keep them eligible. Two of the athletes who had taken these courses later sued the university for reneging on its promise to educate them.[33]

Smith and Willingham discovered that by the late 1990s, Nyang'oro had developed fifty-five bogus courses. Incredibly, some D-I athletes became conversant in obscure, difficult languages. "One of the favorites for athletes was Swahili 101," which they found, "satisfied a language requirement (other schools like the University of Washington offered this one too. A go-to language at Michigan was Ojibwe). Papers were written in English." North Carolina advisors scoured the course catalog for a professor who demanded little work in the "French Drama in Translation" offering, as well as another easy course in "Acting for Non-Majors." It is odd that athletes were attracted to studying languages, drama, and acting even as another less than demanding course—"Phy Ed for Elementary School"—might have made more sense.[34]

In 2010, Willingham blew the whistle on Nyang'oro's racket. "The paper classes were incredibly popular," she said. "But I knew the game would be over at some point, and it was very wrong from an ethical standpoint." Willingham went through the files of 183 Tar Heel football and basketball players, finding that 60 percent of them read somewhere between a fourth- and eighth-grade level, and almost 10 percent of them read below the third-grade level.[35] She recalled that:

> [O]ne player had never—not once—passed a general competency test during his primary and secondary school years. His reading skills (and writing and math skills) had consistently fallen below minimum standards. Year after year he had been promoted to the next grade not by passing benchmark exams but through the exceptional process known as compiling a 'portfolio'—an assemblage of written work accompanied by teacher testimonials, that ostensibly prove a student's sufficient mastery of the basic skills measured on end-of-grade tests."[36]

North Carolina tried to cover up the scandal, but when it became public, the Tarheel athletic department spent some $18 million fighting the NCAA to prevent it from imposing stiff penalties. North Carolina beat the rap, arguing in court that since regular students also could enroll in the paper courses, they did not constitute special treatment for athletes.[37] According to journalist Joe Nocera, "Although the university initially claimed that the scandal had nothing to do with athletics, that was untrue. Kenneth L. Wainstein, a prominent lawyer, reported in October 2014 that nearly half the students in the paper classes were athletes, although athletes comprised only about 4 percent of the total student population." When they were interviewed by Wainstein's investigators, Nyang'oro and co-worker Deborah Crowder said that their motivation in developing the paper courses was to help struggling students, especially "that subset of student-athletes who came to campus without adequate academic preparation."[38]

That, however, left out one other point: North Carolina's paper courses were surely created with money in mind. The *New York Times* called it "the scholastic equivalent of a Cayman Islands tax dodge.[39] "We entice these players to entertain the public and enrich their coaches by performing a vast amount of arduous, dangerous and unpaid work," wrote North Carolina history professor Harry Watson, "with the opportunity for free education and the distant chance to 'go pro' as their only compensation. Then we set up conditions which make the 'education' either meaningless or nearly unattainable. To me, this situation is fundamentally immoral."[40]

Chapter Eight

The paper classes started in 1993 when revered Coach Dean Smith was running the basketball program. Smith promoted "The Carolina Way"—including the fiction that his players' performance in the classroom was as important as their play on the court. The scandal revealed that North Carolina athletics were as corrupt as the phantom papers. Tarheel faithful don't want to hear that the academic fraud began with Smith, and after his 1997 retirement, it continued under Bill Guthridge, Matt Doherty, and Roy Williams.

Like the others, Williams feigned ignorance that his players were taking courses for which they did no work.[41] In 2005, Tarheel guard Rashad McCants helped Williams win the NCAA title. McCants admitted that he seldom went to class, that tutors wrote papers and other assignments for him, and that he got by through taking some of the paper courses. According to ESPN, McCants said that "he even made the dean's list in the spring of 2005 despite not attending any of his four classes for which a received straight-A grades." In his Afro-American Studies courses, McCants received ten As, six Bs, a C, and a D. In other courses, McCants earned three Fs, one D, and six Cs. "I thought it was part of the college experience," McCants said later. "You don't go to class, you don't do nothing, you just show up and play. That's exactly how it was, you know, and I think that was the tradition of college basketball, or college, period, any sport. You're not there to get an education, though they tell you that." McCants revealed that Williams knew about the fraud, but the coach denied it. Willingham said, "I think the coaches knew about the paper class system. Of course they did."[42]

Even if Williams did not have first-hand knowledge of the sham, he certainly wasn't paying any attention to the fifteen enrollments in the paper classes of players on his 2005 championship team. Evidently, Williams did not consider oversight of the academic progress of the players under his charge part of his job. Leaders have long shed responsibility for misdeeds by shielding themselves with underlings who come in handy for taking all the blame.

Jay Smith says that when he arrived at Chapel Hill in 1990, he was enamored of the success of the Tarheel basketball program. "I drank the Kool-Aid," he admitted. However, after the paper course scandal broke, Smith did not trust the administration to tear down the golden calf of its basketball and football programs. Along with Willingham, he decided to write an exposé of the paper course affair titled *Cheated:*

The UNC Scandal, the Education of Athletes, and the Future of Big-Time College Sports. Smith was right; intercollegiate sports at North Carolina underwent no significant changes. In 2019, he noted, "There'd been none of these public forums, no signs of lessons learned." The North Carolina athletic department was seemingly rewarded for its lack of serious reform when, in 2017, the Tarheels won the NCAA basketball championship.[43]

Farther south, Auburn was running its own academic fraud in the 2000s under the guise of so-called "directed-readings courses," mostly in the sociology department. In 2004–05, the head of the department supervised 250 students conducting independent studies; about a quarter of them were athletes, and the average grade was a healthy B+. One defensive back praised the department chair, saying, "He's the kind of teacher that, you know, he wants to help you out, not just pile a lot of stuff on you." Indeed, if a ten-page paper were required, which is about average for a one-credit independent study, the professor would have read 2,500 pages of students' work. On the heels of the directed-readings courses, Auburn moved up to fourth in the NCAA's Academic Progress Rate (APR) ranking. When the independent study fraud was discovered, Auburn mysteriously dropped to 85th out of 120 athletic programs. As usual, Tiger boosters went after the whistleblower rather than calling for giving players a real education.[44]

At the same time, up at Michigan, a psychology professor was running a similar independent study ruse, herding nearly 300 students through his courses from 2004 to 2007. In this case, too, the vast majority of those "studying" independently were athletes. One Wolverine football player echoed his Auburn counterpart, commenting that the professor was not "really a guy who is work-oriented; he's not just bringing you in to write papers and all that stuff." Another player said that independent study had taught him how to use a day planner. The administration at Michigan denied any impropriety.[45] It is as if big-time athletic departments have a network to share ideas about how to skirt academic standards and keep players eligible.

Smith and Willingham are frank in their denunciation of D-I football and men's basketball: "By systematically neglecting the true educational needs of some of their most academically challenged students, precisely so as to facilitate their own pursuit of profits and wins, universities carry out the greatest of all scandals in big-time college sports."[46]

Chapter Eight

Notes

1. Gary Mihoces, "Longtime Lion, Actor Alex Karras Dies at 77," *USA Today*, October 10, 2012, accessed March 5, 2024, https://www.usatoday.com/story/sports/nfl/lions/2012/10/10/alex-karras-obituary-detroit-lions/1623419.
2. Sperber, *Beer and Circus*, 131.
3. Watterson, *College Football*, 57.
4. Davies, *Sports in American Life*, 127.
5. Oriard, *King Football*, 216.
6. Watterson, *College Football*, 223.
7. Davies, *Sports in American Life*, 221. In 2012, the NCAA allowed for multi-year scholarships that could not be cancelled for athletic reasons.
8. George, *Elevating the Game*, 202; see also Shropshire and Williams, *The Miseducation of the Student Athlete*.
9. Byers, *Unsportsmanlike Conduct*, 298.
10. Davies, *Sports in American Life*, 221; and Byers, *Unsportsmanlike Conduct*, 300–1.
11. Strauss, "Football Major, Basketball Minor?"; and Branch, "The Shame."
12. Watterson, *College Football*, 330.
13. Joe Drabe with Ray Glier, "College Basketball; Georgia Suspends Harrick and Withdraws from Postseason," *New York Times*, March 11, 2003, accessed May 2, 2021, https://www.nytimes.com/2003/03/11/sports/college-basketball-georgia-suspends-harrick-and-withdraws-from-postseason.html.
14. Duderstadt, *Intercollegiate Athletics and the American University*, 47.
15. Byers, *Unsportsmanlike Conduct*, 179.
16. Sperber, *College Sports Inc.*, 298–300.
17. Smith, *Pay for Play*, 134–5.
18. George, *Elevating the Game*, 216.
19. Cited in Feinstein, *The Last Amateurs*, 24–25.
20. Cited in Feinstein, *The Last Amateurs*, 24–25.
21. John Morrow, "The Undergraduate Experience," *New York Times Education Life*, April 24, 2005, accessed July 2, 2020, https://www.nytimes.com/2005/04/24/us/education/the-undergraduate-experience-survival-of-the-fittest.html.
22. Morrow, "The Undergraduate Experience."
23. Feinstein, *The Last Amateurs*, 395.
24. Benedict and Keteyian, *The System*, 166.
25. Benedict and Keteyian, *The System*, 177, 182.
26. Watterson, *College Football*, 327-9.
27. Mitch Stacy, "Programs Lean on Online Academics," *Star Tribune*, December 25, 2019, C2.
28. Watterson, *College Football*, 327–9.
29. Smith and Willingham, *Cheated*, 233.
30. Randy Johnson, "Gophers Ibrahim to Return Next Year," *Star Tribune*, December 29, 2020, C5.
31. Branch, "The Shame."

32. Smith and Willingham, *Cheated*, 15.
33. Strauss, "Football Major, Basketball Minor?"
34. Smith and Willingham, *Cheated*, 32, 34, 39.
35. Joe Nocera, "She Had to Tell What She Knew," *New York Times*, May 6, 2014, A23.
36. Smith and Willingham, *Cheated*, 148.
37. Jeremy Bauer-Wolf, "Breaking: NCAA Finds No Academic Fraud by UNC," *Inside Higher Education*, October 16, 2017.
38. Joe Nocera, "Dean Smith Shadow Looms Over U.N.C. as It Struggles With a Scandal's Fallout," *New York Times*, February 12, 2016, accessed June 25, 2020, https://www.nytimes.com/2016/02/13/sports/ncaabasketball/dean-smiths-shadow-looms-over-unc-as-it-struggles-with-a-scandals-fallout.html.
39. Mike McIntire, "The College Sports Tax Dodge," *New York Times*, December 31, 2017, 10A.
40. Nocera, "Dean Smith Shadow."
41. Nocera, "Dean Smith Shadow."
42. ESPN, Steve Delsohn, "UNC's McCants: 'Just Show Up, Play,'" June 5, 2014, accessed January 10, 2021, https://www.espn.com/espn/otl/story/_/id/11036924/former-north-carolina-basketball-star-rashad-mccants-says-took-sham-classes; and Quierra Luck, "Is It Time to Forgive Rashad McCants?" *Sports Illustrated*, March 29, 2020, accessed January 10, 2021, https://www.si.com/college/unc/basketball/rashad-mccants-unc.
43. Marc Tracy, "At North Carolina, College Sports 101," *New York Times*, April 4, 2019, B8.
44. Smith and Willingham, *Cheated*, 208, 210.
45. Smith and Willingham, *Cheated*, 217–9.
46. Smith and Willingham, *Cheated*, xvii.

CHAPTER NINE

Exercises in Futility:
Reforming the Unreformable NCAA

"College athletics reform movements spanning almost 90 years have been remarkably consistent. They never reformed much of anything."

—Former NCAA President Walter Byers, 1995[1]

There is one line that has been repeated every decade since colleges began to play games: "Intercollegiate sports needs reform." Commissions have been formed over and over to try to right the wrongs of college sports, but reformers' efforts have been Sisyphean. One well-meaning reformer after another has fallen on the swords of win-at-all-cost administrators, athletic directors, boosters, and coaches.

Reconciling a system that puts profit and winning games before educational objectives is impossible. Historian Michael Oriard, a longtime critic of the NCAA system, declared that "proposing reforms for bigtime college football is a fool's task."[2] The huge monetary incentives to win have steadily widened the distance between playing fields and fields of study. To put it simply, D-I sports can no longer co-exist with the primary mission of higher education, because the former have devolved into a multibillion-dollar entertainment business.

Some college faculties and presidents knew—and noted—early on that sports were undermining the integrity of their institutions. Their futile attempts to fix the unfixable are another common thread in the history of the NCAA, from the meeting of college leaders with President Teddy Roosevelt at the White House in 1905 to the NCAA's Sanity Code after World War II to the Rice Commission of the late 2010s. University of North Carolina professor Jay M. Smith, who has written on the history of college sports, concludes, "By examining all these earlier episodes of growth followed by handwringing and efforts at reform, which inevitably fail—what they see is there are systemic features in college athletics that hardened over time and became ever more intractable."[3]

The sheer number of reform efforts bears witness to the inherent flaws in the institution of "amateur" sports and the myth of the "student-athlete." Roosevelt's invitation to leaders from Yale, Harvard, and Princeton for a meeting at the White House to deal with the spate of deaths in college football is perhaps the most famous of the early reform movements. None of the few tweaks to the rules fundamentally changed the system or reduced football injuries.

In December 1905, representatives from more than sixty schools met in New York City to tackle the problems of college football, eventually forming what was to become the NCAA to oversee intercollegiate athletics.[4] According to historian Ronald A. Smith, "The original constitution and bylaws were reform documents. The objective of the NCAA, according to the constitution, was the 'regulation and supervision of collegiate athletics throughout the United States' so that they could be 'maintained on an ethical plane in keeping with the dignity and high purpose of education.'"[5]

The association that spawned from a reform movement currently opposes any serious changes to its lucrative system of college sports. Times have changed, but the NCAA has not. The organization now makes so much money that it cannot put itself out of business.[6]

In 1914, Oberlin College's Charles Savage, a member of the NCAA rules committee, ridiculed ineffectual, halfhearted reform measures. His words then could apply today to the NCAA's tortured efforts to find its way out of the dark forest of corruption in college sports. "We are industriously pruning and trimming the athletic tree," observed Savage. "Plucking a leaf here and a diseased blossom there, but we hesitate to lay ax to the root. The coaches and managers in our great colleges leave no stone unturned [so] that victories may result. Money is poured out like water."[7]

After World War I, college football became one of the most important spectator sports in the country. Historian John Sayle Watterson points out the contradiction between what the United States had fought for in France and what was happening on campus: "Ironically, the war to make the world safe for democracy would also make the college gridiron more vulnerable than ever to greed, power, and unsavory practices of big-time football."[8] In 1932, a panel of college officials chaired by Penn president Thomas Gates met to address problems in college football. "We must place athletics in the proper relationship," the panel advised, "to all that we are attempting to do in fitting young men and women for the many-sided responsibilities, opportunities, and pleasures of life." The suggested reforms—ending spring practice, special athletic dormitories, payments to players, and illegal alumni interference—went nowhere.[9]

In 1934, another meeting of university leaders charged with figuring out how to stop illegal payments to players ended in failure.[10] Six years later, the NCAA declared that "no longer will any college be permitted to practice recruiting and subsidization according to what its athletic department regards as fair and legitimate procedure. In short, all financial aid or aid in kind must, in the future, come solely and only through regular established school channels for student aid available to all students."[11] That mandate was also ignored.

The NCAA instituted a "Sanity Code" in 1948 to "prohibit all concealed and indirect benefits for college athletes" and to award athletic scholarships on financial need rather than on a player's athletic talents. Like other reform measures, the Sanity Code was quickly breached. With the advent of televised games and the "insane" money that came with them, universities chose not to adhere to the rules. By the early 1950s, the Sanity Code had been hollowed out, and athletic scholarships were openly allowed. In the late 1950s, the Big Ten restricted scholarships to financial need. Other conferences did not, however, follow suit, and continued to lure potential recruits with ever big financial packages based on athletic talent. Having grown weary of their stab at nobility, the Big Ten ended their lonesome reform effort in 1961.

In 1951, the NCAA formed yet another commission to address the ubiquitous breaking of rules. This time around, a twelve-point program rehashed past and failed attempts to stiffen academic eligibility, limit the number of games, get gambling out of the games, and end illegal payments to players. Once again, the enforcement of the new rules was lax at best. Now the American Council of Education (ACE) got involved, forming a commission of eleven college presidents to look into the illegal practices. "Athletes holding scholarships or grants-in-aid," the commission wrote, "should be required to meet the same standards of academic performance and economic need as are required of all other recipients." It was an effort to restore the notion of the purely amateur sportsman to college athletics, but such a figure never actually took a position on the line of scrimmage or the jump circle. The head of the commission was a football booster, and the body he led resulted in no significant reforms. The presidents of schools who signed the report, such as Michigan State, Nebraska, and SMU, showed "either incurable optimism or outright hypocrisy," according to Watterson.[12]

Rehabilitation of the NCAA's chronic wrongdoers never happens because the organization's sanctions have always been (and still are) too weak. Cheating pays everyone involved—with the exception, that is, of the players. "One of the problems of any reform legislation of the past century," argues Smith, "is that the punishment has generally been so slight that individuals and institutions were willing to chance being caught breaking the rules, for the possible punishment was not a significant deterrent."[13] For example, as a result of a major point-shaving scandal, Kentucky was banned from playing games for one season (1952–53). The Wildcats are a perennial basketball juggernaut. Michigan State was slapped on the wrist for breaking rules in 1953, 1964, and 1970, and yet still emerged to become a powerhouse football and men's basketball school. It appears that the Spartans' misdemeanors were good investments.

Dumping Football

Among all D-I sports, football is the elephant in the locker room. As has been noted, D-I football programs cost the most money to run, with expenses such as building and maintaining stadiums, equipment, the number of coaches and scholarship players, and injuries. Watterson's definitive history of college football chronicles the fruitless and repeated efforts to reform the "lawless, and dishonest underside of [college] football."[14]

The Ivy League deemphasized football in the 1950s, its teams comprising more of a small-college conference than a big-money, high-profile football factory. Dropping football is a modest reform that has worked as well for some D-I schools by drastically reducing athletic budgets. In 1951, Georgetown eliminated football (reinstated in 1970), followed by other Catholic schools, including St. Mary's (Oakland), San Francisco, Santa Clara, Duquesne, Fordham in the 1950s, and Detroit and Marquette in the 1960s. D-I basketball schools without football include NYU, Caltech, University of the Pacific, George Washington, and Boston University.[15]

The example of one high school that dropped football in favor of a greater focus on academics provides evidence that the game does not necessarily benefit a school or foster good behavior. In 2012, a rural school district in Texas faced such dire financial straits that the superintendent suspended every sport. Football was the biggest financial drain, at $1,300 per player annually. In contrast, the district's annual outlay for math was $618 per student. The savings to the district amounted to $150,000 a year. The high school principal shifted the savings to raises for his teachers. With a renewed focus on academics, he said, "80 percent of the students passed their classes, compared with 50 percent the previous fall. About 160 people attended parent–teacher night, compared with six the year before." Teacher Desiree Valdez was elated with the results, saying, "There's been a definite decline in misbehavior. I'm struggling to recall a fight. Before, it was one every couple of weeks." Even the football coach was on board with the changes, despite having coached for two decades. "Learning is going on in 99 percent of the classrooms now," the coach told a reporter, "compared to 2 percent before."[16]

Even though dropping the football program at some schools helped their budget, it is probably not a viable reform option for others today. In 2002, with athletic department deficits mounting, Tulane University President Scott Cowen proposed chopping the football program. Outraged boosters and students wouldn't hear of it, hanging Cowen in effigy. The spooked university president backed off, and the Green Wave continued to roll.[17] In late 2014, the University of Alabama at Birmingham (UAB) axed the football program. At the time the decision was made, the school was covering two-thirds of the athletic department's budget. University President Ray L. Watts said that "football is simply not sustainable." Fans in the football-crazy state balked. Some boosters argued that schools build a national brand by playing on national TV. By the ensuing summer, the UAB Football Foundation had raised $27 million, and the school reinstated the sport. According to a UAB commission named "College Sports Solutions," the resurrected football program would "foster much goodwill and stimulate a substantial amount of spiritual and financial support from alumni, donors, ticket holders, friends, students, faculty, and the community [and] positive national attention to the University."[18] At Vanderbilt, President Gordon Gee went even further by suggesting the school jettison the entire athletic department. Par for the course, the outcry over the suggestion immediately put the kibosh on the idea.[19]

When asked about getting rid of the football program that costs Miami University millions a year, their athletic director said it would be "devastating" to Miami sports.[20] Given the amount of money that the department would be save by dropping football, as well as the spotty attendance at Miami games, one wonders how the word "devastating" applies.

A Half Century of Futile Reform Efforts

The NCAA's last serious efforts to rein in exorbitant spending on D-I football and men's basketball came in the 1970s, but member schools would have none of it. "In the end, 'need' as a grant-in-aid [scholarship] criterion was rejected," Byers recalled, "traveling squad limits were circumvented, grants were restricted to one year at a time, and freshmen were ruled eligible to play varsity games. In the wake of the attempted reforms, the football and basketball seasons were actually lengthened."[21] Robert Atwell, the former president of the ACE, declared, "I'm not sure this beast can be put in the cage. The public attachment to big-time intercollegiate football and basketball is so insane that I don't know if it can be done."[22]

In 1979, a group of twenty-six college presidents chaired by Harvard's Derek Bok called yet again for meaningful reform in college sports. One of Bok's assistants clearly saw it as a fruitless enterprise, declaring, "There isn't any way to reform it." Ideas such as shortening the basketball season fell on deaf ears (the number of games has steadily increased since). Indiana coach Bobby Knight showed his utter disdain for college administrators encroaching on his hallowed turf, saying, "[Are the presidents] qualified to tell the athletic departments what the fuck to do?"[23]

In early 1984, the SMU football scandal prompted some college presidents, headed by Bok and Father Timothy Healy of Georgetown, to call for a new presidents' commission, this time with veto power over the NCAA legislation involving scholastic and financial measures.[24] As usual, that reform movement came to naught. The presidents took none of the blame for allowing the system to deviate from the mission of higher education, pointing instead to coaches, athletic directors, and the NCAA. Byers accused the presidents of hypocrisy: "Presidents glory in all the good things about college athletics and blame others for the bad."[25]

Five years later, the Knight Foundation gave a $2 million grant to finance a commission to study D-I sports—sixty years after the Carnegie Report had castigated college teams for paying players and perpetuating academic fraud. The Knight Report found that little had changed over the course of six decades. In the past few decades, the commission determined, the NCAA had levied sanctions on half of D-I athletic departments. One survey of active and retired professional football players found that a third had received illegal payments while in college. The Knight Commission also discovered overwhelming "evidence of the widening chasm between higher education's ideals and big-time sports." Nonetheless, the commission's recommendations simply rehashed failed reform measures of yore, effectively changing nothing. Significantly, the report did not address the inequity of high-paid coaches and athletic administrators overseeing unsalaried players. Wise old Michigan football coach Bo Schembechler knew that the watered-down recommendations would have no impact: "By the turn of the century, things will return to their normal state. The hubbub will pass, as will the so-called reformers." Schembechler was prescient.[26]

When NCAA violations occur, the proliferation of employees in college administrations and athletic departments allows the higher-ups to avoid responsibility. In other words, it is easy to blame and then fire underlings for not adhering to the rules. More than twenty-five years ago, Byers saw this coming, stating, "Today, the NCAA's structure with layer and layer of administration and managers is designed to obscure responsibility."[27] In 2012, the NCAA issued a series of new edicts to impose stiffer penalties on programs and coaches for repeated infractions.[28] Nothing changed.

Former college and pro coach Dick Vitale has made a big name for himself as a colorful basketball commentator. He truly loves the college game, making his exuberant style at once both over the top and endearing. In *Campus Chaos: Why the Game I Love Is Breaking My Heart* (2000), Vitale wrote a sincere plea to save amateur college basketball as he imagined it. The book is an honest expression of his grief about the state of the game, which he calls "the greatest sport on earth." His main complaints were aimed at the illegal cash payments to players

Chapter Nine

and the growing number of them who were leaving college early to play in the NBA.[29]

The cover of the book features Vitale in front of a white board listing his wish list of reforms: "clean up gambling; control agents & boosters; keep players in school; reform recruiting; and restructure NCAA rules." Like many others who have called for the NCAA to clamp down on violators, Vitale had no concrete, viable implementation measures to suggest. The NBA has no reason to cooperate with the NCAA to regulate when players can declare for the draft. State legislatures, such as those in Alabama, Georgia, Ohio, and Kansas, are disinclined to mess with their highly popular college football and basketball programs. Vitale's call to "uphold respectable standards for academic, moral, and socially acceptable conduct" has been a stated NCAA goal for a hundred years now, but as ever more money has poured into D-I sports, these high-minded words have become increasingly meaningless. The number of scandals has only risen.[30]

Vitale also urged athletic departments to hire more "qualified African-American coaching candidates," again echoing an NCAA' pledge.[31] The dismal record of minority hires in D-I men's basketball and football in the last two decades relative to the proportion of Black players indicates that athletic directors, who are overwhelmingly White, don't perceive a problem.

The NCAA has made insincere, half-hearted efforts to raise academic standards for recruits and current players. In the early 1960s, it mandated a minimum 1.60 GPA (the high standard of a D+) for athletic eligibility and, a decade later, a minimum 2.0 high school GPA [32] These were not very stringent standards, and the latter rule was easily side-stepped with remedial high school courses.

Prior to 1972, the NCAA barred freshmen from playing varsity sports, a policy that allowed incoming athletes to adapt to college coursework. However, as fielding winning teams took priority over athletes' academic performances, the novel idea of giving incoming high schoolers a year to acclimate to college-level coursework went the way of basketball's "no dunking" rule. In 1986, the NCAA passed Proposition 48, which added SAT test scores to recruits' eligibility requirements, but cries of bias against minority athletes squelched that effort. Coaches John Chaney of Temple and John Thompson of Georgetown criticized the NCAA's academic standards as unfair to impoverished minority players, and standard tests as culturally prejudiced.[33]

According to NCAA rules, "Intercollegiate athletics programs shall be maintained as an important component of the educational program, and student-athletes shall be an integral part of the student body." On the recommendation of the Knight Commission, in the early 1990s, college presidents launched an initiative they deemed the Academic Progress Rate (APR). NCAA President Myles Brand proudly proclaimed the APR to be "the most far-reaching effort of its kind." Athletic departments reacted to the imposition of the APR by either steering their athletes toward easy majors or creating entirely new ones comprising sure-to-pass courses. As usual, unscrupulous athletic departments and their academic tutors gutted the reform measure. Like its counterparts of the past, the APR was rarely enforced. "I majored in football," one D-I player quipped.[34]

In 2012, college presidents and athletic directors held a roundtable to discuss D-I reforms. At it, University of Missouri athletic director Mike Alden confessed that changing the academic requirements for athletes was not on the agenda: "I must tell you, as the director of athletics at an institution in the Big 12 Conference, that probably wasn't the thing that was right on the tip of my tongue every day. It wasn't at the forefront of what I was looking at every day when I went to work." Alden said that raising money and winning games, among other things, were priorities.[35]

Mary Willingham, the academic advisor who blew the whistle on North Carolina's paper courses, advocated for academically unprepared players to get at least fifteen months of remedial work before taking a test to get into the school and five-year scholarships to ensure graduation.[36] For D-I coaches focused on winning and for players more interested in getting drafted by the NBA than passing courses, Willingham's high-minded ideas amounted to pure fancy.

In 2015, a professor emeritus from Florida State and the director of public affairs at Syracuse proposed special business and other courses that would actually prepare athletes for a career, in or out of sports. It seems like a good idea on the surface. How rigorous would these classes be? Coaches cannot afford to risk having their athletes declared academically ineligible. Furthermore, like the special dorms, training tables, and facilities for the exclusive use of athletes, an exclusive major for D-I athletes would only serve to further separate athletes from the rest of the student body. The numerous cases of academic scandals among athletes should plant a sufficiently glaring red flag on creating any more programs geared specifically to a small and elite group of students.[37]

Giving university credit for practicing and playing games is yet another contrived proposal to keep the "student" in the student-athlete. With athletes spending so much time practicing for and playing their games, some reformers have actually suggested creating a major in sports, equating receiving credit for one's performance on the field with the credit that a fine arts major might get for a theatrical or musical performance.[38] This is a foolish comparison. Miami University's fine arts program, for example, does not have the athletic department's budget in excess of $25 million, and fine arts students and their mentors do not have to win or go home. These students live in the real world, knowing that positions in art or performance are highly competitive. They need recommendations from professors (not coaches), so fine arts students probably do not want to be excused from class or receive special treatment.

The notion that coaches would give honest grades to their players based on the quality of their play is also ludicrous. If a player has a bad practice or game, would the head or assistant coach really give him an F for the week? What coach is going to flunk a player and risk their academic eligibility? Coaches already teach "theory of coaching" and other easy courses for their players; the grading in these courses is hardly rigorous. Universities do not need any more courses like "Varsity Basketball" or "Varsity Football" in which attendance is the only requirement. Bill Snyder, the respected former football coach at Kansas State, gave most of his players an "A" in such courses. The University of Georgia was forced to let Assistant Basketball Coach Jim Harrick Jr. go for offering athletes courses like "Coaching Principles and Strategies of Basketball." On one final exam, players were challenged with such multiple-choice questions as, "How many points does a 3-point field goal account for?"[39] The correct answer is—and hold on to your seat here—three.

A better idea would be to provide athletes with courses in the business of sports but without any connection to the university—a sort of associate sports degree run by the athletic department. There would be no required GPA or academic requirements to be eligible to play. At least that would maintain the integrity and rigor of other university majors and courses, as well as prevent indifferent athletes from taking up seats in the classroom that other students truly want or need in order to satisfy their major's required coursework.

The Rice Commission

The NCAA has struggled to find a solution to the embarrassment of college players who leave their studies to go pro. Although a few high schoolers, like Kevin Garnett and LeBron James, went on to be successful NBA players, former NBA commissioner David Stern was concerned that too many eighteen-year-olds were flaming out. In 2005, he pushed for "Article X" in the collective bargaining agreement, which mandated that a player had to be nineteen to be eligible for the draft. This led to the "one-and-done" players who play one season of NCAA basketball and then leave school for the pros. The rule takes away at least one year of earning power from NBA-ready players whose families are financially strapped. The player also risks serious injury in that one college season, which can dramatically impact his worth. Here, the case of Kentucky star Nerlens Noel comes to mind, who, after tearing his ACL, went from a potential top draft choice to number six in the 2013 draft, costing him millions of dollars. The market is not free for D-I football and basketball players.

In the latest chapter of the NCAA's blank book of reforms, in 2018, NCAA President Mark Emmert charged former Secretary of State Condoleezza Rice with leading yet another reform commission, this one on college basketball. Rice was hardly an expert on D-I sports, but the commission she headed recommended eliminating the one-and-done ballplayers.[40] It was an ignorant idea because the Rice Commission and the NCAA have no influence on the NBA, which is too successful to stop admitting talented nineteen-year-olds. Clemson's athletic director called on the NBA to end the practice, but the league has no incentive to do that as long as the NCAA provides it with a no-cost farm system.

An increasing number of "blue chip" high school basketball players are foregoing college altogether, opting to go pro playing abroad or in leagues like Overtime Elite. They take thousands of dollars of up-front money from agents and apparel companies. Nearly a decade ago, Arizona senior basketball player Solomon Hill reacted to an investigation into recruiting violations related to UCLA prospect Shabazz Muhammad. Hill pointed to the inevitability that top players would forego college to work out with trainers and nutritionists, all guided by an agent: "It's going to show future classes, 'OK, they're going to put you under investigation, make you look like the bad guy just to make an example of you.' If you don't want to be investigated, just don't go to college. If you take money early, make the decision that you're not going to attend college and you're going to seek training. There's nothing bad with that decision." For his part, Muhammad turned out to be a one-and-done at UCLA.[41]

As of the 2018–2019 season, a player could make the NBA-affiliated G League's $35,000 base salary, with other incentives, if called up to the NBA. In October 2018, the NBA announced that a "specific group of elite [eighteen-year-old] players" could earn as much as $125,000 for a G League season, even though they still had to wait a year to be brought up.[42] The NBA will probably soon begin to subsidize the G League at even higher levels as so many good high schoolers decide to stop wasting their time with the charade of attending college classes for a semester in order to play a single season of D-I hoops.

In 2018, eighteen-year-old Syracuse recruit Darius Bazley didn't show up on a college campus, deciding instead to do a million-dollar "internship" at New Balance, where his agent had negotiated a shoe contract. "They hooked me up," Bazley said.[43] As of 2020, Bazley was averaging 4.5 points with the Oklahoma City Thunder. NBA All-Star Carmelo Anthony has invested in a scheme to pay high school prospects at least $100,000 to skip college, presumably to get a cut of their NBA salary later.[44] Five-star prospect Jalen Green signed a G League contract for a half million dollars in 2020. That's a lot of money to eschew by making a pit stop in college hoops, especially given the risk of career-threatening injury and the relatively short earning potential of pro athletes.[45]

Dick Vitale and others who have proposed reforms are not concerned about whether a player finishes college. Eligibility, not credit hours, is the bottom line. Vitale recognizes the problem of kids who have little interest in attending classes, but then that includes most of the players on top football and basketball teams. "It's a sad commentary," Vitale rightly says, "when coaches tell me they have guys on their staff whose sole responsibility is to get up in the morning and make sure Johnny goes to class. . . . It's an absolute joke." However, Vitale's suggestions to develop an NBA loan program for prospective draftees or a lower NBA pay scale for college players who come out early are unrealistic, and frankly, anti-free market.[46] His ideas leave the NCAA cartel intact.

Vitale held up Mike Krzyzewski's "ideal" Blue Devil program as the gold standard of a commitment to the academic as well as athletic well-being of its players, most of whom stayed through their senior year. "Duke is the one program I thought never would have star players leaving early for the NBA or have key players transferring," Vitale said.[47] Alas, even Coach K caved in to recruiting one-and-dones, such as Jabari Parker and Kyrie Irving. A coach with his stature and respect in the business of college basketball would have made a difference had he instead said that winning was secondary to recruiting players who wanted to get a meaningful four-year degree.

Nerlen Noel's coach at Kentucky, John Calipari, built the program on the one-and-dones. Nonetheless, he claims, "I'm the one guy out there saying we've gotta change this somehow. We've gotta encourage these kids to stay two years. . . . It's wrong for high school kids; it's wrong for college kids; it's wrong for the NBA."[48] Graduating players is of no consequence to Calipari, because Kentucky does not offer a two-year degree.

The NCAA has repeatedly changed the rules of eligibility for players without any consideration of their studies. A "redshirt" player gets an extra year of eligibility by sitting out a season; he can still practice with the team during that redshirt year. In 2018, the NCAA also allowed football players who had only played four games in a season to get another year of eligibility. Redshirts are rarely held out of a season to give the player time to get his academics in order.

The Transfer Portal Merry-Go-Round: Degree Optional

Until recently, players in football, men's baseball, men's ice hockey, and men's and women's basketball could not transfer to another college in order to play for another college team without sitting out from athletics for a year (evidently the NCAA did not care about transfers in soccer, golf, swimming, and other less visible and less lucrative sports, because the rule book placed no such restrictions on them).[49] Players could not contact another school about transferring, and coaches could even step in to prevent the transfer. Of course, coaches have and do not place any such penalties on themselves for leaving a school, even on a moment's notice, for a better job.

In 2011, the NCAA came up with a convoluted rule allowing a graduating player with one year of eligibility left to transfer immediately

Chapter Nine

to another school for graduate study if their original school did not have that specific graduate program. That stipulation no longer applies, so players can choose any school. About a third of the basketball grad transfers finish their master's degree, which is at least a two-year commitment. Less than 30 percent of the football transfers get the sheepskin.[50] Once the season is over, it's one-and-done for the grad transfer too. It is also an advantage for the sports program, because the scholarship only lasts a year. In football, this permits someone like a seasoned reserve quarterback to shop around for a team that needs a starter. It is safe to say that a particular course of graduate study is probably not the deciding factor in such a player's choice of a new school to attend. As of the fall of 2018, 1,200 football players used this convenient rule to play at a different school, including 836 players at 125 FBS schools.[51]

Big-name schools are using the grad transfer rule to poach players from the mid-majors. Assistant coaches are charged with keeping track of players from other schools who might be redshirted, injured, late bloomers, or merely disgruntled with their current team. Illinois State Coach Dan Muller lamented, "It can decimate your program. There have been multiple coaches who have been fired because they haven't won enough—because of grad transfers." Howard University basketball coach Kevin Nickelberry lost several players to the grad transfer rule. "Now, you have larger schools basically just recruiting your experience and taking advantage of what you have developed," he said. "I really don't fault the young men. It's the college coaches and the presidents and everyone else, the NCAA—we decided on this rule." Iowa coach Fran McCaffery called it "the worst rule in the history of college basketball."[52]

In the late 2010s, the NCAA deliberated whether to change the rule that forced transfers to sit out a year. "We walked right up to this question," said MAC commissioner John Steinbrecher, "but the [2018] Rice Commission report [on college basketball] came out and they asked that no further action be taken on transfers at the time." The Rice Commission suggested that "hardship" cases be allowed to transfer with no penalties, but that was a subjective, unenforceable, and inequitable rule.[53] Coaches worried that any disgruntled player would leave, or that big schools would pick off burgeoning stars from smaller colleges.

A player could, however, get a waiver to play in the next season if he or she could prove "hardships or extenuating circumstances," which served to burden the NCAA and athletic departments with more compliance cases with which to deal. The rule change promised to add even more bureaucratic oversight. For example, the NCAA's Indianapolis offices had to pore through a player's family medical records to ascertain whether a player's parent was indeed sick enough to justify the player playing at a new school closer to home. And there was more. According to journalist Dan Wolken, "You had NCAA staffers trying to determine the psychological impact of a racist incident on campus," which might be cited to allow the player to transfer (and play) immediately. Players and parents often hired lawyers to make their case, and the costs of litigation for the schools involved skyrocketed.[54] As coaches continue to tamper with other teams' players, the incidence of academic fraud is bound to increase, and with more players moving around from school to school, it makes a farce of the NCAA's stipulation of "progress toward a degree."

When the pandemic hit in 2020, the NCAA further loosened transfer rules for all athletes. The last time the organization did that was after World War II, in consideration of how the war had disrupted players' lives. But in 2020, keeping the players playing games rather than maintaining academic continuity for the students was the NCAA's main concern, as Chairwoman M. Grace Calhoun of the NCAA Division-I Council acknowledged, "Allowing transfer student-athletes to compete immediately will provide additional opportunities to student-athletes during this difficult time, and perhaps allow games to be played that otherwise might not have been."[55]

In 2021, there were nearly a thousand men's college basketball players "in the portal," anticipating that the NCAA would soon allow free movement from team to team without penalty.[56] The NCAA did indeed finally end the patchwork system of waivers and special cases that spring, allowing any football, men's and women's basketball, or ice hockey player to transfer one time from one school to another without waiting out a year (like other sports). With 850 women basketball players in the portal, UConn coach Geno Auriemma opined, "Three hundred of them are not going to go, because they're going to realize it's not the school they just left [that is the problem], it's them." In the spring of 2022, the Minnesota Gophers women's team lost seven players to the portal, in part because head coach Lindsay Whalen had left the program.[57]

Basketball teams see an exodus of players around the Christmas holiday, the time by which disgruntled players realize they are not likely to get any playing time in the current season. By the same token, many football players tend to leave campus after spring practice, the same time when they find out where they rank on the depth chart. Questions remain. How many transferred players will any one team be allowed to acquire? Will coaches drop their own recruits if a better player from another team becomes available via a transfer? If the answer to the latter means the difference between winning and losing and the coach keeping his job, guess what the answer will be.

The NCAA claims that it is "dedicated to helping college students develop leadership, confidence, discipline, and teamwork through sports." What kind of team building, loyalty, and character building does this free agency engender? As journalist Kevin McNamara put it, "You want a roster filled with kids who fight through adversity, own a great work ethic, and grow together to enjoy success as seniors. It's looking like that might be as gone as a slick post move and the set shot."[58] From 2019 to 2021, one NCAA basketball player went from Drake to Minnesota to Vanderbilt.[59] Although his last stop was to the best academic school, it is unlikely that he changed schools because Vandy offered his desired major. In loosening the transfer rules, the NCAA ignored the "student" in favor of obliging the "athlete."

The NIL and Paying Players

Many voices have suggested succumbing to reality and paying players. However, in clinging to their raison d'etre, NCAA officials have unleashed their formidable legal team to fight against the prospect of sharing its profits and ending the façade of amateur sports. Nevertheless, in recent years, the courts have slowly chiseled away at the foundation of the NCAA's anti-free market front. In early 2021, the US Department of Justice (DOJ) informed the NCAA that there could be antitrust violations in the organization's plan to allow athletes to profit from their images, which "could block athletes from entering into sponsorship agreements [as part of] with their [respective] school's [promotional] deals.... Athletes [also] would not be permitted to endorse products or gambling that conflict with NCAA rules." The assistant director of the DOJ's antitrust division, Makan Delrahim, argued, "Ultimately, the antitrust laws demand that college athletes, like everyone else in our free market economy, benefit appropriately from competition." It is not clear whether former NCAA President Emmert was serious when he expressed his disappointment at the DOJ's stance: "Gosh, it just seems like no good deed goes unpunished."[60]

Allowing players to cash in on their own likenesses was something former UCLA basketball player Ed O'Bannon spent years fighting for in the courts. The NCAA profited from the use of his image in the video game *NCAA March Madness 09*, for which he received nothing. O'Bannon says that his case has to do with justice, not money.[61] In 2014, EA Sports released *NCAA Football 14*—another version of the video game that had earned the company $900 million since it first appeared in 1993. NCAA players saw none of those profits. Lucas Vincent, a defensive tackle from Missouri whose likeness appears in the game, said he couldn't even get a complimentary version of it, let alone any royalties on its sales: "I wanna buy the new NCAA game, but I also don't wanna be poor till September. . . . My likeness is on the game why do I have to pay for it?" The Missouri athletic department ignored his logical complaint, saying, "We prefer to let it go off into the night."[62]

Later in 2019, the California legislature passed a bill legalizing what Ed O'Bannon had long been fighting for—the right to sell his likeness and for players to hire agents. California Governor Gavin Newsom pointed out that athletes were not receiving equal treatment under the law: "Every single student in the university can market their name, image, and likeness," he argued. "They can go and get a YouTube channel, and they can monetize that. The only group that can't are athletes. Why is that?"[63]

In spring 2020, the NCAA proffered the idea to allow players "to profit from their images if the payments came from a third-party, and not directly from the university."[64] A year later, no definitive rules had been established, leaving players with the impression that they could market themselves but could face penalties for doing so. The California law is scheduled to go into effect in 2023. Never slow to react, the NCAA's legal team wasted no time leaping into action to stop the "Fair Pay to Play Act," citing the US Constitution's interstate commerce clause. The organization threatened to expel any school that allowed its players to break the association's monopoly on this practice. Ramogi Huma, the executive director of the National College Players Organization, castigated the system of intercollegiate sports: "NCAA amateurism is a fraud. It's a $14-billion-a-year industry with millionaire coaches. An NCAA ban on California colleges would amount to an illegal group

Chapter Nine

boycott that would violate federal and California antitrust laws."[65] When other states proposed similar legislation, the NCAA issued an ambiguous directive that would permit athletes "to benefit from the use of their name, image and likeness in a manner consistent with the collegiate model."[66]

With states such as Florida, Georgia, and California passing laws to allow college players to market themselves, the NCAA was forced to contemplate changes to its strict prohibition of paying players. Concerned, the organization charged its three athletic divisions with coming up with guidelines by January 2021. The convoluted directive from NCAA Board of Governors Chair Michael Drake desperately hung on to the old fiction that the "student-athlete" was a student first: "The board is emphasizing that change must be consistent with the values of college sports and higher education and not turn student-athletes into employees of institutions."[67] When we hear that a top player has been declared academically ineligible, or has had to miss practice or a weeknight game because of a scheduled class or exam, or the "one-and-done" is no more, then we might take Drake seriously.

The NCAA's wishes notwithstanding, players are becoming savvier about selling their own likeness and profiting from their unique skills. During the 2021 NCAA basketball tournament, Rutgers guard Geo Baker led a protest to let college players ring the bell of market freedom. "The NCAA OWNS [sic] my name image and likeness," Baker argued. "Someone on [a] music scholarship can profit from an album. Someone on academic scholarship can have a tutor service. For [people] who say 'an athletic scholarship is enough,' anything less than equal rights is never enough." Baker made the point by using the hashtag "I am #NotNCAAProperty." He said that players had to stay in isolation so that the tournament could go on. Players, Baker tweeted, got "free deodorant and small boxed meals." When a tweet follower offered to bring food to the players, Baker correctly pointed out that was against NCAA rules.[68]

In 2021, NIL rulings prompted Jason Stahl from the University of Minnesota to begin an organization to advocate for college football players—the College Football Players Association. Former Minnesota Gopher players and regents were among the members of the advisory board.[69] It remains to be seen whether this organizational effort will succeed where others have failed. The right of players to sell their NILs might be an incentive for them to join the association.

With or without a players' organization, immediately after the changes to the NIL laws, players began to cash in. For example, Parker Fox, a seldom-used Minnesota Gopher power forward, made more than $10,000 on deals such as a restaurant's promotion of "Parker Fox Loaded Tater Tots." More than 150 Gopher athletes got endorsements in 2021, about a third of them football players. Management companies have helped athletes broker deals.[70] Former Georgia and Miami football coach Mark Richt joked about his playing days: "When I was playing college football, my priorities were girls, football, and then school. Now, it's going to be money, girls, football, school." The NCAA was not about to let athletes cut their own sponsorship contracts if the deals conflicted with those of the athletic department. So, if Oregon has an agreement with Nike, a Duck player cannot go with Adidas. Whether players can shill beer brands remains to be seen. The ban on college players signing with agents remains.[71]

The NCAA tried to prohibit recruiting athletes with promises to promote their NIL, but like all other attempts to stop illegal recruiting practices, that one was a dead letter. In the spring of 2022, the NCAA also tried but failed to stop "collectives" that helped players' market themselves, equating the collectives with boosters. Athletes are aware of their earning potential and are already asking athletic programs about it.[72] According to Todd Berry, the executive director of the American Football Coaches Association, "I had a coach call me a couple of weeks ago that said he had a booster promising all these high school kids NIL to encourage them to pick State U, so to speak, and these are guys he [the coach] didn't even want to recruit."[73] There were 1,400 men's basketball players in the portal in early 2022, many of whom were looking for better NIL deals. Asked about how often he looks at the portal, Minnesota Gopher basketball coach Ben Johnson replied, "It's an every five-minute thing. It's a sickness."[74]

Some reformers have called for giving D-I players a small cash stipend (in addition to their scholarship). These payments would not reflect the player's market worth but would grant them a few thousand dollars to cover incidental costs, such as buying food after the dining halls are closed. This would, of course, amount to a tiny fraction of the huge salaries going to D-I football coaches. In March 2019, California Judge Claudia Wilken handed down a muddled decision about compensation for players, acknowledging that they should be getting benefits "related to education," but not full-blown salaries. "The extraordinary revenues that defendants derive from these sports," she wrote, "is not commensurate with the value that they create." Wilken basically ruled that the system was unjust but lacking an alternative and, admitting that it was a popular institution, left it intact. The ruling left neither side satisfied.[75]

The NCAA knows that it will be opening a Pandora's Box if cash payments are made to players. One of their lawyers argued in a federal appeals court that paying athletes an hourly wage "launches you on the edge of a slippery slope that rapidly takes you to someplace that you don't want to go."[76] He should have clarified that it was someplace that the big NCAA moneymakers don't want to go.

Illicit money already ends up in players' pockets. What would prevent a booster or coach from slipping an extra several thousand into the envelope? And aside from the twenty or so athletic departments that run a profit, no mid-major like Miami University, whose athletic department sinks millions into the red every year, could afford to pay its players. In 2015, Oliver Luck, the NCAA's former executive vice president, declared, "It would be a bad mistake to create campus employer-employee relationships with student-athletes." Paying college athletes "would distract in a very significant way from pursuing what they really need to pursue—an education. And we need to emphasize the value of that education."[77]

In June 2021, the US Supreme Court unanimously ruled that the NCAA was in violation of the Sherman Antitrust Act in restricting "education-related benefits" to athletes. Justice Neil Gorsuch, writing for the court, found that the NCAA was seeking "immunity from the normal operation of antitrust laws." The ruling will have a far-reaching impact, according to journalist Jessica Gresko: "The NCAA itself cannot bar schools from sweetening their offers to Division I basketball and football players with additional education-related benefits."[78]

Undoubtedly, the dumbest reform idea the NCAA has come up with in recent years is to pay players up to $5,980 for getting high grades (where the NCAA came up with that monetary figure is unknown, as is the requisite GPA). This is, of course, another recipe for corruption. Even with such a rule in place, why wouldn't athletic advisors find their players the easiest classes taught by the most lenient graders? And one can readily imagine an athlete and his advisor confronting a professor about getting a better grade because a lower one will cost the player thousands of dollars. By the way, will regular students get the same financial bonuses for pulling down good grades? And where will this extra money to pay players for good grades come from? Athletic departments already have their hands deep into the pockets of regular students in the guise of their annual student fees, and at most universities, athletic directors also ask the administration year after year to dip into the academic budget for funds to service the debts they have racked up. Former Gopher gymnast John Roethlisberger, who led a movement to reinstate his sport at Minnesota after it got the axe in 2021, commented, "If the option is there to pay [athletes], they'll have to. I don't fault them because they don't really have a choice. The part that's frustrating to me is, our message to the Regents has been that college sports model is completely broken. It's unsustainable, and we need to find solutions."[79]

The Unlevel Playing Field

The NCAA has tried to make the case that without limits on players' compensation, the competitive balance would be thrown off. But that balance does not and never truly did exist in the first place. As athletes market themselves, blue chip players will go to those schools where they can get maximum exposure on primetime TV for their NIL deals. This means that the Alabama, Michigan, and USC football teams, to name a few, will end up with the best players every year, and that top basketball recruits will head to the likes of UCLA, Duke, and Michigan State. If surreptitious cash payments to recruits and players are a problem now, one can only imagine the abuse that sanctioned stipends to players will bring. Academic considerations will be shunted even further to the side.

In reaction to the California legislation allowing players to sell their likeness, Emmert argued, "The whole notion of trying to maintain as fair a playing field as you can is really central to all this. And using sponsorship arrangements, in one way or another, as recruiting inducements is something everybody is deeply concerned about."[80] One must wonder to what competitive balance Emmert is referring. Certainly, no such balance exists in college football or men's basketball. For years, teams from Florida—the University of Florida, Florida State, and Miami—have dominated the football scene, winning or tying for seven national championships. In recent years, it has been a good bet that Notre Dame, Alabama, Clemson, Oklahoma, LSU, Auburn, USC, or Ohio State will make the final four of the NCAA football championship.

Minnesota, Miami-Ohio, and Alabama football compete in the same division, but the odds of the Gophers or the Redhawks meeting the

Chapter Nine

Crimson Tide in the championship are infinitesimal. Since its inception in 2015, there have been twenty-eight spots in the College Football Playoffs. Even so, only eleven different teams have ever participated, with Oklahoma, Ohio State, Clemson, and Alabama securing twenty of those bids. Until Cincinnati did so in 2021–22, no team outside the Power Five conferences or Notre Dame had appeared in the playoffs (Alabama crushed the Bearcats in the semifinal). In fact, that year, the Crimson Tide won its sixth national title in fourteen seasons under Nick Saban, who had compiled a phenomenal record of 170–23. So much for Emmert's fair playing field. Bama is always a good money-line bet.

As in D-I football, year after year, the men's basketball championship is a forum for the usual suspects. It is likely that Duke, North Carolina, Kansas, Michigan State, and Gonzaga will compete for the men's basketball championship every year. In early 2021, for the first time in thirty-nine years, Duke and North Carolina were not ranked in the Associated Press's top twenty-five basketball teams. From 2009 to 2019, the big powers reigned supreme in the championship: Duke, North Carolina, Villanova, and UConn twice each, and Kentucky, Louisville, and Virginia once each.

Honest people with connections to big-time college sports know that the current NCAA system is irredeemable. Legislators know it, college administrators know it, athletic department staffs know it, student-athletes know it, and faculties know it. If the average student who subsidizes intercollegiate sports through mandatory fees is paying attention, they know it too.

Notes

1. Byers, *Unsportsmanlike Conduct*, 337.
2. Oriard, *Bowled Over*, 233.
3. Marc Tracy, "College Sports 101: A U.N.C. Class Reviews a Scandal at Its Source," *New York Times*, April 4, 2019, accessed December 20, 2020, https://www.nytimes.com/2019/04/04/sports/unc-scandal.html.
4. Watterson, *College Football*, 77–79; and Taylor Branch, "The Shame of College Sports."
5. Smith, *Pay for Play*, 53.
6. See Ingrassia, *The Rise of the Gridiron University*, 60.
7. Watterson, *College Football*, 138.
8. Watterson, *College Football*, 140.
9. Smith, *The Myth of the Amateur*, 80–82; and Watterson, *College Football*, 179.
10. Alan Gould, "College Grid Recruiting, Louis' Climb Major Topics," *Montana Standard*, December 22, 1935, 22, accessed January 15, 2021, https://newspaperarchive.com/montana-standard-dec-22-1935-p-22/.

11. Unattributed, "Student Aid to Be Open to All Scholars," *Des Moines Tribune*, January 1, 1940, 12, accessed January 6, 2021, https://www.newspapers.com/image/324157497.

12. Watterson, *College Football*, 227–28, 233.

13. Smith, *Pay for Play*, 209.

14. Watterson, *College Football*, 397ff.

15. Sanderson and Siegfried, "Why American."

16. Amanda Ripley, "The Case Against High-School Sports," *Atlantic Monthly* vol. 312, no. 3 (October 2013), 72–78.

17. Watterson, *College Football*, 415.

18. Ben Strauss and Zach Schonbrun, "It's a Game of Spiraling Costs, So a College Tosses Out Football," *New York Times*, December 3, 2014, A1; and ESPN, Alex Scarborough, "UAB Reinstates Football for 2016," accessed March 29, 2020, https://www.espn.com/college-football/story/_/id/12991674/uab-blazers-football-return.

19. Watterson, *College Football*, 415.

20. Interview with Miami University athletic director, August 12, 2021.

21. Byers, *Unsportsmanlike Conduct*, 240.

22. Duderstadt, *Intercollegiate Athletics*, 304.

23. Sperber, *College Sports Inc.*, 339.

24. Watterson, *College Football*, 355.

25. Byers, *Unsportsmanlike Conduct*, 109.

26. Davies, *Sports in American Life*, 224–226.

27. Byers, *Unsportsmanlike Conduct*, 35.

28. Michael Marot, "NCAA Passes Stronger Rules to Punish Cheating Programs," *Star Tribune*, October 31, 2012, C2.

29. Dick Vitale, *Campus Chaos: Why the Game I Love Is Breaking My Heart* (Indianapolis: Time Out Publishing, 2000), 258.

30. Vitale, *Campus Chaos*, 260–2.

31. Vitale, *Campus Chaos*, 263.

32. Watterson, *College Football*, 305.

33. Craig R. Coenen, review of Ronald Smith, *Pay for Play*, *American Historical Review* 117, no. 5 (December 2012): 1610–1611.

34. Coenen, review of Ronald Smith, *Pay for Play*; and Chudacoff, *Changing the Playbook*, 150.

35. Evans, et al., "Institutional Experience with Academic Reform," 101.

36. Joe Nocera, "She Had to Tell What She Knew," *New York Times*, May 6, 2014, A23.

37. Strauss, "Football Major, Basketball Minor?"

38. See Roger Pielke, Jr., "Why Not a College Degree in Sports," *New York Times*, September 14, 2016, A27.

39. Strauss, "Football Major, Basketball Minor?"

40. Rice Commission Report, September 6, 2018, NCAA.org, accessed December 23, 2022, https://www.ncaa.org/sports/2018/9/6/commission-updates.aspx.

41. Bischoff and Kelley, "Students Pay Big for NCAA Sports."; and Eric Prisbell, "Muhammad Saga Could Alter Thinking," *USA Today*, November 14, 2012, 7C.

42. Victor Mather and Kevin Draper, "N.B.A. G League is Set to Offer an Alternative to 'One and Done,'" *New York Times*, October 19, 2018.

43. Marc Stein, "Who Says College Leads to Better Pay," *New York Times*, October 23, 2018, B7.

44. Alan Blinder, "No Tournament? No Problem for Some Awaiting Draft," *New York Times*, March 21, 2021, 33.

45. Fuller, "Stars Weigh G League and College."

46. Vitale, *Campus Chaos*, 22, 24.

47. Vitale, *Campus Chaos*, 2.

48. Grant Hughes, "Why the NBA's 1-and-Done Rule Is Causing More Harm than Good," August 8, 2013, accessed June 28, 2022, https://bleacherreport.com/articles/1723163-why-the-nbas-one-and-done-rule-is-causing-more-harm-than-good.

49. See Chip Scroggins, "NCAA Scored by Loosening its Reins," *Star Tribune*, June 1, 2018, C3.

50. Luke Thompson, "Degree Rare for Grad Transfers in Revenue Sports," *News Star*, May 27, 2016, accessed June 29, 2022, https://www.thenewsstar.com/story/news/local/2016/05/27/degree-rare-grad-transfers-revenue-sports/85060646/.

51. Unattributed, *USA Today*, September 6, 2018, C1.

52. Nicole Auerbach, "Grad Rule Veers Off Course," *USA Today*, November 17, 2017, accessed March 15, 2022, https://www.usatoday.com/story/sports/ncaab/2017/10/17/college-basketball-grad-transfers-unintended-consequences/537014001/.

53. Ralph D. Russo, "Rules on Transfers Likely to Be Changed by NCAA," *Star Tribune*, April 14, 2021, C3.

54. Dan Wolken, "NCAA Zeroing in On Really Helping Athletes," *USA Today*, February 20, 2020, 5C.

55. AP, "NCAA Grants Waivers for All Transfer Athletes," *Star Tribune*, December 17, 2020, C2.

56. Marcus Fuller, "Mahtomedi's Fox Commits to U," *Star Tribune*, April 16, 2021, C2.

57. Rachel Blount and Andrew Krammer, "The Grass May Not Be Greener for Players in Transfer Portal," Star Tribune, April 1, 2022, C9; and unattributed, "Smith is Seventh Player to Enter Transfer Portal," *Star Tribune*, April 2, 2022, C3.

58. NCAA website, http://www.ncaa.org/about/join-our-team, accessed March 31, 2020.

59. Marcus Fuller, "Former Gophers Center Liam Robbins to Transfer to Vanderbilt," *Star Tribune*, April 12, 2021, accessed June 15, 2021, https://www.Star Tribune.com/former-gophers-center-liam-robbins-to-transfer-to-vanderbilt/600045119/.

60. Unattributed, "NCAA to Delay Vote on Compensation, *Star Tribune*, January 10, 2021, C11.

61. See Ed O'Bannon, *Court Justice: The Inside Story of My Battle Against the NCAA* (New York: Diversion Books, 2018).

62. Austin Murphy, "Full Hearts, Empty Pockets," *Sports Illustrated*, July 22, 2013, 15.

63. Alan Blinder, "Jolting N.C.A.A., California Law Says College Athletes Can Profit," *New York Times*, September 30, 2019, A1.

64. Brakkton Booker, "College Athletes Are Now Closer to Getting Paid After NCAA Board Oks Plan," National Public Radio, April 29, 2020, accessed March 25, 2021, https://www.npr.org/2020/04/29/847781624/college-players-are-now-closer-to-getting-paid-after-ncaa-board-oks-plan.

65. "California Urged to Block Attempt to Pay Athletes," *New York Times*, September 12, 2019, B9.

66. Dan Wolken, "States Lit Fuse for College Athletes," *USA Today*, November 12, 2019, 3C.

67. Ralph Russo, "NCAA Sets Stage for Athlete Pay," *Star Tribune*, October 30, 2019, A1.

68. Cindy Boren, "Prominent NCAA Tournament Players Launch '#NotNCAAProperty' Protest as March Madness Begins," *Washington Post*, March 18, 2021, accessed March 21, 2021.

69. Randy Johnson, "Players Association Aims to Give Athletes A Voice," *Star Tribune*, July 28, 2021, C2.

70. Ryan Faircloth, "U Student-athletes Cashing in Under New NCAA Rules," *Star Tribune*, December 5, 2021, A1

71. Alan Blinder, "As States Act, N.C.A.A. Chief Budges on Pay," *New York Times*, May 9, 2021, A1.

72. Chip Scoggins, "Collectives Sprouting in College Sports, and U Needs One to Keep Up," *Star Tribune*, April 17, 2022, C1; and Randy Johnson, "Road Trip with New Areas to Explore," *Star Tribune*, May 10, 2022, C1.

73. Dan Wolken, "College Football Starts Season Under a Dark Cloud," *USA Today*, September 3, 2021, 1C.

74. La Velle E. Neal III, "Long Shot Brings Big Buzzkill," *Star Tribune*, May 8, 2022, C2.

75. Marc Tracy, "Judge Opens the Door to More Compensation for College Athletes," *New York Times*, March 8, 2019, accessed March 24, 2020, https://www.nytimes.com/2019/03/08/sports/ncaa-amateurism-ruling.html.

76. Maryclaire Dale, "NCAA Asks US Appeals Court to Block Pay for Student-Athletes," *Star Tribune*, February 15, 2023, accessed February 16, 2023, https://www.startribune.com/ncaa-asks-us-appeals-court-to-block-pay-for-student-athletes/600251977/.

77. Steve Cameron, "The NCAA Brings in $1 Billion a Year—Here's Why it Refuses to Pay Its College Athletes," *Business Insider*, March 26, 2019, accessed April 8, 2015, https://www.businessinsider.com/ncaa-college-athletes-march-madness-basketball-football-sports-not-paid-2019-3.

Chapter Nine

78. AP, Jessica Gresko, "High Court Sides with Ex-Athletes in NCAA Compensation Case," *Star Tribune*, June 21, 2021, accessed July 10, 2021, https://www.startribune.com/high-court-sides-with-ex-athletes-in-ncaa-compensation-case/600070451/.

79. Marcus Fuller, "U to Pay Athletes for Academic Success," *Star Tribune*, April 5, 2022, A1.

80. Russo, "NCAA Sets Stage."

CHAPTER TEN

On Defense:
Pom-Pom Presidents, Booster Boards, NCAA Bureaucrats, and the Status Quo

> "I believe the record now clearly shows the major hope for reform lies *outside* the collegiate structure. What the colleges will not do voluntarily should be done for them."
>
> —Former NCAA executive director Walter Byers, 1995[1]

The history of failed reforms of intercollegiate sports, as chronicled in the last chapter, begs the question: Who will change a system that is inherently contradictory to the objectives of higher education? Byers was dismissive of the NCAA's commitment to change: "Today's enlarged NCAA rule book and the beleaguered NCAA enforcement program cannot produce the changes and restore the integrity many seek."[2]

Indiana University professor Murray Sperber agreed with Byers that reform of big-time college sports could not come from within, chastising the NCAA in no uncertain terms: "*The association, in its present form, cannot and does not want to control the commercialism and corruption of College Sports Inc.* [italics Sperber's]"[3] He added this:

> Myth: The NCAA can correct the problem in college sports. Reality: The athletic directors and coaches who control the NCAA deny the existence of any significant problems in college sports.... The bottom line on meaningful NCAA reform is clear: the NCAA cannot solve the systemic problems in college sports because the coaches and ADs who control it are a central source of those problems.[4]

Chapter Ten

Moneymakers and the Status Quo

Radical change to an entrenched bureaucracy like the NCAA will not come from legislators, boards of trustees, or college presidents. Reform will also not come from athletic departments or coaches. With the exception of D-I athletes, the stakeholders in big-time college sports make too much money to incentivize them to change it. If their consciences have not been tweaked by the great many scandals that have dogged D-I sports for so long, why would they stop milking their cash cow now?

At some schools, the members of the boards of trustees are some of the biggest boosters of intercollegiate sports. Many of them are avid sports fans, and may not, as they do with athletics, feel an emotional connection to the university professors who teach, research, and write. Football and men's basketball games are the public face of the university, and some trustees judge the success or failure of a school's team as a measure of their school's prominence. A great many people can tell you which schools have the best football or basketball teams, but not too many can off the top of their heads rattle off which institutions boast the best medical or law schools.

Many trustees are wealthy businesspeople.[5] Coming from the private sector, they see no problem with "branding" their school on its team's record on the field of play. To their minds, advertising through athletics justifies the multimillion-dollar deficits incurred by D-I athletic departments. Although it is a dubious proposition that enormous, even unaffordable, expenditures on sports programs are the best way for a university to get the most for its advertising buck, many trustees feel that way, even when those expenses come at the cost of the university's academic mission. Booster boards accept athletic department scandals as unfortunate byproducts but hardly as deal breakers.

University leaders are also big backers of their athletic programs. "More often than not they have played the role of cheerleader for their own institution," writes Ronald A. Smith, "while calling for reform of the system for all the others. Cheerleading has generally won the day, whereas reforming the system has generally been subscribed to by word and not by action."[6] In the midst of the investigation into Ohio State's football program in the late 2000s, President Gordon Gee joked about his power to control the athletic program and fire coach Jim Tressel: "I'm just hopeful the coach doesn't fire me!"[7]

On Defense

In 1991, the Knight Commission advised that university presidents were key to reforming the system, but there is little chance of that happening. They either have no inclination to institute reforms or have no power to make significant changes.[8] It is trustees who hire and fire university presidents, so the trustees at universities that run big-money sports programs must be in agreement that the sports program is their school's fiscal priority. Historians Elliott Gorn and Warren Goldstein point out that "the very people who have been expected to 'clean up' college athletics—college presidents—have never had the power to do so. Those who did have the power, those who actually controlled college sports programs—boards of trustees and alumni—have consistently refused to tamper with big-time college athletics."[9] No presidential candidate is going to get the job if they tell a search committee that they want to de-emphasize intercollegiate sports. Courageous presidents who have tried to rein in their schools' athletic budgets have met with resistance from trustees and wealthy athletic boosters. One president of a big football school told journalist Gilbert M. Gaul, "We are our own worst enemies. We're all afraid to go first."[10]

Jay M. Smith and Mary Willingham, those who blew open North Carolina's paper course scandal, also hold out no hope for change to come from the top of the Ivory Tower: "The Michigan case [of academic fraud in the mid-2000s] throws into relief one of the greatest obstacles to reform in the world of collegiate sport. At big-time institutions, key administrators and faculty committee positions tend to be dominated by the compromised and the co-opted."[11]

The late North Carolina State basketball coach Jim Valvano knew exactly who the most important university employees were. Valvano coached Chris Washburn, who struggled mightily in the classroom and, after a short NBA career, ended up homeless. Valvano once said the most powerful people on campus were not administrators, implying that coaches were, and that academic ability played no role in admitting players like Washburn: "You think the chancellor is going to tell you what to do? Who to take into school or not to take into school? I doubt it."[12]

Pom-pom waving presidents have feigned at making reforms, but their periodic commissions have not stopped the steady growth in the money their schools spend on sports programs to the detriment of the university's educational mission. "University presidents could stand up like responsible heads of state instead of hiding in the corner anytime athletic boosters or academic department chairs start calling them out," charges former Rutgers athletic director Robert Mulcahy III. "Money has the potential to destroy the integrity—even the morality—of intercollegiate sports as much as it could enrich the system. Reform should begin with a more level-headed system for sharing money across all three divisions. . . . The NCAA is not capable in its current form of solving this problem."[13]

In journalist Alexander Wolff's 1995 open letter in *Sports Illustrated* to Edward T. Foote II, the president of the University of Miami from 1981 to 2001, Wolff contrasted Miami's dedication to winning with New York University's focus on academics, making the latter one of the best schools in the country:

> [During your tenure] your football program dragged Miami's name through the mud, [while] another urban, private university has gone big-time—raising huge amounts of money, going on a building binge and raiding the Ivy League for faculty—without big-time sports. And no one has any less respect for NYU because it doesn't field even a club football team. . . . "As president I take full responsibility," you [Foote] said last week. "The buck stops with me." If you really believe that, don't even think about resigning. . . . Think of your own words. "Those with responsibility for the academic mission of universities—faculties, deans, provosts and presidents, not coaches, athletic directors and alumni associations—must lead," you wrote in 1982. "Universities exist for teaching and research, not winning games."[14]

University presidents and boards of trustees dare not invoke the wrath of rabid alumni fans and boosters by questioning the millions of dollars most schools lose on athletic programs or by addressing the rampant scandals that plague NCAA sports. Yes, college presidents and administrators refer to athletic programs as an attractive "front porch" to their universities. What they don't say is that the house the pretty porch sits in front of has become rundown, or that the porch, too, has begun to rot. Still, college leaders operate under the assumption that their schools will suffer if athletic programs are cut in favor of a greater emphasis on academics and a rebranding of their schools as model educational institutions. Maybe not, as Wolff pointed out in the case of NYU.

On Defense

The NCAA Guards the Bank

We should not expect the bureaucrats at the NCAA headquarters in Indianapolis and their offices around the country to do anything to right the wrongs of D-I sports. Reforming the system has been a fool's errand, in part because the bureaucrats who profit from the Division I system have no incentive to change it. They have too much money on board to scuttle their own ship. Bureaucracies do not reform themselves, and as writer John Feinstein points out, "The NCAA is a classic bureaucracy that makes so many mistakes it is impossible to keep count."[15] The NCAA often deflects any blame by charging delinquent athletic programs with a lack of "institutional oversight." Business leaders often have to cut the fat out of management, but no bureaucrat making a hefty salary in a "non-profit" organization—in this case, the NCAA—eliminates their own job or that of their colleagues. Seventy years ago, Columbia University professor Jesse Feiring Williams said:

> To ask individuals who are the product of forces that produce 16 Bowl Games last January to put an end to such business by acts of personal volition is merely to profess faith in moral magic. To ask individuals who are caught up in the meshes of an economic system to give up Madison Square Garden by simply foregoing thousands of dollars is a species of faith that may move mountains but not athletic boards and councils.[16]

Williams would be shocked to know that in 2021–22, the number of bowl games had grown substantially to forty-four.

No one invested in the NCAA structure is going to initiate a proposal to put their own job in jeopardy. Mark Emmert, unlike his predecessor Walter Byers, could not admit that the system he ran was irredeemable. In the early 2010s, Emmert hinted at making significant reforms: "The integrity of collegiate athletics is seriously challenged today by rapidly growing pressures coming from many directions. We have reached a point where incremental change is not sufficient to meet these challenges. I want us to act more aggressively and in a more comprehensive way than we have in the past. A few new tweaks of the rules won't get the job done."[17] Before retiring in 2023, Emmert made a few meaningless changes, none of which rectified his inherently corrupt system.

The NCAA website boasts that their Indianapolis office is staffed by "more than 500 professionals dedicated to helping college students develop leadership, confidence, discipline, and teamwork through sports."[18] Good luck in finding any reference to academic achievement on the site. When confronted with the NCAA's hypocritical commitment to academics in D-I sports, Emmert often prefaced his comments with the claim that the classroom was his first priority. "I'm a lifelong academic," he said. "I grew up with that tradition, and I never worked at a school that didn't have students on their board, and they were full voting members. They voted on my contract, and I think that's just perfectly appropriate." The *New York Times* pointed out that "there are athletes serving on several important councils, but there is not one on the NCAA Board of Governors. No athletes vote on Emmert's [multimillion-dollar] contract, which was extended late last year through 2023."[19]

The NCAA and its lawyers have dodged every effort to end the monopoly on college sports. In 2022, the organization moved to give more power to schools and conferences, which Emmert called a "declaration of independence." The motive was not so much an altruistic gesture but rather one intended to avoid more lawsuits and court rulings unsympathetic to the NCAA's arguments for maintaining the status quo.[20]

Athletic department employees, who run the show for the NCAA on the ground, also have no incentive to change a system for which they have worked their entire careers. This includes D-I men's basketball and football coaches, who are not only often the highest-paid university employees but even are among the highest-paid public state employees. Athletic departments carefully guard their bailiwicks. Seven universities, four of them from Texas, even insisted that the NCAA notify their athletic departments of a pending investigation.[21]

Given their complicity in running the sham "amateur" and "nonprofit" system for the supposed educational benefit of their athletes, it is probably no surprise that athletic directors decline to respond to tough questions about the current situation in D-I sports. In 2021, repeated requests were sent to the athletic directors of more than a dozen D-I schools for what was promised to be a short interview. In so doing, the request identified the interviewer as a professor of history at Miami University who teaches sports history, among other subjects, and the author of several books on sports. The request disclosed current work on this book, to which their perspectives would be added. Of all the ADs contacted, a total of two—those at Clemson and Miami University—agreed to talk.

No reply whatsoever was received from the ADs at the University of North Carolina, the University of Miami, the University of California-Berkeley, Duke University, Notre Dame, The Ohio State University, or Temple University. Staff members in the athletic departments at USC and Oklahoma replied that the athletic director was unavailable for an interview. The athletic department at the University of Minnesota said that Mark Coyle would not be available for two months. Two days later, an interview with Coyle appeared in the Minneapolis *Star Tribune*, in which he addressed some of the current issues in NCAA sports—the very request of the interview. Evidently, Coyle, a public employee, is selective about to whom he speaks. He also declined to talk to Minnesota Public Radio about the Gopher athletic department's huge budget deficit and his elimination of men's gymnastics, tennis, and track and field, which were done in efforts to cut costs.

Faculty Impotence

Some scholars suggest that reform will have to come from within,[22] but university faculties cannot reassert control over intercollegiate sports. When, in 1898, representatives from the seven schools that eventually made up the Ivy League (minus Yale) met to establish faculty control over college football and baseball, the committee's recommendations fell flat—as have most faculty attempts to reform college sports and reestablish academic priorities ever since.[23]

In the last half-century, faculties at most D-I schools have increasingly lost power relative to regents, presidents, provosts, deans, and financial administrators.[24] According to Gerald Gurney, Donna Lopiano, and Andrew Zimbalist, who have either written about or consulted for athletic programs, "nearly 80 percent of faculty athletics representatives are appointed by college presidents, while only 20 percent are nominated by the faculty and approved by the president."[25] Many athletic departments and coaching staffs have also grown dismissive of the tenured intellectuals sitting pretty in the ivory tower; giving them control over fields of play is anathema. The two constituencies obviously work at cross purposes; coaches must win and can't afford to risk the eligibility of their players by allowing faculty to determine academic standards and limits on spending.[26]

No elitist professors are going to tell D-I coaches what to do, as the Ohio State faculty did to Woody Hayes in 1961. That year, Hayes led the Buckeyes to a 6–0 Big Ten record and the conference championship. At

Chapter Ten

the end of November, the Ohio State Faculty Council voted 28–25 to turn down a bid to play in the Rose Bowl—the "granddaddy" of college bowl games. The professors did so because they concluded that football had become too important at the university—to the point of overshadowing its academic mission. The winter semester started on January 2, making it nearly impossible for students who traveled to Pasadena to watch or play in the January 1 bowl game to get back to Columbus in time to attend their first week of classes. Displeased by this overture to academics, one Buckeye fan worried that the university was going the way of the Ivy League schools: "I hope our university does not pattern itself or imitate some of the effete Eastern Colleges with the consequent loss of vigor, both in mind and body."[27]

When word went out that the Ohio State faculty had stepped in to decline the Rose Bowl bid, thousands of students and Buckeye fans took to the streets of Columbus in protest. To Hayes's credit, he did not spur them on. He was scheduled to give a speech at an alumni dinner in Cleveland when he heard the news. "I'm bitter," he said. "The vote deeply disturbs and dismays me. But I cannot question the faculty's sincerity or their right to act. But I seriously question their judgment."[28] The decision stood, and the football team stayed home rather than travel to Pasadena that year.

Now in need of another team to play in the big game, the Rose Bowl committee turned to the Minnesota Gophers, who had finished second that season. The Gophers accepted the invitation. Ironically, in the late 1950s, the Minnesota faculty had questioned the Big Ten's binding contract with the Rose Bowl, arguing that the weeks of practice before the game were too disruptive to the football players' studies. Nevertheless, the Minnesota Faculty Senate Committee on Intercollegiate Athletics voted 108–33 to allow the Gophers to play in their second straight Rose Bowl. The decision was made in part because the university had received its share of Rose Bowl money in the past, and the faculty did not think it fair to deprive other Big Ten schools of the payout should the Rose Bowl committee have to invite a school from outside the conference.[29]

In 2007, Arizona State kinesiology professor James E. Odenkirk called The Ohio State faculty's rejection of the 1961 Rose Bowl bid the "Eighth Wonder of the World," adding that it is inconceivable to envision such an occurrence ever taking place again.[30] He was right. It is absurd to suggest that a faculty today could stop a D-I team from participating in a bowl game or March Madness, although a few attempts have been made. In 1999, the Drake Group, a think tank dedicated to reforming college sports, called for bringing back faculty oversight of D-I athletics. The idea was quickly squelched. In the wake of the "paper course" scandal that broke in the 2010s, North Carolina history professor Jay M. Smith led a fruitless faculty effort to reform the Tarheels' athletic program. "I naïvely believed that if enough attention were paid to the corruption," he lamented, "it would lead people to call for a change to the system. Instead, the system is treating the scandal at North Carolina as a one-off. As it always does."[31]

While faculty athletic committees still exist, they are simply a nuisance to athletic departments. It is no secret that many who staff in athletic departments are disdainful of the professors who work in the library instead of in the weight room. There is no shortage of prejudice coming from academics toward the staff of athletic departments either.

Athletes' Inaction

Meanwhile, the most exploited class in D-I sports—college athletes—remains powerless to change the system. The NCAA bureaucracy writ large has no incentive to share the hundreds of millions that it pulls in every year. The NCAA thinks that D-I players should be grateful for the coupon to go to a college where many of them earn a meaningless degree and many don't even graduate.

A century ago, Ted Benson, writing for the *Daily Worker*, a Communist newspaper published in New York City, suggested that a college players' union was the only way for athletes to receive the value of their labor. "Our suggestion is for the boys who tote the leather for dear old Alma Mammy to get wise to themselves and form the American Federation of Football Players and Substitutes under the banner of the CIO [Congress of Industrial Organizations]."[32] Decades later, Hall of Fame NBA player Kareem Abdul Jabbar made the same recommendation: "Without a union, these student athletes will be without advocates and will always be at the whim of the NCAA and the colleges and universities that profit from them."[33]

Division I players are hard pressed to form a collective bargaining body. Organizing a union is difficult given the transiency of college players, the distances between schools, and the lack of alternatives to playing D-I sports as a stepping stone to the pros. There are no factory pods to organize. Division I athletes will not jeopardize their careers by going on strike and refusing to play. There will always be teammates

Chapter Ten

who will gladly step into their shoes, or players at other schools who will be happy to be scabs for the opportunity to play for a good team.

Nor have college players found a friend in the courts of law for their organizing efforts. In five fiscal years from 2014 to 2018, the NCAA spent more than $165 million on outside legal fees fighting lawsuits, many of them regarding overcompensation of their own officials and concussions suffered by players. In that time, the organization spent some $400,000 a year lobbying the government to maintain the status quo.[34]

Players do not have the financial resources to see their cases to the end. Although they toil for well more than forty hours a week in practice and in competition, making millions of dollars for their universities, for more than fifty years now, courts have declined to designate them as employees. The NCAA's designation "student-athlete" is a convenient way of avoiding all the legal protections afforded most all other employees in the nation, including the right to unionize.

In the early 2010s, Northwestern quarterback Kain Colter attempted to unionize football players, arguing that they were employees of the university and that academics took a distant second to playing football. Peter Ohr, the regional director of National Labor Relations, agreed, recognizing the right of the Northwestern players to organize. "The record makes clear that the employer's scholarship players are identified and recruited in the first instance because of their football prowess," Ohr declared, "and not because of their academic achievement in high school." He added that "no examples were provided of scholarship players [at Northwestern] being permitted to miss practice and/or games to attend to their studies." The Northwestern administration disagreed with the ruling, and the NCAA, using its vast financial resources, put its lawyers to work fighting the ruling in court. The plaintiffs did not have sufficient financial resources to compete, so the United Steelworkers paid some of their legal bills.[35] Nevertheless, in 2015, Colter and the players officially lost their case: the NCAA could continue its monopoly on college sports and the right to restrict players' free economic choices. Since then, the courts have sided with the athlete's right to life, liberty, and property. Some players' NIL deals run into the millions.

Meaningful change in big-time college sports seems like a last-second shot from half-court. But sometimes, an improbable connection is made to pull out a victory, even when all hope appears lost. By allowing players to sell their NILs, the courts have begun to chip away at the NCAA's monopoly on profits. A coalition of progressive university leaders, from trustees, presidents, and athletic directors, could affect a significant revolution in D-I sports. That would, however, take courage and a willingness to put their jobs on the line to realign sports programs with the true mission of higher education.

Notes

1. Byers, *Unsportsmanlike Conduct*, 369.
2. Byers, *Unsportsmanlike Conduct*, 109.
3. Sperber, *College Sports Inc.*, 349.
4. Sperber, *College Sports Inc.*, 10–11.
5. See Philip Mousavizaheh, "Alumni Raise Concerns at Trustees' Astronomical Wealth Skews Priorities," *Yale News,* December 28, 2022, accessed December 28, 2022, https://yaledailynews.com/blog/2021/10/27/alumni-raise-concerns-that-trustees-astronomical-wealth-skews-priorities/.
6. Smith, *Pay for Play*, ix.
7. John U. Bacon, *Fourth and Long: The Fight for the Soul of College Football* (New York: Simon & Schuster, 2013) 11.
8. Oriard, *Bowled Over*, 277–279.
9. Gorn and Goldstein, *A Brief History of American Sports*, 230. Gorn credits Ronald A. Smith for making this argument in *Sports and Freedom: The Rise of Big-Time Athletics* (Oxford Press, 1990).
10. Gaul, *Billion-Dollar Ball*, xiii.
11. Smith and Willingham, *Cheated*, 226–7.
12. Sperber, *College Sports Inc.*, 18.
13. Mulcahy III, *An Athletic Director's Story*, 180.
14. Wolff, "Broken Beyond Repair."
15. Feinstein, *The Last Amateurs*, 22.
16. Kemper, *College Football*, 96.
17. Branch, "The Shame of College Sports."
18. NCAA website, http://www.ncaa.org/about/join-our-team, accessed March 31, 2020.
19. Marc Tracy, "Waiting for Student Athletes to Become Student Activists," *New York Times*, April 9, 2019, B9. Emmert retired in 2023.
20. Unattributed, "NCAA Pursuit of Big Change Begins with New Constitution," *Star Tribune*, January 21, 2022, C5.
21. Byers, *Unsportsmanlike Conduct*, 14.
22. See, for example, John R. Gerdy, *American Education's Failed Experiment with Elite Athletics* (Jackson, MS: University of Mississippi Press, 2006), 9. "It is no longer in doubt that reform of the current elite model of athletics within our educational system must start on our college campuses."

23. Watterson, *College Football*, 49.

24. See Benjamin Ginsberg, *The Fall of the Faculty: The Rise of the All-Administrative University and Why It Matters* (Oxford: Oxford University Press, 2011).

25. Gurney, et al., *Unwinding Madness*, 10, 209ff. They also recommend restoring institutional control of athletics. Meaningful reform of college sports has rarely come from within.

26. See Watterson, *College Football*, 393.

27. Kemper, *College Football*, 30.

28. John D. McCallum, *Big Ten Football Since 1895* (Radnor, PA: Chilton Book Co., 1976), 125.

29. Mike Wilkenson, *The Autumn Warrior: Murray Warmath's 65 Years in American Football* (Edina, MN: Burgess International Group, 1992), 160. The Rose Bowl's contract with the Big Ten and the Pacific Coast Conference had lapsed.

30. James E. Odenkirk, "The Eighth Wonder of the World: Ohio State University's Rejection of a Rose Bowl Bid in 1961." *Journal of Sport History* 34, no. 3 (Fall 2007): 391.

31. Nocera, "Dean Smith Shadow."

32. Oriard, *King Football*, 246.

33. Kareem Abdul-Jabbar, "Stop Keeping College Athletes Poor and Trapped, *Time*, July 25, 2014, accessed March 8, 2022, https://time.com/3030399/kareem-abdul-jabbar-college-sports-players-unionize/.

34. Steve Berkowitz, "NCAA President Mark Emmert Had Net pay of $2.9 million in 2017 Calendar Year," *USA Today*, May 24, 2019, accessed March 24, 2020, https://www.usatoday.com/story/sports/college/2019/05/23/ncaa-president-mark-emmert-2-9-million-net-salary-2017/1207369001/.

35. Michael Tarm, "Northwestern Football Team Can Unionize," *Star Tribune*, March 27, 2014, 1A.

CHAPTER ELEVEN

A New Game Plan:
Free Market Campus Sports, the American Way

> "The marriage of commercial sports and higher education was not inevitable. Nor is it inevitable that the forces binding them together will—or should—hold indefinitely."
>
> —Allan Sanderson and John Siegfried[1]

Meaningful reform of the current D-I intercollegiate sports system is seemingly impossible. The NCAA system gelled at about the same time that the first Model-T came off the assembly line. Obviously, drivers a century ago would barely recognize the cars of today, just as sports authorities back in 1908 would be flabbergasted at what has happened to their ideal amateur model of college sports. The big-time college sports machine is broken beyond repair. As nostalgic as some might be about the classic car, the NCAA vehicle is bound for the junkyard.

The Rice Commission of 2018—the NCAA's latest publicity stunt to convince legislators and the public that it wanted real change—called for allowing players to hire an agent, permitting undrafted players to return to school, placing both restrictions and transparency requirements on shoe and clothing company deals, a lifetime ban on cheating coaches, and an end to the "one-and-done" players. Still, none of those recommendations, even if adopted, would fundamentally change the system, which is exactly what NCAA head Mark Emmert intended. His $2.7 million-a-year job never came into question—but then, he had hired Condoleezza Rice, a diplomat, for the job. The Rice Commission, like so many halfhearted attempts to keep the corrupt system afloat, sailed into the sunset without making a ripple.

Historian Taylor Branch has been a vocal critic of intercollegiate sports for years, but unfortunately, there is little chance that his recommendations—which echo past reform efforts—would have any chance of fundamentally changing a system that works at cross purposes. "The most basic reform would treat the students as what they are—adults with rights and reason of their own—and grant them a meaningful voice in NCAA deliberations," he says. "A restoration of full citizenship to 'student-athletes' would facilitate open governance, making it possible to enforce pledges of transparency in both academic standards and athletic finances."[2] It is not clear how this "full citizenship" would bring "open governance," given that administrators and athletic directors would still have the power to make final decisions. And would faculties, as watchdogs for academic fraud, have any greater oversight?

Purists who want to fix the current system ignore the long history of rulebreaking in college sports and the futile attempts to square competitive D-I sports with academic achievement. From 2001 to 2010, nearly half of the NCAA's top football schools were sanctioned for rule violations. Serious breaches of academic rules doubled in the 2000s.[3] Former NCAA head Walter Byers saw no way to reconcile the contradictory goals of higher education and big-time sports. "I'm gradually coming to the conclusion that there has to be a major rearrangement on the part of the institutions of higher learning as to what they want to do with their athletic programs," he said. "I think there is an inherent conflict that has to be resolved."[4] Anachronistic, dysfunctional, corrupt systems run by rich bureaucrats are irredeemable. They must be dismantled.

The Anti-Free Market, Corporatist NCAA

Furthermore, the current corporatist NCAA system is inherently undemocratic and anti-capitalist. For decades, the NCAA has tenaciously defended its monopoly, protected by politicians, athletic departments, and, until recently, the courts. The NCAA has maintained restrictions on players exercising their constitutional rights to private property—in this case, athletes' freedom to market themselves. Liberal economists, free market politicians, and strict constitutional constructionists can't defend this anti-capitalist system with a straight face. Of course, it is nothing novel in the free market system for management to try to minimize the cost of labor or fight workers in the courts to prevent unions or any other legal efforts to give workers a greater share of the profits. However, the courts' recent rulings to allow players to sell their NIL is a crucial first step on the way to bringing down the entire NCAA structure.

According to NCAA bylaws, "Student participation in intercollegiate athletics is an avocation, and student-athletes should be protected from exploitation by professional and commercial enterprises."[5] In essence, the only thing that the profit-making, professional, and commercial enterprise is protecting college players from is getting in on the action. There is no other organization in the country that prevents entertainers and athletes—including actors, musicians, artists, tennis players, and golfers, among others—from getting paid for work.

The Sherman Act of 1890 outlaws "every contract, combination, or conspiracy in restraint of trade," and any "monopolization, attempted monopolization, or conspiracy or combination to monopolize." According to the Federal Trade Commission, Sherman defines "certain acts [that] are considered so harmful to competition that they are almost always illegal. These include plain arrangements among competing individuals or businesses to fix prices, divide markets, or rig bids."[6] The premise of the antitrust act is that a business without competition inevitably leads to economic exploitation.

There is no doubt that the NCAA and its members, including the Power Five conferences, monopolize and conspire to eliminate competition. They fix prices, divide markets, and rig bids for television and merchandising contracts. The players get none of the cash profits.[7] The NCAA desperately hangs on to the myth of the student-athlete, because without that premise, the IRS would come calling to take a chunk out of their revenues. To keep its status as a non-profit organization, the NCAA cleverly keeps its lobbyists housed in the same Washington, D.C., building with other reputable higher education institutions, just to make it look like the NCAA is in that business too.[8]

The NCAA is also in violation of US labor laws, which preclude "discrimination against a job applicant... because of the person's race, color, religion, [or] sex."[9] While the majority of football and men's basketball players are Black, athletic departments are overwhelmingly staffed by White males.[10] The 1935 Wagner Act "gave employees the right, under Section 7, to form and join unions, and it obligated employers to bargain collectively with unions."[11] The NCAA has fought tooth and nail against lawsuits to grant players workers' rights, including their right to form unions.

In recent years, the courts have been reluctant to invoke Sherman to bust any big business, including the NCAA. Judges have consistently sided with corporate America as it has chiseled away at workers' compensation and collective bargaining rights. The NCAA treats its players like independent contractors, an end run for employers to get around paying their workers benefits. The NCAA is no different from other big industries that have tried to corner the market to increase profits and eliminate competition.

Undoubtedly, many will contend that a revolution in D-I college sports cannot happen. Interestingly, several years ago, former University of Michigan president James J. Duderstadt outlined many of the recommendations below but discounted them as "draconian," "extreme," and "unrealistic." One of the "unrealistic" proposals he cited was to pay the players, making the dubious claim that education is most athletes' priority: "Perhaps the pay-for-play approach would make sense if the primary reason that student-athletes enrolled in the university was to participate in sports. But, at least for most of these individuals, the purpose of enrolling is to get a college education." Duderstadt added that "high school players would be faced with the decision of going pro and trying to make the big time or becoming real college students."[12] What is to prevent paid college athletes from using money earned to pay for and attend classes?

Duderstadt also argued that it would be virtually impossible "to split off big-time sports from higher education—most particularly, football and basketball—and make them independent professional franchises." He did not clarify why this could not be done. It would just take like-minded schools to eliminate the stipulation that players have to enroll in school, and for athletic directors to use their profits to pay players, like any other free market enterprise.[13]

Instead of the "draconian" proposals, Duderstadt trotted out the failed reforms that have been proposed for the last century, including more faculty control of sports, ending special treatment for athletes and coaches, and connecting athletics to academic budgets. Although his ideas, such as reducing the number of teams in the NCAA basketball tournament, eliminating platoon football, and curbing the influence of sports media and professional leagues, are principled, they are wholly impractical.[14]

The Game Plan

What, then, is to be done with the dysfunctional marriage between D-I sports and the university? The answer is to make college teams into club teams. Rather than a complete divorce, a separation is necessary,

A New Game Plan

with club teams maintaining cordial relations between the college campus and themselves for the sake of the family—namely, the players and the fans.

Many respected scholars have made similar proposals. Years ago, Indiana University professor Murray Sperber, who has written extensively on intercollegiate sports, recommended that college athletic programs become "self-sufficient separate businesses." High school players would be drafted and paid, and taxes on clubs would be assessed.[15] Sperber's plan is the only way to steer toward a reconciliation of big-time sports and the mission of higher education.

Professor Ellen J. Staurowsky from Ithaca College and Professor Emeritus Allen L. Sack from the University of New Haven also called for athletic departments to separate from universities and become self-financing clubs.[16] Another expert on college sports, Professor John Sayle Watterson of James Madison University, has advocated for the separation of football from the university while keeping it on campus and not requiring that players attend classes at their club's school. As Watterson puts it, "Football would no longer be the dry rot eating at the foundation of the academic edifices. The lawless, and dishonest, underside of football which has existed for more than a century could become lawful."[17] For years, journalist Rick Telander has called for the professionalization of college football. Noted lawyer Jeffrey Kessler, a specialist in sports law, has it right: "Make football and men's basketball autonomous commercial enterprises subject to all rules of a free market, thus separating them operationally from the university athletic departments."[18]

These revolutionary proposals would, if implanted, end the NCAA's monopoly on intercollegiate sports in favor of a truly American, capitalist, free-market system in which workers can bargain for their wages and working conditions. What is more American than letting the free market work? Separating the business of sports from the university will end the hypocrisy for the people running the current "amateur," "nonprofit" system.

Step 1. *Create separate, stand-alone, self-financing clubs on campus.*
The teams will pay their administrators, coaches, and players what their independent budgets will allow. There will be with no connection to the university administratively, financially, or academically. The clubs will be run like businesses, and players, say, for the Duke Basketball

Association or the Notre Dame Football Club, will have the option to enroll in the university, and can play for the club as long as they wish to do so.

This is a transition from inter-collegiate to inter-campus athletics, as a complete divorce of the current D-I football and men's basketball teams from the college scene is wholly unrealistic. Sports provide a tight-knit community of students, alumni, boosters, townspeople, regions, and states. For many students, games on campus are great fun. In this age of rising mental health issues and social isolation, more communal joy is needed. Alabama football belongs in Tuscaloosa, and North Carolina and Duke basketball on Tobacco Road. The popularity of college football and men's basketball teams in rural states like Nebraska and Kansas make it unrealistic to separate them from their universities or to call them anything but the Cornhuskers and Jayhawks. In 2005, Lynne M. Tronsdal, the late former assistant vice president for student retention at the University of Arizona, pointed college sports in the direction of town clubs. "What we need to have are athletes who play for a municipality," she said. "Call them the Tucson Wildcats and let them get paid. And then we can all just stop fooling ourselves."[19]

Step 2. *Run self-sufficient campus clubs like a professional franchise.*
From its inception, intercollegiate sports have connected alumni to their schools. While keeping the school's name, the separation of teams from the academic side of a university will give alumni the opportunity to donate as much money as they want to athletic facilities, club management, and the players themselves. Division I sports is already a big business. Boosters can come out of hiding and sponsor their favorite clubs. Professional leagues and moneymaking campus clubs can subsidize affiliate youth clubs. If there is money to be made, the NBA and NFL will want to help finance these club teams.

Businesses will jump at the chance to stamp their brand on campus clubs. In the 1920s, famous Notre Dame football coach Knute Rockne pulled down $75,000 annually for a sponsorship from the Studebaker car company. In 1927, he made another $22,000 from writing a football column and books on the game.[20] If Rockne made that enormous sum in those days, one can imagine what club coaches and players could make today. There is no shortage of companies like Nike, Walmart, and Amazon that will compete to put their logos on club teams.

A New Game Plan

Universities used to build memorial stadiums to honor the sacrifices of American soldiers in war, but rampant commercialism has put an end to that sentimental practice. Stadium branding comes with a hefty price tag these days, such as U.S. Bank Field at the University of Minnesota, Kroger Field at the University of Kentucky, and Pratt & Whitney Stadium at UConn. Huge donations from individuals get their names on the marquee, such as Joan C. Edwards Stadium at Marshall University or (Edward Hudson) Lane Stadium at Virginia Tech. If another donor antes up, sometimes the playing surface is given a different name, such as Worsham Field at Lane Stadium.

Enterprising campus clubs can sell seatbacks, weight rooms, yard markers, goal posts, and anything else that can sport a placard. And, of course, the public address announcer can peddle anything. "The starting lineup is sponsored by Ford." "Johnny's touchdown calls for a Budweiser." "Kayla's three-pointer was brought to you by Kentucky Fried Chicken." "The Miami Redhawks thank its partner Kaytee Gourmet Bird Seed Cakes."

This sort of blatant advertising is already happening. In 2021, the Michigan State Spartans were "presented by Rocket Mortgage."[21] Nike, Under Armour, and Adidas are targeting big D-I programs like North Carolina, Kansas, and Duke in basketball, and Alabama, Clemson, and Ohio State in football. As of 2020, Kansas had a $196 million deal with Adidas, Ohio State had a $252 million agreement with Nike, and UCLA had a $280 million contract with Under Armour.[22] With that kind of money floating around, it is no surprise that the FBI uncovered illegal shoe deals that company reps were giving to college recruits.[23]

Beer companies have been trying to get their hands on college sports for a long time, but athletic departments have not wanted to taint the façade of their squeaky-clean "amateur" image by sanctioning students' inebriation—as if drinking was not happening before, during, and after every big college contest played. That high-minded prohibition against alcohol advertising ended when the Covid pandemic of 2020 hit D-I athletic budgets hard. With truncated schedules, reduced television revenues, and zero gate revenue, men's basketball and football—the moneymaking sports—could not cover their own costs, let alone the outlay for non-revenue sports. In early 2021, after years of debate, the University of Minnesota joined eleven other Big Ten schools and a majority of other D-I universities by approving about $300,000 in licensing deals with alcoholic beverage companies, with one caveat: the Minnesota Board of Regents mandated that mascot Goldy Gopher stay sober and off the beer cans—as though Minnesota students would eschew the brew if Goldy wasn't peddling it. Deals could also be made with brewpubs and student-run breweries. Rodrigo Tojo Garcia, a student representative on the board, acknowledged, "The advertising that would come about as a result of this policy will undoubtedly end up having some effect on students who are below the legal drinking age." Regent David McMillan remarked, "If we really want to reverse course and make a bigger difference in terms of student consumption of alcohol, we probably need to back all the way to decisions long ago about selling alcohol in our venues."[24]

For a licensing fee, clubs, with corporate money, could use the university's name, sell endorsements, broadcasting rights, and merchandise, such as the Minnesota Gopher Football Club, Miami University Basketball Club, or Duke University Lacrosse Club. Campus clubs would also have to pay to use the university's athletic facilities. In some cases, the university could sell the venues to the campus team. These revenues could be plowed back into academics, enhancing the main mission of colleges—to educate, research, and serve the community. The monies could also go to an expansion of intramural sports for the physical health of all students.

Some critics might argue that rich clubs like Alabama football or Duke basketball will reap most of the advertising money, thereby upsetting the competitive balance. Maybe so, but no such balance exists today anyway. With few exceptions, the same schools end up in the college football finals and make deep runs into the March Madness basketball tournament.

The D-I revenue sports—men's basketball and football—can easily transition into professional clubs. Top D-I teams are worth a lot of money. Elite FBS football programs are worth well more than $100 million. In 2011, the Texas Longhorns topped the list at an estimated $133 million, surpassing $100 million in revenue. Michigan was worth $120 million, and Notre Dame $103 million.[25]

Non-revenue sports, such as swimming, lacrosse, softball, and gymnastics, can be organized into self-sufficient clubs and seek sponsorships as well. There are enough boosters out there to subsidize them. For example, in 2019, Miami University received a big anonymous donation to help build a $3.8 million indoor equestrian center. In 2014, former

A New Game Plan

Miami University quarterback and star Pittsburgh Steeler quarterback Ben Roethlisberger donated $1 million for a football practice facility at his alma mater.[26]

University trustees and presidents fear that if sports were separated from the university and players were not connected to the classroom, donations like Roethlisberger's would dry up. The opposite is true; if he and other wealthy alumni like LSU's Odell Beckam Jr. were allowed to get in on recruiting, hang out in the locker room, and dole out goodies without risking NCAA sanctions, donations might well increase. Alumni and boosters would be free to pump as much money as they wanted into the clubs. They could, for example, pay for special living and training facilities, charter airplanes, and other amenities to which the players are accustomed. Agents, too, could come out into the open.

Donations to the university for academics could rise as well. Many benefactors might be inspired by a university that promotes its academic excellence. For example, "in 1986, the year after Tulane shut down its basketball program in the wake of a point-shaving scandal, donations to that school leaped by $5 million. Wichita State raised $26 million in a special drive in '87, the year in which it dropped football."[27] Top schools like the University of Chicago and the Ivy Leaguers are surely not hurting for donations, even if they don't compete at the highest levels of D-I sports. Harvard has an endowment of more than $40 billion, while the University of Chicago has $8.5 billion in its kitty.

Those who staff university development offices, which have ballooned in size in the last few decades, can focus on soliciting gifts for academic programs, scholarships, and endowed chairs. The mission of university development offices should not be to seek funds from alumni and others for athletics. Some of the money saved from sports could be dedicated to television and other media outlets for ads that highlight a school's professors, majors, academic excellence, and career opportunities.

Step 3. *Pay the players.*

Walter Byers was ahead of his time in the 1990s when he recommended that players should be allowed to get paid advertisements, but to maintain the fiction of amateurism, Byers suggested that the player's earnings go into a trust fund they could tap into upon graduation. He also favored paying players a small cash stipend above and beyond their tuition scholarships. "All I accomplished with those efforts," Byers recalled, "was a hardening of the NCAA position on 'amateurism.' Players must be shielded from exploitation and the taint of commercial gold, the NCAA officially reiterated in the early 1990s, and it then confirmed that the gold belonged to the coaches and the colleges."[28]

It goes without saying that campus club players would be able to market themselves—something that has already begun. As noted, in 2021, the US Supreme Court ruled 9–0 that players could profit from their NIL. The decision leaves open the possibility that the entire NCAA system of preventing athletes from getting paid to play their sports might come crashing down. Justice Brett Kavanaugh pointed out the obvious when he wrote, "The NCAA's business model would be flatly illegal in almost every other industry in America. The bottom line is that the NCAA and its member colleges are suppressing the pay of student athletes, who collectively generate billions of dollars in revenue for colleges every year."[29]

Since then, an academic advisor at the University of California-Berkeley said that, with the NIL ruling, "the landscape is completely changing."[30] Former Big Ten Commissioner Kevin Warren agreed. "We're at an inflection moment in college athletics," he said, and went on to list selling likenesses, switching conferences, and the expansion of football playoffs as other issues facing the NCAA.[31]

Shortly after the NIL decision was handed down, Alabama quarterback Bryce Young landed a million dollars' worth of endorsement deals.[32] A Wisconsin basketball player started his own clothing line. Athletic departments added more employees charged with helping to set up marketing opportunities for current players as well as recruits. Some universities are already preparing for the day when players are paid. Louisiana State, Nebraska, and Texas are connecting with marketing agencies to help their athletes navigate sponsorship deals.[33]

Allowing players to market themselves has also had an immediate impact on recruiting. Head coaches are now the biggest promoters of NIL to prospects, trying to lure players to their programs by letting them know they will get maximum exposure in order to enhance the worth of their likeness deals. In 2021, Texas Tech hired a relatively unknown head football coach because of his connections to players from Texas, in part to convince prospective players that Tech, too, could help them promote their NIL in their home state.[34]

Former Northwestern head football coach Pat Fitzgerald expressed misgivings about how the system was going to work. "Right now, there's a lot of head coaches getting on a dais and singing a bunch of songs," he charged, "and they have no idea what they are singing. 'We've got the greatest NIL'. They're all full of it. Nobody knows what they are doing. They're all faking it, and I'll be the first to admit it."[35] Unscrupulous characters are bound to pounce on young athletes to capitalize on their financial opportunities. Michigan defensive end Aidan Hutchinson was optimistic about his prospects of selling his likeness, but he soon became disillusioned. "It was pretty exciting at first," he said. "Two weeks later, people are hitting me up and it's like, 'I really don't want to deal with any of that… I just want to play ball.'"[36] At least if he could make money, his playing football would have nothing to do with his studies and staying academically eligible.

"It's fascinating to watch schools go from 'NIL will end college sports' to 'pick our school because we offer the best NIL opportunities,'" says economist Ted Tatos. "It's almost as though they always knew their previous position was utter nonsense." *New York Times* columnist Joe Nocera agrees: "The NCAA still maintains that paying players an actual salary would bring about the ruination of college sports. No one believes it anymore."[37]

There would be no shortage of local businesses that would want a piece of the new campus clubs. For example, a Nebraska regional restaurant chain offered an endorsement deal to the first one-hundred Cornhuskers who applied, regardless of what sport they played. Some colleges put a ban on players' endorsements of alcohol, but it was not clear whether that included restaurants that sold it.[38] In 2021, Built Bar, a sports nutrition company, gave 36 walk-ons on BYU's football team what amounted to a full athletic scholarship.[39]

Campus clubs would render the problems stemming from NIL in intercollegiate sports moot. One journalist pointed out that "the NCAA was careful to stress that the new NIL policy 'preserves the commitment to avoid pay-for-play.'"[40] Players would be free agents to pursue their careers without any of the NCAA's anti-free market restrictions. If campus clubs pay their players, the athletes would not have to chase these endorsement contracts to make a living.

The Clemson athletic director viewed the NIL ruling as good for players. He thought that if agents were registered, it would prevent them from making surreptitious payments to influence recruits to attend a certain school or to keep players from leaving a school. He added that rules had been bent before, and likely would be again. He was opposed to paying the players a salary and collective bargaining, declaring that he would get out of college sports if that happened. Finally, he was opposed to getting rid of the term "student-athlete."[41]

Regardless of what any athletic director thinks, paying campus club players is the right thing to do. Today, basketball and football players are mandated to serve a one-to three-year unpaid apprenticeship, making intercollegiate sports the only entertainment business in the United States that restricts the free market. As Justice Kavanaugh put it in the Supreme Court's decision in 2021 on paying college athletes a small cash stipend: "Nowhere else in America can businesses get away with agreeing not to pay their workers a fair market rate on the theory that their product is defined by not paying their workers a fair market rate." The Supreme Court ruled that the NCAA was running an illegal monopoly and that players should receive "modest, education-related payments." It was a limited decision, but the wheels of justice are in (albeit slow) motion.[42]

The court's decision will not fundamentally change anything, except to give revenue producing programs at the Power Five conferences an additional advantage. Mid-majors like Miami University cannot afford to pay players in addition to their scholarships. "The question before the court was a fairly narrow one, and the court responded with a narrow ruling," Alan Blinder of the *New York Times* says, "but what they did was trim the NCAA sails. They said that their power was not absolute and unchallenged."[43]

It is not at all clear how schools would determine what small amount to pay players. In a 2014 *New Yorker* opinion piece, journalist Adam Gopnik wrote, "If you pay all [college] athletes, women cross-country runners alongside left tackles, then no one can possibly construct a rational fee scale." Gopnik is exactly right, but why have pay steps anyway? If campus clubs were to be responsible for their own budgets and fundraising, the market would determine the amount of athletes' compensation, if any. Gopnik makes that point himself: "If you pay only those athletes in the few men's sports that make money, you're accepting that those sports are essentially a stand-alone business, not to be considered in any way part of the broader mission of the university, which is what the critics of college sports say is the problem with having them in the first place."[44]

In 2014, University of Delaware President Patrick T. Harker wrote an editorial for the *New York Times* in which he argued that smaller D-I schools would not be able to compete for good players if schools had to pay them. "This would only further lessen the priority on learning," he contended. "If scholarship athletes already find it hard to balance schoolwork with team commitments, under arrangements that obligate educational opportunity, think how much harder it would be if they were being paid to play."[45]

Harker is correct only if schools still stipulated that athletes on club teams had to attend classes. Would anyone really care if the athletes don't go to school? Some idealists might argue that a separate, self-sufficient club system will diminish fans' interest in the "college" game, as well as the connection that the student body has to its athletes, who could play for many years. Given the cocoon that D-I programs have created for themselves on campus, that link between campus life and athletes has become tenuous anyway.

Nocera points out that diehard supporters of D-I college sports have their heads buried in the sand when it comes to its operation as a big business: "Fans want to believe that the players on the field are all students. And they want to believe that the players have the same loyalty to the university that they do. Paying the players would destroy that illusion, the NCAA believes."[46]

The one-and-dones barely go to school anyway, and the flood of disgruntled players who leave teams through the transfer portal are not seeking a better educational opportunity elsewhere. In 2014, NCAA President Mark Emmert testified in an antitrust case against his organization, clinging to this romantic notion that fans cared about the players' academic side: "Fans appreciate the fact that these are indeed college athletes. They recognize that they are students. They recognize that they are not the greatest athletes. To convert college sports into professional sports would be tantamount to converting it into minor-league sports. And we know, in the United States, minor-league sports are not particularly successful."[47] Contrary to Emmert's prediction, rabid partisan fans have not turned away from their college teams in the "transfer portal" era because everyone knows that players are more or less just hired guns, do not regularly attend classes, and have little loyalty to a team or a school.

During the global pandemic of 2020, the NCAA fought hard to prevent universities from paying players. When some schools developed "internships" and paid "educational expenses" for players, the organization went to court to stop the practice, losing its case. The NCAA argued that the ruling "effectively created a pay-for-play system for all student-athletes, allowing them to be paid both 'unlimited' amounts for participating in 'internships'" and an additional $5,600 or more each year they remain eligible to play their sport. Although there is no evidence that fans disowned the many players who prolonged their college careers to six and even seven years during the covid pandemic, the NCAA's lawyer contended that the payments to players "will eradicate the distinction between college and professional athletes, causing many consumers to lose interest as college sports are perceived as just another minor league."[48]

Campus clubs run as business enterprises would decide for themselves how much to pay the front office, coaches, and players. At least the university would no longer be complicit in the discrimination against the unpaid D-I men's basketball and football athletes, the majority of whom are Black.

Step 4. *Schools can decide whether they want their club players to enroll in college, giving the players the option to take courses.*

A well-paid football or basketball player could easily afford tuition for a useful course of study in challenging courses that actually prepare them for a future other than in playing sports or help them hone the necessary skills to succeed after their athletic career ends. As everyone knows, only a small percentage of D-I athletes make it to the pros, anyway. Players who pay for their education will likely be more motivated to take their studies seriously and enroll in courses important for their intellectual development and future careers—and do so without having constantly to worry about maintaining eligibility. Alabama or UCLA could still have their names on their campus football and basketball clubs without having to compromise their school's academics.

Different academic requirements among the clubs would create intriguing rivalries. What is more fun than a David vs Goliath matchup in March Madness, say an Ivy League team against Kansas or Duke? Wouldn't it be even more fun with a clash between the eggheads from the Northwestern University Wildcat Club, which requires its players to be enrolled in the university, and the pros from the North Carolina Tarheel Basketball Club, which does not?

Like-minded schools can form their own conferences, but without any rules about academic standards, which too often results in cheating. Universities would not have to allow the creation of specialty courses

A New Game Plan

for athletes, classroom seats would not be taken up by athletes who have no interest in learning, and professors would not be asked to spend time providing extra accommodations to student athletes—perks not afforded regular students.

Clemson's athletic director said he was opposed to separating sport programs from the university, arguing that part of the campus experience for the non-athlete is the fun of going to games and rooting for the Tigers.[49] The Miami University athletic director, who comes from a D-3 background, agreed, indicating that he liked the academic side of D-I sports. "If it goes pro, I'm out."[50] Club teams will not take away from the fun of on-campus games. Some universities will continue to feature their self-financed campus teams as a draw to the school.

Schools could mandate that their club players attend classes and have their teams play in conferences with similar requirements. The university would self-regulate, and the NCAA and its 430-page book of niggling rules and bloated bureaucracy would be scrapped.

Step 5. *Create regional conferences of club teams with regional rivalries, lower travel costs, and like-minded athletic and academic missions.*

Teams playing in faraway places incur exorbitant travel costs. Miami University's ice hockey team used to play in the same conference with the University of Anchorage, not exactly a puddle-jumper flight away from Oxford, Ohio, or a heated rivalry in the making. Miami is now in the National Collegiate Hockey Conference with Denver University, Colorado College, and the University of North Dakota, still not within driving distance. At the same time, North Dakota's traditional ice hockey rivalry with the Minnesota Gophers has gone by the wayside.

Regional conferences make sense. For eample, Miami University always draws bigger basketball and football crowds when hosting nearby teams, none of whom are in the same conference. Miami club teams could form a conference with neighboring D-I schools, including Xavier, Wright State, Dayton, Toledo, Ball State, Butler, Indiana University-Purdue University Indianapolis, Northern Kentucky, and Morehead State, all within a three-hour bus ride from Oxford. Club teams could negotiate new interconference tournaments, with the smaller schools actually getting a chance to win a title. Big money clubs like Clemson and Alabama in football, or Duke and Kentucky in basketball, could form their own conferences.

Chapter Eleven

The NCAA defends its monopoly by arguing that, without them at the helm, college sports would be balkanized, resulting in a patchwork of different regulations and eligibility requirements from region to region. In February 2020, South Dakota Senator John Thune argued that "having each state doing their own thing is problematic. Sports is something that cuts across party lines, it cuts across geography and it's so ingrained in our culture. Everyone wants to see that if nothing else in our country works, they want to see our sports work."[51] What is wrong with regional rivalries and a return to local institutional oversight?

Clubs could also form conferences with nearby institutions with similar academic standards. It would then be up to each school to decide on academic requirements, thereby avoiding the nearly continuous academic scandals of the current system—this, despite the proliferation of compliance positions in the NCAA today.

Step 6. *Conferences could mandate age limits and transfer rules.*
From 2016 to 2022, basketball guard Charlie Moore played at Cal-Berkeley, Kansas, DePaul, and Miami (Florida). In 2022, one North Dakota State offensive lineman set a record by playing in his 65th college game. Also in 2022, a Kansas Jayhawk played his seventh year of college basketball. As long as he helps Kansas win, no Jayhawk partisan is going to squawk.

No one expresses outrage that some players have stayed that long with a program or questions their choice of majors or their progress toward a degree. These days, with players moving around so frequently, all fans are rooting for is the laundry their team wears. Some 78,000 Alabama fans show up for a spring football game; do you suppose any of those fans care about how long certain players have or will play in Tuscaloosa, or whether they are working toward a degree? If it must be, clubs can mandate that their players audit a financial investment class; even that would be enough to keep the myth of the student-athlete alive.

Decades ago, colleges decided that required courses for a degree would take four years to complete. The same time limit was then arbitrarily applied to an athlete's eligibility, although in recent years with the use of redshirts, graduate transfers, and transfer portal exceptions, many athletes have managed to prolong their college careers. During the pandemic, some players came back for several years beyond four, about which no one seemed to care. At Minnesota, three of the most important Gopher players—All-American running back Mohamed Ibrahim, quarterback Tanner Morgan, and star wide-out Chris Autman-Bell—returned for a sixth year. Gopher center Eric Curry also remained in the basketball program for six years.

The NCAA's one-time transfer exception has wreaked havoc on the college game. Players change schools more than pros change teams. In the middle of 2021, 2,400 FBS football players had entered the so-called transfer portal, as had 2,700 D-I men and 1,660 women basketball players. As one sports columnist put it, "Coaches must recruit three places now: High school, transfer portal, and their current roster." Tampering with other D-I sports rosters is inevitable, and athletic departments will have to add yet another layer of coaches who scout prospects from every other team in the country.[52] Mississippi head football coach Lane Kiffin said that building a program now is tougher because unlike in the professional leagues, whose players are under contract, "These guys [college athletes] are free agents every single year."[53] Why not, then, let players sign deals with campus club teams?

Step 7. *Money not spent on D-I budgets goes to academics, lowering tuition.*

The monies saved on D-I intercollegiate sports could go instead to academic programs. Ironically, when the University of Chicago got rid of football in 1939, the locker rooms under the football stadium were converted into a nuclear lab, in which the research conducted contributed to the making of the first atomic bomb (admittedly a controversial scientific achievement).[54]

Schools could drastically reduce the annual student fee, of which about half is devoted to subsidizing D-I intercollegiate sports. If a school so chooses, using the savings for an ad campaign extolling its academic programs would be a better way to promote the school than putting a mediocre football or men's basketball team on ESPN. Perhaps the savings might even go to hiring more and better tenure-track professors, something that would have a direct impact on the student body and help universities attend to their primary objective: educate.

Step 8. *Create expanded intramural programs giving all students the opportunity to play sports.*

More spending on intramural programs would return college sports back to its original form, when students organized their own teams and scheduled regattas and baseball, soccer, and rugby games with nearby universities. The millions saved on eliminating the university's subsidy of D-I sports would help fund intramural teams, encouraging more students to play games, rather than just the few elites. Universities could also develop more sophisticated fine arts programs, including music and dance, which enhance the physical and mental health of students.

There is no question that physical exercise is an important part of a well-rounded education. In 1990, a US federal court judge stated that "even in the increasingly commercial modern world this court believes there is still validity to the Athenian concept of a complete education derived from fostering the full growth of both mind and body."[55] True enough, but the financial outlay for big-time sports and a select few elite college athletes today comes at the expense of the health and physical education for all students. Julie Sullivan, former president at the University of St. Thomas, extolled the virtues of sport. "If you want to establish that level of excellence [such as Villanova or Marquette]," she said, "you want to meet that level in academics and athletics. Athletes develop entrepreneurial skills. Resilience. Collaboration, communication, grittiness, and ability of to face adversity." Either out of ignorance, naivete, or willful omission, Sullivan failed to mention that the multimillion dollar outlays for D-I sports would benefit only about 500 of the nearly 9,000 students at St. Thomas, and that athletic facilities that were once accessible for all students were now off-limits to them, reserved for the D-I athletes.[56] In the winner-take-all world of college sports, the body of the D-I athlete is what counts. Going D-I will hardly improve St. Thomas's academic profile; the school accepts nearly 90 percent of all applicants.[57]

The money in D-I sports is simply too big to bring intercollegiate sports back to some idyllic nineteenth-century century marriage of mind and body. After retiring, Byers took the organization to task for its duplicity, while appealing for a return to the mythic image of the college amateur athlete that has never existed:

> Throughout my career I had fought for the amateur ideal against such big-time coaches as Barry Switzer, Joe Paterno, and Jerry Tarkanian. I supported any rule that sought to keep college athletics more a student activity than a profession. Although we lost one engagement after another, I hoped we could recapture some philosophy of yesteryear. It finally became clear that the new

A New Game Plan

generation of coaches and staff didn't know and didn't care to learn about the old ideals.[58]

The original objective of college sports—to provide a healthy, recreative, and amusing outlet for students—has long been compromised. Athletic departments compete with other schools in the race for bigger and better facilities for their D-I athletes. These venues are often off-limits for the regular student, even when they are not being used. Current club teams have to beg, borrow, and steal to get a place to work out. The club director at Miami University told one gymnast that the women's practice facility was so old as to be considered unsafe; the university would eventually have to axe the gymnastics club as well as the youth program it ran. Miami has no plans to build a new venue for the club. "Kinda sad to think about how much money is in the university and especially how much money is spent on football and basketball," the gymnast said, "but it does not get distributed to club teams to encourage participation in sports."[59]

In 2013, Spelman College, a historically Black all-women's school, decided that the $900,000 it was spending annually on athletics (this out of a total university budget of $100 million) was unsustainable and unjustifiable. "I was startled," remarked Spelman president Beverly Tatum. "It seemed like a lot of money for 80 students [on the teams]." The athletes comprised only 4 percent of the student population. After attending a basketball game, Tatum thought, "None of these women were going to play basketball professionally—I mean even recreationally. I thought of all the Black women I knew, and they did not tend to spend their recreational time playing basketball. So, a little voice in my head said, let's flip it." Tatum decided to address the startlingly high rates among Black women of heart disease, diabetes, and other illnesses related to diet and sedentary lifestyles. About 50 percent of the first-year Spelman students were "obese or had high blood pressure, Type 2 diabetes, or some other health condition." By ending intercollegiate athletics, Tatum directed the nearly $1 million saved to be spent on physical education for all students, adding physical education courses to the curriculum and giving all students access to fitness facilities.[60]

In a sense, robust intramural athletics programs would turn the clock back to more than a century ago when James Naismith invented basketball to keep his charges active in the winter months. It is no secret that people who exercise regularly are more physically and mentally healthy.

Studies even show that people who are avid sports fans are less angry, uptight, and anti-social.[61] One psychologist from the Wharton School of Business writes, "Peak happiness lies mostly in collective activity. . . . We find our greatest bliss in moments of collective effervescence. . . the synchrony you feel when you slide into rhythm with strangers on a dance floor, colleagues in a brainstorming session, cousins at a religious service or teammates on a soccer field. . . . Collective effervescence happens when joie de vivre spreads throughout a group."[62]

The ruthless quest to get a scholarship to play D-I sports and maybe go on to ink a pro contract has sapped the fun out of games. Youth sports at that level is work. Utah State University's Families in Sport Lab found that "the more parents spend on youth sports, the more likely their kids are to lose interest [in the sport]." Assistant professor Travis Dorsch summed it up succinctly: "More pressure means less enjoyment."[63] Norway has a commitment to "Children's Right to Sports"—beginning athletics for kids at an early age but without competition until age thirteen. "There seems to be a lot of emphasis on including everybody," says one young Norwegian alpine skier. "Whether or not you are really good or not, it's pretty much the same experience for everyone."[64]

Clubs bring people together. One of the big problems in the United States is the lack of recreational leagues. Americans are truly "Bowling Alone," and the political, ethnic, and urban-rural divide is growing.[65] The satisfaction of winning a game with other people is exhilarating, and it can lead to life-long friendships. Americans need more of this kind of camaraderie. Dusty Baker, the successful long-time MLB manager, once asked his good friend Bill Russell, who won eleven championships with the Boston Celtics, what the key was to their success. "He told me that they loved each other," Baker remembered. "And love can take you to heights you never thought you could get to. And they feed off of each other and pull for each other on a daily basis. And one guy falls down, and the next guy, you know, picks him up."[66]

The model for campus club teams might be found in the European system of self-financing sports clubs. In these clubs, elite athletes are paid for playing in the top divisions, but the club also sponsors lower-level teams. Clubs charge membership dues and field teams at all age and ability levels. If the top team in the club is revenue generating, its profits help subsidize the club's youth teams. The European club system enables individuals at different ability levels to participate in sports, and to do so until old age. Players are not allowed to change clubs during the season, however. The absurd reality of American college sports is that most athletes' careers end at the age of twenty-two.

Big programs like Alabama football or Duke basketball can fund junior varsity teams that play their own games with other schools. If the Alabama Football Club chooses to subsidize the lower-level campus club teams, in whatever sport, more students will get the health benefits of playing sports and the fun of experiencing some intercollegiate or intramural competition.

Sports is integrating. Kids of various backgrounds playing games together may be the best organic sensitivity training there is. Club sports now, because of the money necessary to run them, tends to favor wealthy White students. The money saved on D-I sports could go to intramural and lower-level club teams that can benefit any student who wants to play, as well as return sports to the realm of play rather than work.

Some might argue that African Americans and other minorities will lose opportunities to go to college if the current system is changed. On the contrary, the millions of dollars saved from funding D-I athletics could free up scholarship money for a great many minority students whose primary motivation to go to college is to learn. In the long run, sports are not the way out of poverty for the vast majority of youngsters—even some highly talented ones—anyway.

Women, too, will benefit. Their clubs could be separate entities run mainly by women. Baylor women's basketball coach Kim Mulkey posed the question, "Is it time to separate [from the men]? I don't know. Can we sustain it financially? I don't know. But those are the discussions that need to be had at the higher levels by people who are a lot smarter than me."[67]

Some critics of the idea to separate intercollegiate sports from the university argue that it will undermine Title IX and the opportunities for women to get involved in sports. Self-financed clubs in Europe and elsewhere, however, support women's sports far more than does the United States.[68] Women's college sports clubs would find plenty of sponsors. If there is money to be made by putting a corporate logo on a women's uniform, court, or field, businesses will pony up. Transitioning to women's college clubs would also be smart marketing to more than half of the US population.

An expanded intramural and college club team system would also give more women opportunities to play sports. For reasons that are unclear—a high percentage of women who play high school sports don't go on to do so in college, whether on an organized team or casually. An all-women's pickup basketball game is a rare sight at college gyms.

Furthermore, the transition to clubs would give more women the chance to manage and coach athletic teams. Whenever sports organizations have merged men's and women's programs, men have dominated the decision-making positions. Women, for example, lost their autonomy when women's track and field was allowed into the Olympics in 1928.[69] Before Title IX, women ran their own sports, but when athletic departments merged, women were edged out. Today men hold most of the positions in athletic departments, and men disproportionally hold the top jobs.

Men's and women's clubs would proliferate in any sport that is financially sustainable. Not every campus would be able to offer a club team in every sport, but how many lacrosse, gymnastics, and field hockey teams are needed? Many men's and women's sports like wrestling, golf, volleyball, soccer, and baseball have high expenses related to coaches, referees, venues, scorekeepers, and announcers, while usually playing in front of sparse crowds. That's a lot of overhead for a few hundred spectators.

Step 9. *Implement a five-year plan.*
It would be unfair to all those employed in D-I athletic departments or the athletes if these changes were made overnight. A five-year (or longer) transition period would give athletic departments time to adjust to the end of funding from the university and find commercial sponsors, and employees time to find work in the new campus clubs or in some other job. The big athletic departments like those at Michigan and Notre Dame would find the transition easy, because the revenue-producing sports would no longer have to carry the financial burden of funding non-revenue sports (campus club leaders can voluntarily decide to subsidize other sport clubs). Campus clubs would have time to form new conferences, make schedules, and devise their bylaws. The five-year transition would also give players already on a scholarship the opportunity to graduate.

The D-I sports system is already breaking down, under siege from the NIL ruling and the coming of small cash payments to players. The professionalization of college players will continue apace. It is time to accelerate the process and send the aging body of the NCAA to hospice.

Step 10. *Inaugurate the Robert Hutchins Award*

These recommendations are a call to a coalition of like-minded of trustees, presidents, athletic directors, and coaches of D-I schools who want to reconcile the troubled marriage of big-money college sports with the mission of their academic institutions. These proposals are intended to tweak the consciences of those who run D-I sports programs and would, if implemented, liberate them from the contradictions of D-I sports, of which they are fully aware. Everyone connected with the NCAA system would be able to bank their paychecks with a clear conscience.

A few courageous leaders could start a movement to change the system. Presidents affecting these changes could be given a Robert Hutchins Award, in honor of the brave University of Chicago president who famously folded up Chicago's football program in 1939, hardly to the detriment of that elite academic institution.

These leaders will undoubtedly put their jobs in jeopardy for advocating an end to the current system of D-I sports, but they will be remembered for their determination to stand up for the true mission of their educational institutions.

Notes

1. Sanderson and Siegfried, "Why American."
2. Branch, "The Shame."
3. Sheldon Anderson editorial in *The Miami Student,* January 22, 2013.
4. Bruce Weber, "Walter Byers, Ex-N.C.A.A. Leader Who Rued Corruption, Dies at 93," *New York Times,* May 27, 2015, accessed March 5, 2021, https://www.nytimes.com/2015/05/28/sports/walter-byers-ex-ncaa-leader-who-rued-corruption-dies-at-93.html.
5. Nocera and Strauss, "Here's How," 213.
6. Federal Trade Commission, "The Antitrust Laws," accessed February 1, 2021, https://www.ftc.gov/tips-advice/competition-guidance/guide-antitrust-laws/antitrust-laws.
7. See Jim Spencer, "Sen. Amy Klobuchar Pushes to Overhaul Antitrust Laws," *Star Tribune,* February 4, 2021, accessed February 24, 2021, https://www.startribune.com/klobuchar-pushes-to-overhaul-antitrust-laws/600018940/.
8. Sperber, *Beer and Circus,* 217.
9. US Government, "Labor Laws and Issues," accessed February 1, 2021, https://www.usa.gov/labor-laws; and US Equal Employment Opportunity Commission, accessed February 1, 2021, https://www.eeoc.gov/overview.
10. "NCAA Demographics Database Spreadsheet: Student Athletes and Coaching Staff," ncaa.org, 2022, accessed December 29, 2022, https://www.ncaa.org/sports/2013/11/20/diversity-research,aspx.

Chapter Eleven

11. National Labor Relations Board, "1935 Passage of the Wagner Act," accessed February 1, 2021, https://www.eeoc.gov/overview.

12. Duderstadt, *Intercollegiate Athletics*, 275–277, 280.

13. Duderstadt, *Intercollegiate Athletics*, 275–277, 280.

14. Duderstadt, *Intercollegiate Athletics*, 281–3, 299, 302.

15. Sperber, *College Sports Inc.*, 349.

16. Sack and Staurowsky, *College Athletes for Hire*, 142.

17. Watterson, *College Football*, 388, 397.

18. Rick Telander, *The College Football Problem: How Money and Power Corrupted the Game and How We Can Fix That* (Champaign, IL: Sports Publishers, 2020); and Smith and Willingham, *Cheated*, 242.

19. John Morrow, "The Undergraduate Experience," *New York Times Education Life*, April 24, 2005, accessed July 2, 2020, https://www.nytimes.com/2005/04/24/us/education/the-undergraduate-experience-survival-of-the-fittest.html.

20. Watterson, *College Football*, 146.

21. Jack Baer, "Michigan State Announces Basketball Team Will Now Be Called 'MSU Spartans Presented by Rocket Mortgage," Yahoo!, March 11, 2021, accessed March 22, 2022, https://sports.yahoo.com/michigan-state-basketball-team-msu-spartans-presented-by-rocket-mortgage-223057968.html.

22. Will, "The Real March Madness."

23. Adam Gopnik, "Team Spirit," *The New Yorker*, May 12, 2014, 24.

24. Peter Warren, "U Approves Alcohol Sponsorships," *Star Tribune*, February 13, 2021, C2; and Rachel Blount, "U Regents Take Up Push for Alcohol Sponsorship Deals, *Star Tribune*, December 5, 2020, C3.

25. "Lucre Bowl," *Sports Illustrated*, January 21, 2013, 20.

26. Unattributed, "Roethlisberger Invests $1 Million in Miami Student-Athletes," Miami Athletic Fund, accessed February 11, 2020, https://www.miamiathleticfund.org/s/916/gradchamps/interior.aspx?sid=916&gid=1&pgid=8699&cid=16178&ecid=16178&crid=0&calpgid=8523&calcid=15839#:~:text=Roethlisberger%20and%20his%20wife%2C%20Ashley,creating%20their%20own%20great%20moments.,.

27. Wolff, "Broken Beyond Repair."

28. Byers, *Unsportsmanlike Conduct*, 13.

29. Chip Scoggins, "Score One for NCAA Resisters." *Star Tribune*, June 27, 2021, C1.

30. Interview with University of California-Berkeley academic advisor, September 29, 2021.

31. Randy Johnson, "Players Cheer Their Newfound Financial Freedom," *Star Tribune*, July 23, 2021, C4.

32. Johnson, "Players Cheer."

33. Tess DeMeyer, "The College Athletes Who Are Allowed to Make Big Bucks: Cheerleaders, *New York Times*, November 29, 2020, accessed May 26, 2021, https://www.nytimes.com/2020/11/29/sports/the-college-athletes-who-are-allowed-to-make-big-bucks-cheerleaders.html?action=click&module=Editors%20Picks&pgtype=Homepage.

34. Dan Wolken, "College Hires May Shift," *USA Today*, November 11, 2021, C1.
35. Johnson, "Players Cheer."
36. Johnson, "Players Cheer."
37. Joe Nocera, "The Difference Between Unpaid and Paid Student-Athletes? Not Much, It Turns Out," *New York Times*, October 25, 2021, B8.
38. Kent Youngblood, "College Athletes Can Finally Cash In," *Star Tribune*, July 1, 2021. C1.
39. Laine Higgins, "The Decade When Everything Changed," *Wall Street Journal*, August 28-29, 2021, A12.
40. Youngblood, "College Athletes Can Finally Cash In."
41. Interview with Clemson athletic director, September 16, 2021.
42. Tom Wright-Piersanti, "Change Comes to the N.C.A.A.," *New York Times*, June 22, 2021, accessed June 22, 2021, https://www.nytimes.com/2021/06/22/briefing/ncaa-scotus-ruling.html.
43. Wright-Piersanti, "Change Comes to the N.C.A.A."
44. Adam Gopnik, "Team Spirit," *The New Yorker*, May 12, 2014, 23.
45. Patrick T. Harker, "Student Athletes Shouldn't Unionize," *New York Times*, April 2, 2014, A25.
46. Nocera, "The Difference."
47. Nocera, "The Difference."
48. Jessica Gresko and Mitch Stacy, Associated Press, August 11, 2020, accessed April 15, 2022, https://apnews.com/article/sports-athlete-compensation-college-sports-elena-kagan-football-d6a2133175bc1405ae0c46d9180f4721.
49. Interview with Clemson athletic director, September 16, 2021.
50. Interview with Miami University athletic director, August 12, 2021.
51. Alan Blinder, "Senators Express Frustration, and So Does the N.C.A.A.," *New York Times*, February 12, 2020, B10.
52. Chip Scoggins, "Wooing Recruits Over and Over Again," *Star Tribune*, June 3, 2021, C1.
53. Laine Higgins, "The Decade When Everything Changed," *Wall Street Journal*, August 28-29, 2021, A12.
54. Davies, *Sports in American Life*, 122.
55. Branch, "The Shame."
56. James Walsh, "St. Thomas President Raised University's National Profile," *Star Tribune*, March 30, 2022, B3.
57. University of St. Thomas (MN), *U.S. News & World Report: Education*, accessed May 21, 2022, https://www.usnews.com/best-colleges/university-of-st-thomas-minnesota-2345.
58. Byers, *Unsportsmanlike Conduct*, 8-9.
59. Interview with Miami student, November 2, 2022.
60. Amanda Ripley, "The Case Against High-School Sports," *Atlantic Monthly* vol 312, no. 3 (October 2013), 72–78; and Mike Tierney, "With Budget and Health Aims, College Drops N.C.A.A. Sports, *New York Times*, April 14, 2013, 1A.
61. See Larry Omsted, *Fans* (NY: Algonquin, 2021).
62. Adam Grant, "The Joy We've Been Missing," *New York Times*, July 11, 2021, 3.

63. William Hageman, "Investing in Kids' Athletic Future Risky," *Star Tribune*, June 11, 2014, E1.

64. Matthew Futterman, "It's Norway's Games Again," *New York Times*, February 20, 2022, SP1.

65. See Robert Putnam, *Bowling Alone: The Collapse and Revival of American Community* (New York: Simon and Shuster, 2000).

66. Gabe Lacques, "Astros May Never Silence Boos with Fifth ALCS Trip in a Row," *USA Today*, October 14, 2021, 3C.

67. Alan Blinder, Jeré Longman, and Gillian R. Brassil, "Women's Basketball Battles Second-Class Treatment," *New York Times*, April 4, 2021, 26.

68. Jenna Ortiz, "Why Are WNBA Players in Russia?" *Arizona Republic*, March 6, 2022, accessed July 2, 2022, https://www.azcentral.com/story/sports/wnba/mercury/2022/03/06/why-brittney-griner-russia-what-you-need-know/9402897002/; and John Kessel, "The Path to Being a Pro Volleyball Player," *USA Volleyball*, undated, https://usavolleyball.org/resource/the-path-to-being-a-pro-volleyball-player/, accessed July 5, 2022.

69. See Florence Carpentier and Jean-Pierre Lefevre, "The Modern Olympic Movement, Women's Sport and the Social Order During the Inter-war Period," *The International Journal of the History of Sport* 23 (no. 7, November 2006): 1112-1127.

CHAPTER TWELVE

Student-Athletes for Sale:
Making Millions on NIL Deals

The NCAA edifice is collapsing. College athletes can now make money on their celebrity, and athletic departments have become marketing agents to help their players ink NIL deals. If players are not satisfied with the money, they can enter the transfer portal to find another athletic program that can guarantee a better payday. Effectively, players are now free agents every year. As of late 2023, seasoned quarterbacks were demanding a million or more in NIL deals from their new teams. Academic considerations seldom play any role in these decisions.

NCAA bureaucrats, athletic directors, and coaches, some of whom pull down multimillion-dollar salaries, decry the chaos and professionalization of the "non-profit," "amateur" enterprise that remunerates them so well. The current NCAA moneymakers pay lip service in support of their players' NIL opportunities but lament the constant turnover of team rosters and inevitable corruption. "What it is," says Big Ten commissioner Tony Petitti, "is a great mechanism for student-athletes to benefit from their name, image, and likeness through real marketing opportunities. . . . However, it is important to say that much of what is happening now under the guise of NIL is not true NIL but rather a move to a pay-for-play system that is driving recruitment and the transfer portal. This system operates away from and without institutional control, nor does it comply with Title IX." Petitti hopes that Congress will pass legislation to somehow reinstate institutional control and preserve the "academic athletic model," but the genie is already out of the bottle.[1]

Petitti is right on two counts. There is nothing to prevent deep-pocketed boosters from handing over cash to recruits and players promising to peddle their NIL, even if the marketing side of the deal doesn't happen. This chicanery is already going on. Second, if schools are forced to pay players, non-revenue sports, including women's sports, will indeed have to be cut. This is yet another reason to separate athletic departments from university budgets and let teams fend for themselves as business enterprises. On the one hand, there may not be a women's field hockey or lacrosse team on every college campus, and it is not fair to charge non-athletes fees to subsidize these NCAA sports. On the other, the money in NIL for some high-profile women athletes is far greater by staying in college than what they can make in the less-watched pro leagues. For example, LSU's Flau'jae Johnson and University of Iowa's Caitlyn Clark get *more* exposure and money-making opportunities by playing college basketball than by going to the WNBA. As of early 2023, Johnson had deals worth nearly $670,000. Clark's came in at $192,000. One sports media analyst estimates that the rights to the 2025 women's NCAA basketball tournament are worth around $100 million. A record 9.9 million viewers tuned into the 2023 tournament on ABC. The WNBA's deal with ESPN for 2025, which covers the entire season and the playoffs, amounts to only $33 million. The bottom line for Johnson and Clark is to play college ball as long as possible.[2]

It must be hard for the NCAA's satraps to maintain their faith in the purity of amateur sports as embodied in the student-athlete, a term Petitti likes to use. Team camaraderie and continuity are becoming relics—as is any semblance of a meaningful college education for many D-I men's basketball and football players.

Most critics of the professionalization of college sports call for reforms to come from within the NCAA and its member institutions. Such self-regulation is wishful thinking. The NCAA continues to defend its monopoly in the courts and to Congress. Some critics suggest that the NCAA purposely replaced retiring president Mark Emmert with former Massachusetts governor Charlie Baker because Baker has the political savvy to lobby Congress to regulate players' NIL deals and to ensure that athletes are not considered employees, which would give them protection under national labor laws.[3]

The NCAA is fighting for its life in the courts. In 2022, Arizona State swimmer Grant House filed a request for class certification seeking backpay for players' lost NIL monies. The NCAA claims that it might be on the hook for more than one billion dollars if it loses the case.[4]

Selling their NIL is one way for college athletes to make money, but paying them a salary for their work *on* the field is inevitable. The liberation of athletes from the NCAA monopoly is analogous to the demise of the oligopolistic Hollywood studio system in the 1950s, when film actors were no longer contractually tied to one studio, or to the end of MLB's reserve clause in the 1970s. In another pending case—*Johnson v. NCAA*—the NCAA is contesting the designation of athletes as university employees who therefore must be paid.[5] Shamelessly, the NCAA has invoked the 13th Amendment—which abolished slavery—to defend the current system. The amendment also exempted prison labor from compensation, and the NCAA has argued that this precedent should be applied to college athletes.[6] It is clear from these and other cases that serious reform will *not* emanate from inside the current power structure.

The NCAA's phony "student-athlete" system has one foot in the grave, just as amateurism in soccer, cricket, the Olympics, and other profitable spectator sports died in the last century. Big money is talking, and amateurs are listening.

Notes

1. Randy Johnson, "Hazing a Hot Topic for Braun and Petitti," *Star Tribune*, July 27, 2023, C1.

2. Tim Crean, "Caitlyn Clark Works for Free with 1 of Her Biggest NIL Partners," *Sportscasting*, March 31, 2023, accessed July 30, 2023, https://www.sportscasting.com/caitlin-clark-works-free-biggest-nil-partners/; Billy Witz, "It's a New Broadcast World. Can the N.C.A.A. Take Advantage," *New York Times*, June 18, 2023, 26; and Howard Megdal, "The WNBA's New Deal with ION By the Numbers," *Forbes*, April 26, 2023, accessed July 30, 2023, https://www.forbes.com/sites/howardmegdal/2023/04/26/the-wnbas-new-deal-with-ion-by-the-numbers/?sh=2c7cebfbba41.

3. See Nicole Auerbach, "With Charlie Baker, the NCAA is Banking on a Political Path Out of Its Troubles," *The Athletic*, December 15, 2022, accessed July 31, 2023, https://theathletic.com/4006731/2022/12/15/ncaa-president-charlie-baker-political-career/.

4. Thomas Baker, "If NIL Suit is Considered Class Action, It Could Cost NCAA More Than $1 billion," *Forbes*, May 5, 2023, accessed July 29, 2023, https://www.forbes.com/sites/thomasbaker/2023/05/05/if-nil-lawsuit-is-deemed-class-action-it-could-cost-ncaa-more-than-1-billion/?sh=47eb939144b2.

5. Richard Johnson, "Johnson v. NCAA Explained: What's at Stake in Wednesday's Hearing," February 15, 2023, accessed July 29, 2023, https://www.si.com/college/2023/02/15/johnson-v-ncaa-court-hearing-employment-status.

6. Bill Saporito, "The NCAA Keeps Running Plays Against Pay for Student-Athletes," *Washington Post*, May 25, 2023, A19.

AFTERWORD

Past Critics

There are a number of seminal works on the same topic to which an interested reader might turn. For many years, non-governmental organizations, college professors, journalists, players, and former NCAA bureaucrats have denounced big-money college sports. For example, in 1929, the Carnegie Foundation discovered that only about one-fourth of colleges and universities that offered athletics were running "ethical" programs.[1] Sixty years later, Indiana University professor Murray Sperber highlighted the problems of NCAA sports in his groundbreaking book, *College Sports Inc.: The Athletic Department vs the University* (1990), which he followed up with *Beer and Circus: How Big-Time College Sports is Crippling Undergraduate Education* (2001).

Walter Byers, former executive director[2] of the NCAA and creator of the term "student-athlete," was an important witness in Sperber's case against D-I college sports. After retiring, Byers had a change of heart, bluntly stating in *Unsportsmanlike Conduct: Exploiting College Athletes* (1995) that "colleges have expanded their control of athletes in the name of amateurism—a modern-day misnomer for economic tyranny."[3]

History of education professor John R. Thelin supplemented Sperber's works in *Games Colleges Play: Scandal and Reform in Intercollegiate Athletics* (1994), a survey of the history of intercollegiate athletes from its inception, citing the repeated scandals that have dogged the system. John R. Gerdy, the author of several books on college sports, makes clear his take on college sports in the title of his book *Air Ball: American Education's Failed Experiment with Elite Athletics* (2006).

Sports management professors Allen L. Sack and Ellen J. Staurowsky echoed Sperber's and Thelin's criticism of the NCAA in *College Athletes for Hire: The Evolution and Legacy of the NCAA's Amateur Myth* (1998), as did economists Andrew S. Zimbalist in *Unpaid Professionals* (1999) and Charles Clotfelter in *Big Time Sports in American Universities* (2011). Another important work is John Sayle Watterson's *College Football: History, Spectacle, Controversy* (2000). Historian Brian Ingrassia also addressed the role that college football was supposed to play in training young men's bodies, minds, and spirits, and this troubled and peculiarly American connection between football and higher education in *The Rise of the Gridiron University: Higher Education's Uneasy Alliance with Big-Time Football* (2012). John U. Bacon's *Fourth and Long: The Fight for the Soul of College Football* (2013) is another valuable contribution to the debate over the efficacy of big-time football on the college campus.

Ronald A. Smith, in *Pay for Play: A History of Big-Time College Athletic Reform* (2011), explored the futile attempts to reform a college sports system that was broken from the start. Smith followed that up with the *Myth of the Amateur: A History of College Athletic Scholarships* (2021). Scholars Kenneth L. Shropshire and Collin D. Williams indict the NCAA and offer reforms to the system in *The Miseducation of the Student Athlete: How to Fix College Sports* (2017). Education professor Gerald Gurney, along with Donna Lopiano and Andrew Zimbalist, also suggested reforms to the NCAA, mainly D-I football, in *Unwinding Madness: What Went Wrong with College Sports and How to Fix It* (2017).

Author Jeff Benedict and journalist Armen Keteyian tell the sad story of repeated football scandals in *The System: The Glory and Scandal of Big-Time College Football* (2014). *New York Times* columnist Joe Nocera and *Washington Post* reporter Ben Strauss, in *Indentured: The Inside Story of the Rebellion Against the NCAA* (2016), add their voices calling attention to the fiscal inequities in college sports. *Chicago Sun-Times* sports columnist Rick Telander joins the chorus of critics in *The College Football Problem: How Money and Power Corrupted the Game and How We Can Fix That* (2020).

Players have also entered the fray. Former UCLA star basketball player Ed O'Bannon, who for years fought to gain the rights to sell his own likeness from his college days, wrote *Court Justice: The Inside Story of My Battle Against the NCAA and My Life in Basketball* (2018). Former Duke basketball player turned commentator and analyst Jay Bilas has been critical of a system that denied justice for O'Bannon and other college athletes: "The NCAA makes its own rules," Bilas charged, "and their rules are bad."[4]

Afterword

The story comes full circle back to Sperber's *College Sports, Inc.* with public policy professor James T. Bennett's *Intercollegiate Athletics, Inc.: How Big-Time College Sports Cheat Students, Taxpayers, and Academics* (2020), who once again brings into clear focus the detrimental financial impacts of D-I sports on academics. If something isn't done to radically change the current business model of college athletics, this list of critiques will go on and on.

Notes

1. Rader, *American Sports*, 192.
2. The title was changed to president in 1988.
3. Cited in Doug Tucker, "Walter Byers Decries NCAA in New Book," *News Record*, (AP), August 28, 1995, accessed January 18, 2022, https://greensboro.com/walter-byers-decries-ncaa-in-new-book/article_7f7b299c-3926-577d-93b5-5e694ede6933.html.
4. Matt Giles, "The Case of Jay Bilas vs. the NCAA Will Now Be Heard," *The Atlantic*, November 23, 2017, accessed October 28, 2020, https://www.theatlantic.com/entertainment/archive/2017/11/the-case-of-jay-bilas-vs-the-ncaa-will-now-be-heard/546425/.

REFERENCES

Selected Newspapers
Star Tribune (Minneapolis)
New York Times
USA Today
Wall Street Journal
Washington Post

Books

Belanger, Kelly. *Title IX and the Fight for Equity in College Sports*. Syracuse: Syracuse University Press, 2016.

Benedict, Jeff, and Armen Keteyian. *The System: The Glory and Scandal of Big-Time College Football*. New York: Doubleday, 2013.

Byers, Walter. *Unsportsmanlike Conduct: Exploiting College Athletes*. Ann Arbor: University of Michigan Press, 1995.

Cahn, Susan K. *Coming on Strong: Gender and Sexuality in Women's Sport*. Urbana, IL: University of Illinois Press, 2015.

Chudacoff, Howard P. *Changing the Playbook: How Power, Profit, and Politics Transformed College Sports*. Urbana, IL: University of Illinois Press, 2015.

Clotfelter, Charles. *Big Time Sports in American Universities*. Cambridge: Cambridge University Press, 2011.

Cohan, William D. *The Price of Silence: The Duke Lacrosse Scandal, the Power of the Elite, and the Corruption of Our Great Universities*. New York: Scribner, 2014.

Davies, Richard O. *Sports in American Life: A History*. Chichester: Wiley-Blackwell, 2012.

Demas, Lane. *Integrating the Gridiron: Black Civil Rights and American College Football*. New Brunswick, NJ: Rutgers University Press, 2010.

Duderstadt, James J. *Intercollegiate Athletics and the American University: A University President's Perspective*. Ann Arbor: University of Michigan Press, 2003.

Dunnavant, Keith. *The Fifty-Year Seduction: How Television Manipulated College Football from the Birth of the Modern NCAA to the Creation of the BCS*. New York, NY: Thomas Dunne Books, 2004.

References

Edwards, Harry. *The Revolt of the Black Athlete*. Ontario: Collier-McMillan Limited, 1985.

Feinstein, John. *The Last Amateurs: Playing for Glory and Honor in Division I College Basketball*. Boston: Little, Brown, and Company, 2000.

Gaul, Gilbert M. *Billion-Dollar Ball: A Journey Through the Big-Money Culture of College Football*. New York: Viking, 2015.

Gerdy, John R. *Air Ball: American Education's Failed Experiment with Elite Athletics*. Jackson, MS: University Press of Mississippi, 2006.

George, Nelson. *Elevating the Game: Black Men and Basketball*. New York: Harper Collins, 1992.

Gorn, Elliott J., and Warren Goldstein. *A Brief History of American Sports*. Urbana, IL: University of Illinois Press, 2004.

Gurney, Gerald, Donna Lopiano, and Andrew Zimbalist. *Unwinding Madness: What Went Wrong with College Sports and How to Fix It*. Washington, D.C.: Brooking Institution, 2017.

Harris, Reed. *King Football: The Vulgarization of the American College*. New York: The Vanguard Press, 1932.

Hoberman, John. *Darwin's Athletes: How Sports Has Damaged Black America and Preserved the Myth of Race*. New York: Houghton-Mifflin, 1997.

Hurd, Michael. *Black College Football, 1892–1992: One Hundred Years of History, Education, and Pride*. Virginia Beach, VA: Donning Publishers, 1993.

Ingrassia, Brian. *The Rise of the Gridiron University: Higher Education's Uneasy Alliance with Big-Time Football*. Lawrence, KS: University Press of Kansas, 2015.

Kemper, Kurt E. *Before March Madness: The Wars for the Soul of College Basketball*. Urbana, IL: University of Illinois Press, 2020.

Kemper, Kurt E. *College Football and American Culture in the Cold War Era*. Urbana, IL: University of Illinois Press, 2009.

Lapchick, Richard. *Broken Promises: Racism in American Sports*. New York: St. Martin's Press, 1984.

McCallum, John D. *Big Ten Football Since 1895*. Radnor, PA: Chilton Book Co., 1976.

Meggyesy, Dave. *Out of Their League*. Berkeley, CA: Ramparts Books, 1970.

Mulcahy, Robert E., III. *An Athletic Director's Story and the Future of College Sports in America*. New Brunswick, NJ: Rutgers University Press, 2020.

Nocera, Joe, and Ben Strauss. *Indentured: The Inside Story of the Rebellion Against the NCAA*. New York: Penguin Random House, 2016.

O'Bannon, Edward. *Court Justice: The Inside Story of My Battle Against the NCAA*. New York: Diversion Books, 2018.

Omsted, Larry. *Fans*. New York: Algonquin Press, 2021.

Oriard, Michael. *Bowled Over: Big-Time College Football from the Sixties to the BCS Era*. Chapel Hill, NC: University of North Carolina Press, 2009.

Oriard, Michael. *King Football: Sport and Spectacle in the Golden Age of Radio and Newsreels, Movies and Magazines, the Weekly and the Daily Press*. Chapel Hill, NC: University of North Carolina Press, 2001.

References

Putnam, Robert. *Bowling Alone: The Collapse and Revival of American Community*. New York: Simon and Shuster, 2000.

Rader, Benjamin G. *American Sports: From the Age of Folk Games to the Age of Televised Sports*. Sixth Edition. Upper Saddle River, NJ: Pearson/Prentice Hall, 2009.

Sack, Allen L., and Ellen J. Staurowsky. *College Athletes for Hire: The Evolution and Legacy of the NCAA's Amateur Myth*. Westport, CT: Praeger Publishers, 1998.

Schultz, Jaime. *Women's Sport: What Everyone Needs to Know*. Oxford: Oxford University Press, 2018.

Shaw, Gary. *Meat on the Hoof*. New York: St. Martin's Press, 1972.

Shropshire, Kenneth L., and Collin D. Williams. *The Miseducation of the Student Athlete: How to Fix College Sports*. Philadelphia, PA: Wharton School Press, 2017.

Smith, Jay M., and Mary Willingham. *Cheated: The UNC Scandal, the Education of Athletes, and the Future of Big-Time College Sports*. Lincoln, NE: Potomac Books, 2015.

Smith, Ronald A. *The Myth of the Amateur: A History of College Athletic Scholarships*. Austin, TX: University of Texas Press, 2021.

Smith, Ronald A. *Pay for Play: A History of Big-Time College Athletic Reform*. Urbana, IL: University of Illinois Press, 2011.

Smith, Ronald A. *Sports and Freedom: The Rise of Big-Time College Athletics*. Oxford: Oxford University Press, 1988.

Smith, Ronald A. *Wounded Lions: Joe Paterno, Jerry Sandusky, and the Crises in Penn State Athletics*. Urbana, IL: University of Illinois Press, 2016.

Sperber, Murray. *Beer and Circus: How Big-Time College Sports is Crippling Undergraduate Education*. New York: Henry Holt and Co., 2001.

Sperber, Murray. *College Sports Inc.: The Athletic Department vs The University*. New York: Henry Holt and Co., 1990.

Spivey, Donald. *Racism, Activism, and Integrity in College Football: The Bates Must Play Movement*. Durham, NC: Carolina Academic Press, 2021.

Telander, Rick. *The College Football Problem: How Money and Power Corrupted the Game and How We Can Fix That*. Champaign, IL: Sports Publishing, 2020.

Telander, Rick. *The Hundred Yard Lie: The Corruption of College Football and What We Can Do to Stop It*. Urbana, IL: University of Illinois Press, 1996.

Thelin, John R. *Games Colleges Play: Scandal and Reform in Intercollegiate Athletics*. Baltimore, MD: Johns Hopkins University Press, 1994.

Thomason, Andy. *Discredited: The UNC Scandal and College Athletics' Amateur Ideal*. Ann Arbor, MI: University of Michigan Press, 2021.

Vitale, Dick. *Campus Chaos: Why the Game I Love Is Breaking My Heart*. Indianapolis: Time Out Publishing, 2000.

Walsh, Christopher J. *Where Football is King: A History of the SEC*. Lanham, MD: Taylor Trade Publishing, 2006.

Ware, Susan. *Title IX: A Brief History with Documents*. Long Grove, IL: Waveland Press, 2007.

References

Watterson, John Sayle. *College Football: History, Spectacle, Controversy.* Baltimore: Johns Hopkins Press, 2000.

Wilkenson, Mike. *The Autumn Warrior: Murray Warmath's 65 Years in American Football.* Edina, MN: Burgess International Group, 1992.

Zimbalist, Andrew. *Unpaid Professionals: Commercialism and Conflict in Big-time College Sports.* Princeton: Princeton University Press, 1999.

Articles and Chapters in Anthologies

Baker, Aaron. Review of "League of Denial" (2013), *Journal of Sport History* 43, no. 1 (Spring 2016): 102–3.

Branch, Taylor. "The Shame of College Sports." *The Atlantic*, October 2011. https://www.theatlantic.com/magazine/archive/2011/10/the-shame-of-college-sports/308643/.

Carpentier, Florence, and Jean-Pierre Lefevre. "The Modern Olympic Movement, Women's Sport and the Social Order During the Inter-war Period." *The InteInational Journal of the History of Sport* 23, no. 7 (November 2006): 1112–1127.

Colás, Yago. "Our Myth of Creation: The Politics of Narrating Basketball's Origin." *Journal of Sport History* 43, no. 1 (Spring 2016): 37–54.

Demas, Lane. "The Test of Time: Revisiting Stagg's University and College Football Historiography." *Journal of Sport History* 39, no. 1 (Spring 2012): 111–121.

Draper, Alan. "Innocence Lost: Division III Sports Programs." *Change* 28, no. 6 (1996): 46–49.

Evans, John P., et al. "Institutional Experience with Academic Reform: A Panel Discussion." *Journal of Intercollegiate Sport* 5, no. 1 (2012): 98–120.

Edwards, Harry. "The Decline of the Black Athlete." In *The Unlevel Playing Field: A Documentary History of the African American Experience in Sport*, edited by David K. Wiggins and Patrick B. Miller, 435–437. Urbana, IL: University of Illinois Press, 2003.

Giles, Matt. "The Case of Jay Bilas vs. the NCAA Will Now Be Heard." *The Atlantic*, November 23, 2017. Accessed October 28, 2020. https://www.theatlantic.com/entertainment/archive/2017/11/the-case-of-jay-bilas-vs-the-ncaa-will-now-be-heard/546425/.

Hobson, J. Hardin. "Football Culture at New South Universities: Lost Cause and Old South Memory, Modernity, and Martial Manhood." In *The History of American College Football: Institutional Policy, Culture, and Reform*, edited by Christian K. Anderson and Amber C. Fallucca, 37–63. New York: Routledge, 2021.

Kane, Mary Jo, Perry Leo, and Lynn K. Holleran. "Issues Related to Academic Support and Performance of Division I Student-Athletes: A Case Study at the University of Minnesota." *Journal of Intercollegiate Sport* 1, no. 1 (2008): 98–129.

Kerr, Robert L. "Last Stand for a Less Commercialized Game: Contesting Football's Place in Higher Education in NCAA v. Board of Regents." In *The History of American College Football: Institutional Policy, Culture, and Reform*, edited by

References

Christian K. Anderson and Amber C. Fallucca, 167–195. New York: Routledge, 2021.

Kimball, Richard Ian. "Football Culture at New South Universities: Lost Cause and Old South Memory, Modernity, and Martial Manhood." In *The History of American College Football: Institutional Policy, Culture, and Reform*, edited by Christian K. Anderson and Amber C. Fallucca, 37–63. New York: Routledge, 2021.

Lazaroff, Daniel E. "The NCAA in Its Second Century: Defender of Amateurism or Antitrust Recidivist." *Oregon Law Review* 86, no. 2 (2007): 329–371.

Llewellyn, Matthew P., and John Gleaves. "A Universal Dilemma: The British *Sporting Life* and Complex, Contested, and Contradictory State of Amateurism." *Journal of Sport History* 41, no. 1 (2014): 95–116.

Naqvi, S. Kaazim. "O-H! I-O! Black Students, Black Athletes, and Ohio State Football, 1968-1976." *Journal of Sport History* 40, no. 1 (Spring 2013): 111–126.

Mann, Owen. "The Cultural Bond? Cricket and the Imperial Mission." *The International Journal of the History of Sport* 27, no. 13 (September 2010): 2192.

McDaniels, Pellom, III. Review of *Pay for Play* by Ronald A. Smith. *Journal of Sport History* 39, no. 3 (Fall 2012): 567–569.

Miniowski, Łukash, and Tomasz Jacheć. "Illusory Facets of Sport: The Case of the Duke University Basketball Team." *Physical Culture and Sport Studies and Research* 75 (October 2017): 43–54.

Nathan, Daniel A. "'I'm Against It!' The Marx Brothers' *Horse Feathers* as Cultural Critique: Or, Why Big-Time College Football Gives Me a Haddock." In *All-Stars and Movie Stars: Sports in Film and History*, edited by Ron Briley, Michael K. Schoenecke, and Deborah A. Carmichael, 40–54. Lexington: University of Kentucky Press, 2008.

O'Toole, Kathleen M. "John L. Griffith and the Commercialization of College Sports on Radio in the 1930s." *Journal of Sport History* 40, no. 2 (Summer 2013): 241–257.

Odenkirk, James E. "The Eighth Wonder of the World: Ohio State University's Rejection of a Rose Bowl Bid in 1961." *Journal of Sport History* 34, no. 3 (Fall 2007): 389–395.

Sage, George H. "Racial Inequality and Sport." In *Sport in Contemporary Society: An Anthology*, edited by D. Stanley Eitzen, 275–285. New York: Macmillan, 2000.

Sanderson, Allen, and John Siegfried. "Why American Universities Sponsor Commercial Sports." *Milken Institute Review*, July 31, 2018. Accessed September 21, 2019. http://www.milkenreview.org/articles/why-american-universities-sponsor-commerical-sports?IssueID=29.

Schultz, Jaime. "The Test Time: Revisiting *Stagg's University* and College Historiography." *Journal of Sport History* 39, no. 1 (Spring 2012): 111–121.

Scott, Brianna, Thomas Paskus, Michael Miranda, Todd Petr, and John McArdle. "In-Season vs. Out-of-Season Academic Performance of College Student-Athletes." *Journal of Intercollegiate Sports* 1, no. 1 (2008): 202–226.

References

Steinbach, Paul. "Authors React to Cancellation of NCAA Colloquium," *Athletic Business*, March 2013. Accessed August 5, 2021. https://www.athleticbusiness.com/scholars-react-to-cancellation-of-ncaa-colloquium.html.

Thelin, John R. "Academics and Athletics: A Part and Apart in the American Campus." *Journal of Intercollegiate Sport* 1, no. 1 (2008): 72–81.

Wiggins, David K. "'The Color of My Writing': Reflections on Studying the Interconnection Among Race, Sport, and American Culture." *Journal of Sport History* 43, no. 3 (Fall 2016): 306–320.

INDEX

Academic Progress Rate (APR), 207, 219
alcohol and college sports, 43–45, 60, 255–56
Alden, Mike, 219
Alexis Jr., Lucien, 140
Allen, Tom, 85
Alston, Shawne, 70
Amateur Athletic Union (AAU), 14, 149, 153; youth teams, 151
amateurism, 11–14, 68, 104; in college sports, 4, 5, 7, 11, 14, 16–17, 19, 27, 69, 72, 92, 104; in the Olympics, 14
American Association of University Professors (AAUP), 16, 19, 58
Andries, Jamie, 72
Anthony, Carmelo, 222
Archambault, Russ, 203
"arms race" (for athletic facilities), 47–48, 50
Ashe, Arthur, 152
Association of Governing Boards of Universities and Colleges (AGB), 109–10
Association of Intercollegiate Athletics for Women (AIAW), 153–54
athletic departments: administrators' salaries, 73–74; debt, 57–58, 85; employees, 73
Atwell, Robert, 216
Auriemma, Geno, 79, 225
Autman-Bell, Chris, 265

Baker, Charlie, 276

Baker, Dusty, 268
Baker, Geo, 228
Barbour, Sandy, 159
Barnett, Gary, 128
Bates, Leonard, 140
Bauman, Joel, 72
Baylor, Elgin, 37
Bazley, Darius, 222
Becker, Mark, 49, 74
Beckham Jr., Odell, 128–29
Berry, Todd, 96, 229
"Black Fourteen" (Wyoming football players), 142
Blaik, Bob, 198
Blaik, Red, 105, 198
"bodybag games," 55–56
Boeheim, Jim, 77, 106
Bok, Derek, 216
Boles, L.C., 19
Bosworth, Brian, 98, 126
Bowden, Bobby, 79, 98–99, 156, 203
Bowden, Tommy, 156
Bowen II, Brian, 130
Bowl Championship Series (BCS), 24
Branch, Taylor, 145, 147–48, 249
Brand, Myles, 219
Brandon, Dave, 36, 41
Brewster, Tim, 80
Bright, Johnny, 100, 141
Briles, Art, 108
Brodhead, Richard, 37
Brooks, John, 200–01
Brown v. Board of Education, 5

Index

Brown, Dale, 131
Brown, Jim, 67, 74
Brown, Larry, 93, 118, 121–22
Bryant, Bear, 23, 76, 118
Burke, Morgan, 70
Burrow, Joe, 202
Bush, Reggie, 126, 128
Byers, Walter, 22–23, 25–26, 47, 53, 57, 74, 91, 98, 118, 144, 154, 216–17, 237, 241, 250, 257, 266, 279

Calhoun, Jim, 118–19
Calhoun, M. Grace, 225
Calipari, John, 93, 118, 130, 199, 223
Callaway, Rick, 133
Camp, Walter, 15
campus club sports, 253ff
Canham, Dan, 23
Carnegie Foundation report (1929), 17, 18, 19, 35, 197, 217, 279
Carr, Marcus, 126
Carroll, Pete, 118, 128–29
Casey, Dwane, 119
Casteen, John, 109
Chalmers, Mario, 93
Chalmers, Ronnie, 93
Chaney, John, 152, 200, 218
Ciarrocca, Kirk, 79
Claeys, Tracy, 108
Clarett, Maurice, 123
Clark, Caitlyn, 276
Clements, Bill, 98
Coker, Larry, 120
college athletes: academic eligibility, 15; economic exploitation of, 143; promise of a pro contract, 149ff, 252
college coaches: changing jobs, 117ff; rules violators, 118ff; salaries, 15–16, 35, 51–52, 59, 60, 70, 73, 76–80
College Football Association (CFA), 24
Colter, Kain, 246
conference shifts, 83, 84–86
Cooper, John, 77
Coubertin, Pierre de, 13
Covid pandemic, 68, 80–81, 110, 117, 126, 129, 225, 255; and cutting sports,

Covid, pandemic (*continued*) 41–42, 255; and cutting professors, 81
Cowen, Scott, 215
Coyle, Mark, 41, 48, 60, 158, 243
Crawford, Gregory, 51, 74
Creamer, David, 52, 54
Cross, George L., 79
Curry, Bill, 49
Curry, Eric, 265

Davies, Charles "Chick", 76
Davison, Fred, 199
Dawkins, Christian, 130
Dawkins, Darryl, 69
Day, Jason, 77
"death penalty" (on D-I sports program), 39, 95, 98
Delaney, Jim, 24
Dennison,, Ray H., 25
Devaney, Bob, 91
Dewine, Mike, 51
Dietzel, Paul, 105
Division-II schools shifting to Division-I, 49, 83
Dodds, DeLoss, 48, 57
Doherty, Matt, 206
donors and winning teams, 42–43, 58, 257
Douglas, Paul F., 144
Doyle, Chris, 124
Drake, Michael, 74, 228
Duderstadt, James J., 4, 37, 79, 199, 252
Durkin, D.J., 105
Dye, Pat, 110

Eaton, Lloyd, 141
Edwards, Harry, 152–53
Eliot, Charles, 34, 104
Emmert, Mark, 55, 75, 103, 131, 221, 226, 231, 241, 242, 249
Erickson, Dennis, 120
Ernst, Gordon, 133
European club sports, 7
Evashevski, Forest, 20

Falwell Jr., Jerry, 108

Index

Fields, Justin, 202
Fisher, Jimbo, 77
Fisher, Steve, 99, 118
Fitzgerald, Pat, 258–59
Fleck, P.J., 52, 60, 79, 80
Floyd, Elson, 36
Fluker, D.J., 99
Flutie, Doug, 39; "Flutie Factor", 39
Football Bowl Series (FBS), 59, 158–59, 224
Foote II, Edward T. (Tad), 102, 240
Fournette, Leonard, 71
Fox, Parker, 229
Frazier, Keith, 121–22
Fuzak, John, 154

G League, 222
Gabel, Joan, 36
Gaither, Jake, 142
Gallagher, Patrick D., 158
Gallico, Paul, 43,
gambling on college sports, 12, 28n6, 45–47, 82, 96
Gangelhoff, Jan, 203
Garnett, Kevin, 221
Gates Jr., Henry Louis, 151
Gates, Thomas, 213
Gee, Gordon, 215, 238
gender inequality in college sports, 5, 153ff; discrimination against women coaches and administrators, 158–59
"gentlemen's agreements," 140
Gilbert, Sam, 95
Gipp, George, 198
Glades Central High School, 149–50
Gordon, Eric, 111
Grace, W. G., 13
graduation rates: comparison of Black and White students, 148–49
Graham, Michael, 200
Grange, Red, 20, 67
Grant, Bud, 92
Green, Jalen, 222
Greene, Cornelius, 143
Greiner, William, 55
Grier, Bobby, 141

Griffin, Marvin, 141
Gulick, Leonard, 104
Guthridge, Bill, 206
Gutting, Gary, 37

Hamilton, Lloyd, 151
Harker, Patrick T., 260–61
Harper, William Rainey, 15
Harrell, Gary, 56
Harrick, Jim, 199
Hartman, Sid, 92
Haskins, Clem, 203
Hayes, Woody, 52, 96, 123, 143, 243–44
Haywood, Mike, 51
Healy, Timothy, 216
Heinel, Donna, 133
Hernandez, Aaron, 122
Hester, Jesse Lee, 149
Hill, Soloman, 221–22
Historically Black Colleges and Universities (HBCUs), 55–56, 139, 142
Hobbs, Patrick, 84
Holder, Mike, 101
Holman, Nat, 97
Holtz, Lou, 156
Holtz, Skip, 156
Horn, Stephen, 23
Horse Feathers (1932), 15, 33
House, Grant, 276
Huff, George, 18
Huggins, Bob, 24
Huma, Ramogi, 227
Hutchins, Robert, 271
Hutchinson, Aidan, 259

Iba, Hank, 20
Ibrahim, Mohamed, 264
Intercollegiate Athletic Association (IAA), 17
International Olympic Committee (IOC), 13, 163n60
Irving, Kyrie, 223

Jabbar, Kareem Abdul, 245
Jackson, Victoria L., 147

Index

James, Adam, 125
James, LeBron, 221
Jenkins, Martin, 70
Johnson, Ben, 36, 158, 229
Johnson, Flau'jae, 276
Johnson, Jimmy, 120
Jones, K.C., 143
Jordan, Ralph "Shug", 128
Junker, Joe, 132

Kaler, Eric, 74
Karras, Alex, 197
Kellogg, Clark, 133
Kelly, Brian, 52, 126
Kemp, Sean, 133
Kerr, Steve, 111
Kiffin, Lane, 129, 265
Kiffin, Monte, 79, 156
Knight Commission, 59, 217, 219, 239
Knight, Bobby, 23, 79, 109–10, 200, 216
Krzyzewski, Mike, 24, 37, 79, 223

Lawrence, Trevor, 71
Leach, Mike, 118, 124–25
Littlepage, Craig, 35
Lombardi, Nathan, 53
Love, Kevin, 110
Luck, Oliver, 230
Lyke, Heather, 158

Mack, Chris, 100
MACtion, 47
Mahan, Patrick J., 18
Malagi, Ulric, 121
Malone, Moses, 69
Manley, Dexter, 199
Manning, Danny, 93
Manning, Ed, 93
Maravich, Pete, 93
Maravich, Press, 93
"March Madness" (NCAA D-I Basketball Championship), 8, 22, 24–25, 38, 40, 68, 69, 72, 103, 156, 244
Martin, Chuck, 51
Martin, Cuonzo, 93
Marx brothers, 15, 21, 33

Mason, Glen, 123
Maxon, Robert, 39
McCaffery, Fran, 224
McCants, Rashad, 206
McCaw, Ian, 108
McDaniels, Pellom III, 3
McDermott, Greg, 145
McNair, Jordan, 105
Meggyesy, Dave, 105
Meiklejohn, Alexander, 16
Meyer, Ron, 118
Meyer, Urban, 98, 118, 122–24
"mid-major" universities, 50–52
Middlebrooks, Marilyn, 202
Miles, Les, 98, 100, 118, 120
Miller, Sean, 130–31
Mills, Chris, 119, 133
Mills, Claud, 119
Mills, Terry, 199
Mitchell, Sam, 69
Mixon, Joe, 126
Moore, Charlie, 264
Moos, Bill, 125
Morgan, Tanner, 265
Muhammad, Shabazz, 221–22
Mulcahy III, Robert, 58, 102
Mulkey, Kim, 80, 269
Muller, Dan, 224
Musburger, Brent, 46
"Muscular Christianity", 104

Naismith, James, 12, 104, 267
Name, Likeness, Image (NIL), 71–73, 78, 226ff, 258–59, 275ff
Nantz, Jim, 72
Napier, Shabazz, 71, 96, 119
National Association of Intercollegiate Athletics (NAIA), 142
National Invitational Tournament (NIT), 24, 142, 155
NCAA: employees' salaries, 75; rules, 17, 27, 53, 67, 69, 74, 93, 95–96, 154, 201, 218–19, 250; rules-breaking, 23, 35, 91–95, 97ff, 117ff
Neuheisel, Rick, 120–21
Newsom, Gavin, 227

Index

Newton, Cam, 71, 122–23
Nickelberry, Kevin, 224
Nielsen, Kent, 56
Niumatalolo, Ken, 78
Nocera, Joe, 205
Noel, Nerlens, 221, 223
Nurmi, Paavo, 14
Nyang'goro, Julius, 204

O'Bannon, Ed, 71, 227, 280
Ogunleye, Adele, 151
Ollie, Kevin, 79, 119, 120
Olson, Lute, 77, 201
Olympic Games, 4, 13, 14, 163n60, 270
online courses (for athletes), 202
Orgeron, Ed, 98, 118, 120, 128–29
Owens, Jesse, 92

Painter, Matt, 93
"paper" courses, 203ff, 219
Parker, Jabari, 223
Parseghian, Ara, 52
Paterno, Joe, 79, 109, 110, 200, 203, 266
paying college players: illegally, 19–21, 34, 69, 70–71, 92, 96–98, 99, 100, 101–2, 118, 121, 123ff, 252; legally, 229–31, 257, 258ff, 275ff
Pearl, Bruce, 118, 129, 130
Person, Chuck, 130
Phillips, Lawrence, 99
Phillips, Pattie, 158
Pickens, T. Boone, 39
Pierce, Chester, 140
Pinkel, Gary, 202
Pitino, Richard, 156
Pitino, Rick, 77, 118, 130–32
Pont, John, 52
Porter, Michael Jr., 93
Porter, Michael Sr., 93
Pritchett, Henry, 17
professors' salaries, 75–77
Proposition 48, 152, 200, 218

racial inequality in college sports, 5, 139ff; discrimination against Black athletes, 140, 143; discrimination against Black coaches and administrators, 157ff, 218
Ramsey, Eric, 110
Recruiting of high school athletes, 18, 20, 48, 121, 125ff
Reeve, Cheryl, 158
reforming the NCAA, 211ff, 237ff, 252; and dropping football programs, 214–16
Reid, Bill, 16, 76
Rice Commission, 131, 211, 221, 224, 249
Richardson, Book, 131
Richt, Mark, 229
Rickey, Branch, 14
Riley, Lincoln, 126
Robertson, Oscar, 27
Robeson, Paul, 140
Robinson, John, 202
Robinson, Rumeal, 199
Rockne, Knute, 76, 198, 254
Roethlisberger, John, 231
Roethlisberger, Ben, 257
Roosevelt, Teddy, 187, 211–12
Rose, Derrick, 199
Ross, Kevin, 198
Royal, Darrell, 23, 105
Rupp, Adolph, 20, 96, 143
Russell, Bill, 143, 268
Russell, Brian, 202

Saban, Nick, 77–80, 99, 100, 129, 131, 145–46
Sampson, Kelvin, 118, 122
Sandusky, Jerry, 109, 110, 203
Sanford, Mike Jr., 79
Sanity Code, 21, 211, 213
Savage, Charles, 212
Saylor, David, 53
scandals, 91, 92, 97–103, 111; academic 4, 97, 101–2, 105, 121–122, 197ff; admissions, 132ff; criminal, 97, 99, 101, 106ff; point-shaving, 96–97; and academic tutors, 201ff
Schellenberger, Howard, 120

Index

Schembechler, Bo, 52, 217
Schiano, Greg, 102
Self, Bill, 93, 118
separation of sports from universities, 253ff
Shalala, Donna, 45
Shapiro, Nevin, 102
Shaw, Gary, 105
Sherman Anti-trust Act, 24, 251
Sherrill, Jackie, 52
Singer, William, 132
Small, Albion, 16
Smith, Dean, 200–1, 206
Smith, Gene, 81
Smith, Gregg, 120
Smith, Jay M., 204, 206–7, 211, 239, 245
Smith, Zach, 124
Snyder, Bill, 220
Sperber, Murray, 58, 127–28, 237, 253, 279, 281
Spurrier, Steve, 79, 99
Stagg, Amos Alonzo, 15–16
Stahl, Jason, 228
Stallings, Kevin, 126
Stanford Steve, 46
Starn, Orin, 37
Steinbrecher, John, 224
Stern, David, 221
Stoops, Bob, 126
"student-athlete," 4–5, 25, 26–27, 68, 93, 212, 220, 251, 277; and workers' compensation, 25–26
student fees (for athletics), 33, 35, 50–55, 84
Sullivan, Julie, 266
Sullivan, William, 37
Sutton, Eddie, 118–19, 133, 156
Sutton, Sean, 133, 156
Swinney, Dabo, 78, 80, 145
Switzer, Barry, 23, 98–99, 126, 266

Tarkanian, Jerry, 77, 91, 119, 266
Tatum, Beverly, 267
television, and D-I sports, 21–25, 57, 74, 81–82, 84–85, 95, 155
Thomas, Joab, 144
Thompson III, John, 156

Thompson, Jr., John, 75, 106, 125, 133, 152, 200–1, 218
Thorpe, Jim, 14
Thorson, Clayton, 70
Title IX, 5, 79, 153–54, 156, 159, 270
"tramp athletes", 16, 126
transfer portal, 19, 21, 126, 223, 264, 265
transgender women, 160–61,
Tressel, Jim, 124, 238
Trice, Jack, 141
Tronsdal, Lynne M., 201, 254

"vacating" wins, 203
Vaccaro, Sonny, 146
Valvano, Jim, 77, 239
Van Horn, Edward Gary, 26
Van Pelt, Scott, 46
VanDerveer, Tara, 155
Vermeil, Dick, 203
Vincent, Lucas, 227
Vitale, Dick, 217–18, 222–23

Wade, Will, 100, 130–31
Wagner, Dajuan, 93
Wagner, Milt, 93
Waldrep, Kent, 26
Walker, Randy, 52
Ward, Charlie, 71
Warren, Kevin, 81, 258
Washburn, Chris, 200, 239
Watson, Harry, 205
Watts, Ray L., 215
Wettstone, Karl F., 18
Whalen, Lindsay, 225
Whitworth, J.B., 141
Wiggins, Dave, 152
Wilken, Claudia, 229
Williams, Jesse Feiring, 241
Williams, Roy, 118, 206
Willingham, Mary, 204–7, 219, 239
Winston, Jameis, 107–8
Wolff, Alexander, 240
Wooden, John, 76–77, 95

Yost, Fielding, 16
Young Men's Christian Association (YMCA), 104